Me & My Brothers

Volume 10

Hari Tokeino

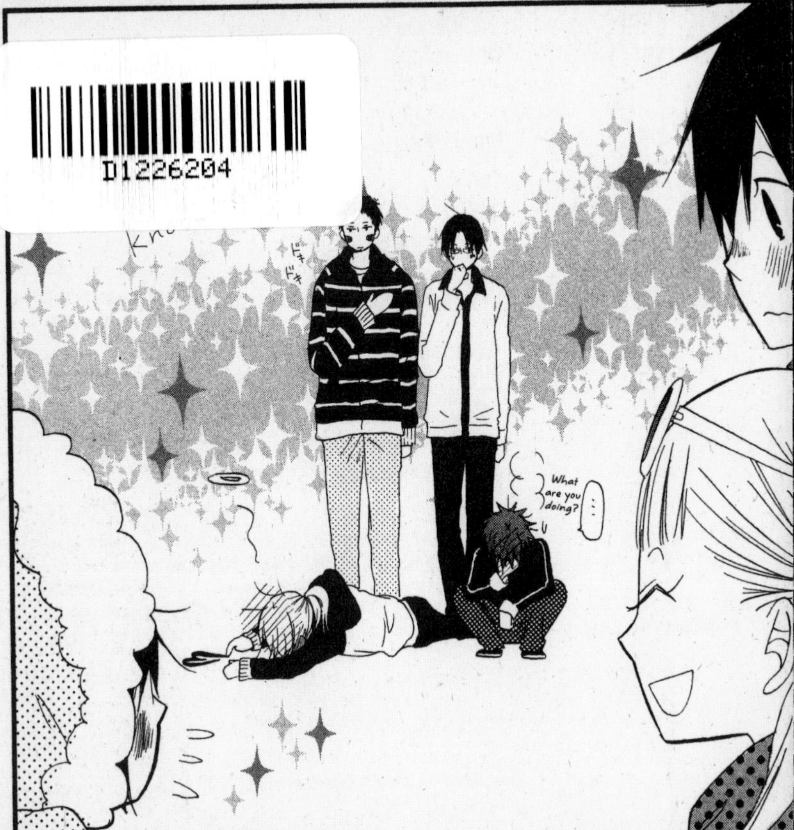
What are you doing?
...

Me & My Brothers Volume 10
Created by Hari Tokeino

Translation - Alethea & Athena Nibley
English Adaptation - Katherine Schilling
Retouch and Lettering - Star Print Brokers
Production Artist - Rui Kyo
Graphic Designer - Al-Insan Lashley

Editor - Cindy Suzuki
Print Production Manager - Lucas Rivera
Managing Editor - Vy Nguyen
Senior Designer - Louis Csontos
Art Director - Al-Insan Lashley
Director of Sales and Manufacturing - Allyson De Simone
Associate Publisher - Marco F. Pavia
President and C.O.O. - John Parker
C.E.O. and Chief Creative Officer - Stu Levy

A **TOKYOPOP** Manga

TOKYOPOP and 🐾 are trademarks or registered trademarks of TOKYOPOP Inc.

TOKYOPOP Inc.
5900 Wilshire Blvd. Suite 2000
Los Angeles, CA 90036

E-mail: info@TOKYOPOP.com
Come visit us online at www.TOKYOPOP.com

ISBN: 978-1-4278-1714-3

First TOKYOPOP printing: December 2009
10 9 8 7 6 5 4 3 2 1
Printed in the USA

Me & My Brothers

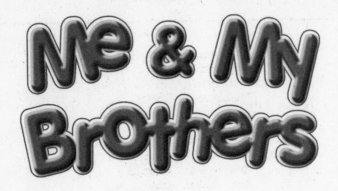

Volume 10

Hari Tokeino

TOKYOPOP®

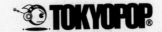

HAMBURG // LONDON // LOS ANGELES // TOKYO

Contents

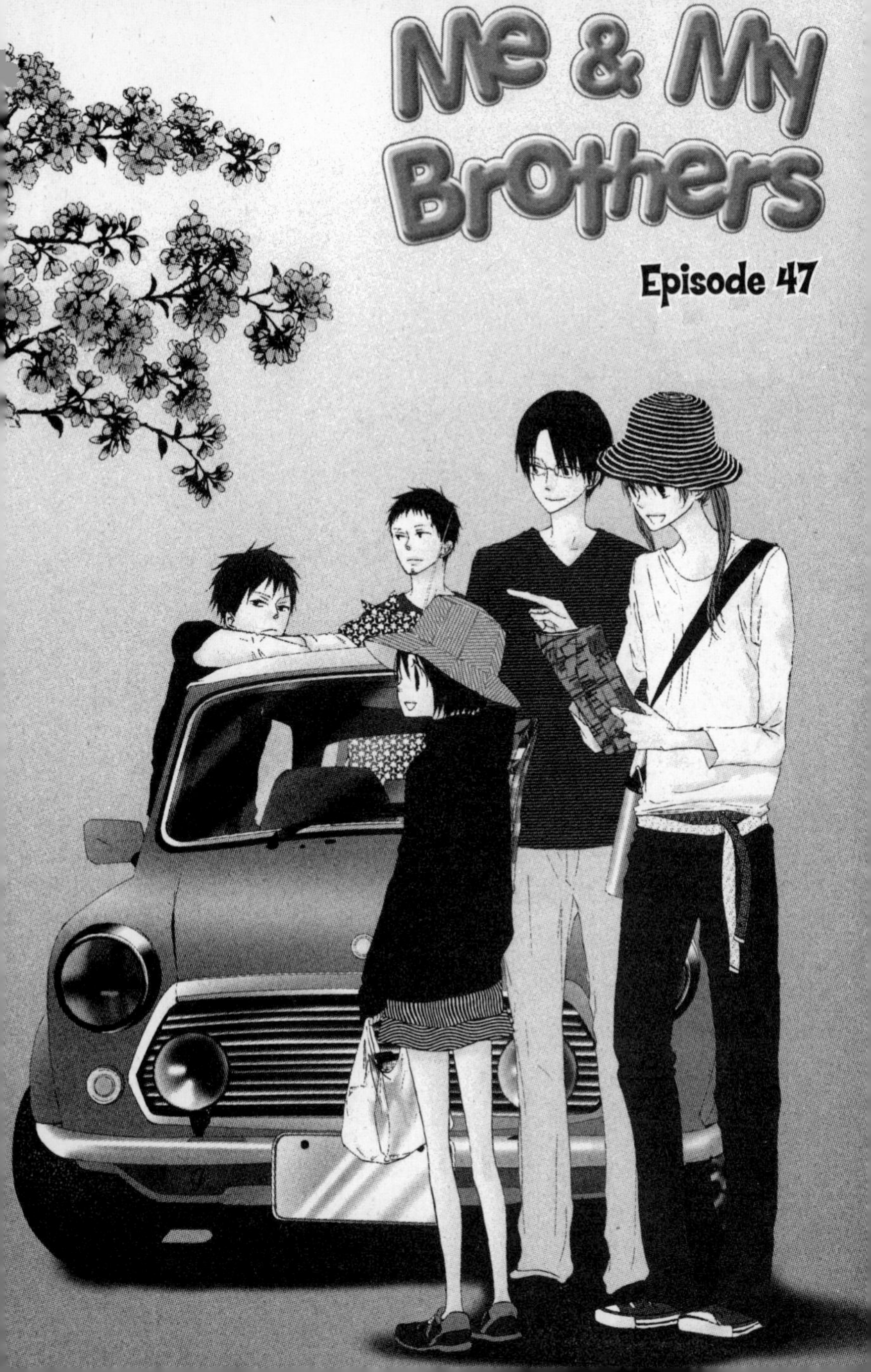
Me & My Brothers
Episode 47

CHARACTERS PROFILE

ME & MY BROTHERS

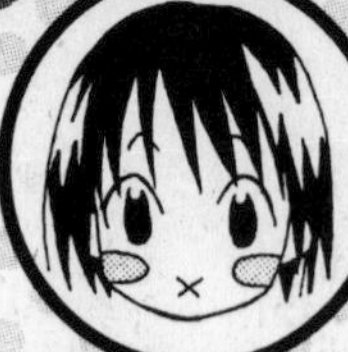

SAKURA MIYASHITA:
THE YOUNGEST. A FIRST-YEAR IN HIGH SCHOOL. THE ONLY GIRL IN THE MIYASHITA FAMILY. SHE IS NOT BLOOD RELATED TO HER FOUR BROTHERS. SHE LOVES MASASHI.♥

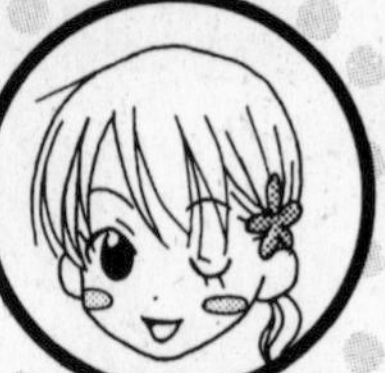

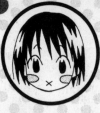

MASASHI MIYASHITA:
THE ELDEST. ROMANCE NOVELIST. ACCORDING TO HIM, HE SOUNDS LIKE A WOMAN BECAUSE OF HIS JOB. HE'S THE LEADER OF THE FOUR SAKURA-SPOILERS.

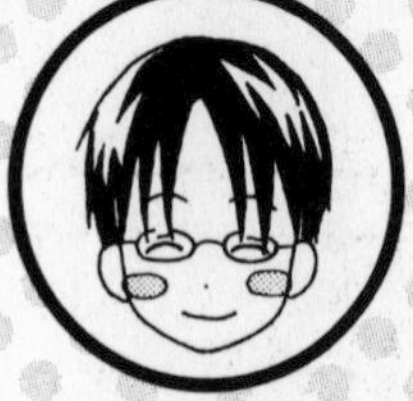

TAKASHI MIYASHITA:
THE 2ND BROTHER. A JAPANESE TEACHER. HE'S A GENTLEMAN.

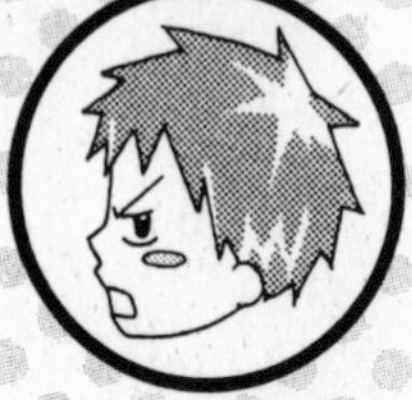

TSUYOSHI MIYASHITA:
THE 3RD BROTHER. FULL-TIME PART-TIMER. HE TALKS ROUGH, BUT IS ACTUALLY QUITE BASHFUL.

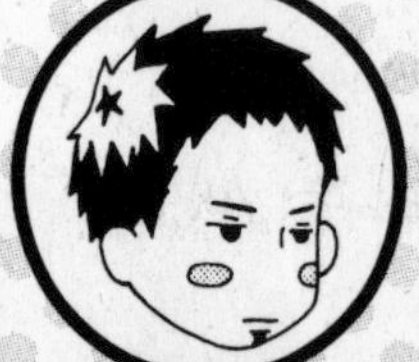

TAKESHI MIYASHITA:
THE 4TH BROTHER. COLLEGE SOPHOMORE. HE LOOKS OLD, BUT HE IS THE YOUNGEST OF THE FOUR BROTHERS. HE'S QUIET AND LOVES GARDENING.

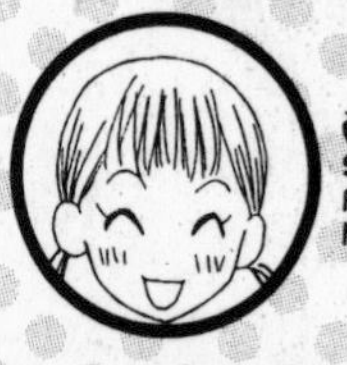

NAKA-CHAN:
SAKURA'S BEST FRIEND. HER FAMILY NAME IS TANAKA.

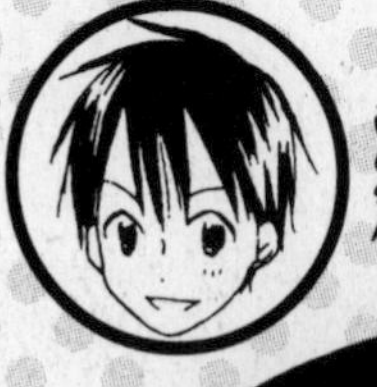

SUZUKI:
ON THE SCHOOL SOCCER TEAM. HE HAS A CRUSH ON SAKURA.

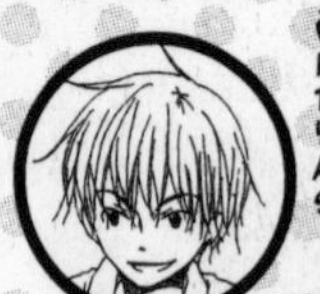

KATAGIRI:
HE CONFESSED HIS LOVE TO SAKURA IN THEIR SECOND YEAR OF MIDDLE SCHOOL AND THEN TRANSFERRED SCHOOLS. BUT NOW...

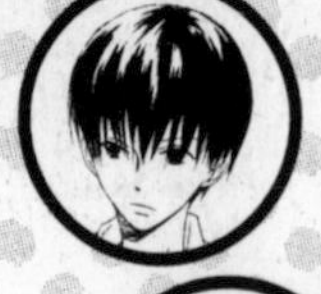

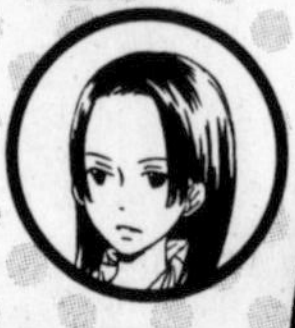

NANA & NENE OZUKA:
THE TWINS IN SAKURA'S SCHOOL SOCCER CLUB. BOTH IN THE 11TH GRADE.

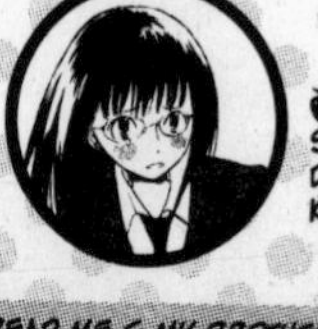

SONOMURA:
SAKURA'S CLASSMATE. DOES SHE LIKE KATAGIRI?!

STORY

SAKURA, AGE 14, LOST HER GRANDMOTHER AND WAS ALL ALONE IN THE WORLD. IN THESE CIRCUMSTANCES, *GASP!* FOUR BROTHERS APPEAR BEFORE SAKURA! ACTUALLY, HER BROTHERS ARE THE SONS OF THEIR FATHER AND HIS FIRST WIFE, AND SAKURA IS THE DAUGHTER OF HER MOTHER AND HER MOTHER'S EX-BOYFRIEND TAIZOU. THEY AREN'T RELATED BY BLOOD, BUT THEY BEGIN TO LIVE TOGETHER AGAIN AFTER ELEVEN YEARS ♥. FINALLY, SAKURA KISSES MASASHI AND CONFESSES HER LOVE TO HIM! COULD MASASHI BE RETURNING HER FEELINGS AS WELL...?

EASE READ *ME & MY BROTHERS* 1–9 FOR MORE DETAILS!

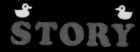

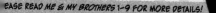

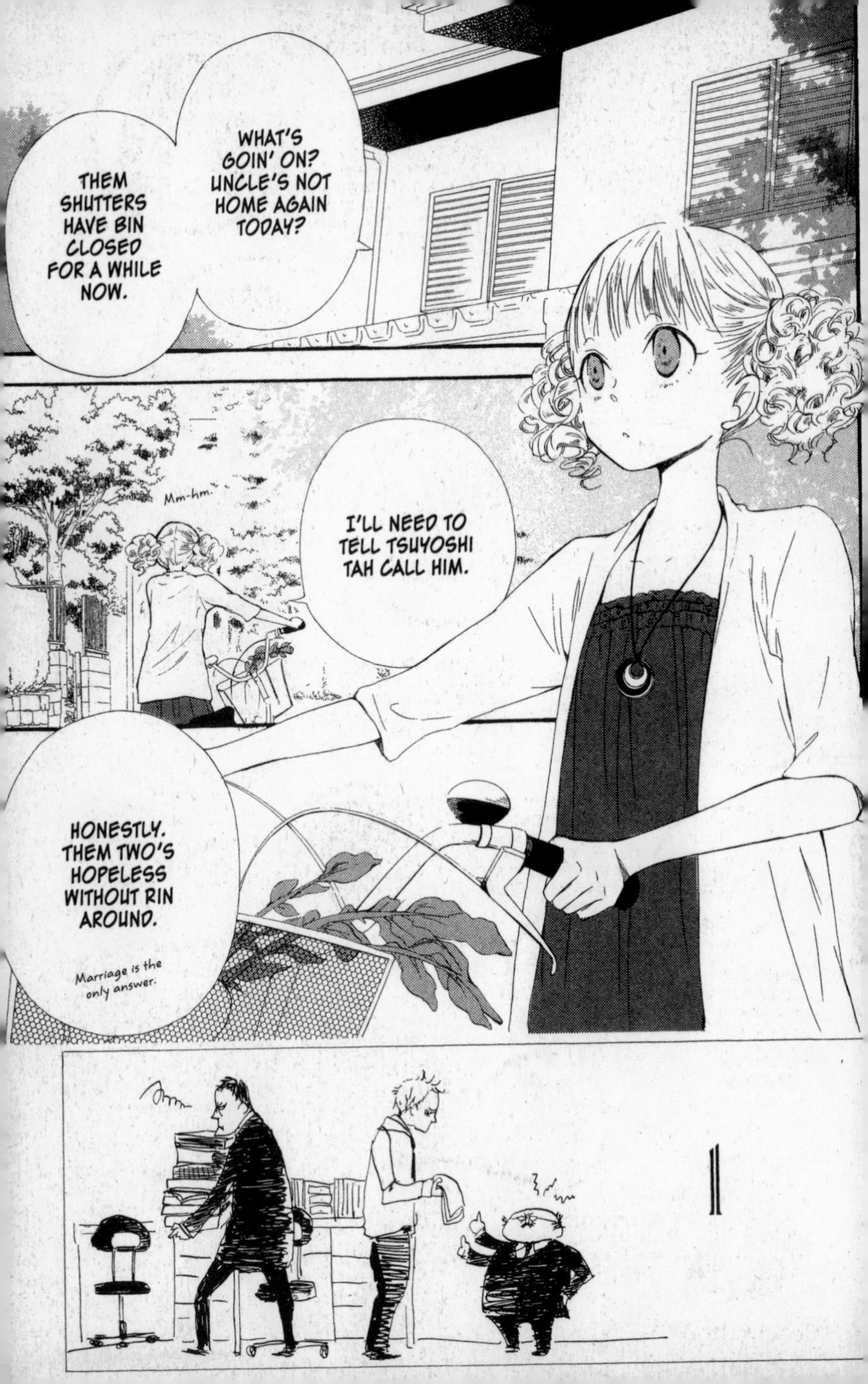
WHAT'S GOIN' ON? UNCLE'S NOT HOME AGAIN TODAY?
THEM SHUTTERS HAVE BIN CLOSED FOR A WHILE NOW.
I'LL NEED TO TELL TSUYOSHI TAH CALL HIM.
Mm-hm.
HONESTLY. THEM TWO'S HOPELESS WITHOUT RIN AROUND.
Marriage is the only answer.

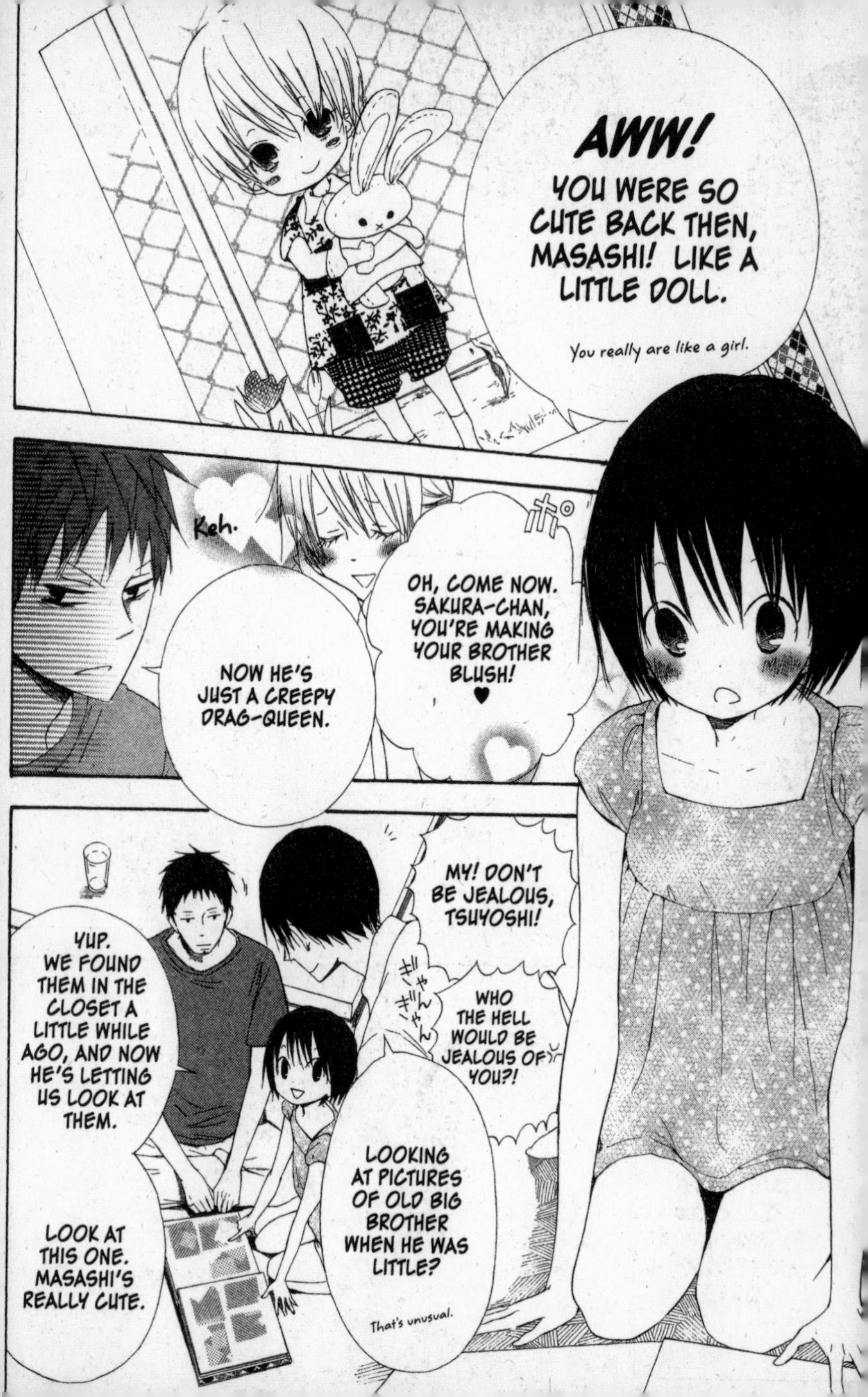
AWW!
YOU WERE SO CUTE BACK THEN, MASASHI! LIKE A LITTLE DOLL.
You really are like a girl.
ポ
OH, COME NOW. SAKURA-CHAN, YOU'RE MAKING YOUR BROTHER BLUSH! ♥
Keh.
NOW HE'S JUST A CREEPY DRAG-QUEEN.
MY! DON'T BE JEALOUS, TSUYOSHI!
WHO THE HELL WOULD BE JEALOUS OF YOU?!
ぎゃんぎゃん
LOOKING AT PICTURES OF OLD BIG BROTHER WHEN HE WAS LITTLE?
That's unusual.
YUP. WE FOUND THEM IN THE CLOSET A LITTLE WHILE AGO, AND NOW HE'S LETTING US LOOK AT THEM.
LOOK AT THIS ONE. MASASHI'S REALLY CUTE.

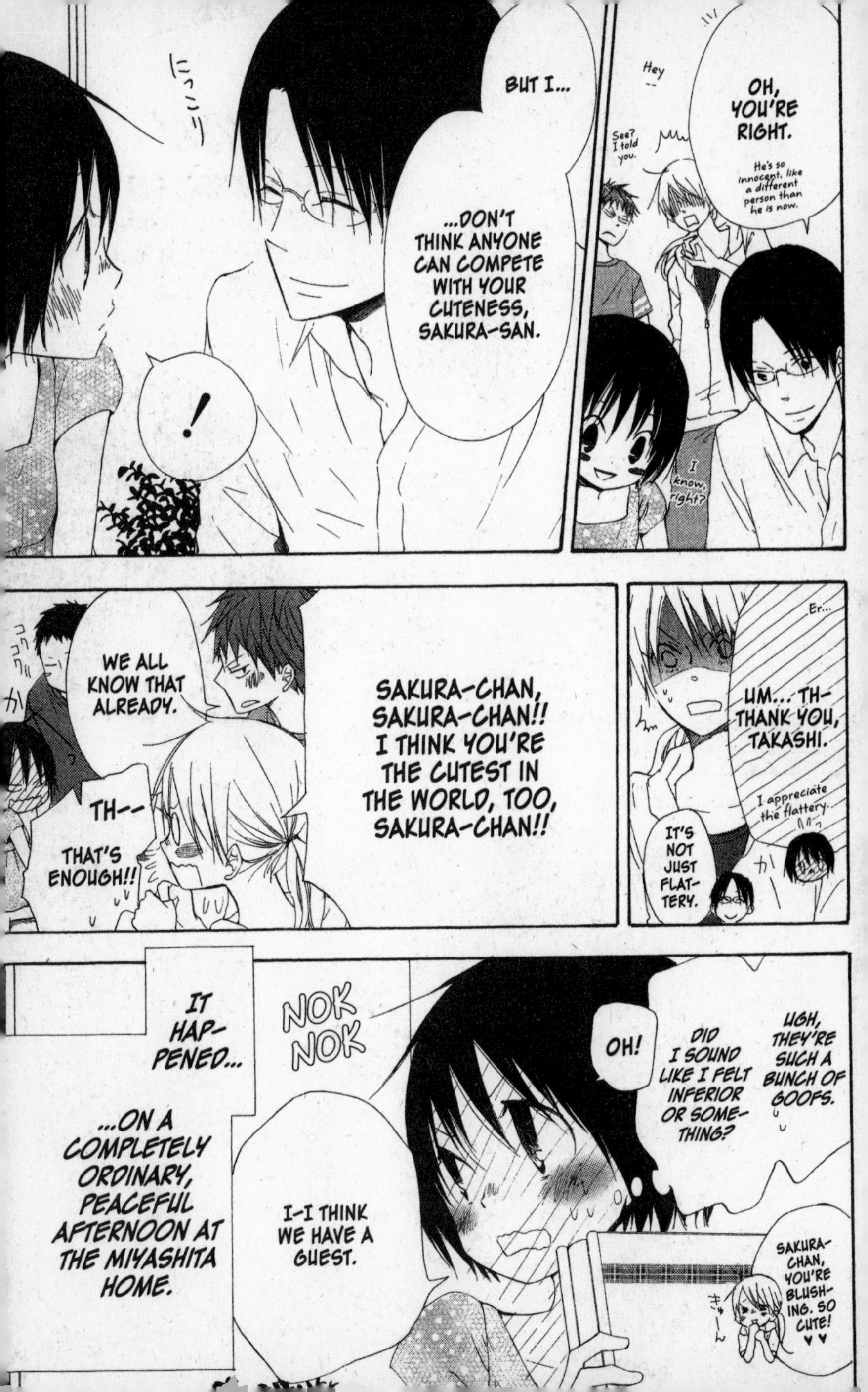
Hey --
OH, YOU'RE RIGHT.
He's so innocent, like a different person than he is now.
See? I told you.
I know, right?
にっこり
BUT I...
...DON'T THINK ANYONE CAN COMPETE WITH YOUR CUTENESS, SAKURA-SAN.
!
Er...
UM... TH-THANK YOU, TAKASHI.
I appreciate the flattery.
IT'S NOT JUST FLATTERY.
か
SAKURA-CHAN, SAKURA-CHAN!! I THINK YOU'RE THE CUTEST IN THE WORLD, TOO, SAKURA-CHAN!!
WE ALL KNOW THAT ALREADY.
コクコク
か
TH--
THAT'S ENOUGH!!
UGH, THEY'RE SUCH A BUNCH OF GOOFS.
DID I SOUND LIKE I FELT INFERIOR OR SOMETHING?
OH!
SAKURA-CHAN, YOU'RE BLUSHING. SO CUTE! ♥♥
きゅーん
I-I THINK WE HAVE A GUEST.
NOK NOK
IT HAPPENED...
...ON A COMPLETELY ORDINARY, PEACEFUL AFTERNOON AT THE MIYASHITA HOME.

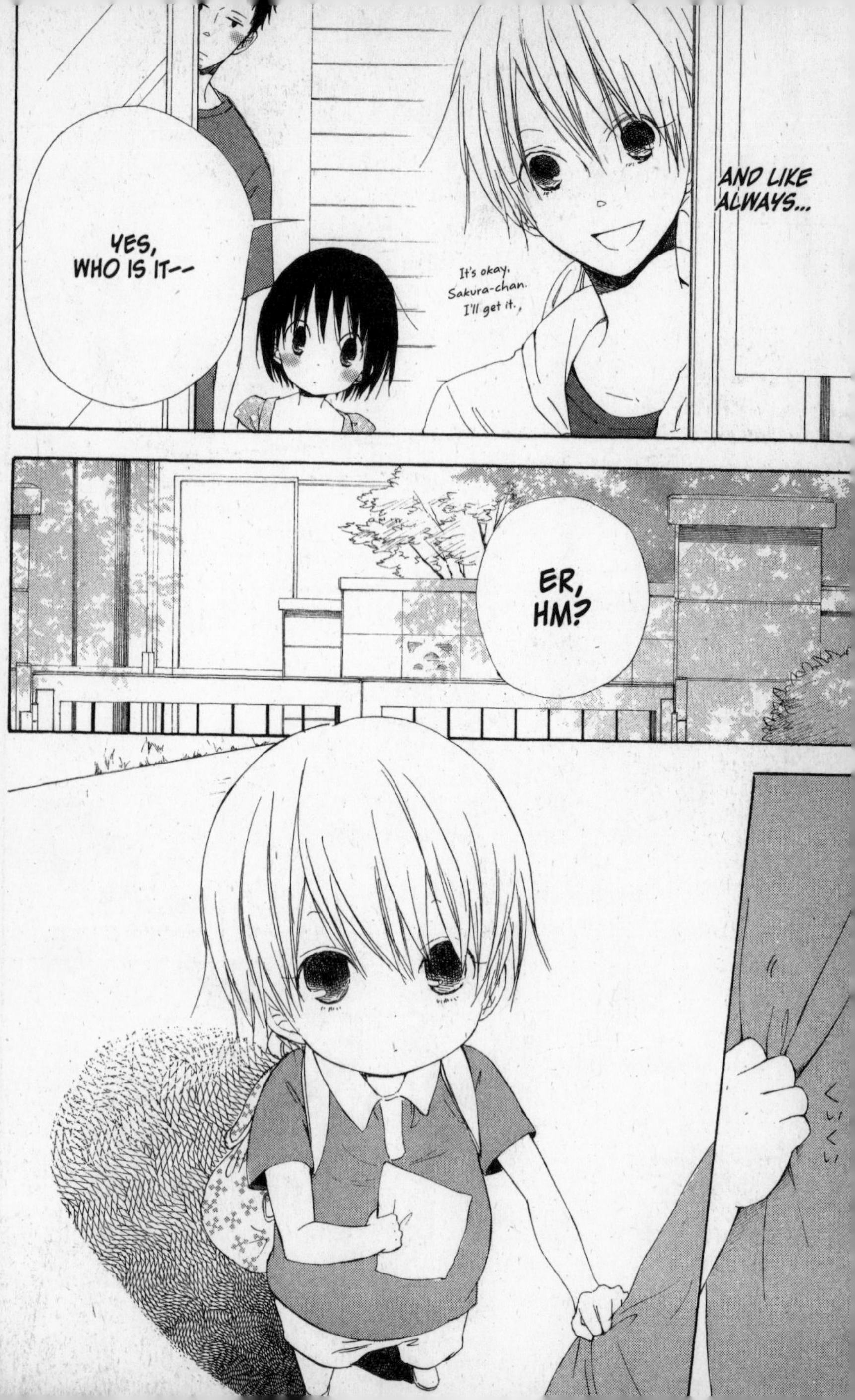
AND LIKE ALWAYS...
YES, WHO IS IT--
It's okay, Sakura-chan. I'll get it.
ER, HM?
くいくい

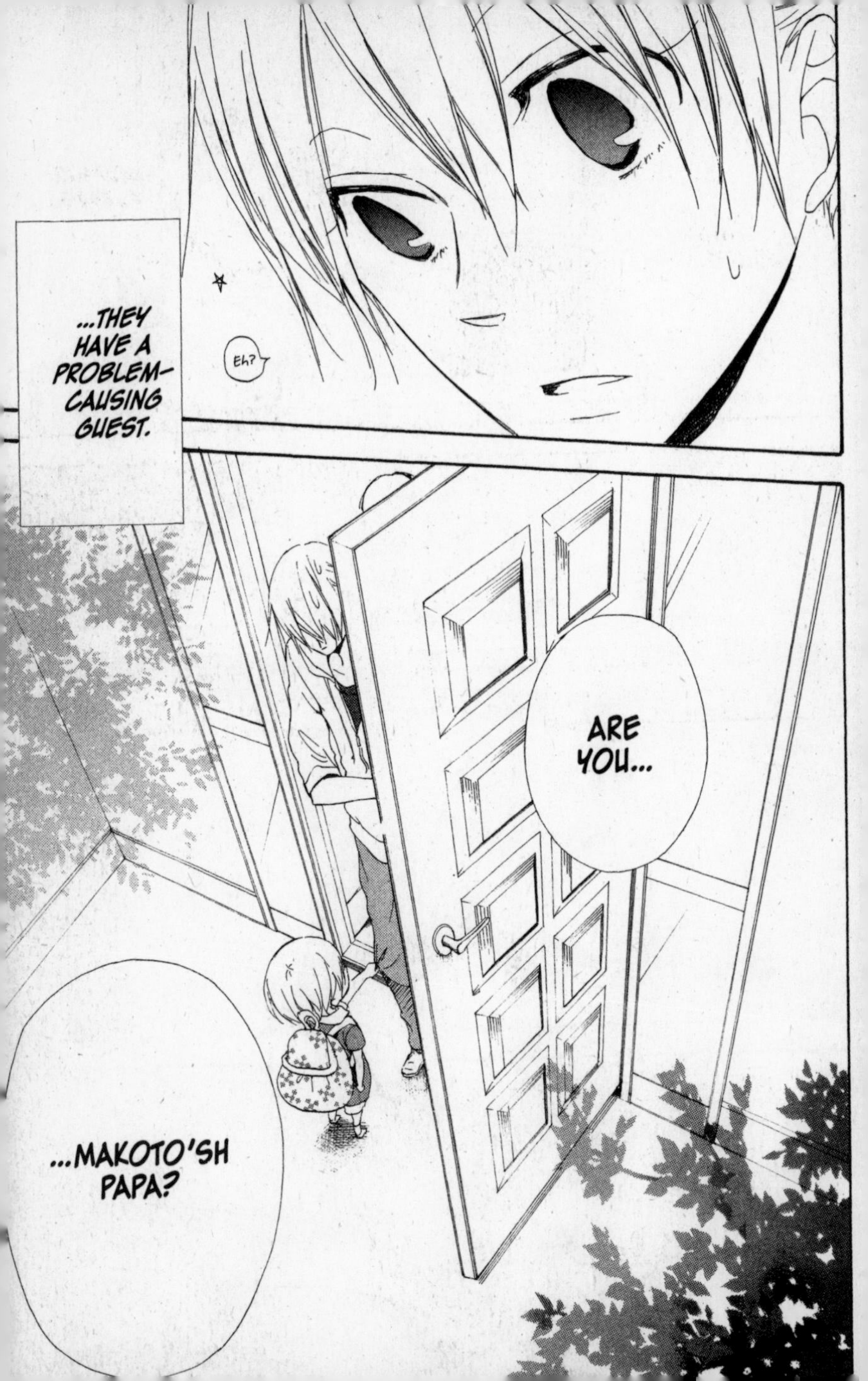
...THEY HAVE A PROBLEM-CAUSING GUEST.
Eh?
ARE YOU...
...MAKOTO'SH PAPA?

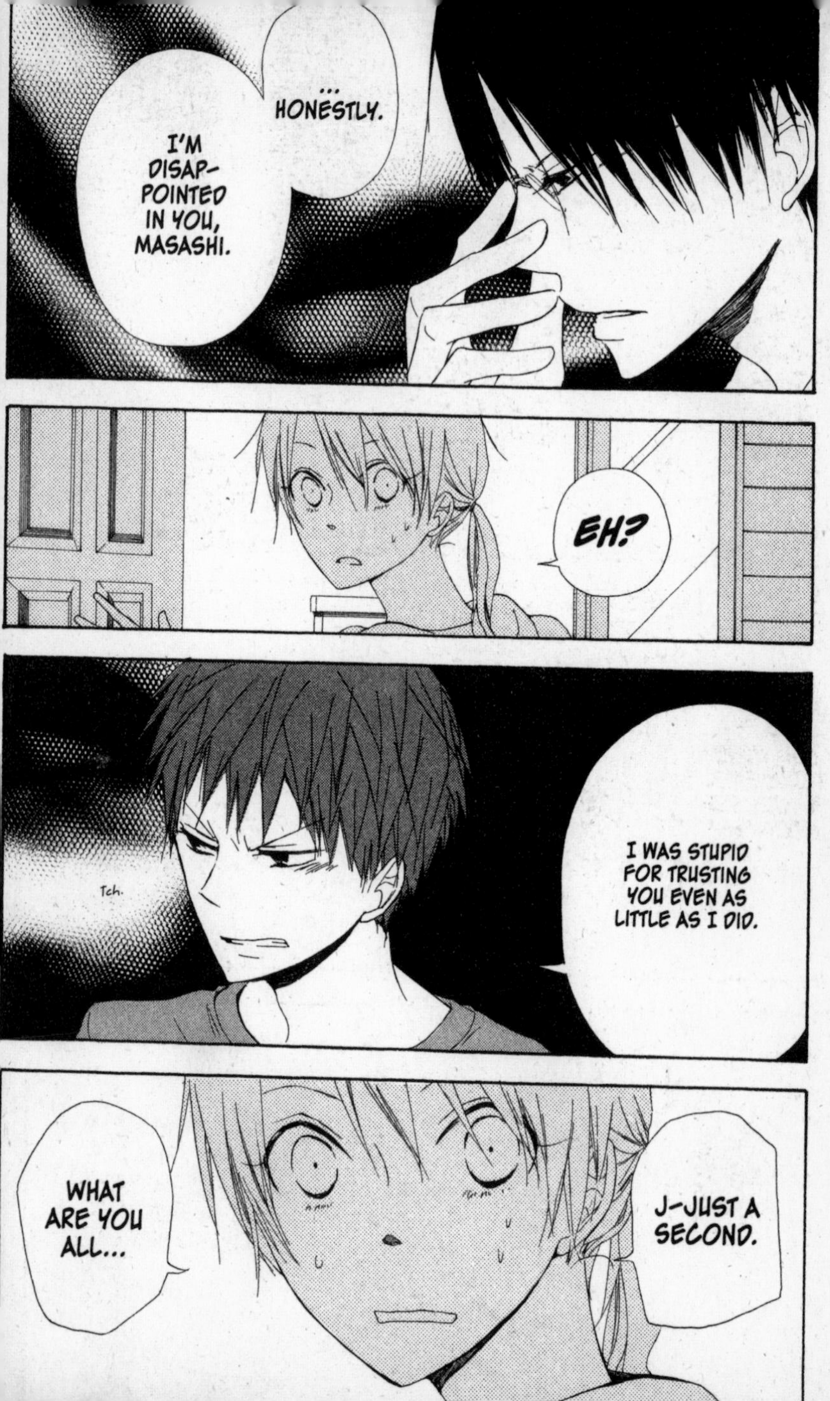
... HONESTLY.
I'M DISAP-POINTED IN YOU, MASASHI.
EH?
I WAS STUPID FOR TRUSTING YOU EVEN AS LITTLE AS I DID.
Tch.
J-JUST A SECOND.
WHAT ARE YOU ALL...

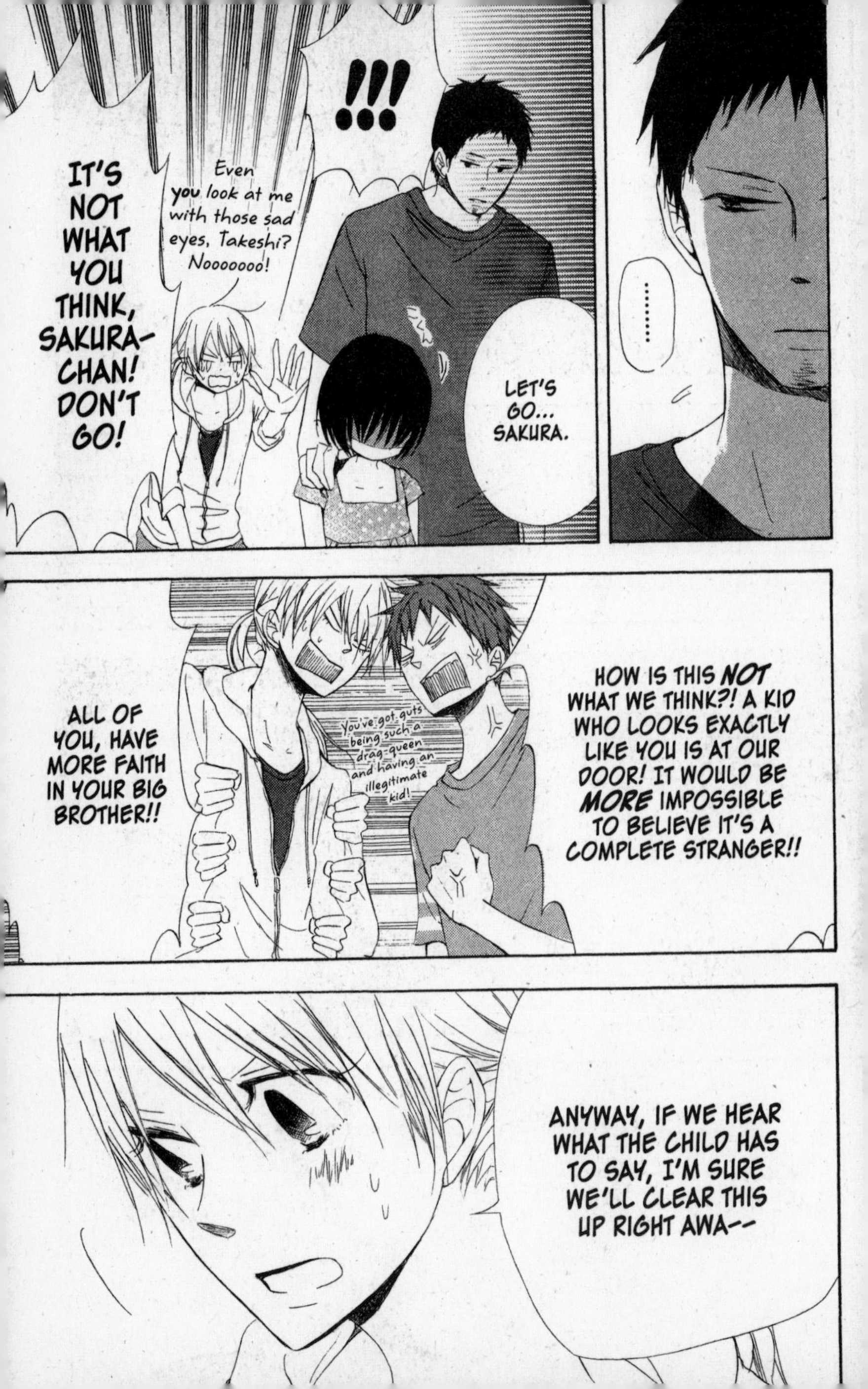
......
LET'S GO... SAKURA.
!!!
Even you look at me with those sad eyes, Takeshi? Nooooooo!
IT'S NOT WHAT YOU THINK, SAKURA-CHAN! DON'T GO!
HOW IS THIS NOT WHAT WE THINK?! A KID WHO LOOKS EXACTLY LIKE YOU IS AT OUR DOOR! IT WOULD BE MORE IMPOSSIBLE TO BELIEVE IT'S A COMPLETE STRANGER!!
You've got guts being such a drag-queen and having an illegitimate kid!
ALL OF YOU, HAVE MORE FAITH IN YOUR BIG BROTHER!!
ANYWAY, IF WE HEAR WHAT THE CHILD HAS TO SAY, I'M SURE WE'LL CLEAR THIS UP RIGHT AWA--

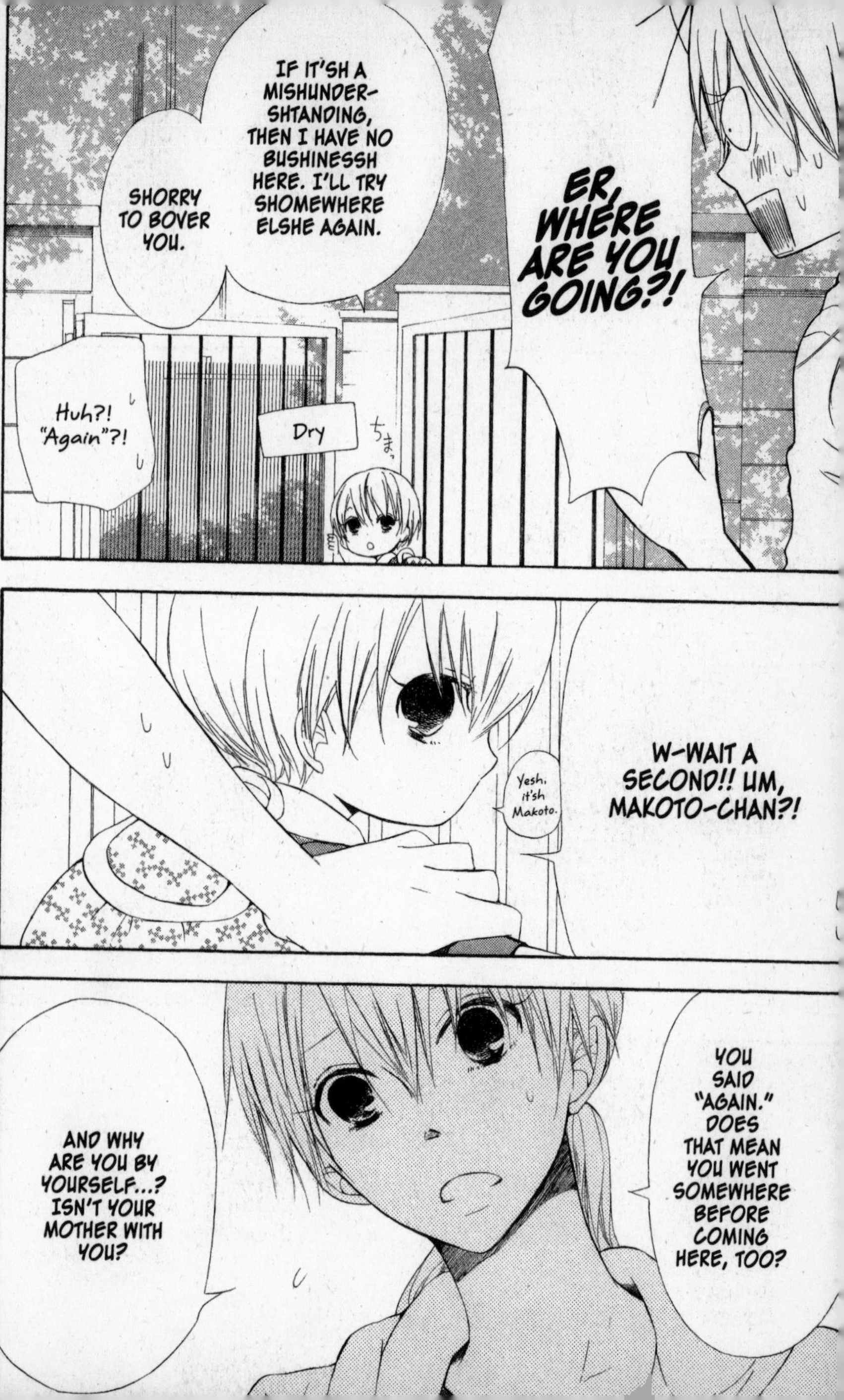
IF IT'SH A MISHUNDER-SHTANDING, THEN I HAVE NO BUSHINESSH HERE. I'LL TRY SHOMEWHERE ELSHE AGAIN.
SHORRY TO BOVER YOU.
ER, WHERE ARE YOU GOING?!
Dry
ちま
Huh?! "Again"?!
W-WAIT A SECOND!! UM, MAKOTO-CHAN?!
Yesh, it'sh Makoto.
YOU SAID "AGAIN." DOES THAT MEAN YOU WENT SOMEWHERE BEFORE COMING HERE, TOO?
AND WHY ARE YOU BY YOURSELF...? ISN'T YOUR MOTHER WITH YOU?

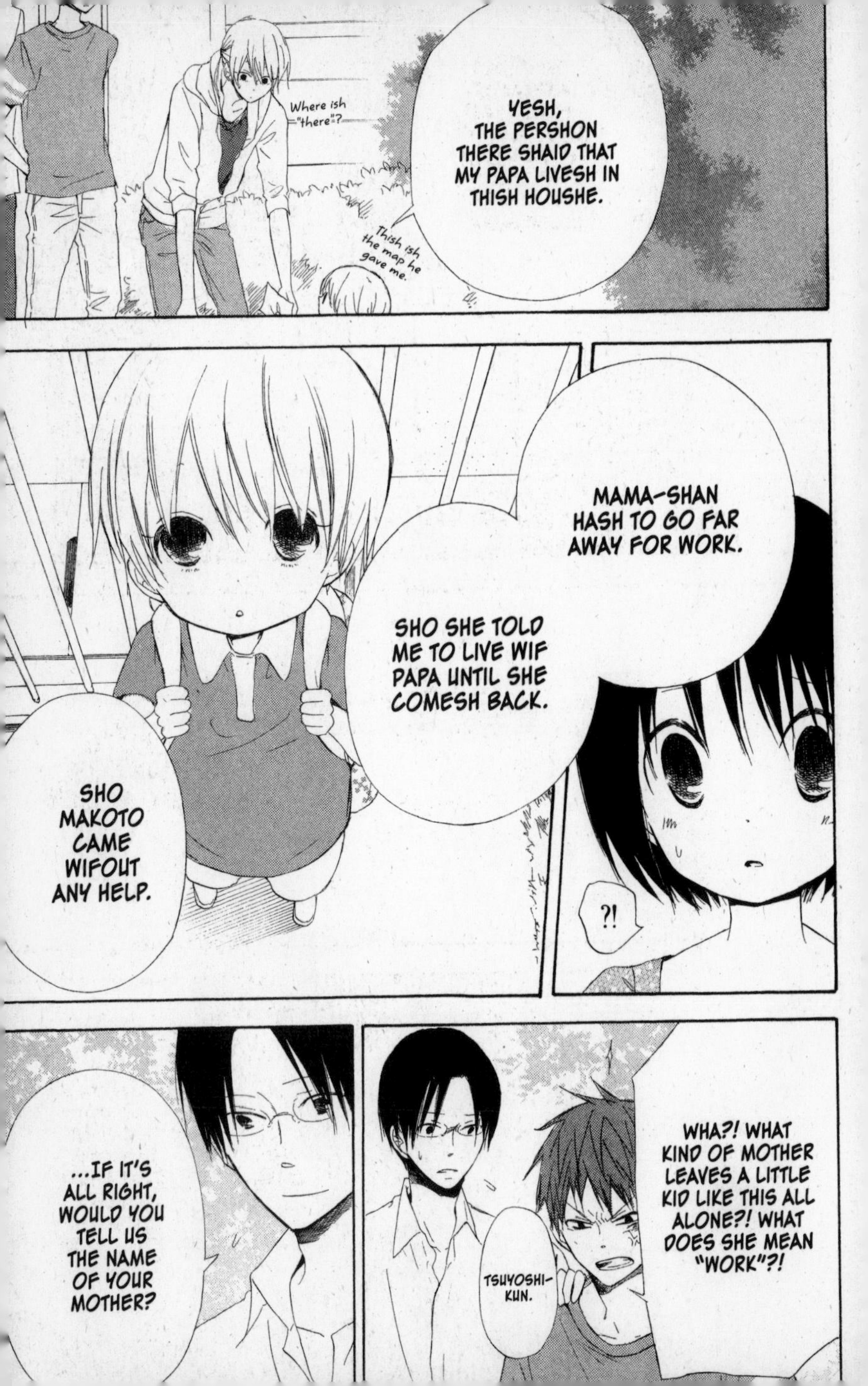
YESH, THE PERSHON THERE SHAID THAT MY PAPA LIVESH IN THISH HOUSHE.
Thish ish the map he gave me.
Where ish "there"?
MAMA-SHAN HASH TO GO FAR AWAY FOR WORK.
?!
SHO SHE TOLD ME TO LIVE WIF PAPA UNTIL SHE COMESH BACK.
SHO MAKOTO CAME WIFOUT ANY HELP.
WHA?! WHAT KIND OF MOTHER LEAVES A LITTLE KID LIKE THIS ALL ALONE?! WHAT DOES SHE MEAN "WORK"?!
TSUYOSHI-KUN.
...IF IT'S ALL RIGHT, WOULD YOU TELL US THE NAME OF YOUR MOTHER?

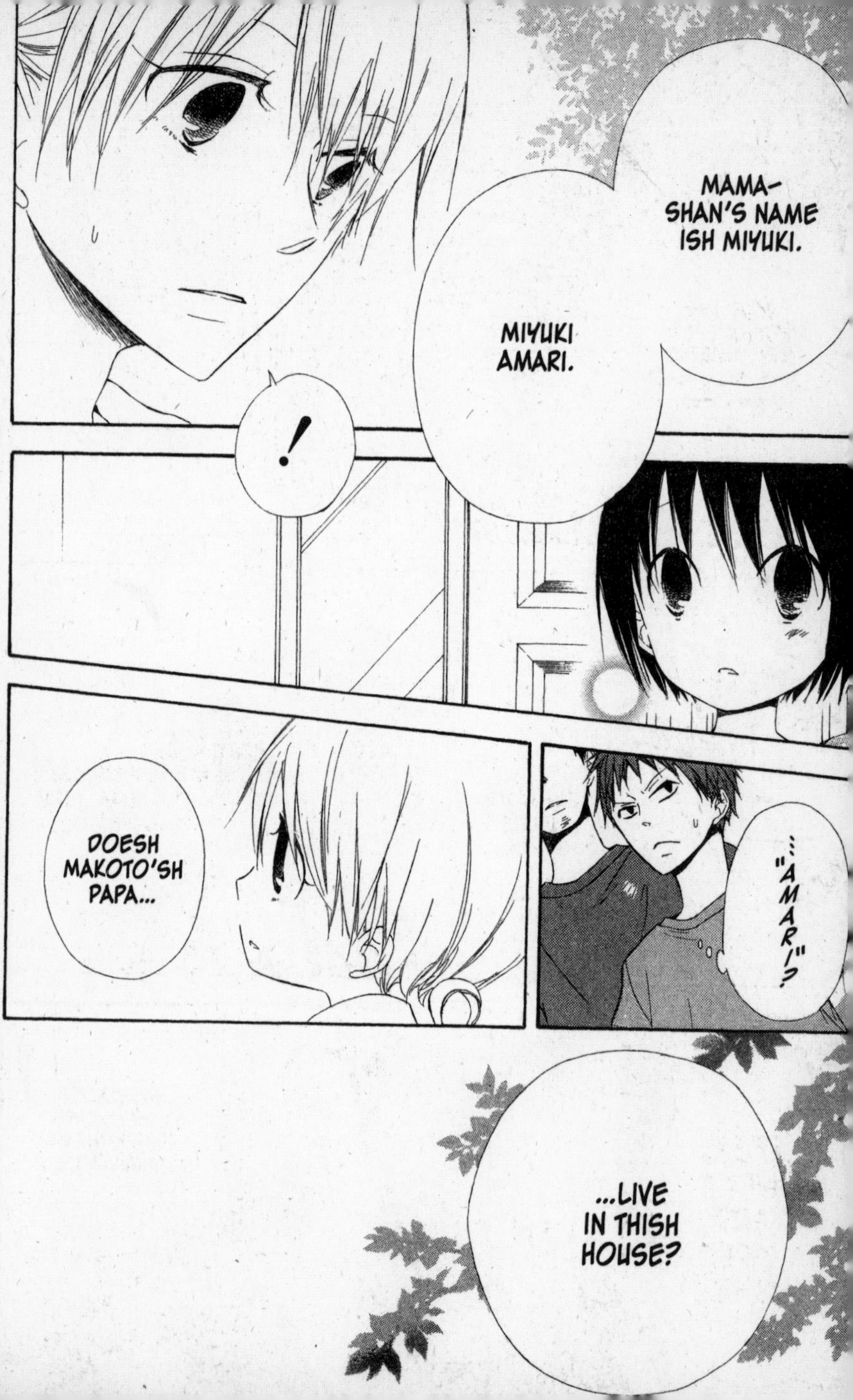

MAMA-SHAN'S NAME ISH MIYUKI.
MIYUKI AMARI.
!
..."AMARI"?
DOESH MAKOTO'SH PAPA...
...LIVE IN THISH HOUSE?

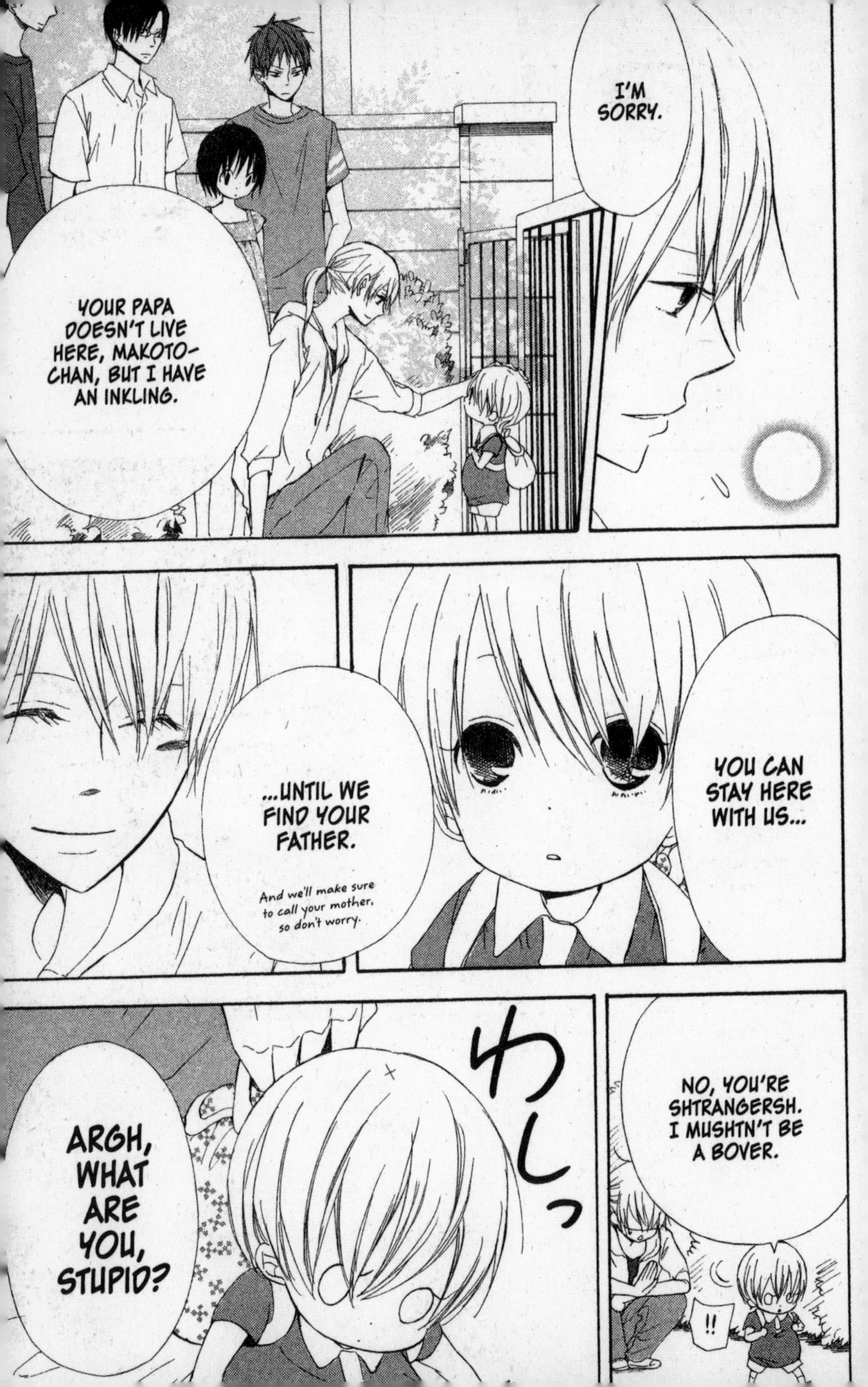
I'M SORRY.
YOUR PAPA DOESN'T LIVE HERE, MAKOTO-CHAN, BUT I HAVE AN INKLING.
YOU CAN STAY HERE WITH US...
...UNTIL WE FIND YOUR FATHER.
And we'll make sure to call your mother, so don't worry.
NO, YOU'RE SHTRANGERSH. I MUSHTN'T BE A BOVER.
!!
めしっ
ARGH, WHAT ARE YOU, STUPID?

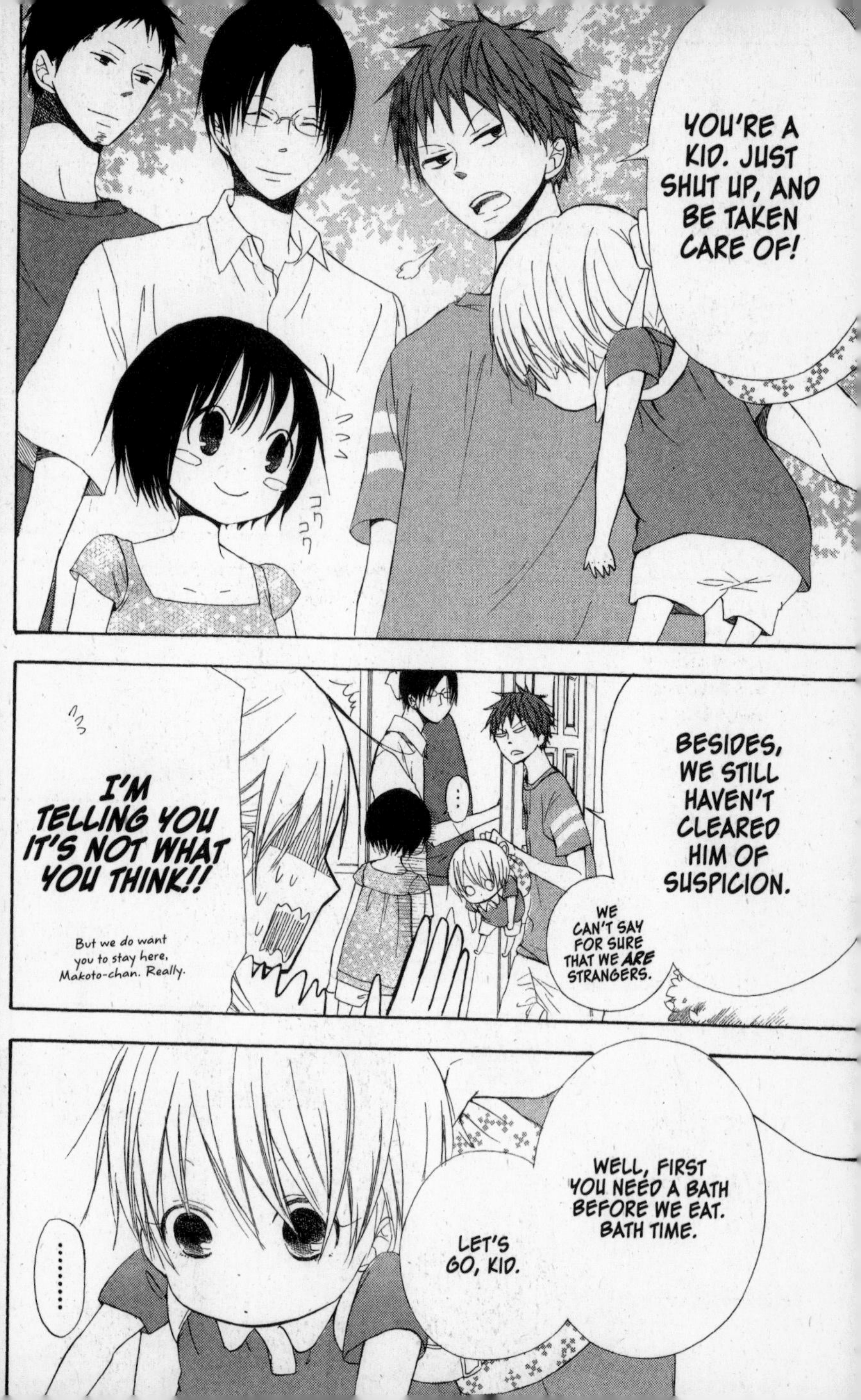
YOU'RE A KID. JUST SHUT UP, AND BE TAKEN CARE OF!
BESIDES, WE STILL HAVEN'T CLEARED HIM OF SUSPICION.
WE CAN'T SAY FOR SURE THAT WE *ARE* STRANGERS.
...
I'M TELLING YOU IT'S NOT WHAT YOU THINK!!
But we do want you to stay here, Makoto-chan. Really.
WELL, FIRST YOU NEED A BATH BEFORE WE EAT. BATH TIME.
LET'S GO, KID.
....

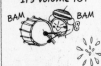

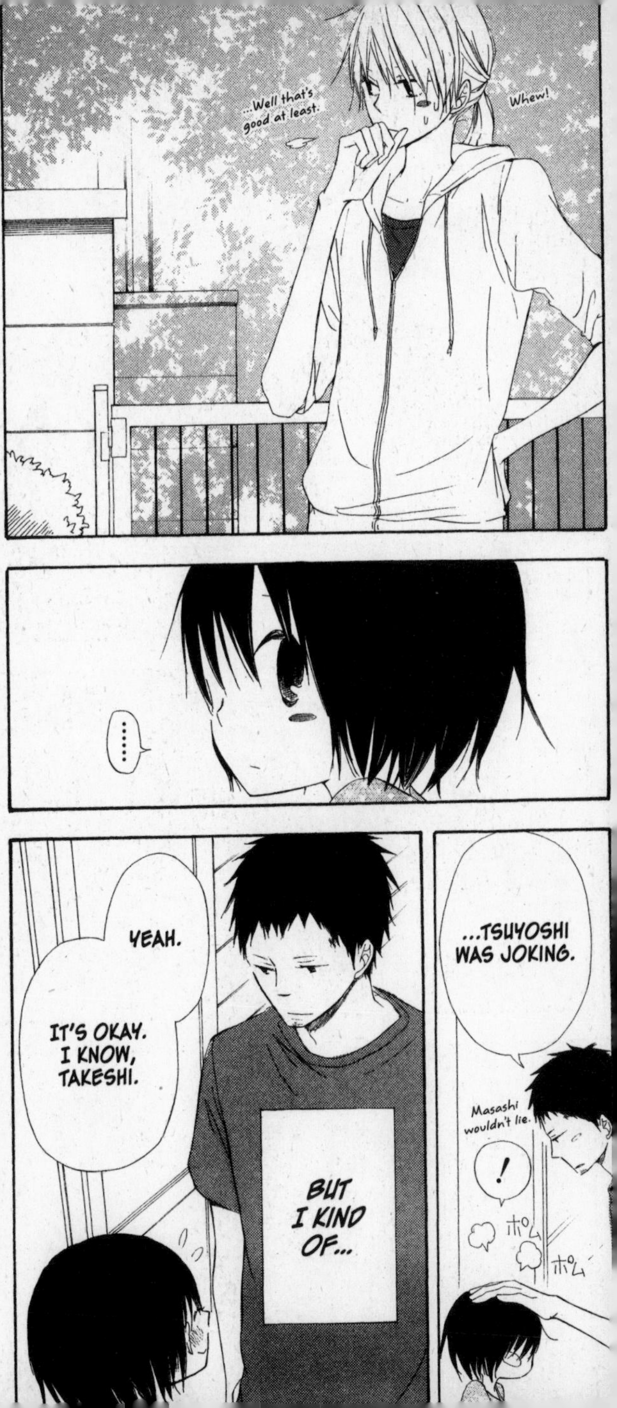
Whew!
...Well that's good at least.
......
...TSUYOSHI WAS JOKING.
!
Masashi wouldn't lie.
ポム
ポム
YEAH.
IT'S OKAY. I KNOW, TAKESHI.
BUT I KIND OF...

1

Hello!
Amazing!
Incredible!
It's volume 10!

BAM BAM

It's all thanks to all you readers! Thank you very much!

When I'm about to lose heart drawing the rough draft before a deadline, your letters and everything really do encourage me.

...And yet my responses are delayed. I'm sorry.

Shape up!

Eh heh...

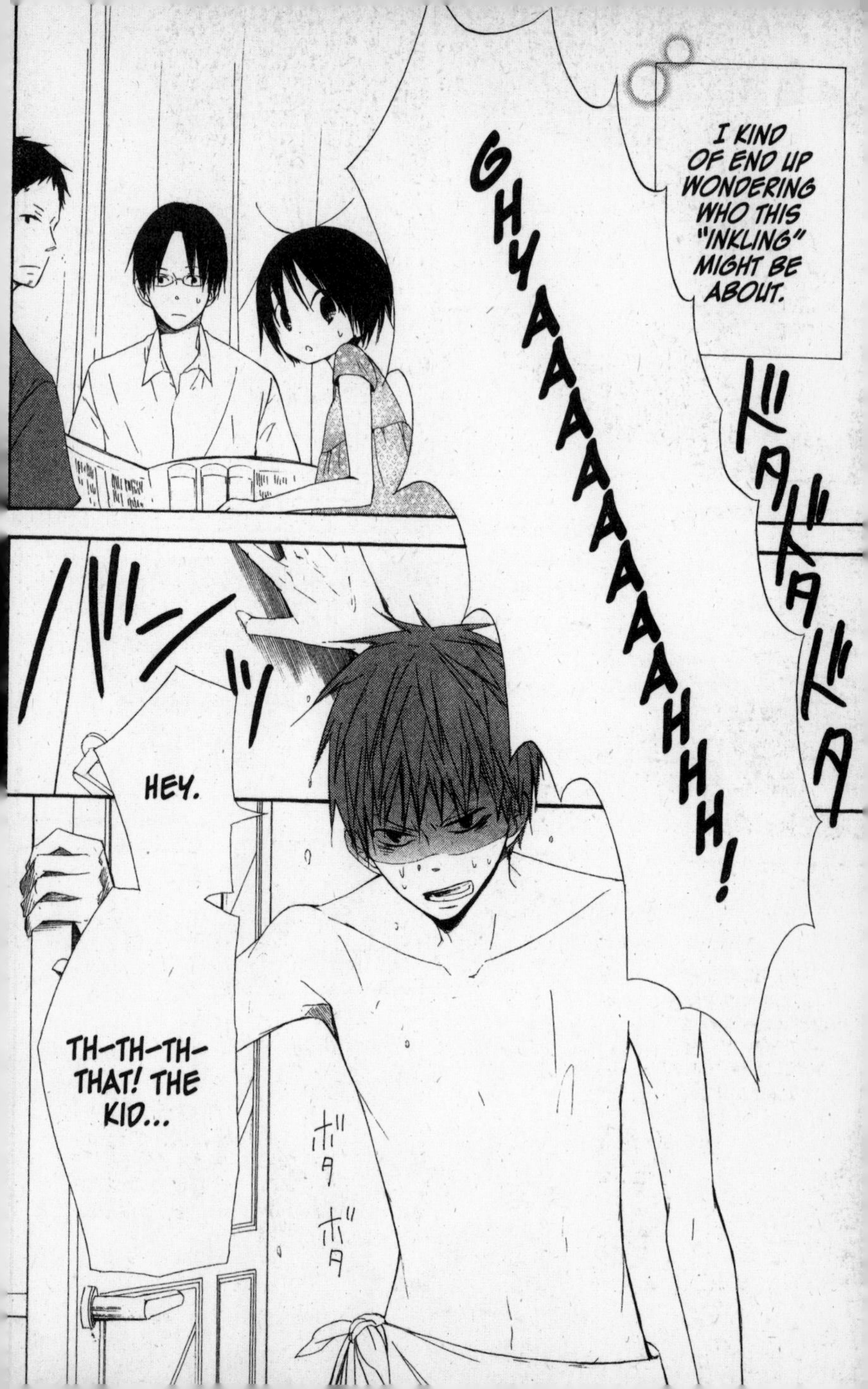
I KIND OF END UP WONDERING WHO THIS "INKLING" MIGHT BE ABOUT.
ドAドAドA
GHYAAAAAAAAAHHH!
バーンッ
HEY.
TH-TH-TH-THAT! THE KID...
ボタ ボタ

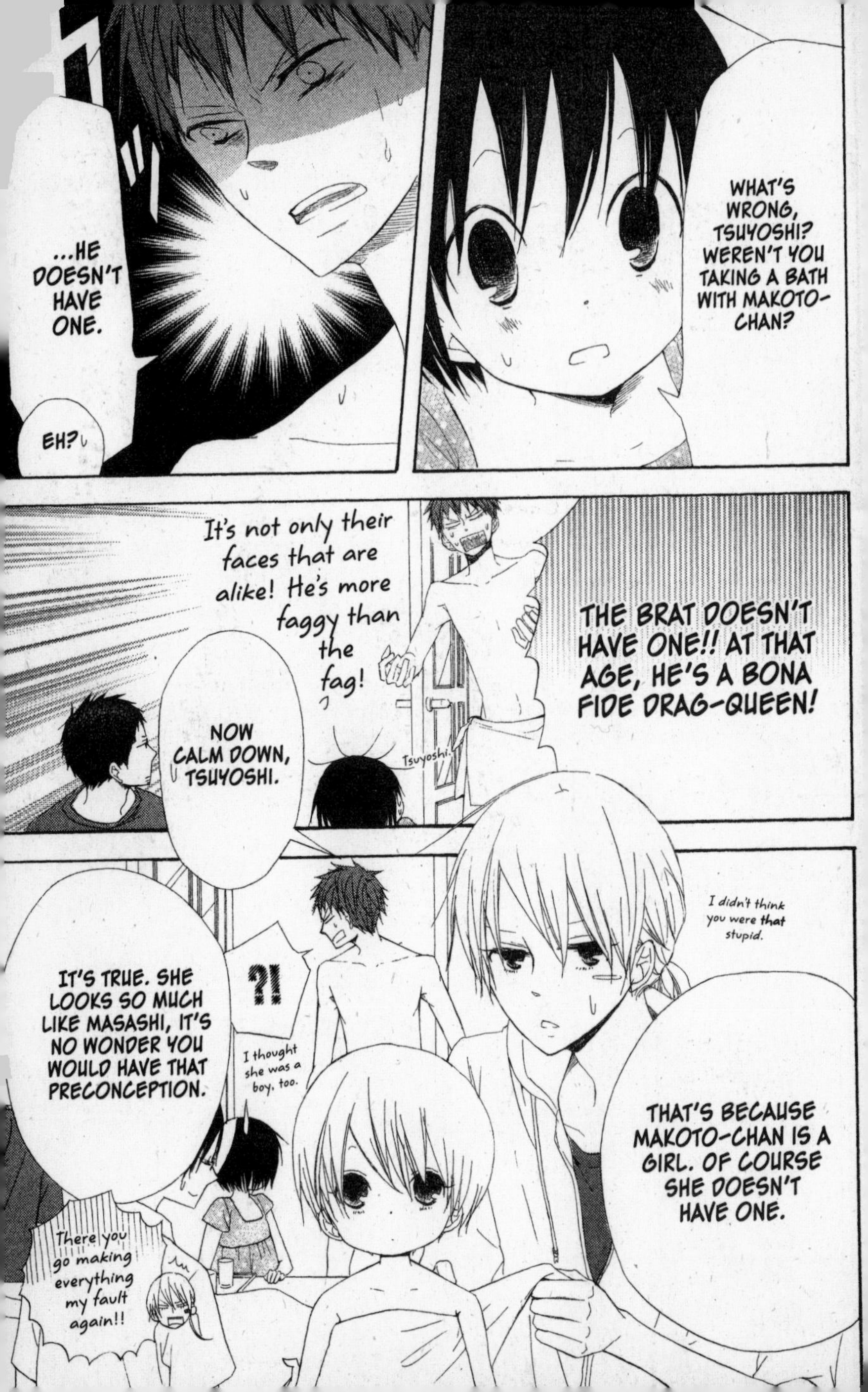
WHAT'S WRONG, TSUYOSHI? WEREN'T YOU TAKING A BATH WITH MAKOTO-CHAN?
...HE DOESN'T HAVE ONE.
EH?
THE BRAT DOESN'T HAVE ONE!! AT THAT AGE, HE'S A BONA FIDE DRAG-QUEEN!
Tsuyoshi.
It's not only their faces that are alike! He's more faggy than the fag!
NOW CALM DOWN, TSUYOSHI.
THAT'S BECAUSE MAKOTO-CHAN IS A GIRL. OF COURSE SHE DOESN'T HAVE ONE.
I didn't think you were that stupid.
?!
I thought she was a boy, too.
IT'S TRUE. SHE LOOKS SO MUCH LIKE MASASHI, IT'S NO WONDER YOU WOULD HAVE THAT PRECONCEPTION.
There you go making everything my fault again!!

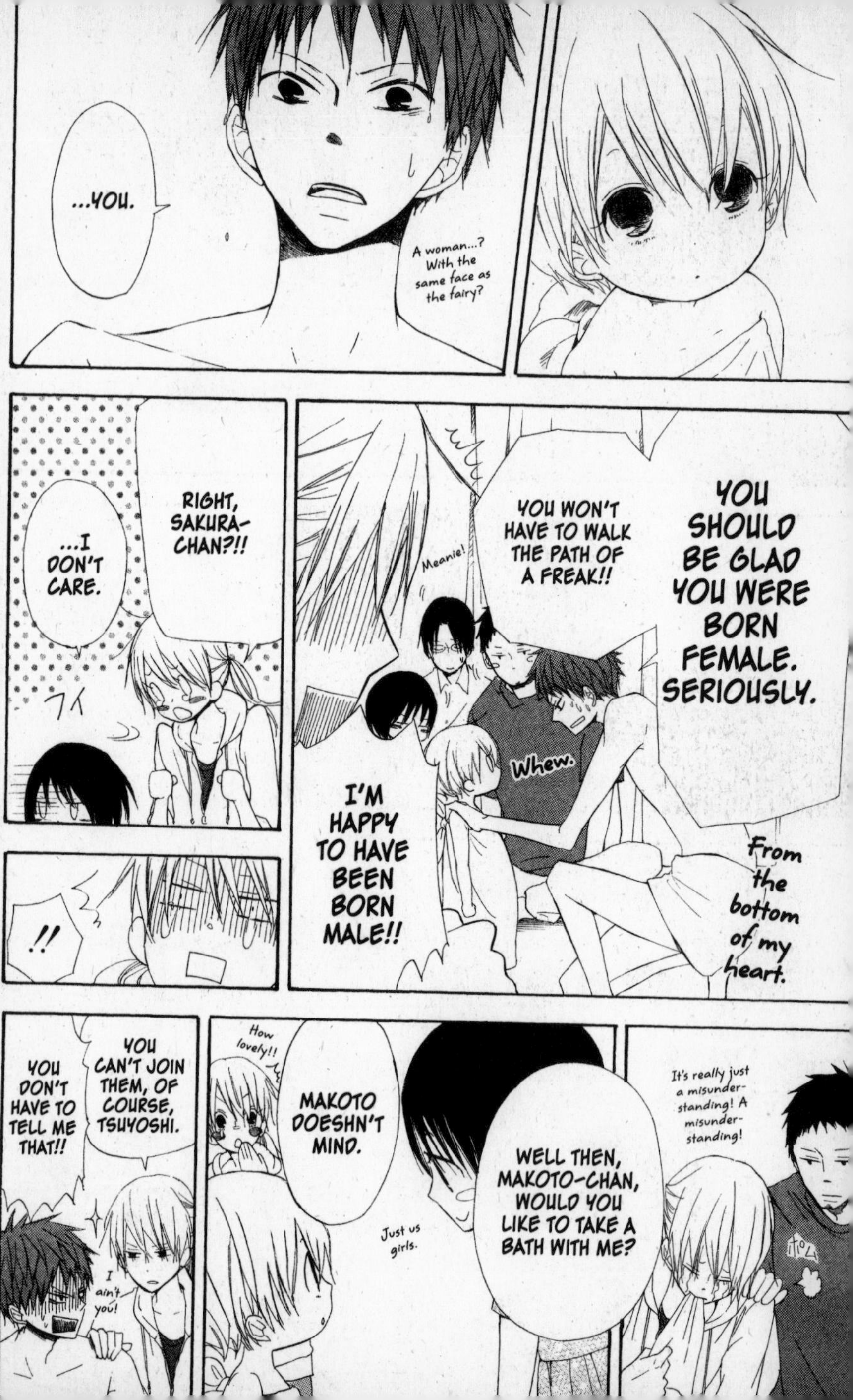
...YOU.
A woman...? With the same face as the fairy?
YOU SHOULD BE GLAD YOU WERE BORN FEMALE. SERIOUSLY.
YOU WON'T HAVE TO WALK THE PATH OF A FREAK!!
Meanie!
From the bottom of my heart.
Whew.
I'M HAPPY TO HAVE BEEN BORN MALE!!
RIGHT, SAKURA-CHAN?!!
...I DON'T CARE.
!!
It's really just a misunderstanding! A misunderstanding!
WELL THEN, MAKOTO-CHAN, WOULD YOU LIKE TO TAKE A BATH WITH ME?
Just us girls.
MAKOTO DOESHN'T MIND.
How lovely!!
YOU CAN'T JOIN THEM, OF COURSE, TSUYOSHI.
YOU DON'T HAVE TO TELL ME THAT!!
I ain't you!

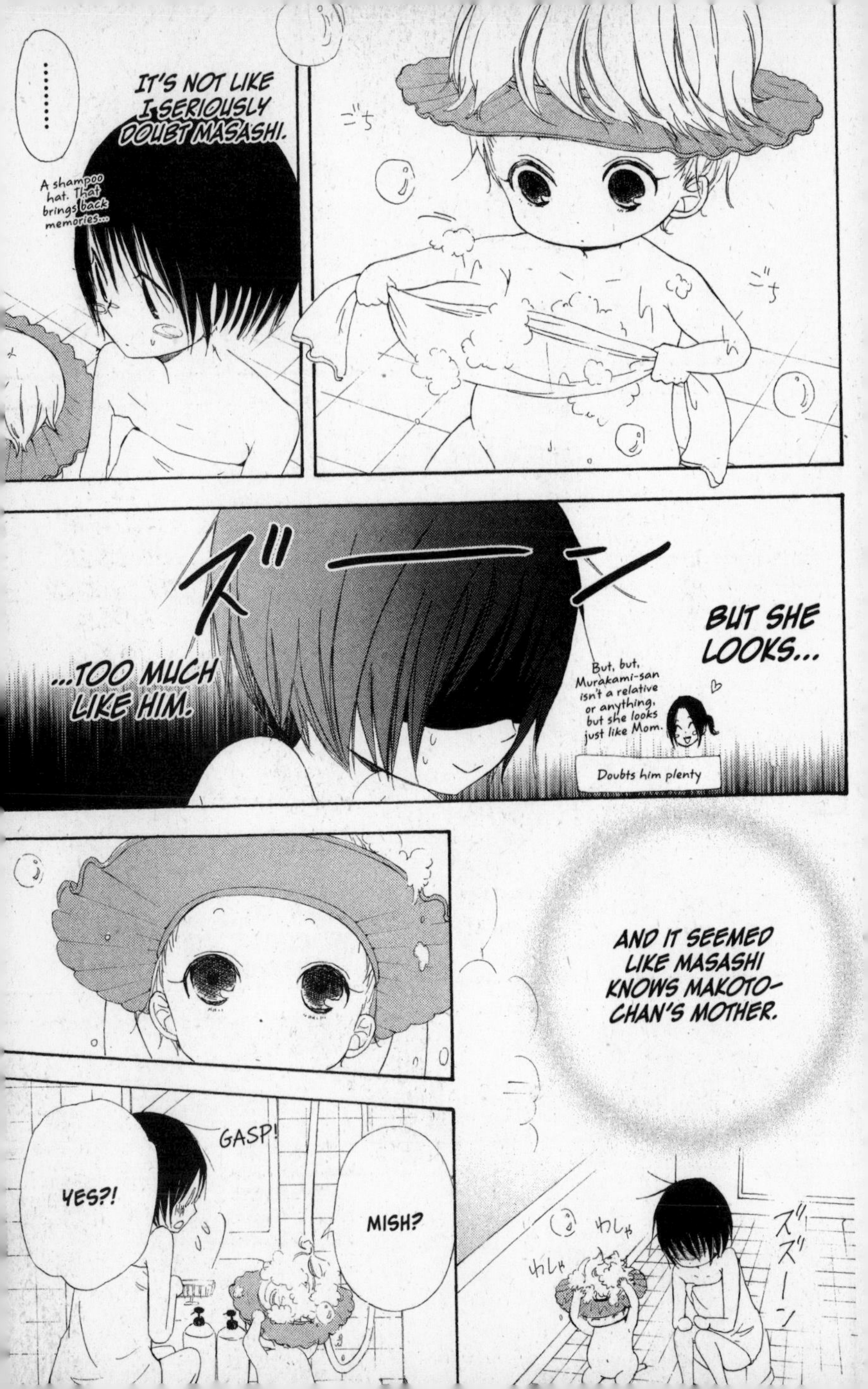
ごち
ごち
IT'S NOT LIKE I SERIOUSLY DOUBT MASASHI.
......
A shampoo hat. That brings back memories...
BUT SHE LOOKS...
But, but, Murakami-san isn't a relative or anything, but she looks just like Mom.
Doubts him plenty
ズーーーン
...TOO MUCH LIKE HIM.
AND IT SEEMED LIKE MASASHI KNOWS MAKOTO-CHAN'S MOTHER.
わしゃ
わしゃ
ズーン
ズーン
MISH?
GASP!
YES?!

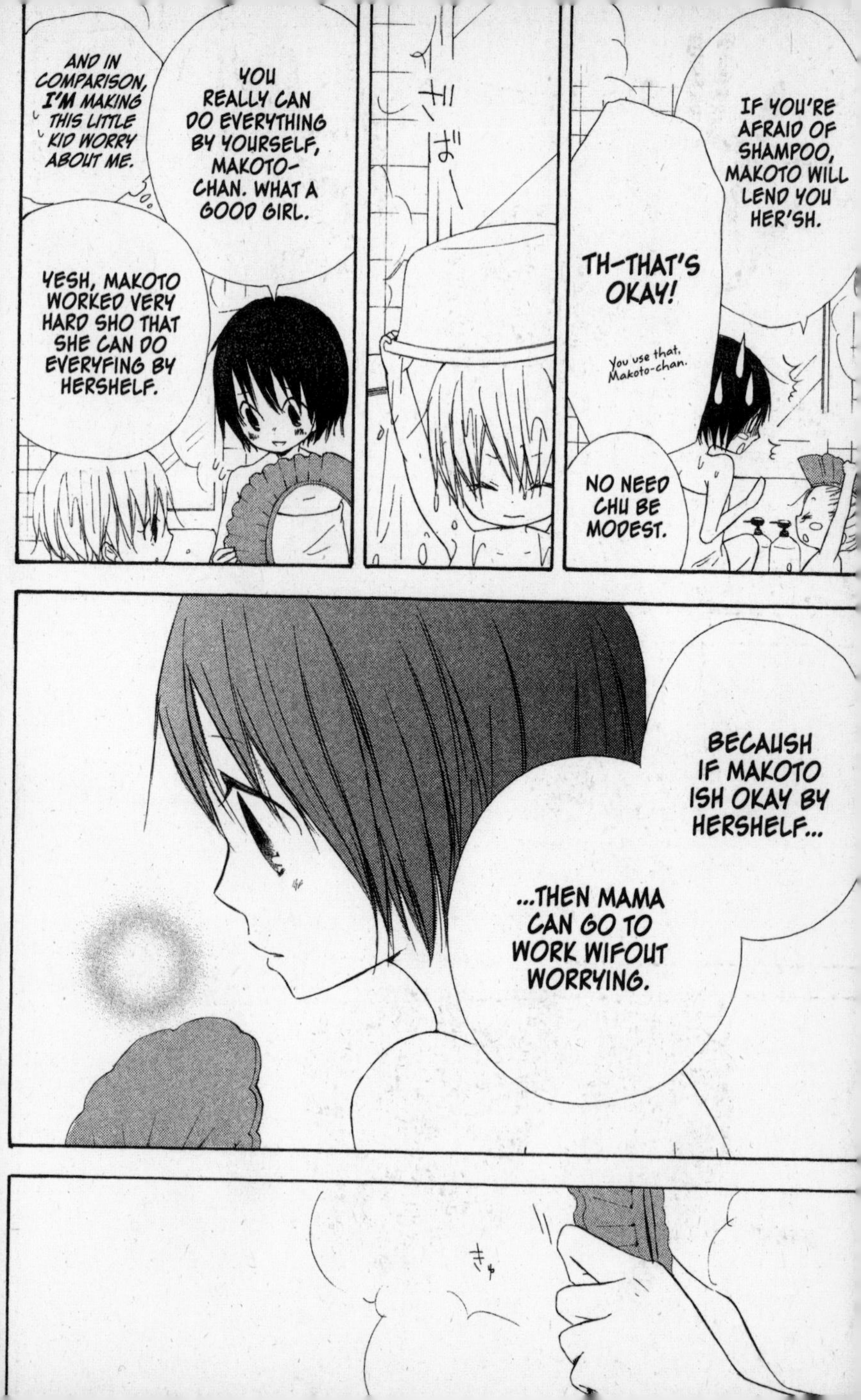
IF YOU'RE AFRAID OF SHAMPOO, MAKOTO WILL LEND YOU HER'SH.
TH-THAT'S OKAY!
You use that, Makoto-chan.
NO NEED CHU BE MODEST.
YOU REALLY CAN DO EVERYTHING BY YOURSELF, MAKOTO-CHAN. WHAT A GOOD GIRL.
AND IN COMPARISON, I'M MAKING THIS LITTLE KID WORRY ABOUT ME.
YESH, MAKOTO WORKED VERY HARD SHO THAT SHE CAN DO EVERYFING BY HERSHELF.
BECAUSH IF MAKOTO ISH OKAY BY HERSHELF...
...THEN MAMA CAN GO TO WORK WIFOUT WORRYING.
きゅ

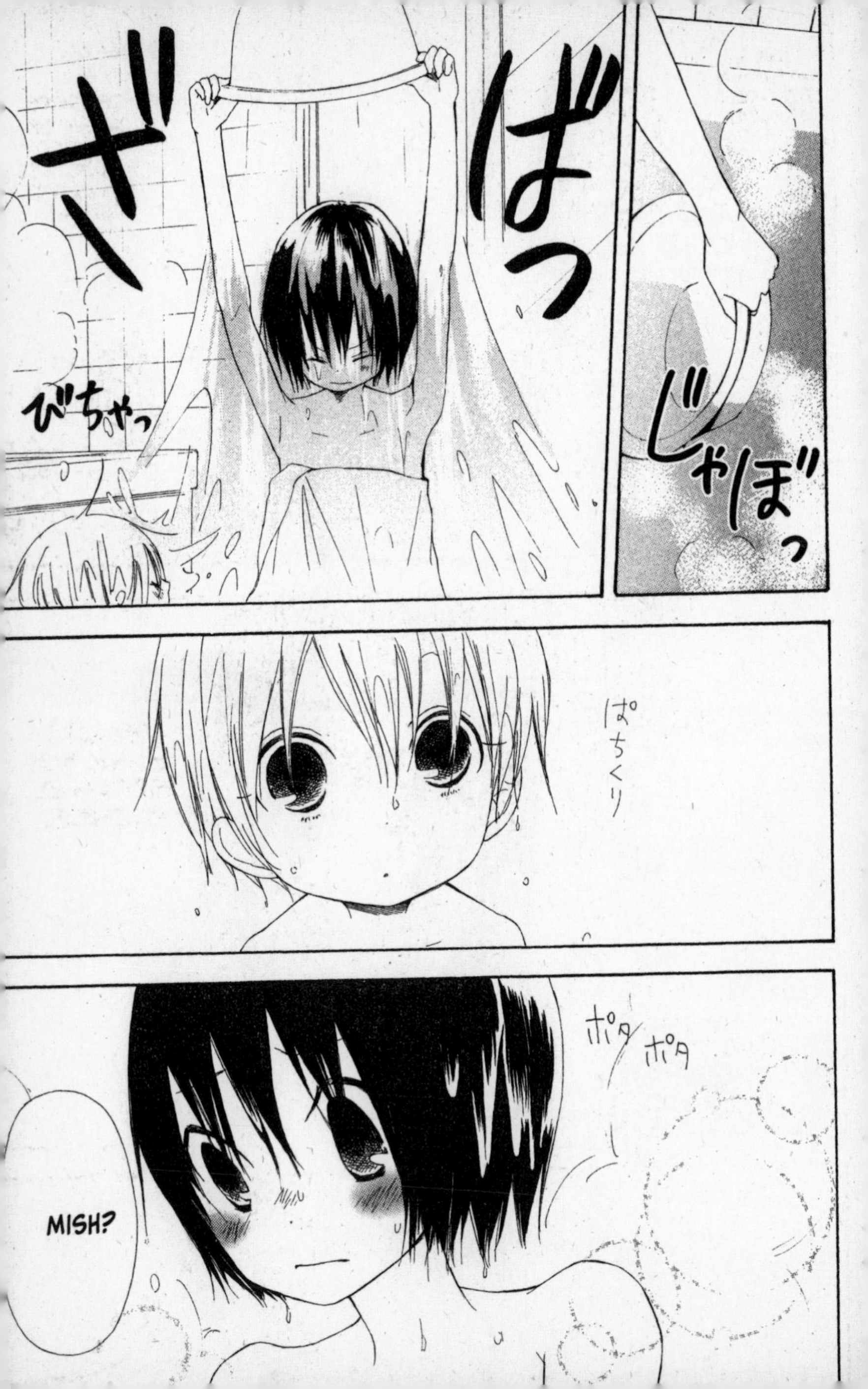
じゃぼっ
ばっ
ザ
びちゃっ
ぱちくり
ポタ ポタ
MISH?

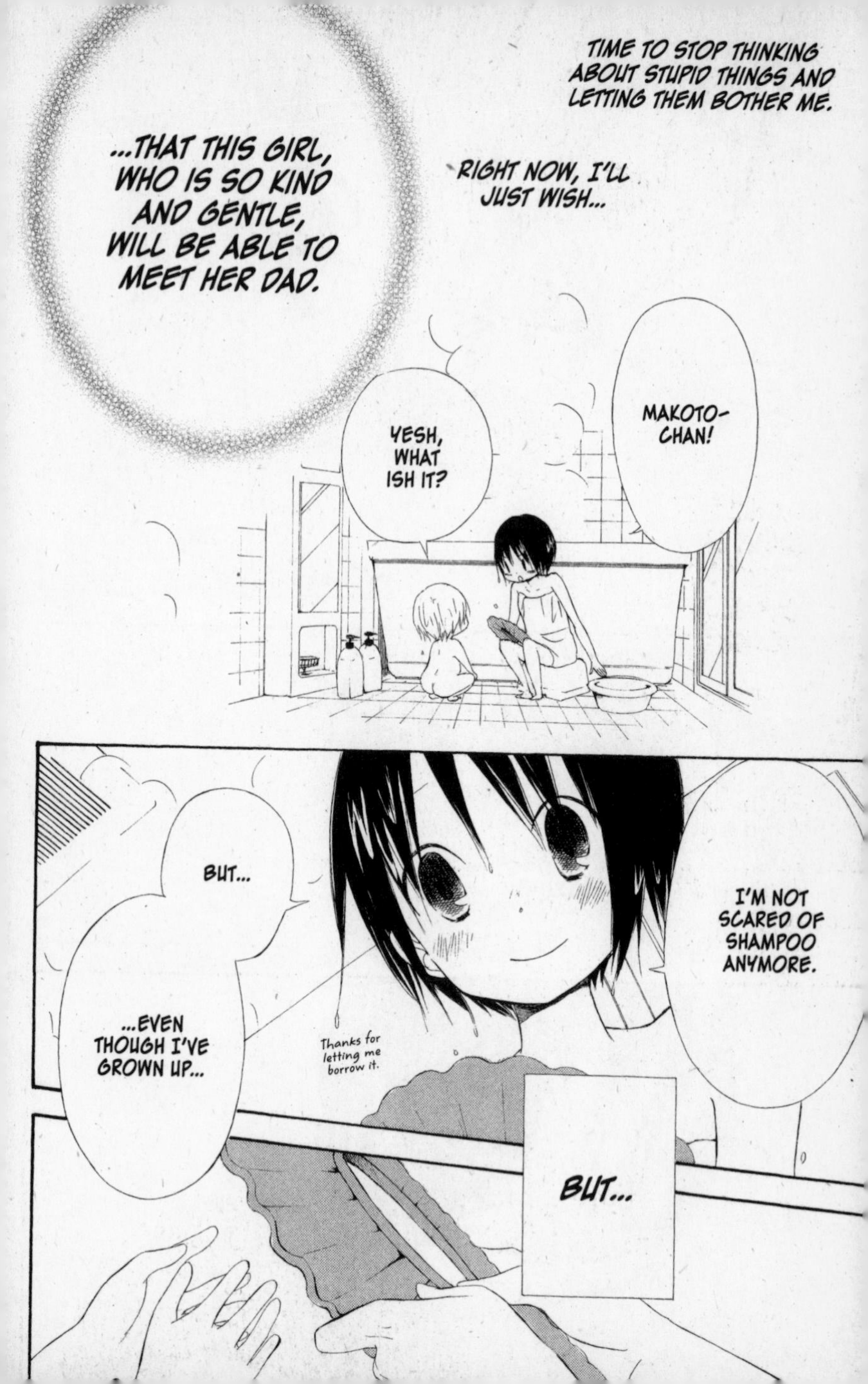

TIME TO STOP THINKING ABOUT STUPID THINGS AND LETTING THEM BOTHER ME.
RIGHT NOW, I'LL JUST WISH...
...THAT THIS GIRL, WHO IS SO KIND AND GENTLE, WILL BE ABLE TO MEET HER DAD.
MAKOTO-CHAN!
YESH, WHAT ISH IT?
I'M NOT SCARED OF SHAMPOO ANYMORE.
Thanks for letting me borrow it.
BUT...
...EVEN THOUGH I'VE GROWN UP...
BUT...

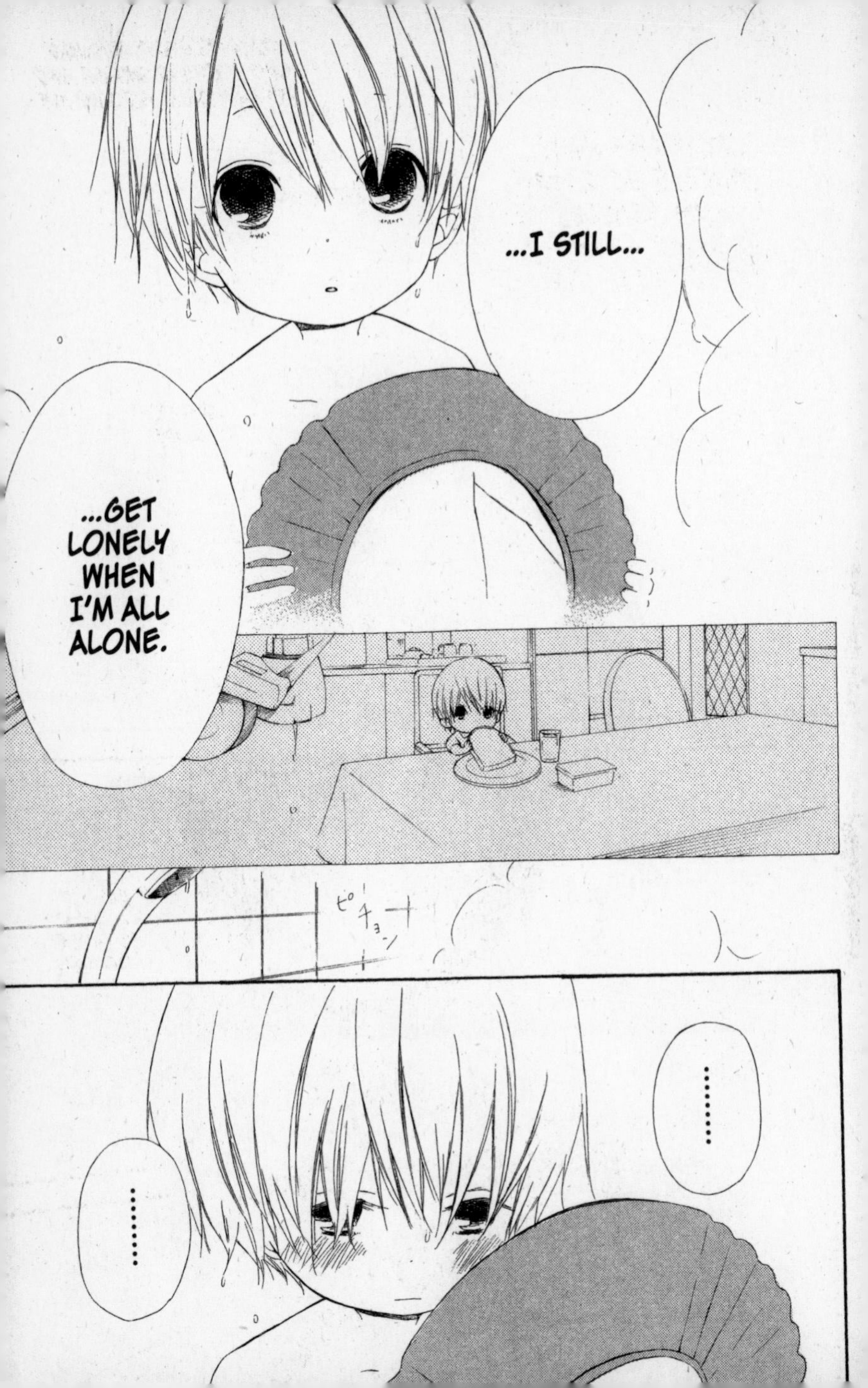
...I STILL...
...GET LONELY WHEN I'M ALL ALONE.
ピチョン
....
....

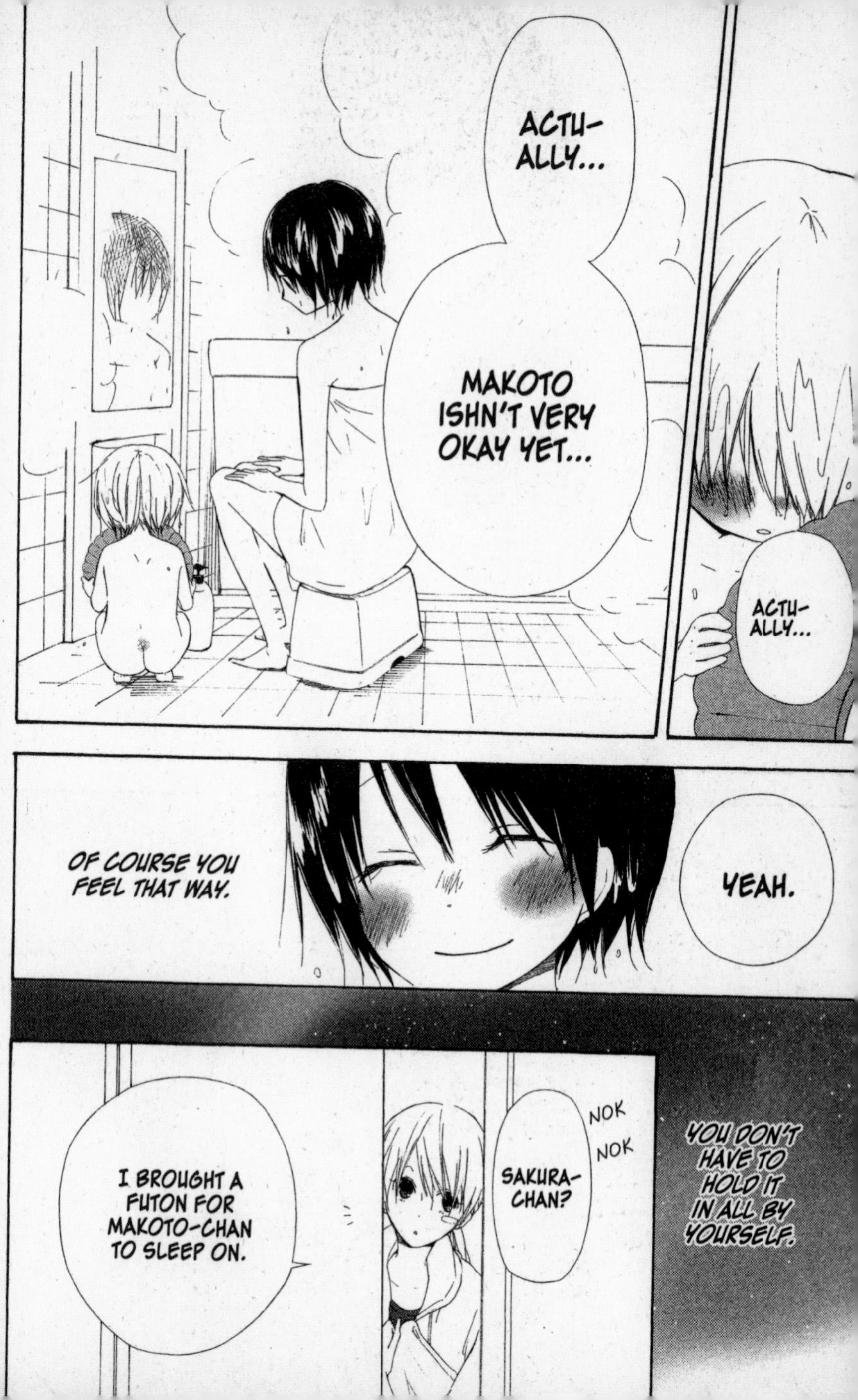
ACTU-ALLY...
ACTU-ALLY...
MAKOTO ISHN'T VERY OKAY YET...
YEAH.
OF COURSE YOU FEEL THAT WAY.
YOU DON'T HAVE TO HOLD IT IN ALL BY YOURSELF.
NOK NOK
SAKURA-CHAN?
I BROUGHT A FUTON FOR MAKOTO-CHAN TO SLEEP ON.

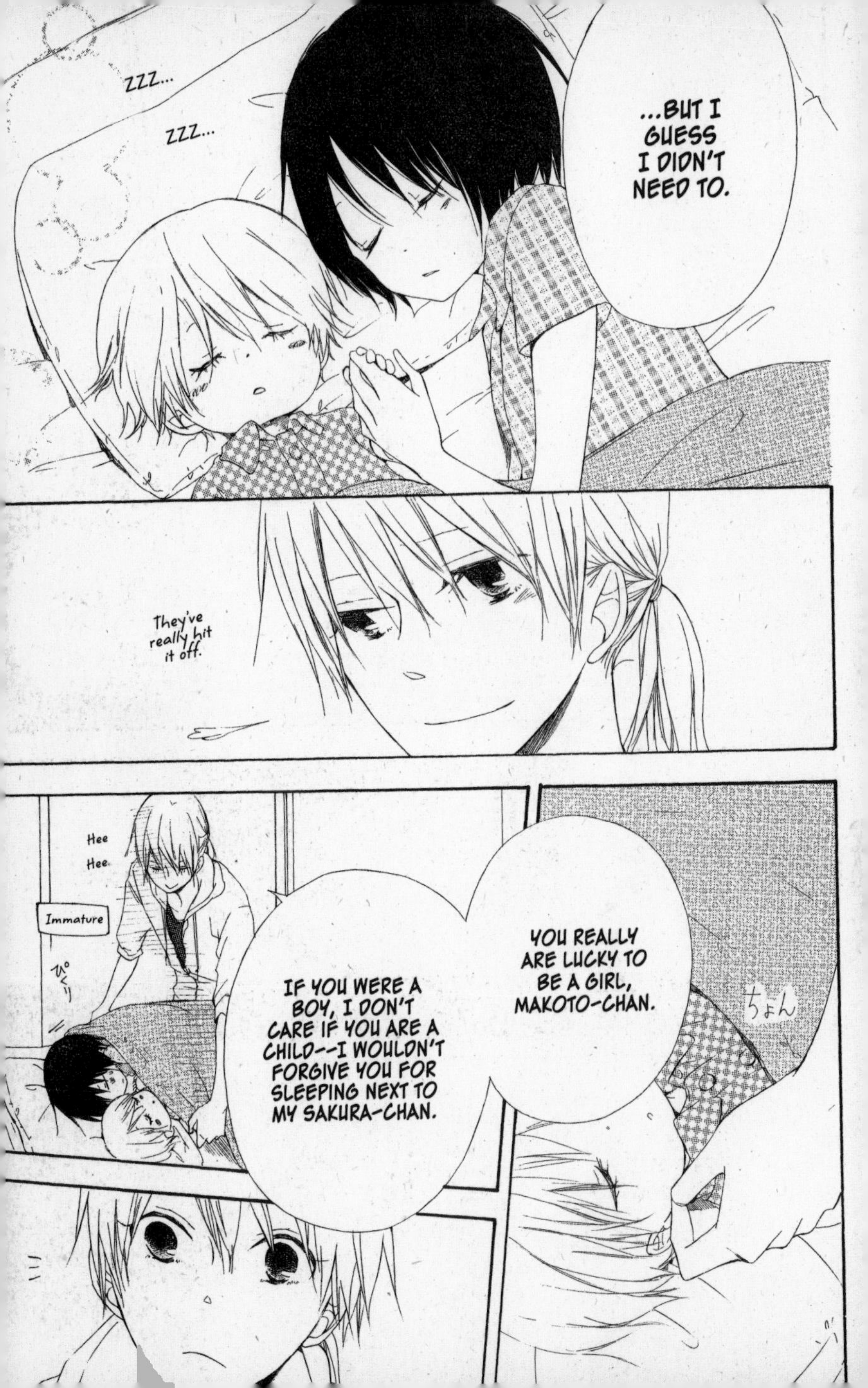
...BUT I GUESS I DIDN'T NEED TO.
ZZZ...
ZZZ...
They've really hit it off.
ちょん
YOU REALLY ARE LUCKY TO BE A GIRL, MAKOTO-CHAN.
IF YOU WERE A BOY, I DON'T CARE IF YOU ARE A CHILD--I WOULDN'T FORGIVE YOU FOR SLEEPING NEXT TO MY SAKURA-CHAN.
Hee Hee
Immature
ぴくり

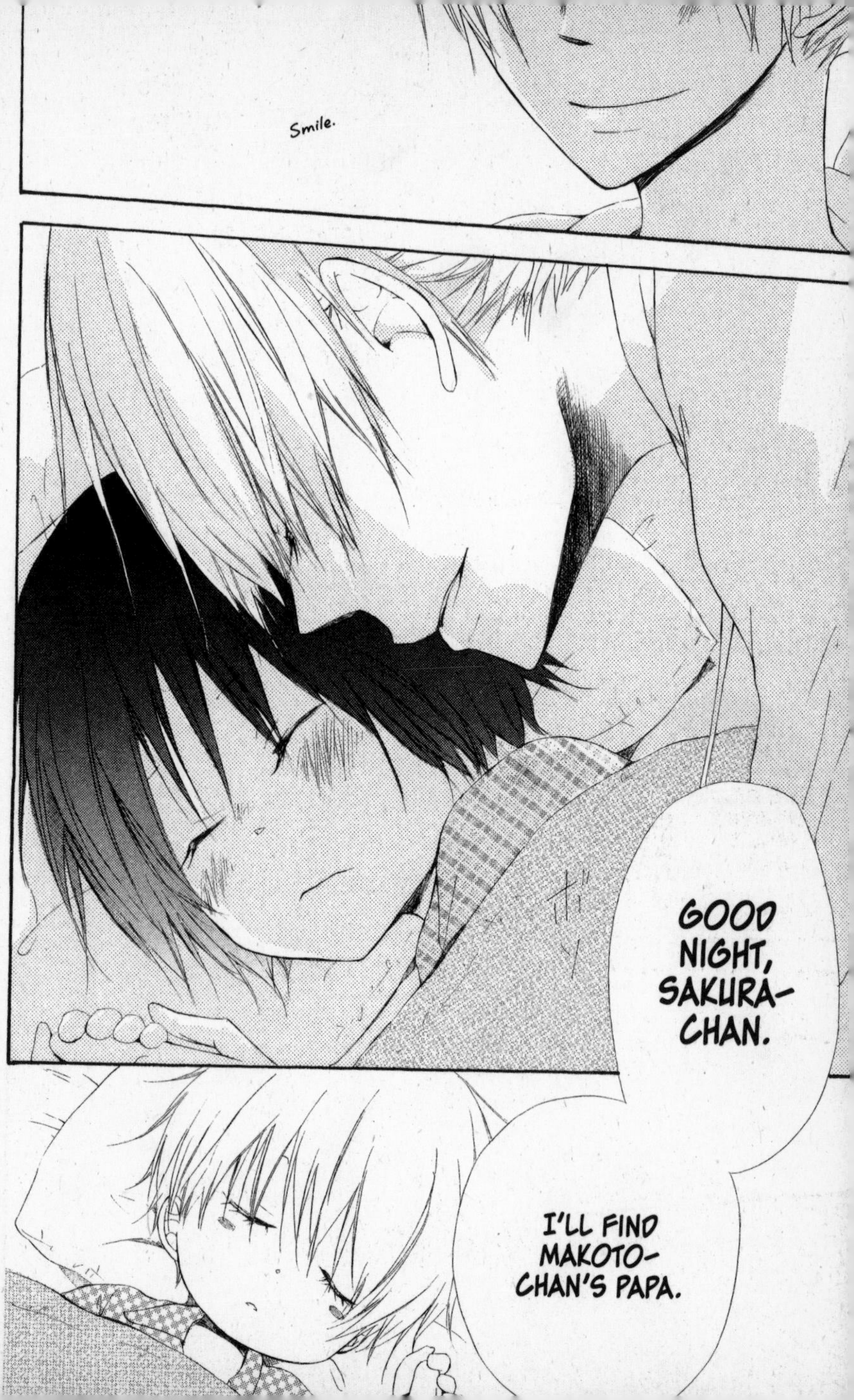
Smile.
GOOD NIGHT, SAKURA-CHAN.
I'LL FIND MAKOTO-CHAN'S PAPA.

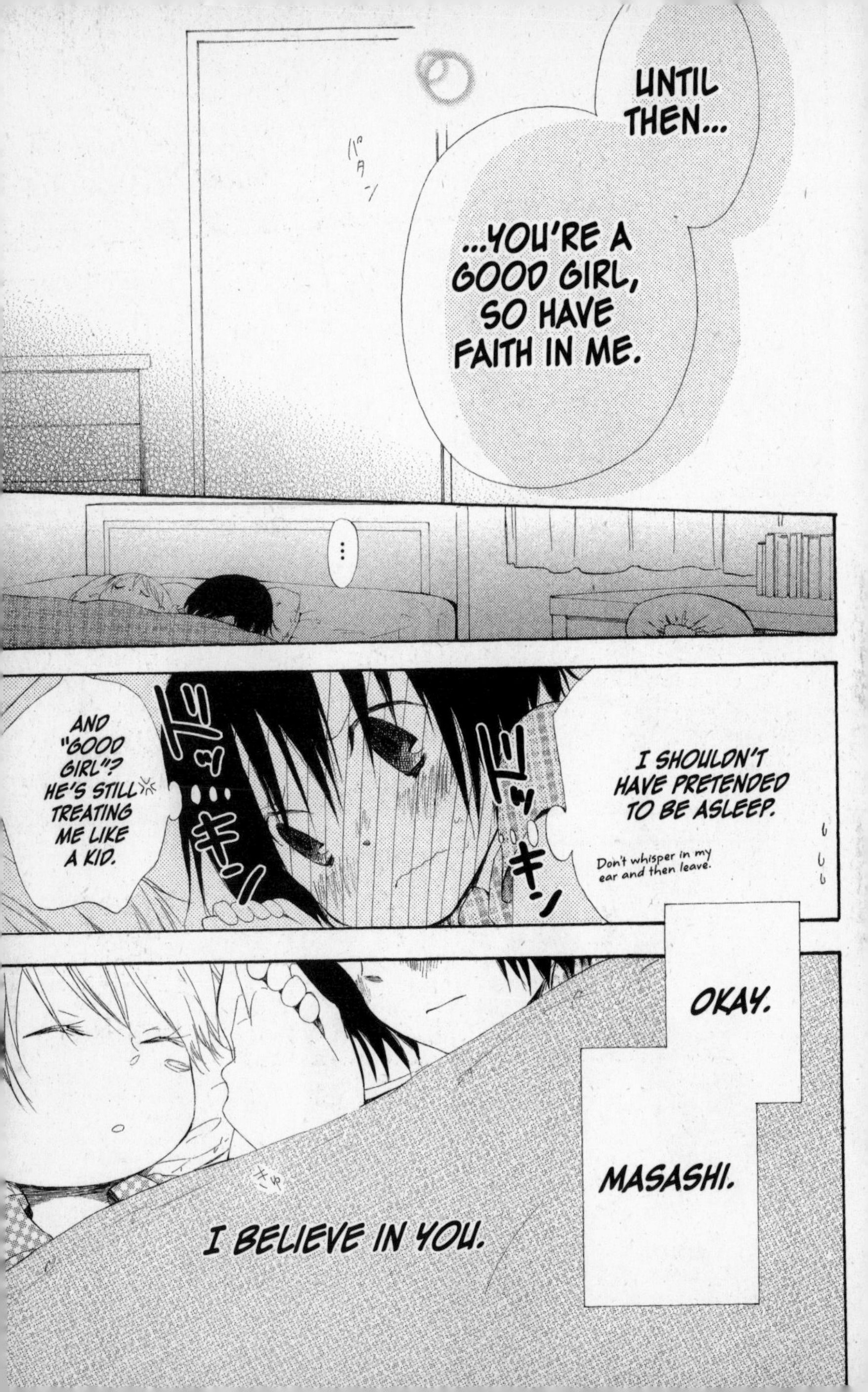
UNTIL THEN...
...YOU'RE A GOOD GIRL, SO HAVE FAITH IN ME.
...
I SHOULDN'T HAVE PRETENDED TO BE ASLEEP.
Don't whisper in my ear and then leave.
AND "GOOD GIRL"? HE'S STILL TREATING ME LIKE A KID.
OKAY.
MASASHI.
I BELIEVE IN YOU.

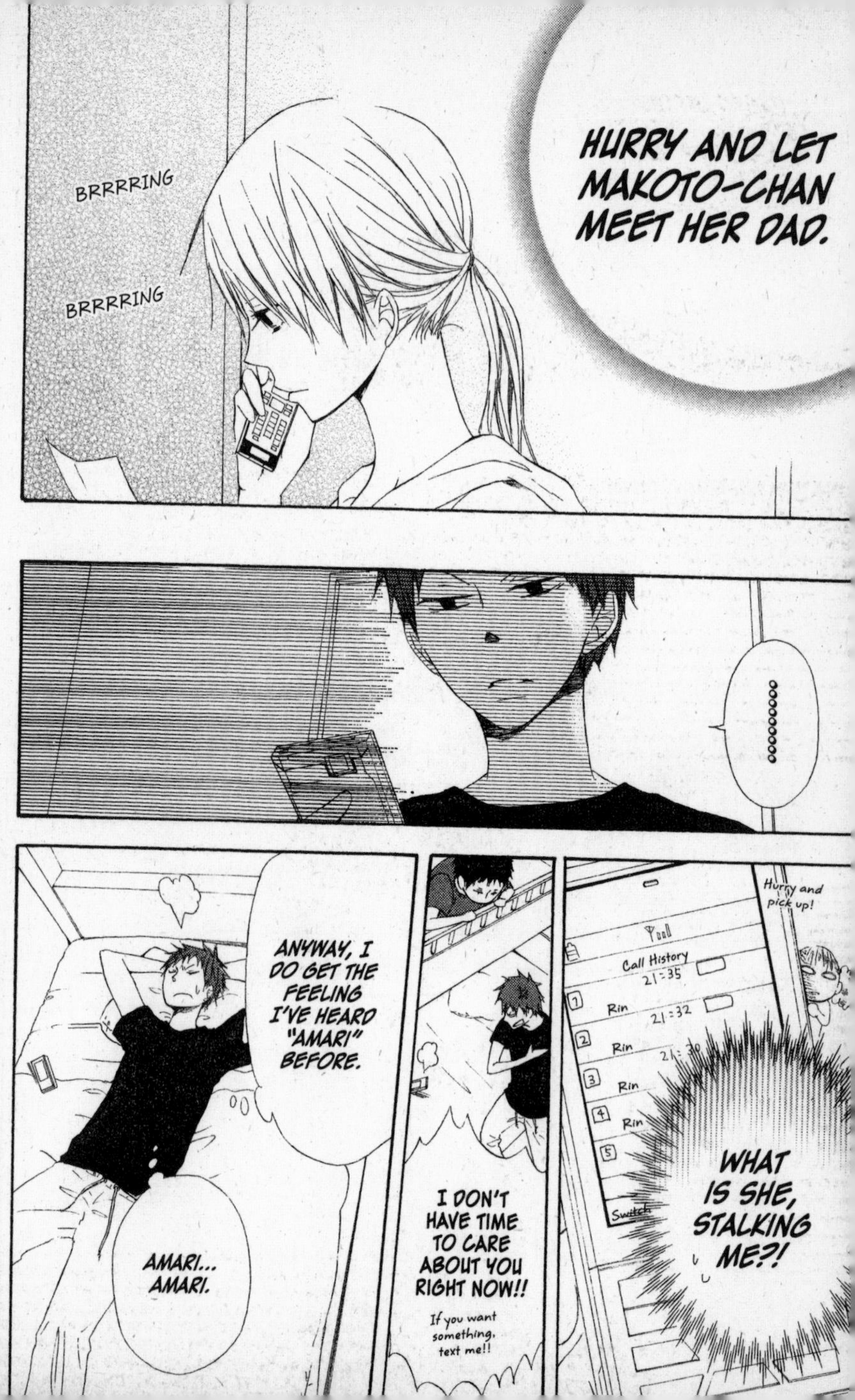
HURRY AND LET MAKOTO-CHAN MEET HER DAD.
BRRRRING
BRRRRING
....
Hurry and pick up!
Call History
21:35
1 Rin 21:32
2 Rin
3 Rin
4 Rin
5
Switch
WHAT IS SHE, STALKING ME?!
I DON'T HAVE TIME TO CARE ABOUT YOU RIGHT NOW!!
If you want something, text me!!
ANYWAY, I DO GET THE FEELING I'VE HEARD "AMARI" BEFORE.
AMARI... AMARI.

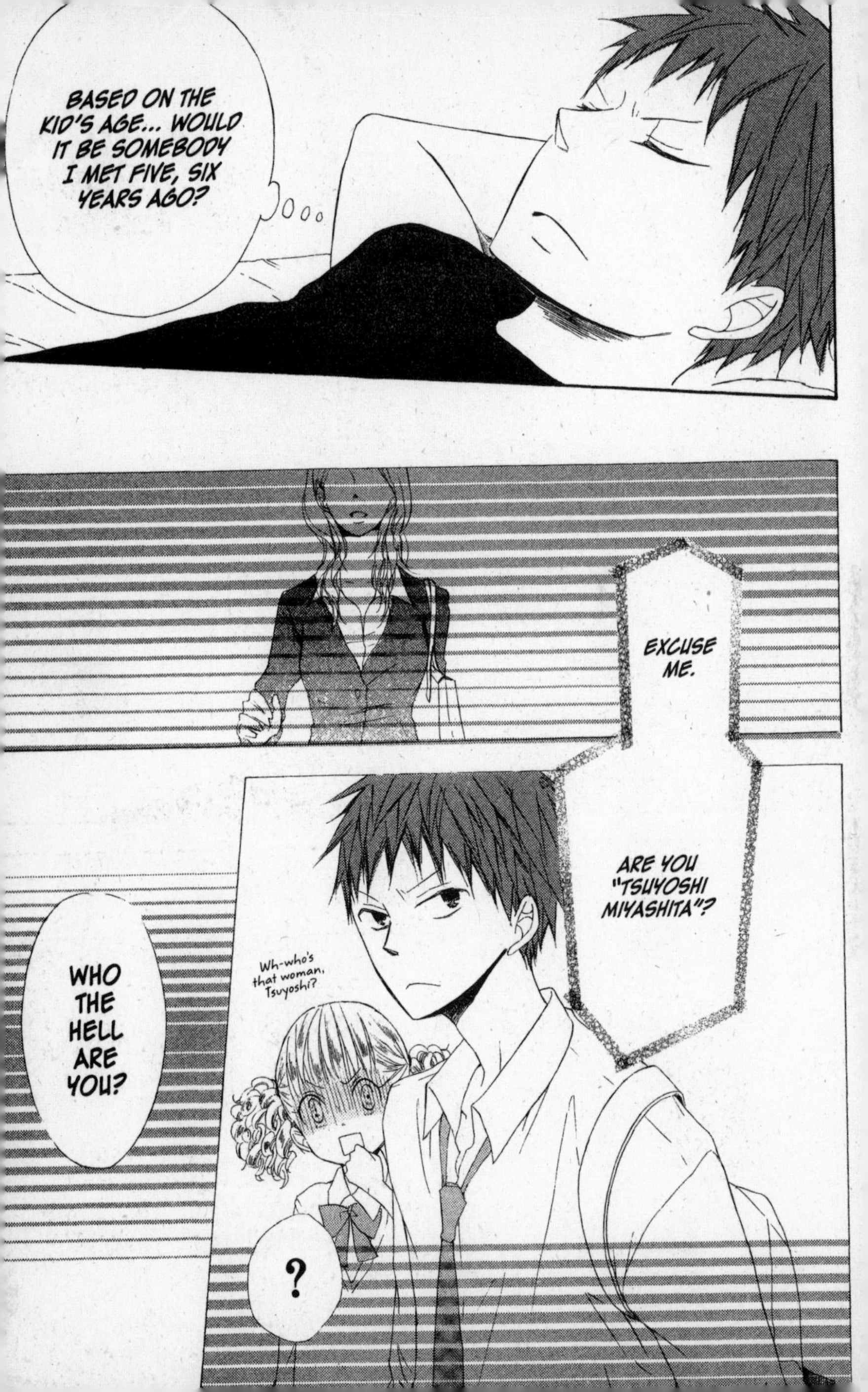
BASED ON THE KID'S AGE... WOULD IT BE SOMEBODY I MET FIVE, SIX YEARS AGO?
EXCUSE ME.
ARE YOU "TSUYOSHI MIYASHITA"?
Wh-who's that woman, Tsuyoshi?
?
WHO THE HELL ARE YOU?

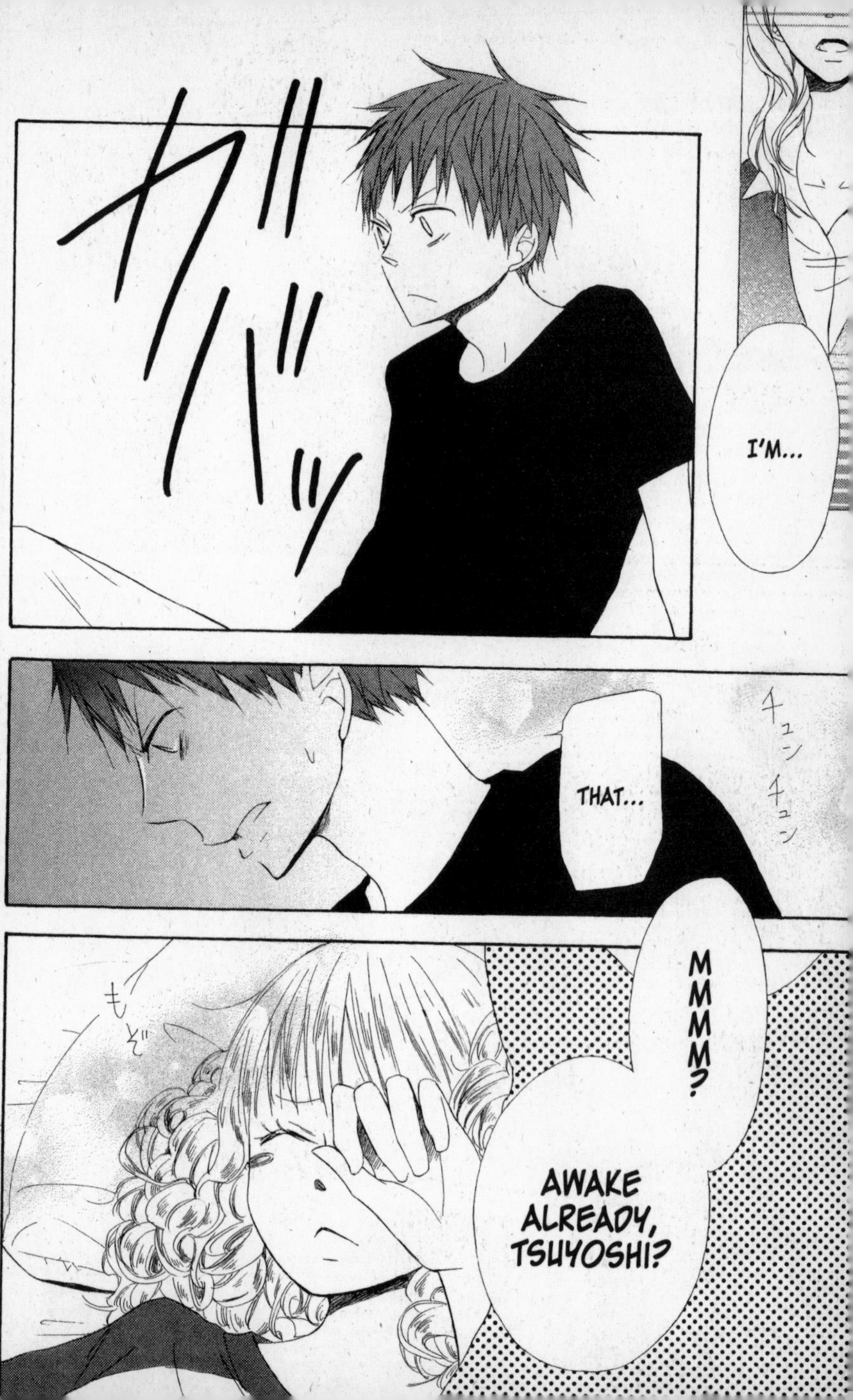
I'M...
ガバッ
THAT...
チュン チュン
MMMM?
AWAKE ALREADY, TSUYOSHI?
もぞ

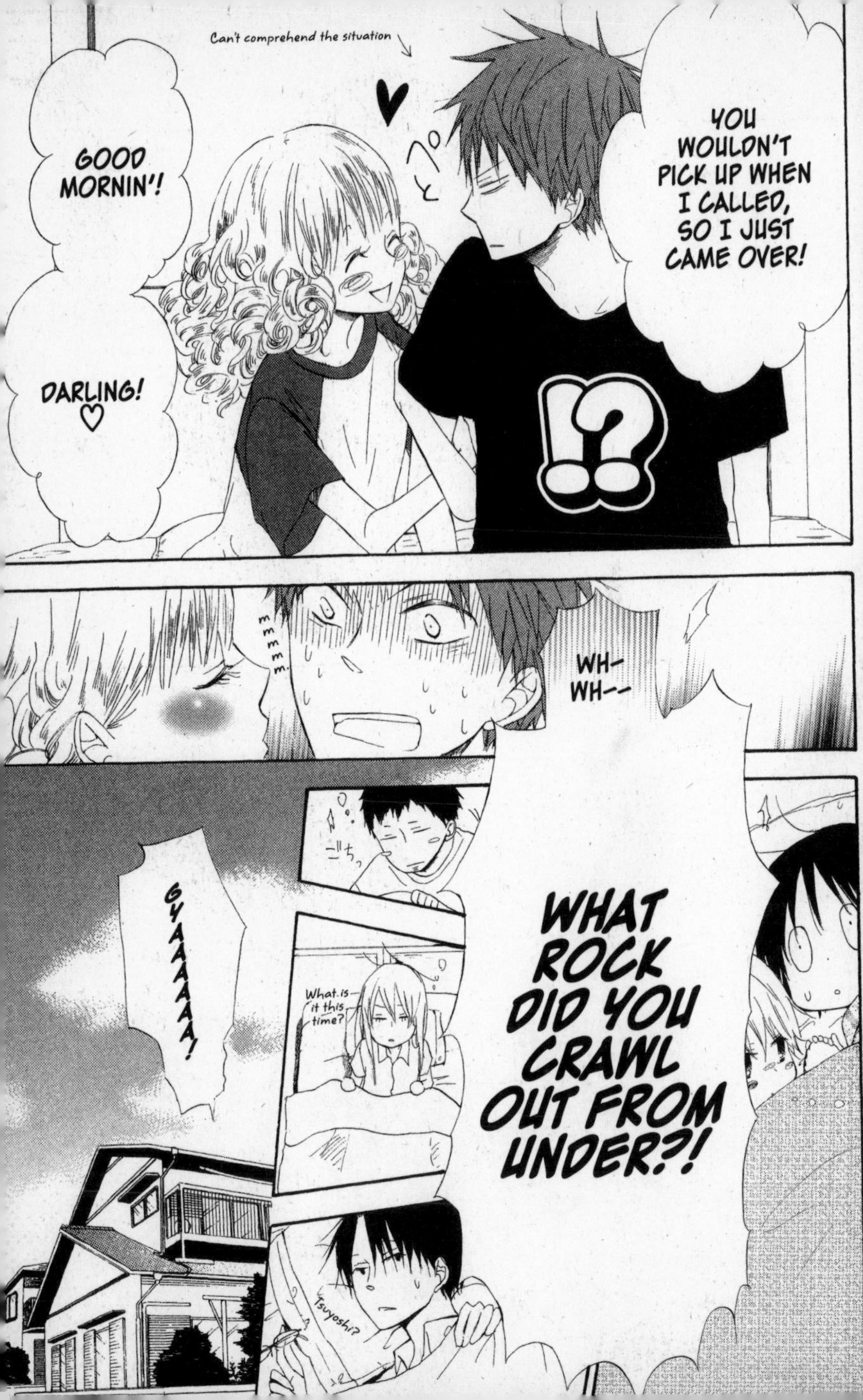
YOU WOULDN'T PICK UP WHEN I CALLED, SO I JUST CAME OVER!
Can't comprehend the situation
GOOD MORNIN'!
DARLING! ♡
WH- WH--
mmmmm.
WHAT ROCK DID YOU CRAWL OUT FROM UNDER?!
ごちっ
What is it this time?
Tsuyoshi?
GYAAAAAA!

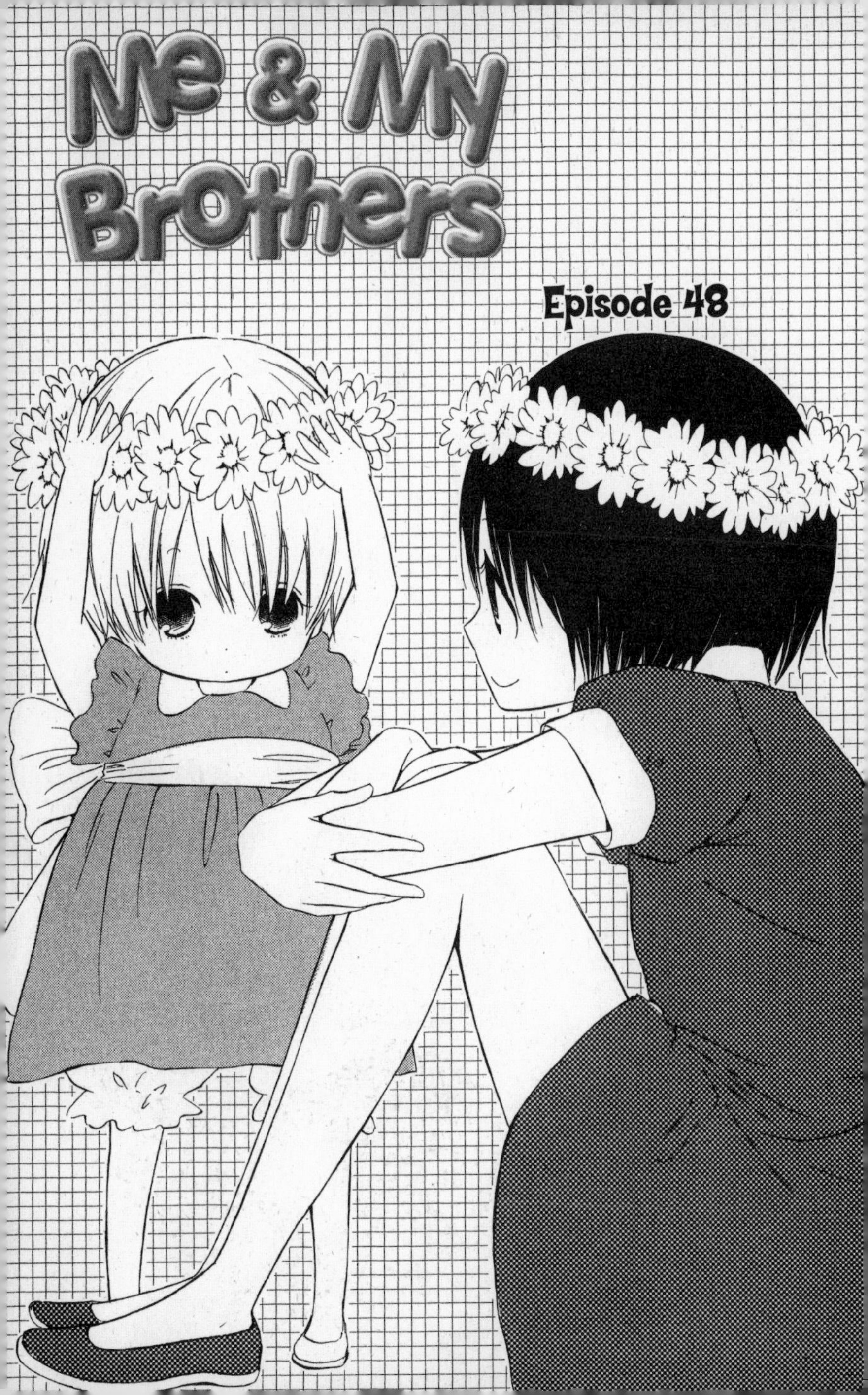
Me & My Brothers
Episode 48

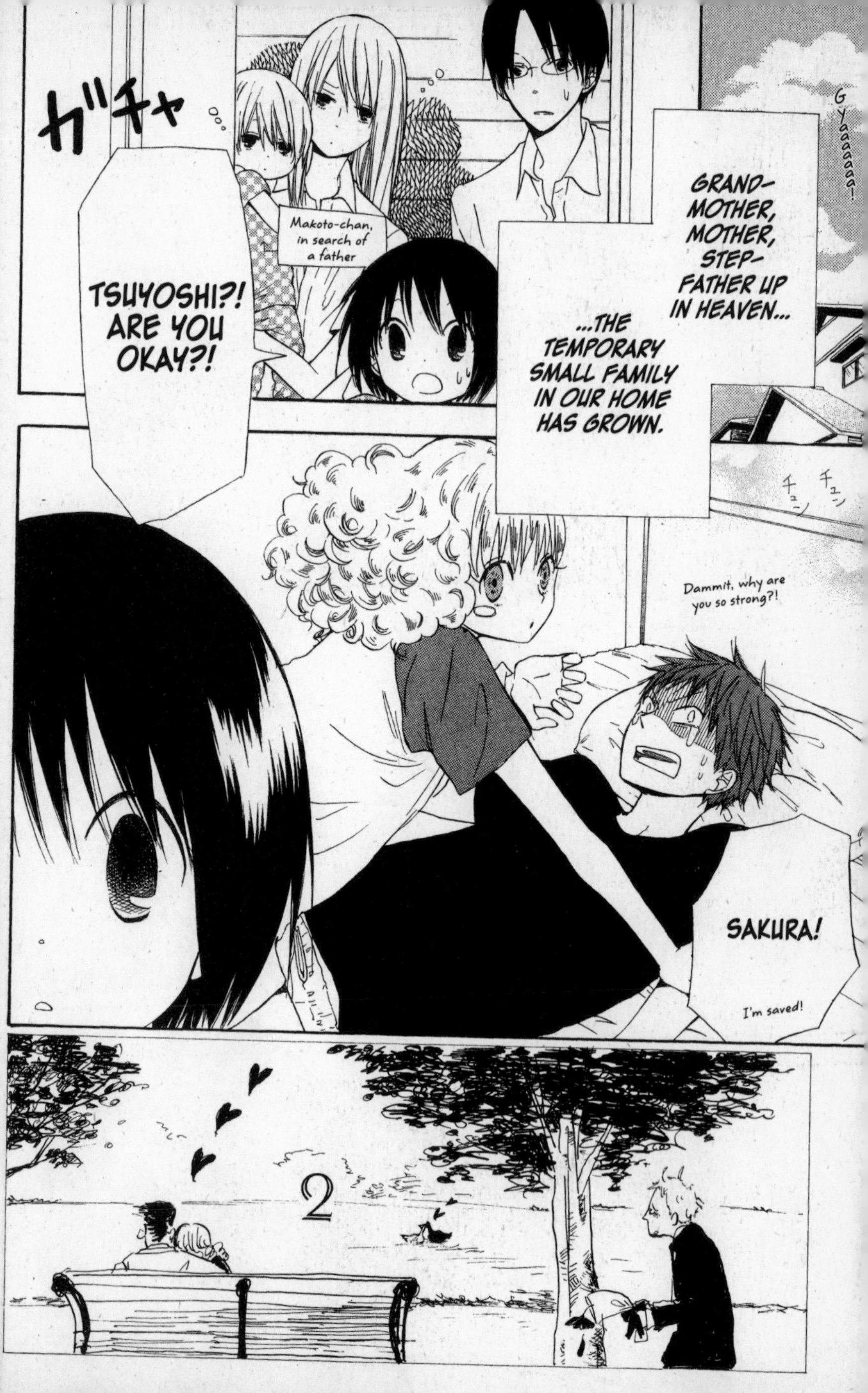
Gyaaaaaaa!
GRAND-MOTHER, MOTHER, STEP-FATHER UP IN HEAVEN...
...THE TEMPORARY SMALL FAMILY IN OUR HOME HAS GROWN.
チュン チュン
ガチャ
Makoto-chan, in search of a father
TSUYOSHI?! ARE YOU OKAY?!
Dammit, why are you so strong?!
SAKURA!
I'm saved!
2

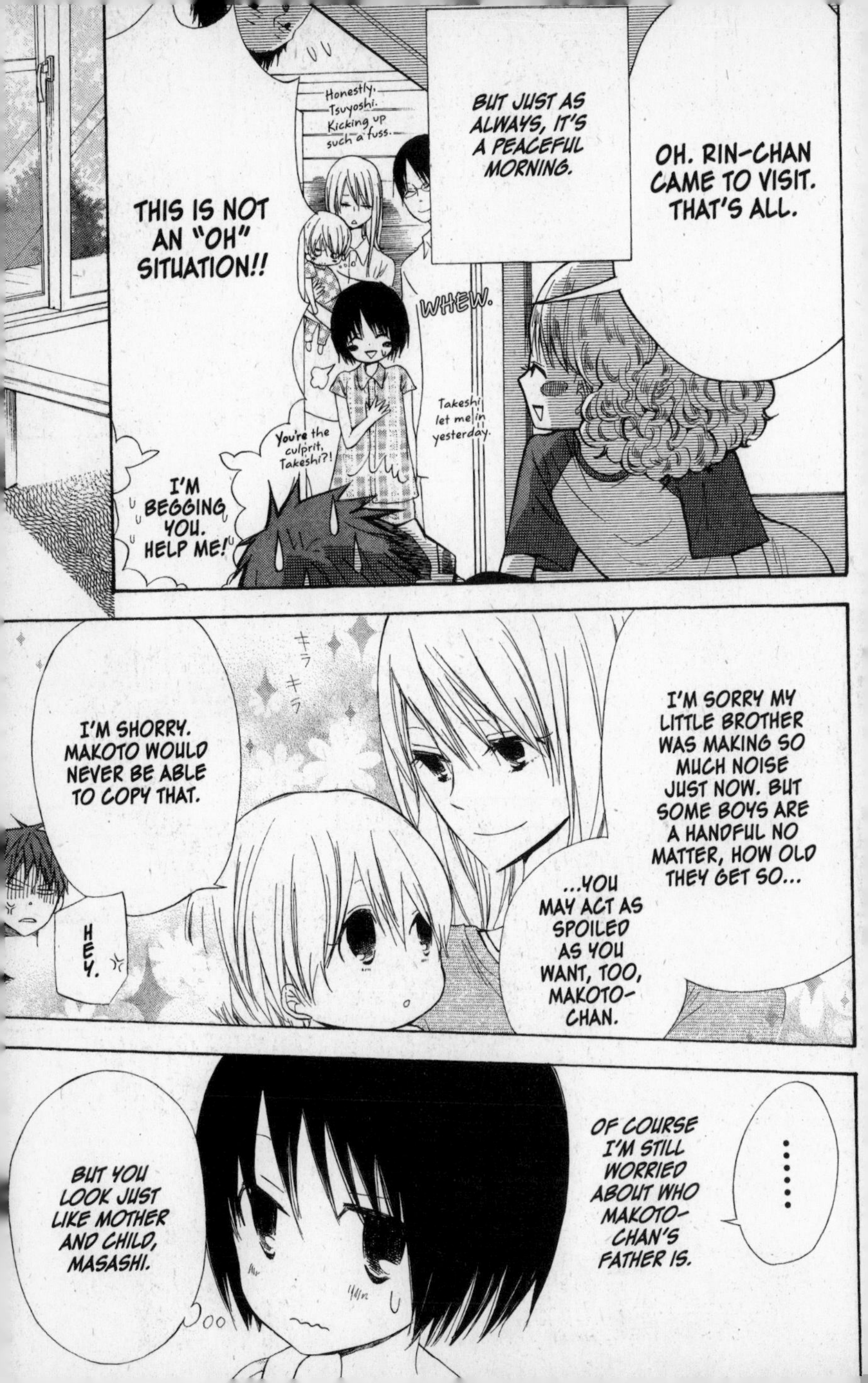

OH. RIN-CHAN CAME TO VISIT. THAT'S ALL.
Takeshi let me in yesterday.
BUT JUST AS ALWAYS, IT'S A PEACEFUL MORNING.
WHEW.
Honestly, Tsuyoshi. Kicking up such a fuss.
THIS IS NOT AN "OH" SITUATION!!
You're the culprit, Takeshi?!
I'M BEGGING YOU. HELP ME!
I'M SORRY MY LITTLE BROTHER WAS MAKING SO MUCH NOISE JUST NOW. BUT SOME BOYS ARE A HANDFUL NO MATTER, HOW OLD THEY GET SO...
...YOU MAY ACT AS SPOILED AS YOU WANT, TOO, MAKOTO-CHAN.
キラ キラ
I'M SHORRY. MAKOTO WOULD NEVER BE ABLE TO COPY THAT.
HEY.
......
OF COURSE I'M STILL WORRIED ABOUT WHO MAKOTO-CHAN'S FATHER IS.
BUT YOU LOOK JUST LIKE MOTHER AND CHILD, MASASHI.

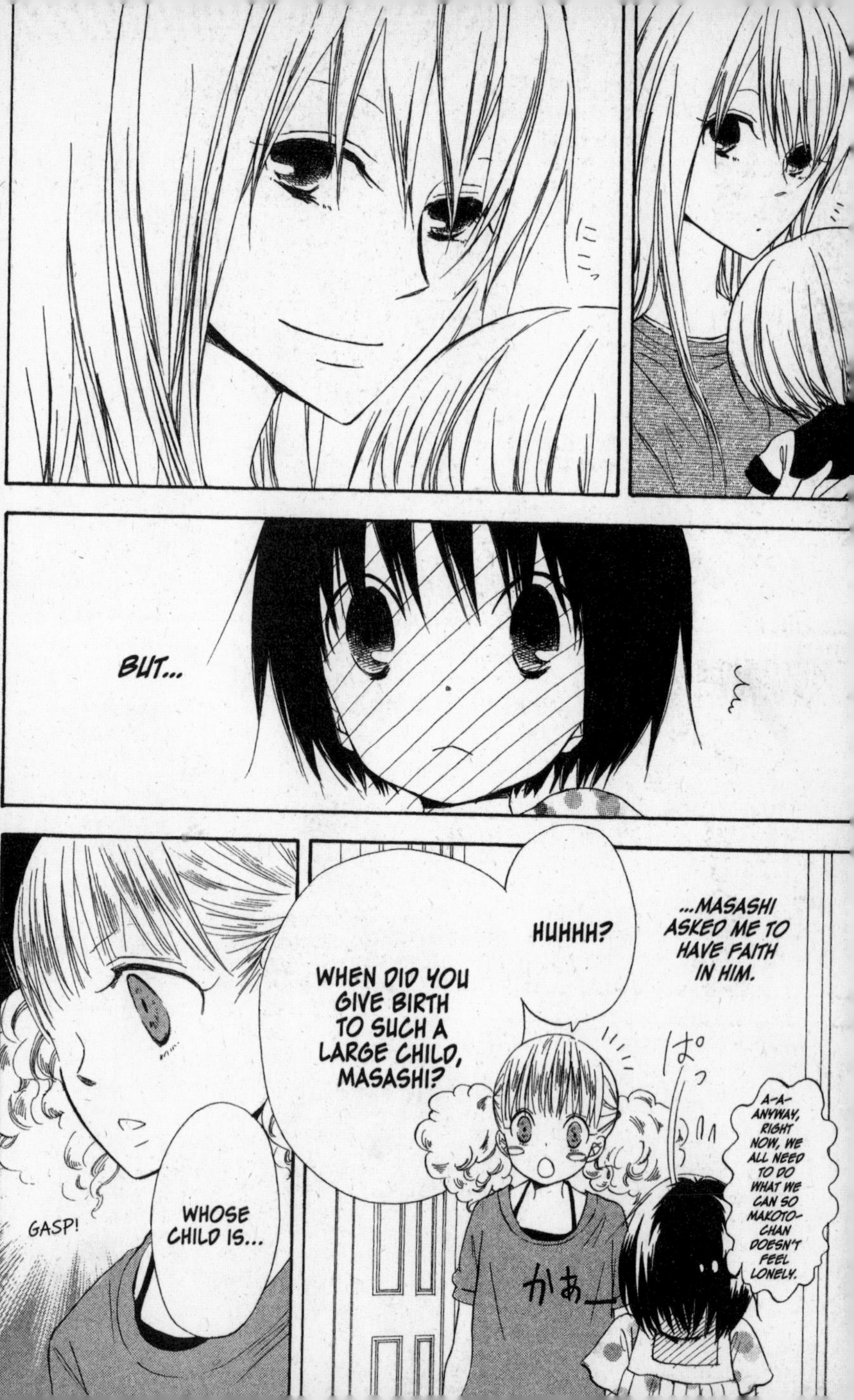
BUT...
...MASASHI ASKED ME TO HAVE FAITH IN HIM.
HUHHH?
WHEN DID YOU GIVE BIRTH TO SUCH A LARGE CHILD, MASASHI?
ぱっ
A-A-ANYWAY, RIGHT NOW, WE ALL NEED TO DO WHAT WE CAN SO MAKOTO-CHAN DOESN'T FEEL LONELY.
かあー
WHOSE CHILD IS...
GASP!

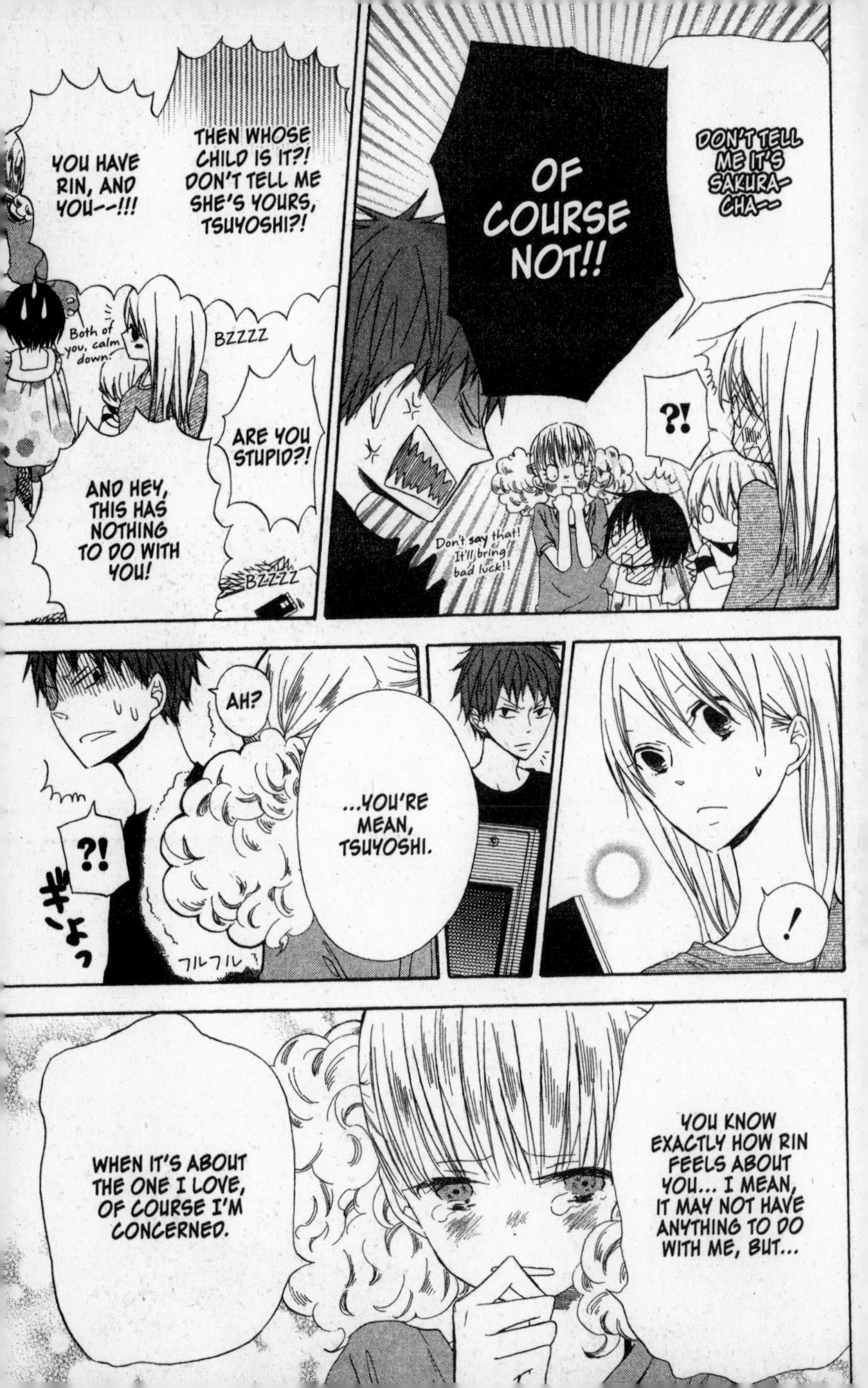
DON'T TELL ME IT'S SAKURA-CHA--
OF COURSE NOT!!
?!
Don't say that! It'll bring bad luck!!
THEN WHOSE CHILD IS IT?! DON'T TELL ME SHE'S YOURS, TSUYOSHI?!
YOU HAVE RIN, AND YOU--!!!
BZZZZ
Both of you, calm down.
ARE YOU STUPID?!
AND HEY, THIS HAS NOTHING TO DO WITH YOU!
BZZZZZ
!
AH?
...YOU'RE MEAN, TSUYOSHI.
?!
ギョッ
フルフル
YOU KNOW EXACTLY HOW RIN FEELS ABOUT YOU... I MEAN, IT MAY NOT HAVE ANYTHING TO DO WITH ME, BUT...
WHEN IT'S ABOUT THE ONE I LOVE, OF COURSE I'M CONCERNED.

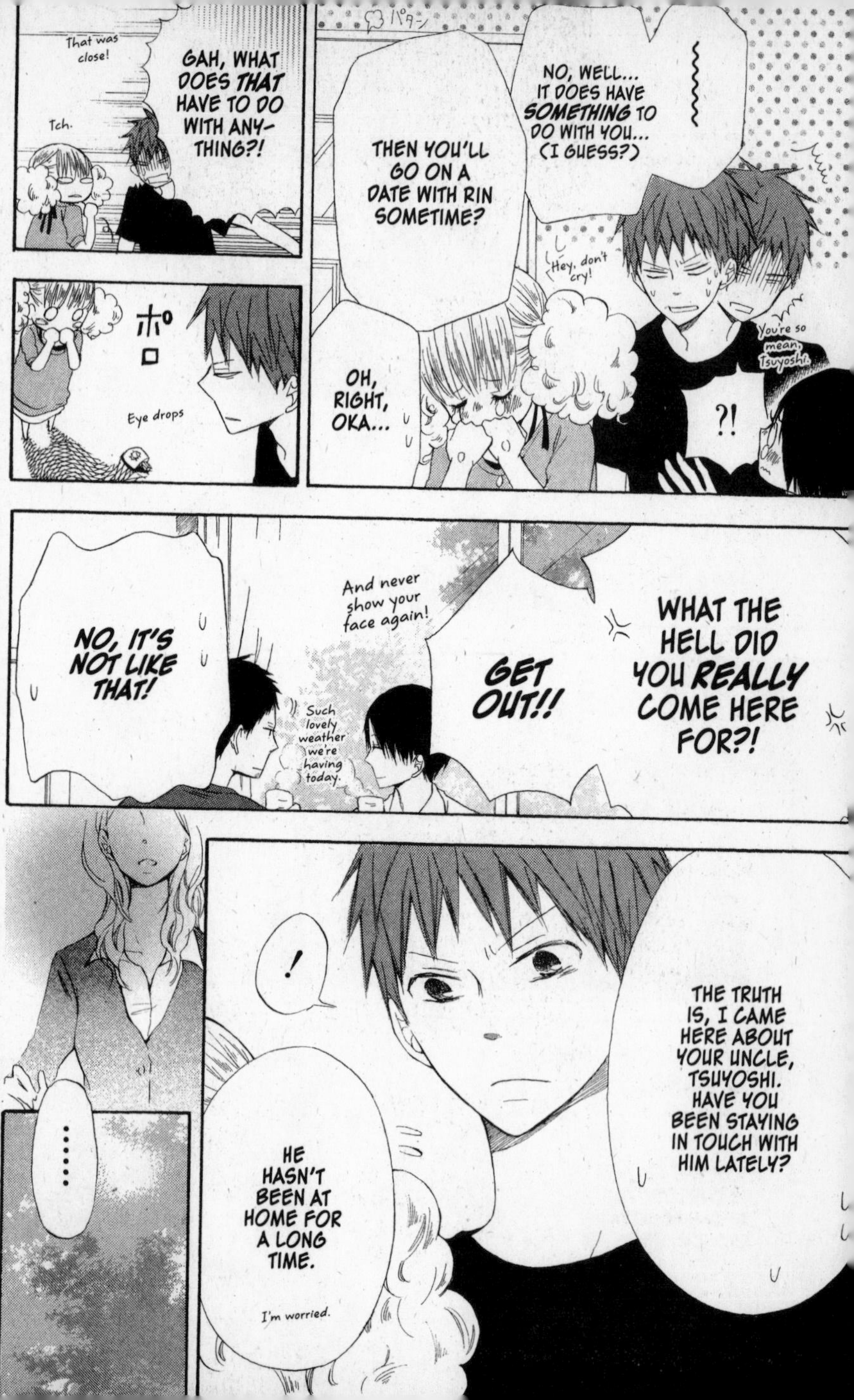
パタン
NO, WELL... IT DOES HAVE SOMETHING TO DO WITH YOU... (I GUESS?)
THEN YOU'LL GO ON A DATE WITH RIN SOMETIME?
Hey, don't cry!
You're so mean, Tsuyoshi.
?!
OH, RIGHT, OKA...
GAH, WHAT DOES THAT HAVE TO DO WITH ANY-THING?!
That was close!
Tch.
ポロ
Eye drops
WHAT THE HELL DID YOU REALLY COME HERE FOR?!
GET OUT!!
And never show your face again!
Such lovely weather we're having today.
NO, IT'S NOT LIKE THAT!
THE TRUTH IS, I CAME HERE ABOUT YOUR UNCLE, TSUYOSHI. HAVE YOU BEEN STAYING IN TOUCH WITH HIM LATELY?
!
HE HASN'T BEEN AT HOME FOR A LONG TIME.
I'm worried.
......

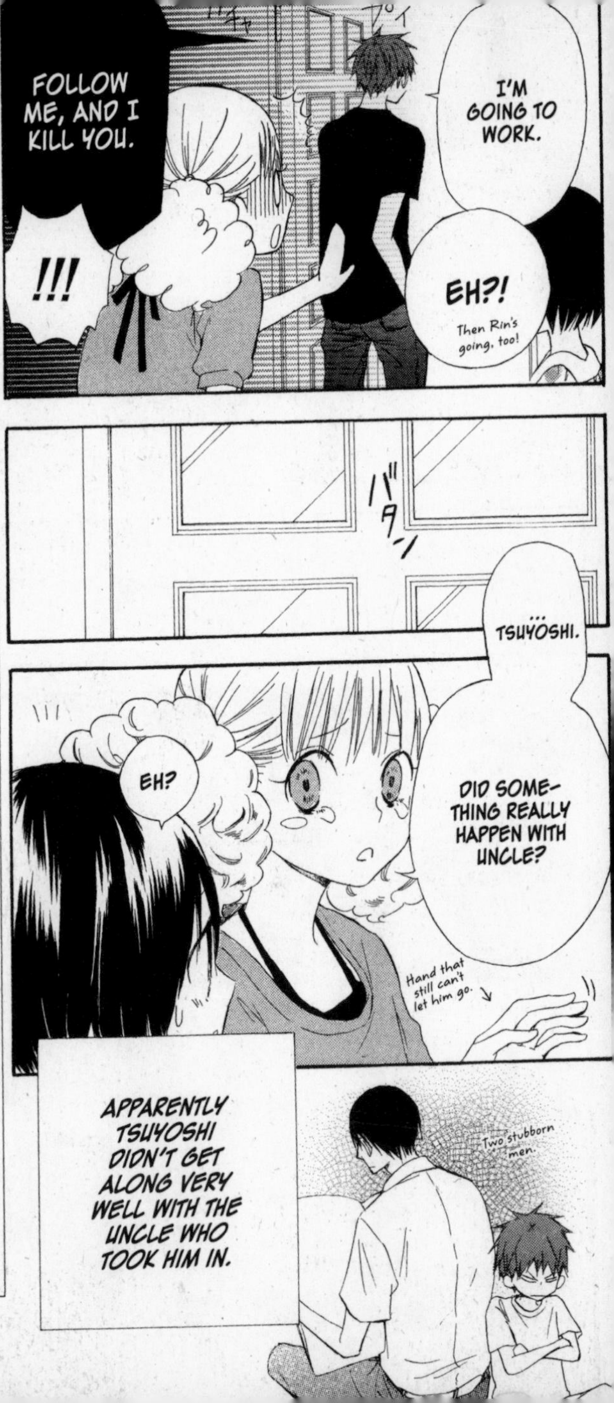
I'M GOING TO WORK.
EH?!
Then Rin's going, too!
FOLLOW ME, AND I KILL YOU.
!!!
...TSUYOSHI.
DID SOMETHING REALLY HAPPEN WITH UNCLE?
EH?
Hand that still can't let him go.
APPARENTLY TSUYOSHI DIDN'T GET ALONG VERY WELL WITH THE UNCLE WHO TOOK HIM IN.
Two stubborn men.

2

This time, I drew Makoto-chan because I wanted to draw a small child, but my father really complimented me on the aotan.

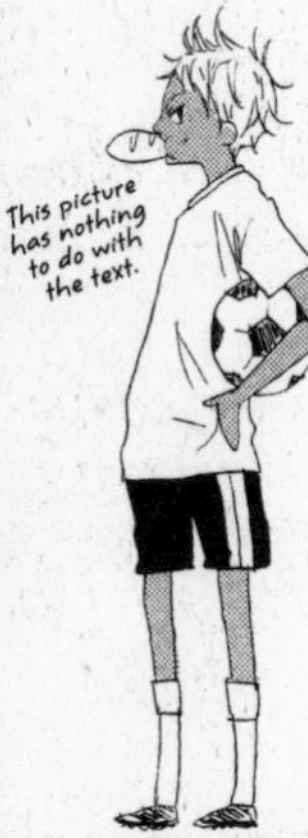
This picture has nothing to do with the text.

Apparently he was impressed that I knew that children have aotan on their bottoms.

By the way, an aotan is a blue mark on the skin, just for your information.

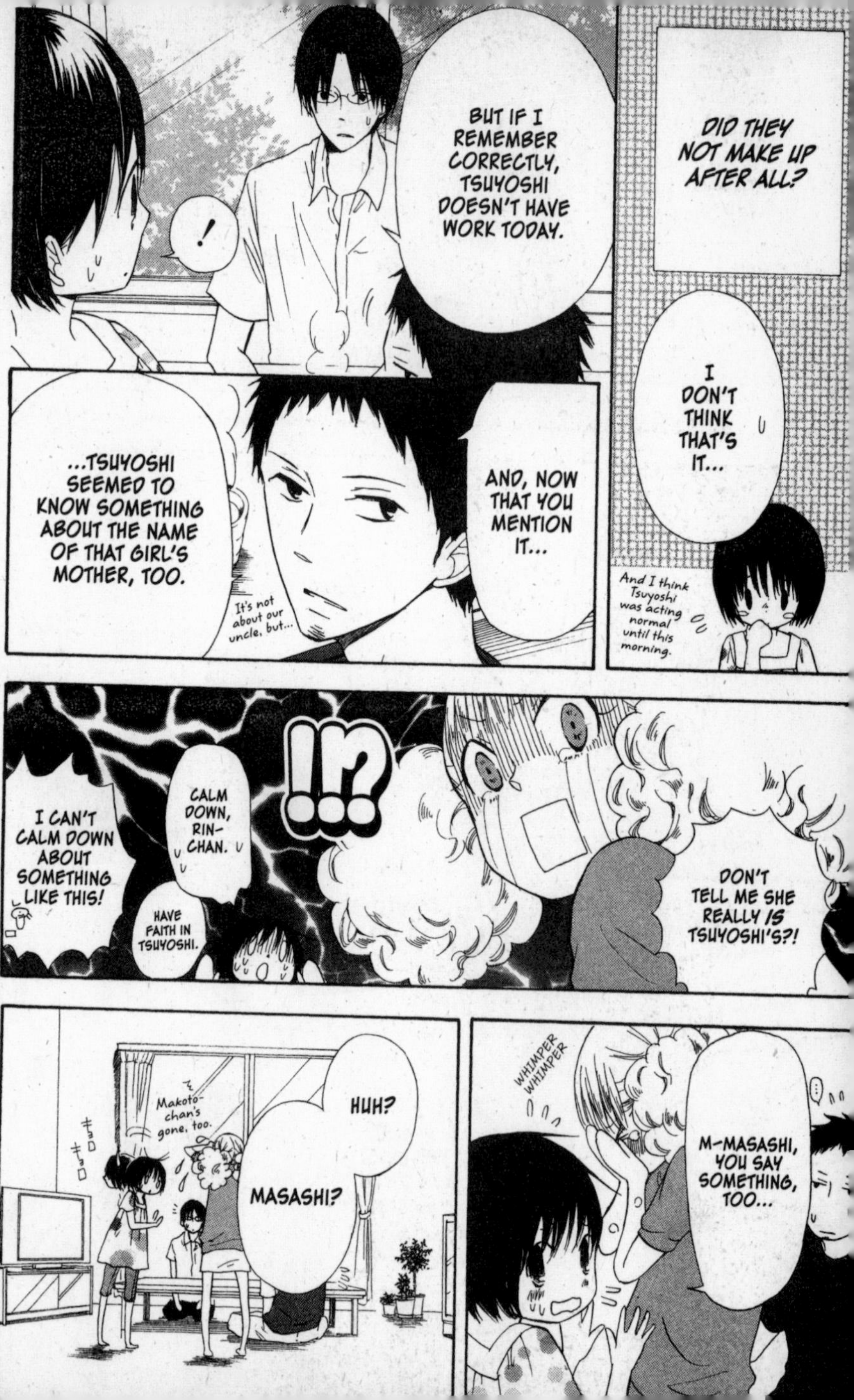
DID THEY NOT MAKE UP AFTER ALL?
I DON'T THINK THAT'S IT...
And I think Tsuyoshi was acting normal until this morning.
BUT IF I REMEMBER CORRECTLY, TSUYOSHI DOESN'T HAVE WORK TODAY.
!
AND, NOW THAT YOU MENTION IT...
...TSUYOSHI SEEMED TO KNOW SOMETHING ABOUT THE NAME OF THAT GIRL'S MOTHER, TOO.
It's not about our uncle, but...
!?
DON'T TELL ME SHE REALLY *IS* TSUYOSHI'S?!
CALM DOWN, RIN-CHAN.
HAVE FAITH IN TSUYOSHI.
I CAN'T CALM DOWN ABOUT SOMETHING LIKE THIS!
WHIMPER WHIMPER
...
M-MASASHI, YOU SAY SOMETHING, TOO...
HUH?
MASASHI?
Makoto-chan's gone, too.
キョロ キョロ

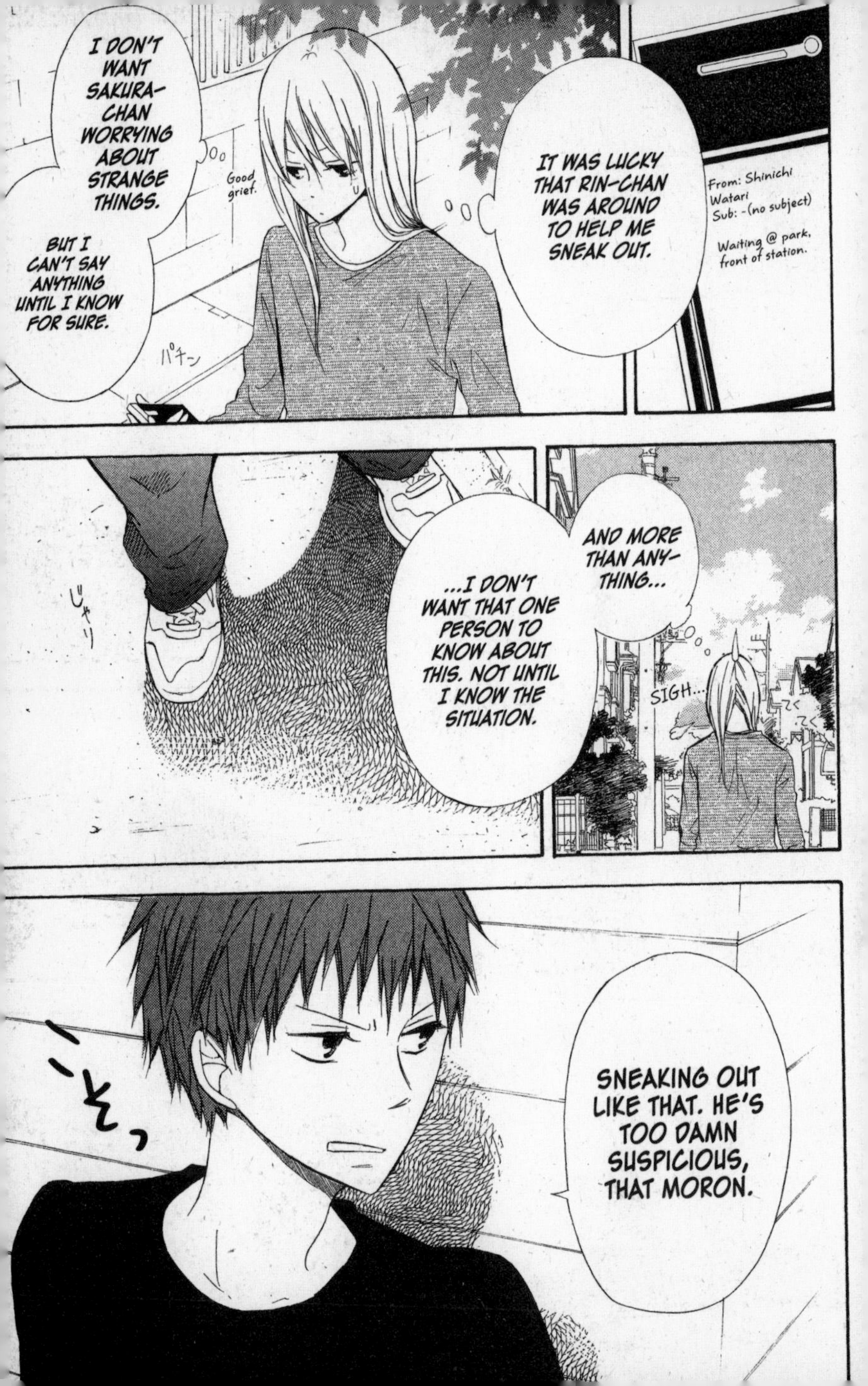
From: Shinichi Watari
Sub: -(no subject)
Waiting @ park, front of station.
IT WAS LUCKY THAT RIN-CHAN WAS AROUND TO HELP ME SNEAK OUT.
I DON'T WANT SAKURA-CHAN WORRYING ABOUT STRANGE THINGS.
Good grief.
BUT I CAN'T SAY ANYTHING UNTIL I KNOW FOR SURE.
パチン
AND MORE THAN ANY-THING...
SIGH...
てく てく
...I DON'T WANT THAT ONE PERSON TO KNOW ABOUT THIS. NOT UNTIL I KNOW THE SITUATION.
じゃり
SNEAKING OUT LIKE THAT. HE'S TOO DAMN SUSPICIOUS, THAT MORON.

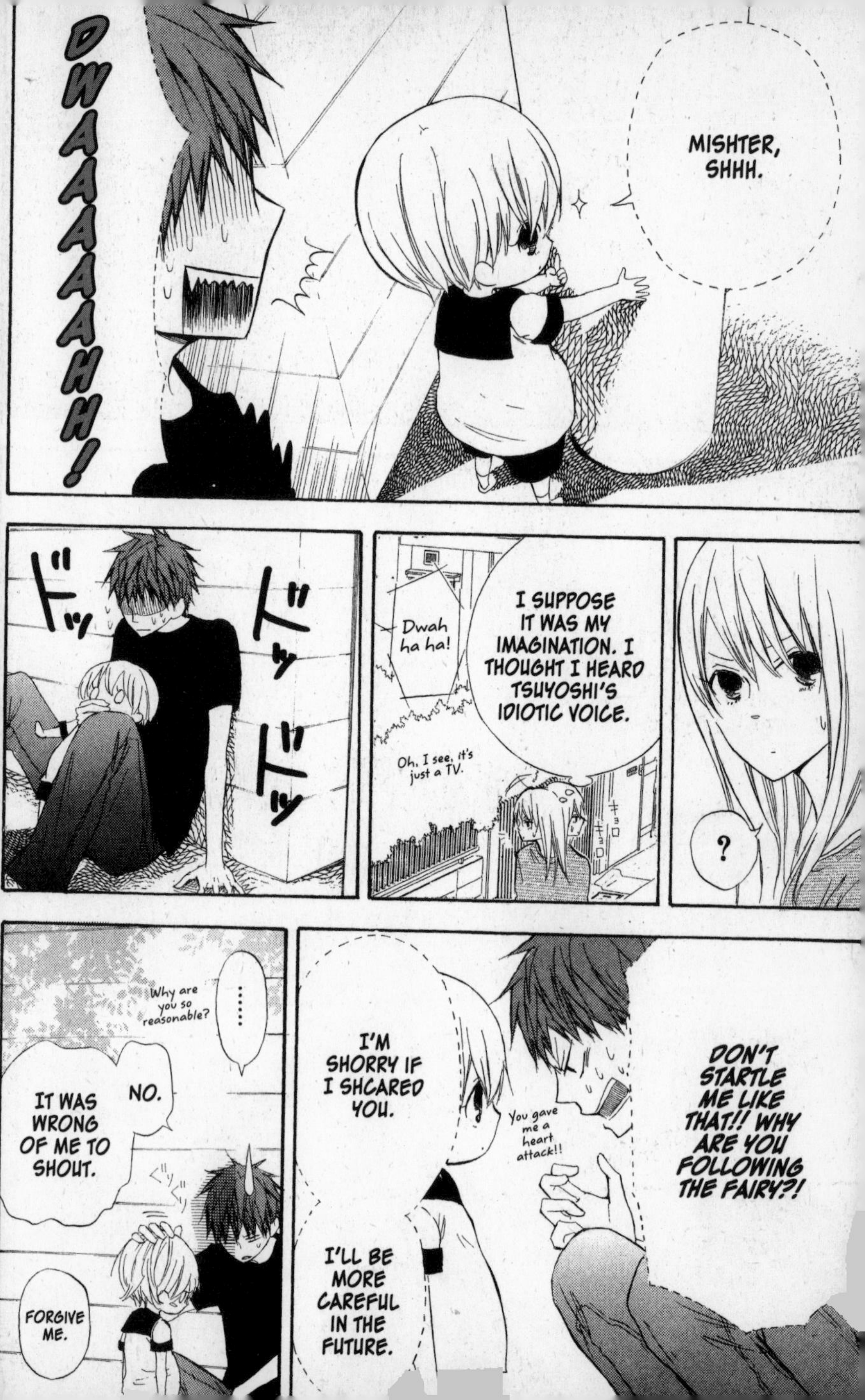
MISHTER, SHHH.
DWAAAAAHH!
?
I SUPPOSE IT WAS MY IMAGINATION. I THOUGHT I HEARD TSUYOSHI'S IDIOTIC VOICE.
Dwah ha ha!
Oh, I see, it's just a TV.
キョロ キョロ
ドッ
ドッドッ
DON'T STARTLE ME LIKE THAT!! WHY ARE YOU FOLLOWING THE FAIRY?!
You gave me a heart attack!!
I'M SHORRY IF I SHCARED YOU.
I'LL BE MORE CAREFUL IN THE FUTURE.
......
Why are you so reasonable?
NO.
IT WAS WRONG OF ME TO SHOUT.
ぐりぐり
FORGIVE ME.

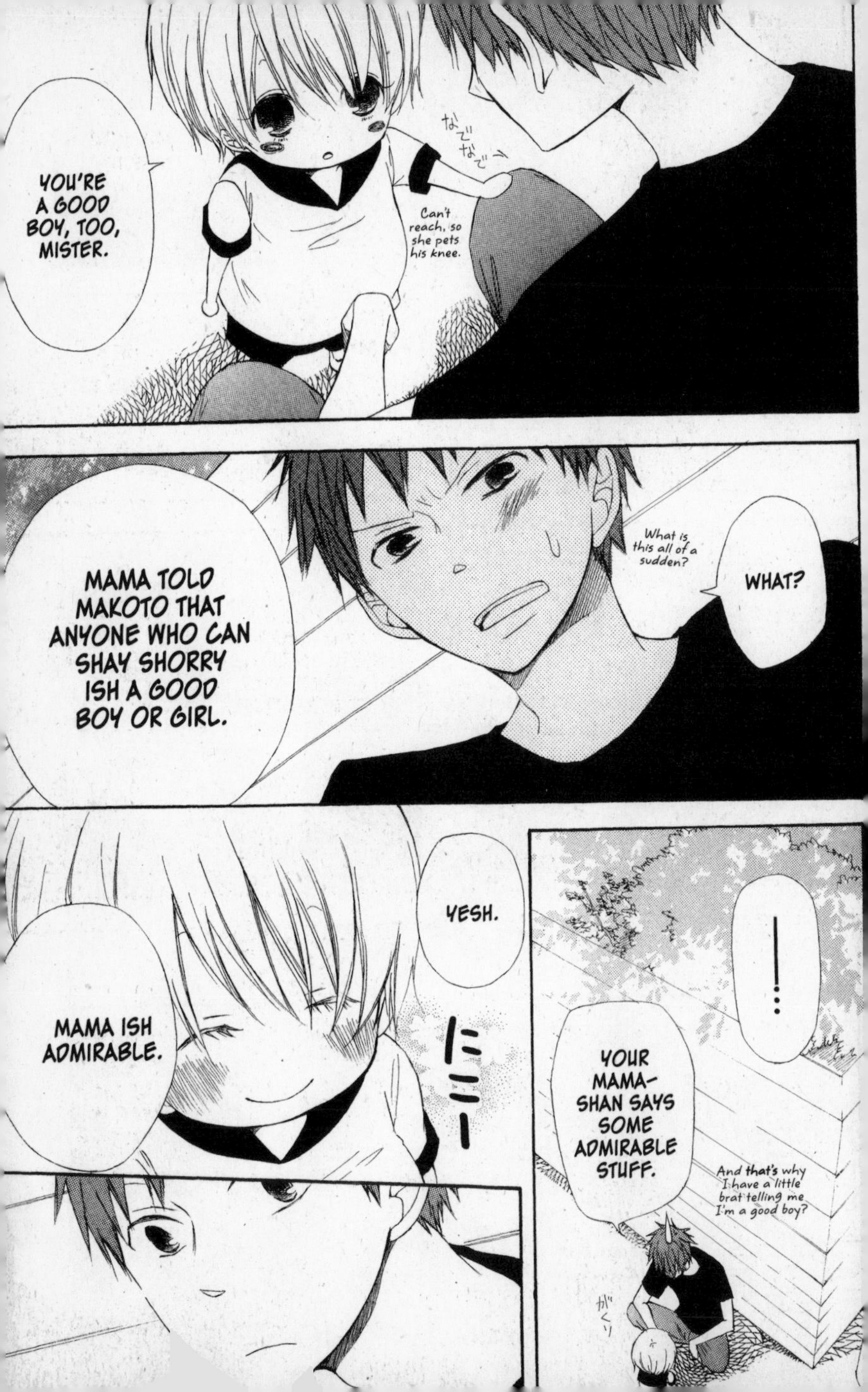
なでなで
Can't reach, so she pets his knee.
YOU'RE A GOOD BOY, TOO, MISTER.
What is this all of a sudden?
WHAT?
MAMA TOLD MAKOTO THAT ANYONE WHO CAN SHAY SHORRY ISH A GOOD BOY OR GIRL.
!...
YOUR MAMA-SHAN SAYS SOME ADMIRABLE STUFF.
And that's why I have a little brat telling me I'm a good boy?
がくり
YESH.
MAMA ISH ADMIRABLE.

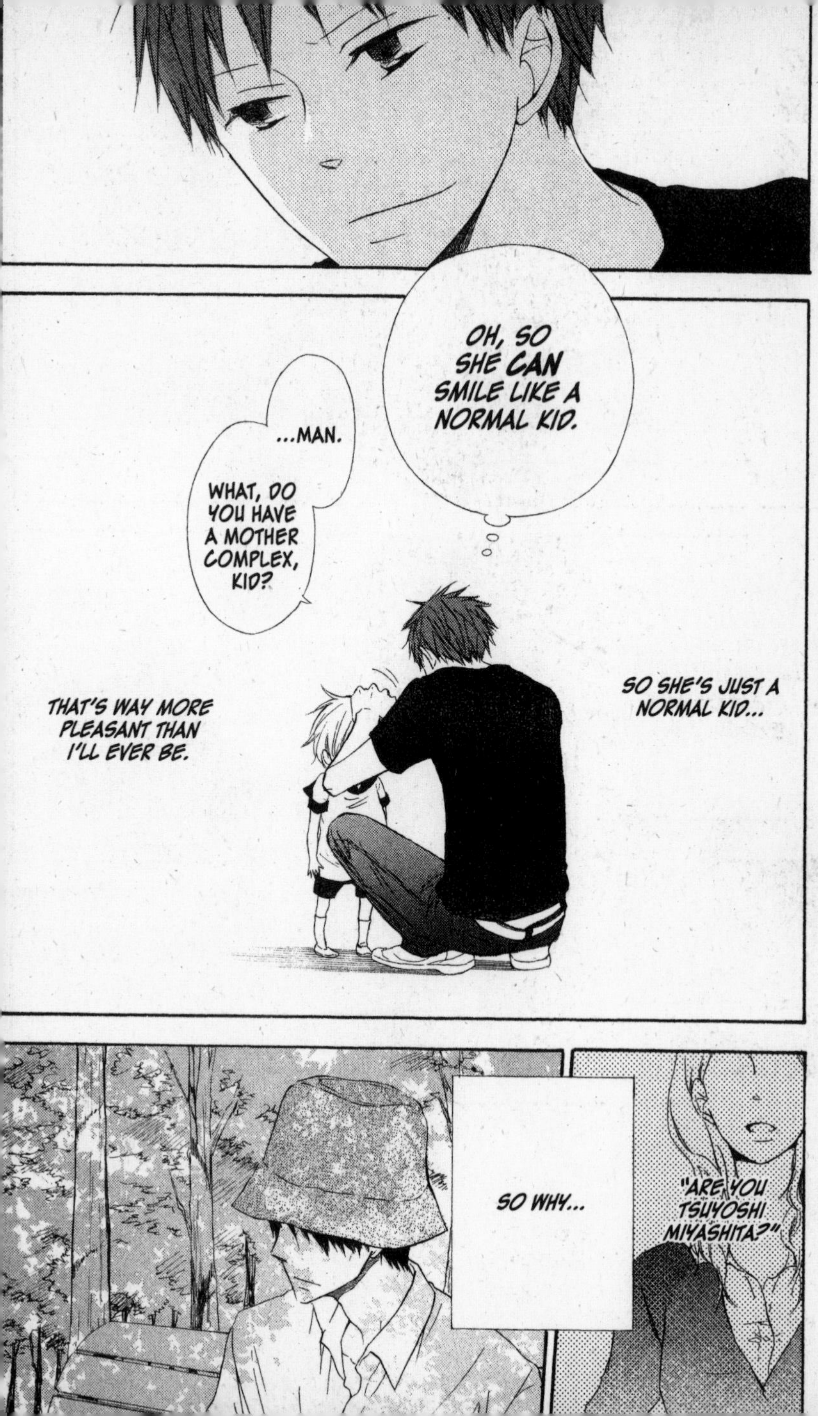
OH, SO SHE CAN SMILE LIKE A NORMAL KID.
...MAN.
WHAT, DO YOU HAVE A MOTHER COMPLEX, KID?
SO SHE'S JUST A NORMAL KID...
THAT'S WAY MORE PLEASANT THAN I'LL EVER BE.
"ARE YOU TSUYOSHI MIYASHITA?"
SO WHY...

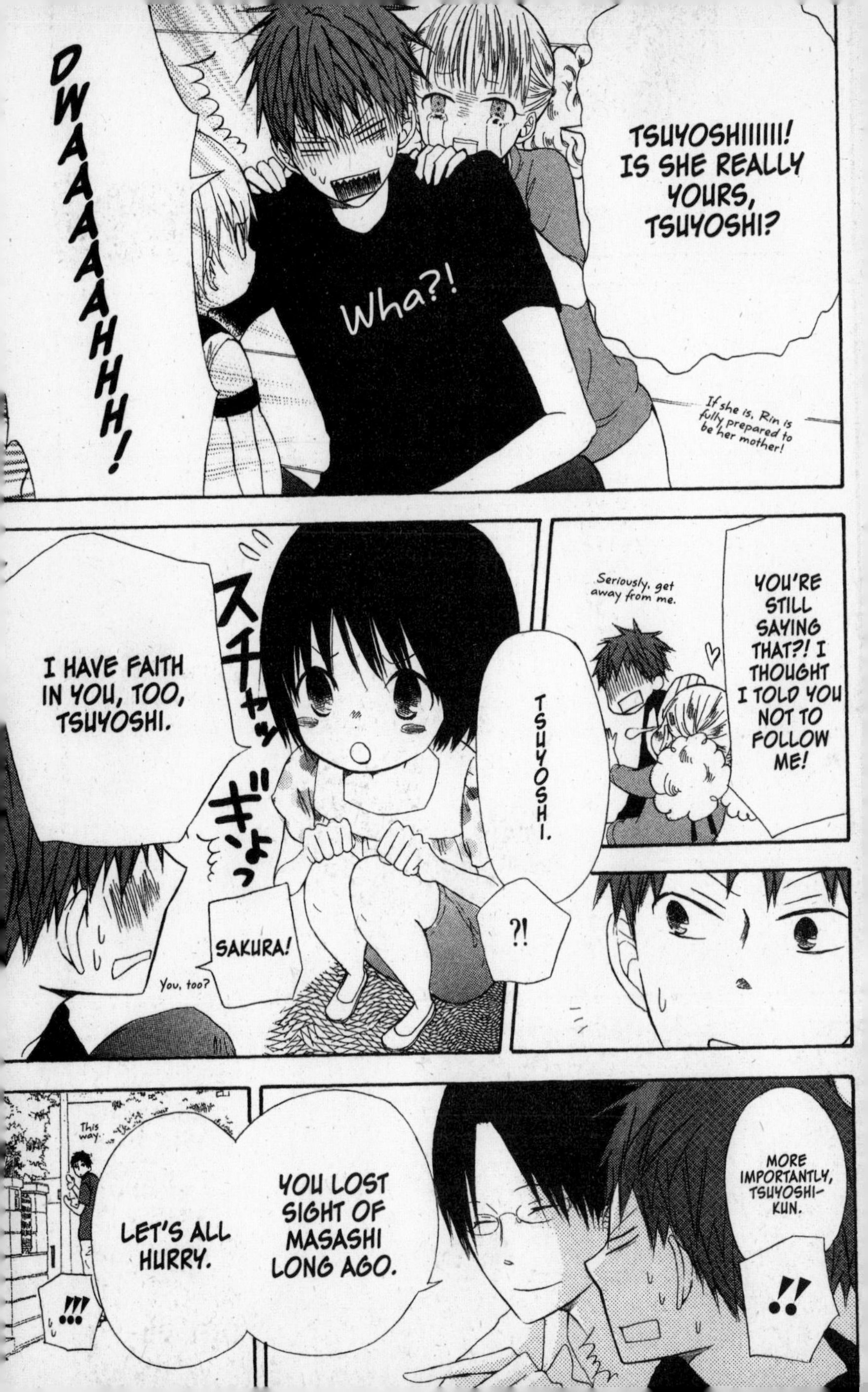
TSUYOSHIIIIIII! IS SHE REALLY YOURS, TSUYOSHI?
If she is, Rin is fully prepared to be her mother!
Wha?!
DWAAAAAHHH!
YOU'RE STILL SAYING THAT?! I THOUGHT I TOLD YOU NOT TO FOLLOW ME!
Seriously, get away from me.
TSUYOSHI.
スチャッ
I HAVE FAITH IN YOU, TOO, TSUYOSHI.
ギョっ
?!
SAKURA!
You, too?
MORE IMPORTANTLY, TSUYOSHI-KUN.
YOU LOST SIGHT OF MASASHI LONG AGO.
!!
LET'S ALL HURRY.
This way.
!!!

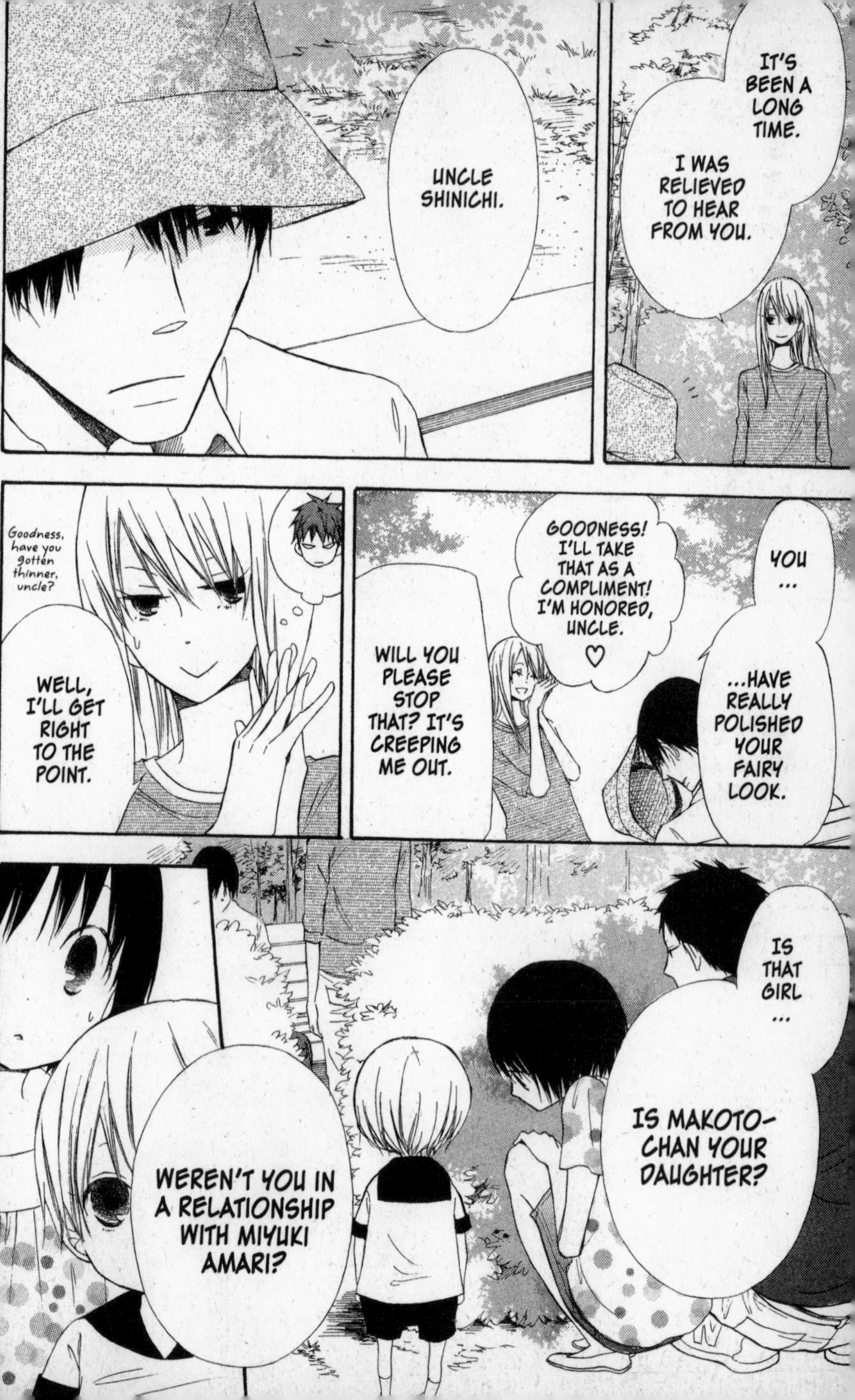
IT'S BEEN A LONG TIME.
I WAS RELIEVED TO HEAR FROM YOU.
UNCLE SHINICHI.
YOU ...
...HAVE REALLY POLISHED YOUR FAIRY LOOK.
GOODNESS! I'LL TAKE THAT AS A COMPLIMENT! I'M HONORED, UNCLE. ♡
WILL YOU PLEASE STOP THAT? IT'S CREEPING ME OUT.
Goodness, have you gotten thinner, uncle?
WELL, I'LL GET RIGHT TO THE POINT.
IS THAT GIRL ...
IS MAKOTO-CHAN YOUR DAUGHTER?
WEREN'T YOU IN A RELATIONSHIP WITH MIYUKI AMARI?

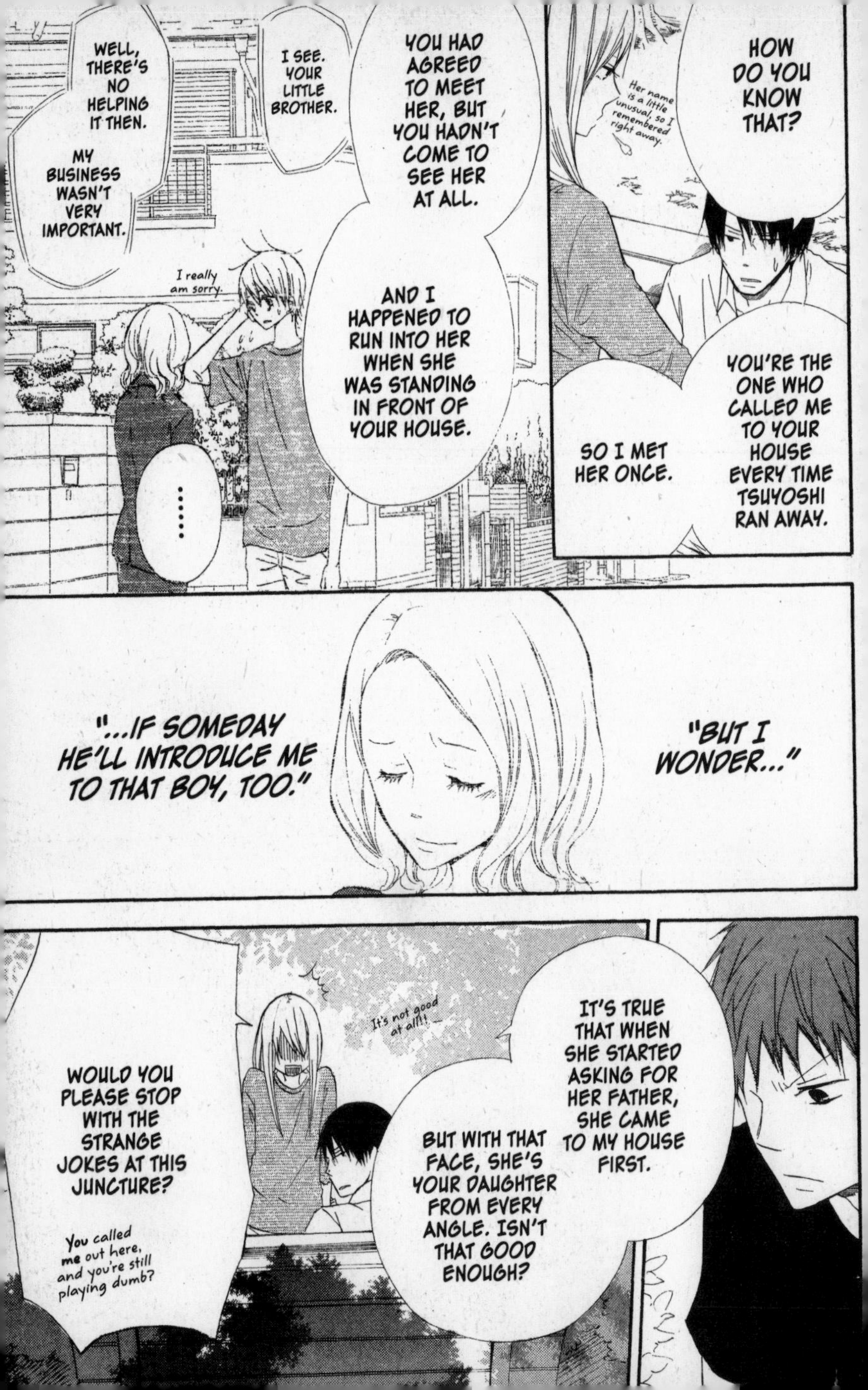
HOW DO YOU KNOW THAT?
Her name is a little unusual, so I remembered right away.
YOU'RE THE ONE WHO CALLED ME TO YOUR HOUSE EVERY TIME TSUYOSHI RAN AWAY.
SO I MET HER ONCE.
YOU HAD AGREED TO MEET HER, BUT YOU HADN'T COME TO SEE HER AT ALL.
AND I HAPPENED TO RUN INTO HER WHEN SHE WAS STANDING IN FRONT OF YOUR HOUSE.
I SEE. YOUR LITTLE BROTHER.
WELL, THERE'S NO HELPING IT THEN.
MY BUSINESS WASN'T VERY IMPORTANT.
I really am sorry.
......
"BUT I WONDER..."
"...IF SOMEDAY HE'LL INTRODUCE ME TO THAT BOY, TOO."
IT'S TRUE THAT WHEN SHE STARTED ASKING FOR HER FATHER, SHE CAME TO MY HOUSE FIRST.
BUT WITH THAT FACE, SHE'S YOUR DAUGHTER FROM EVERY ANGLE. ISN'T THAT GOOD ENOUGH?
It's not good at all!!
WOULD YOU PLEASE STOP WITH THE STRANGE JOKES AT THIS JUNCTURE?
You called me out here, and you're still playing dumb?

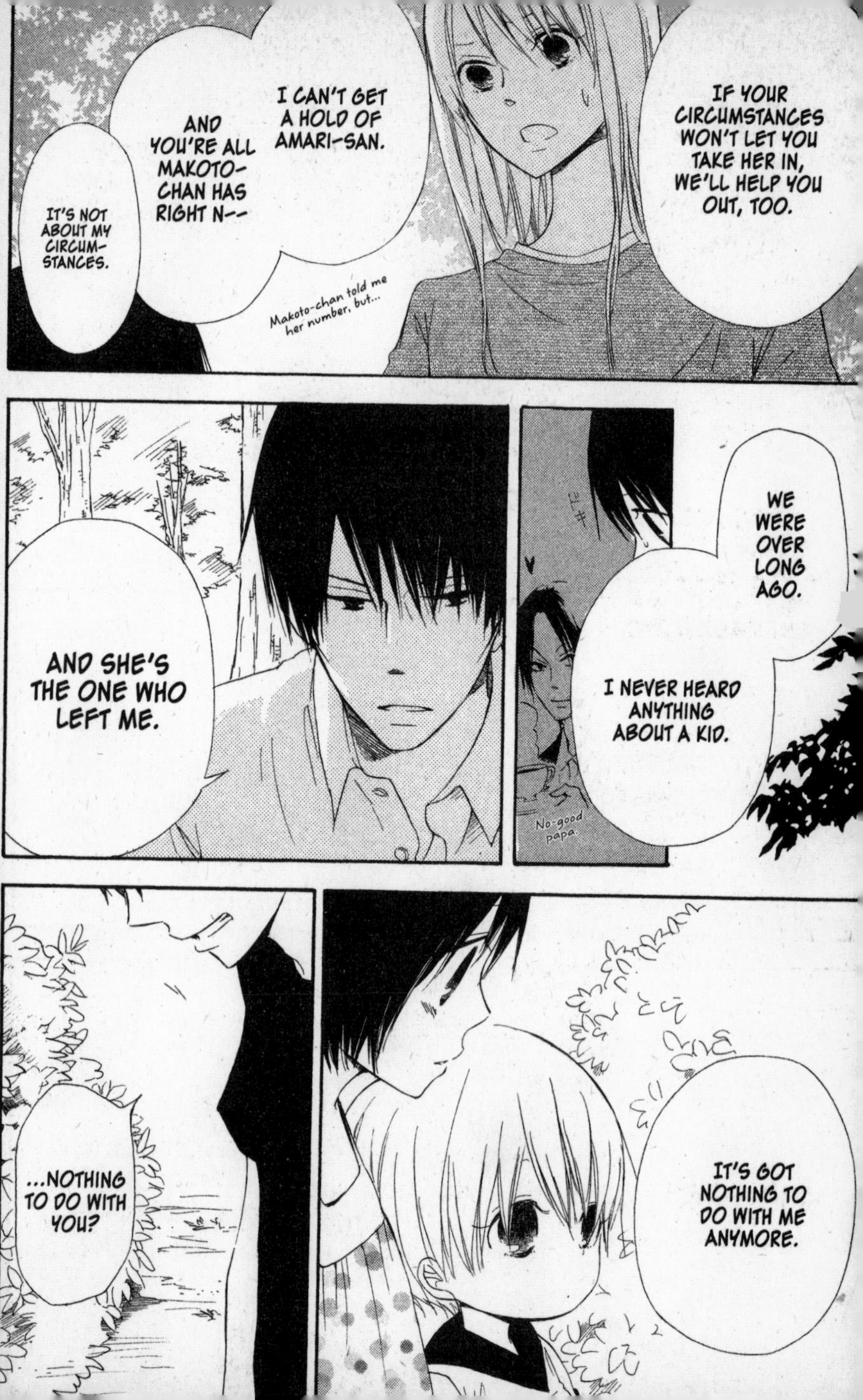
IF YOUR CIRCUMSTANCES WON'T LET YOU TAKE HER IN, WE'LL HELP YOU OUT, TOO.
I CAN'T GET A HOLD OF AMARI-SAN.
AND YOU'RE ALL MAKOTO-CHAN HAS RIGHT N--
Makoto-chan told me her number, but...
IT'S NOT ABOUT MY CIRCUMSTANCES.
WE WERE OVER LONG AGO.
I NEVER HEARD ANYTHING ABOUT A KID.
No-good papa.
AND SHE'S THE ONE WHO LEFT ME.
IT'S GOT NOTHING TO DO WITH ME ANYMORE.
...NOTHING TO DO WITH YOU?

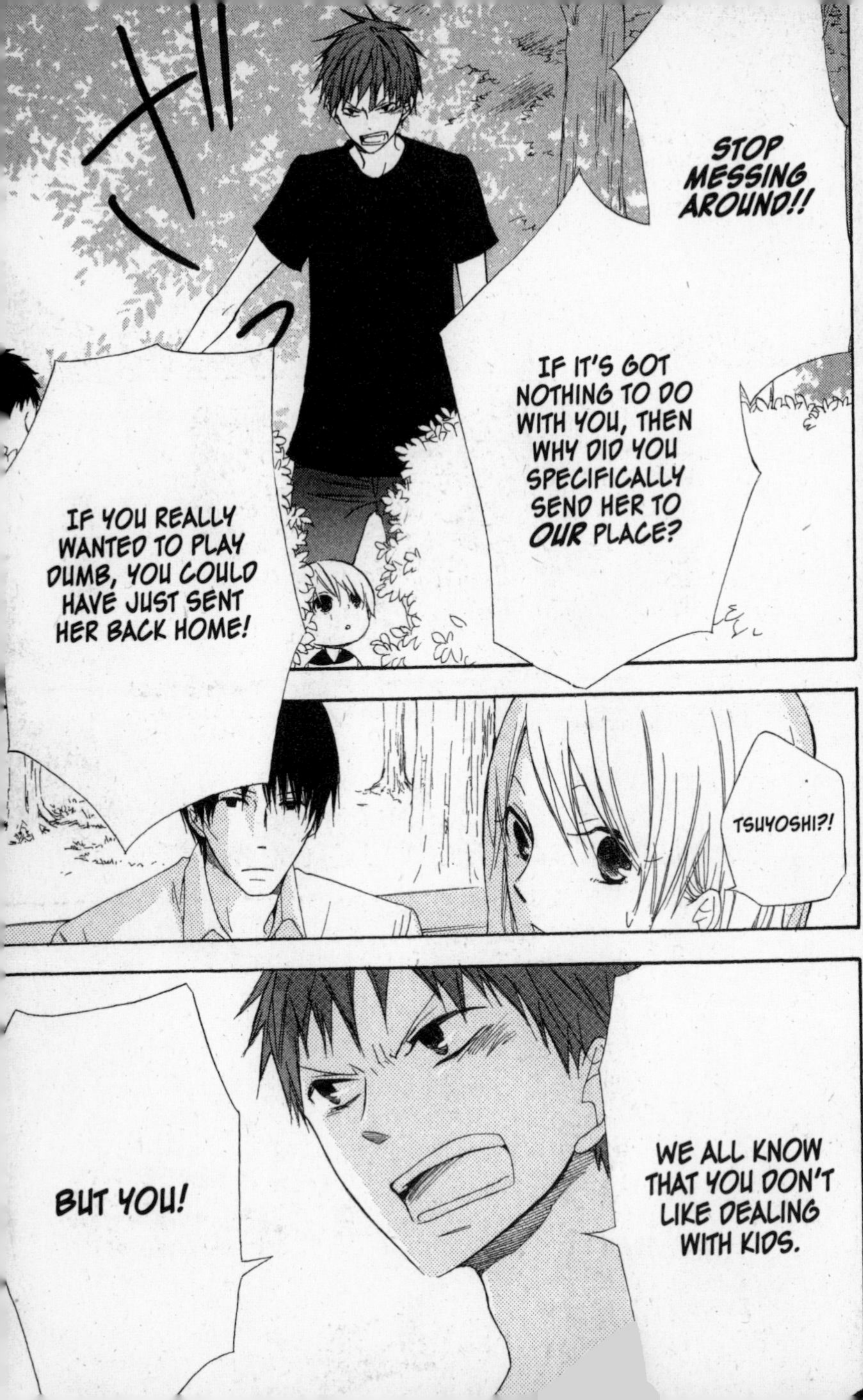
STOP MESSING AROUND!!
IF IT'S GOT NOTHING TO DO WITH YOU, THEN WHY DID YOU SPECIFICALLY SEND HER TO *OUR* PLACE?
IF YOU REALLY WANTED TO PLAY DUMB, YOU COULD HAVE JUST SENT HER BACK HOME!
TSUYOSHI?!
WE ALL KNOW THAT YOU DON'T LIKE DEALING WITH KIDS.
BUT YOU!

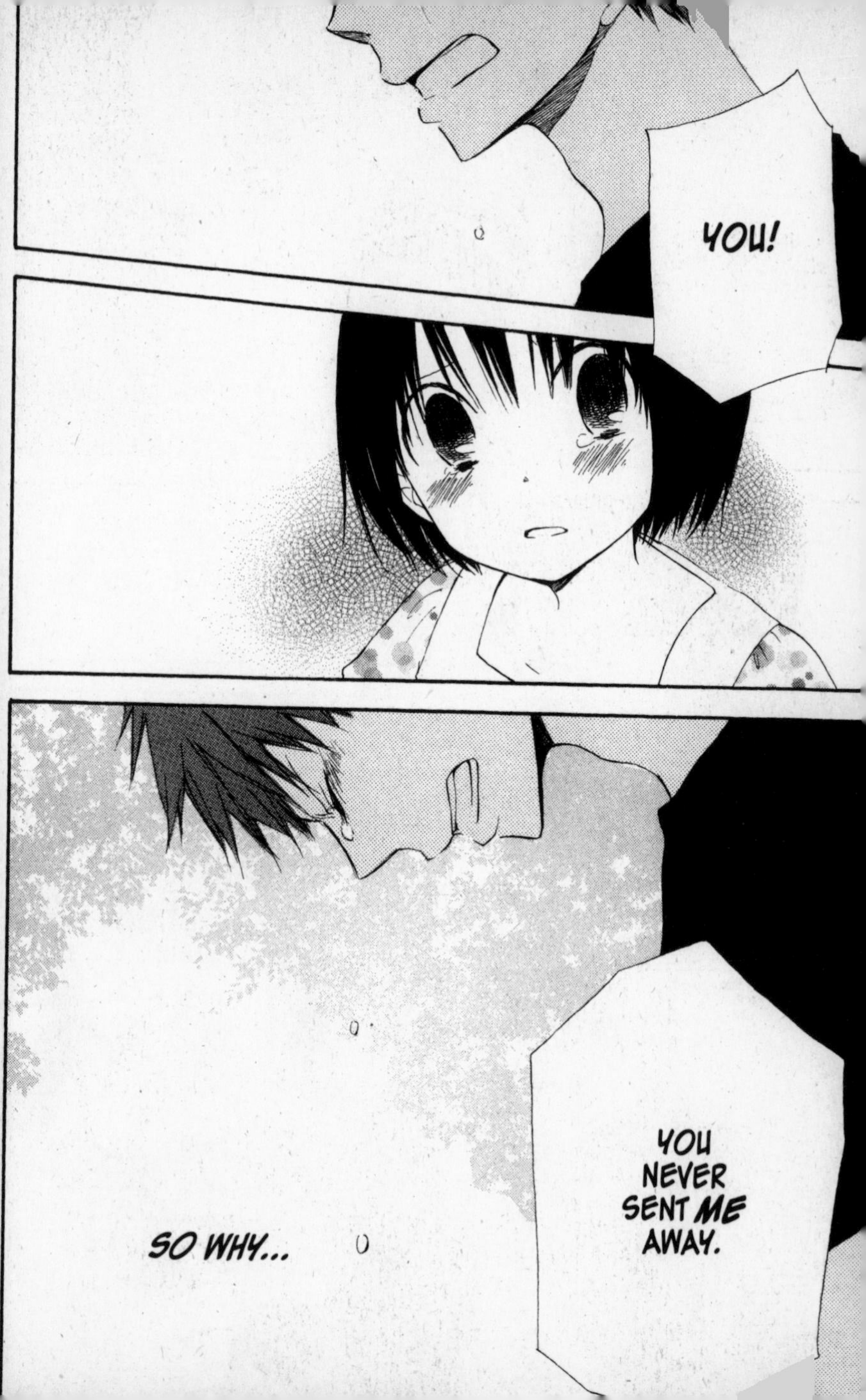
YOU!
YOU NEVER SENT *ME* AWAY.
SO WHY...

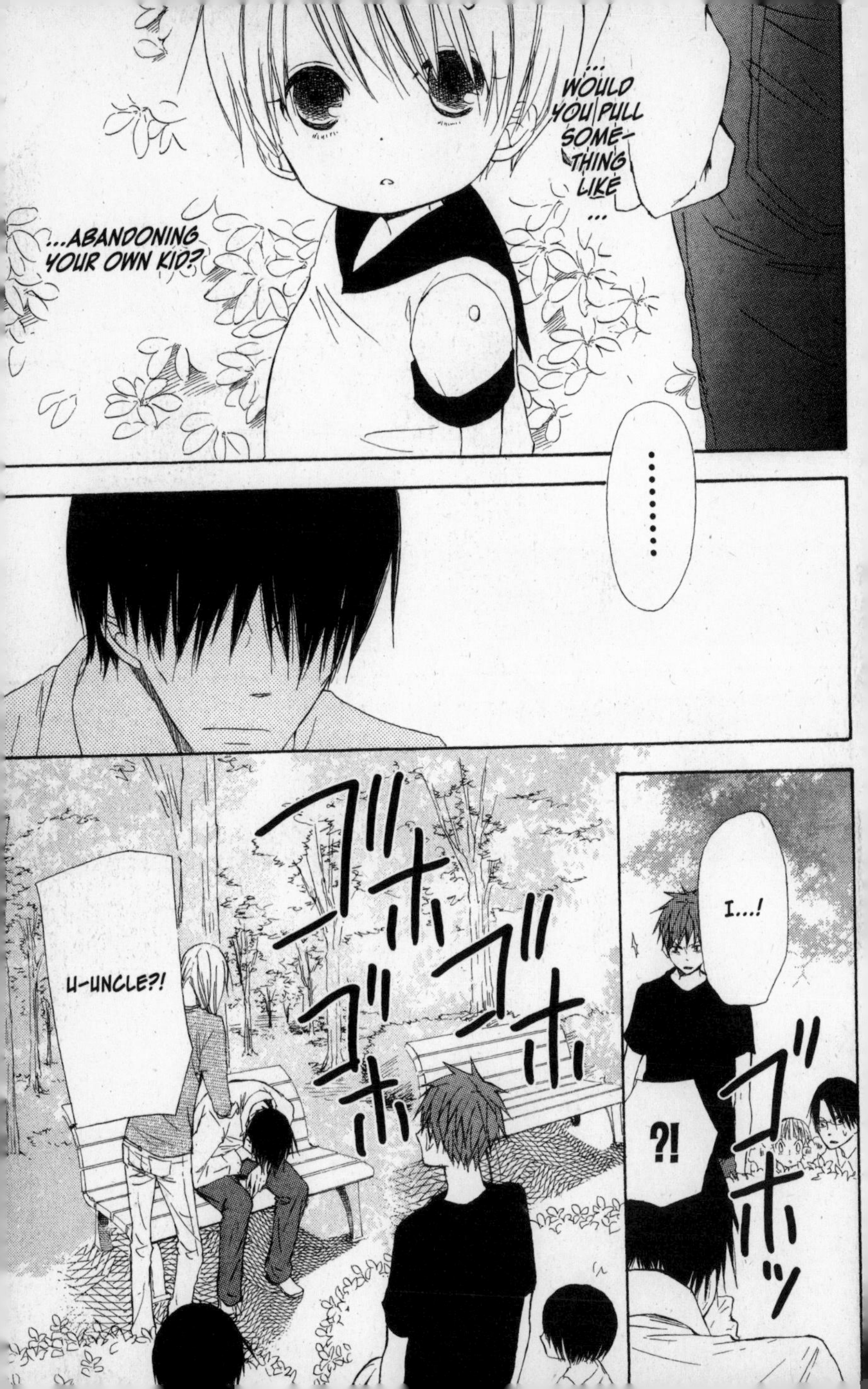
...WOULD YOU PULL SOME-THING LIKE...
...ABANDONING YOUR OWN KID?
......
I...!
?!
ゴホッ
ゴホゴホ
U-UNCLE?!

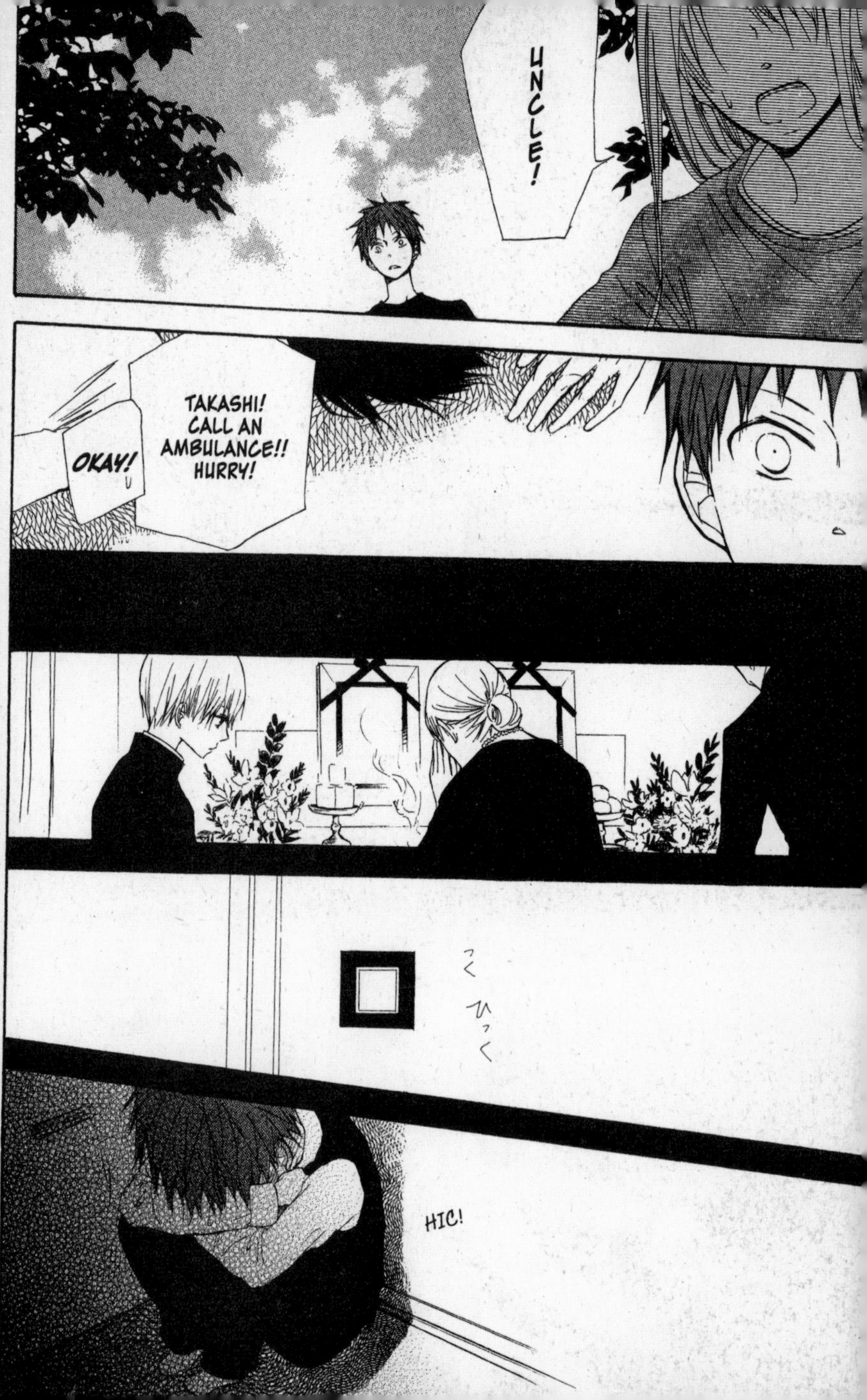
UNCLE!
TAKASHI! CALL AN AMBULANCE!! HURRY!
OKAY!
HIC!

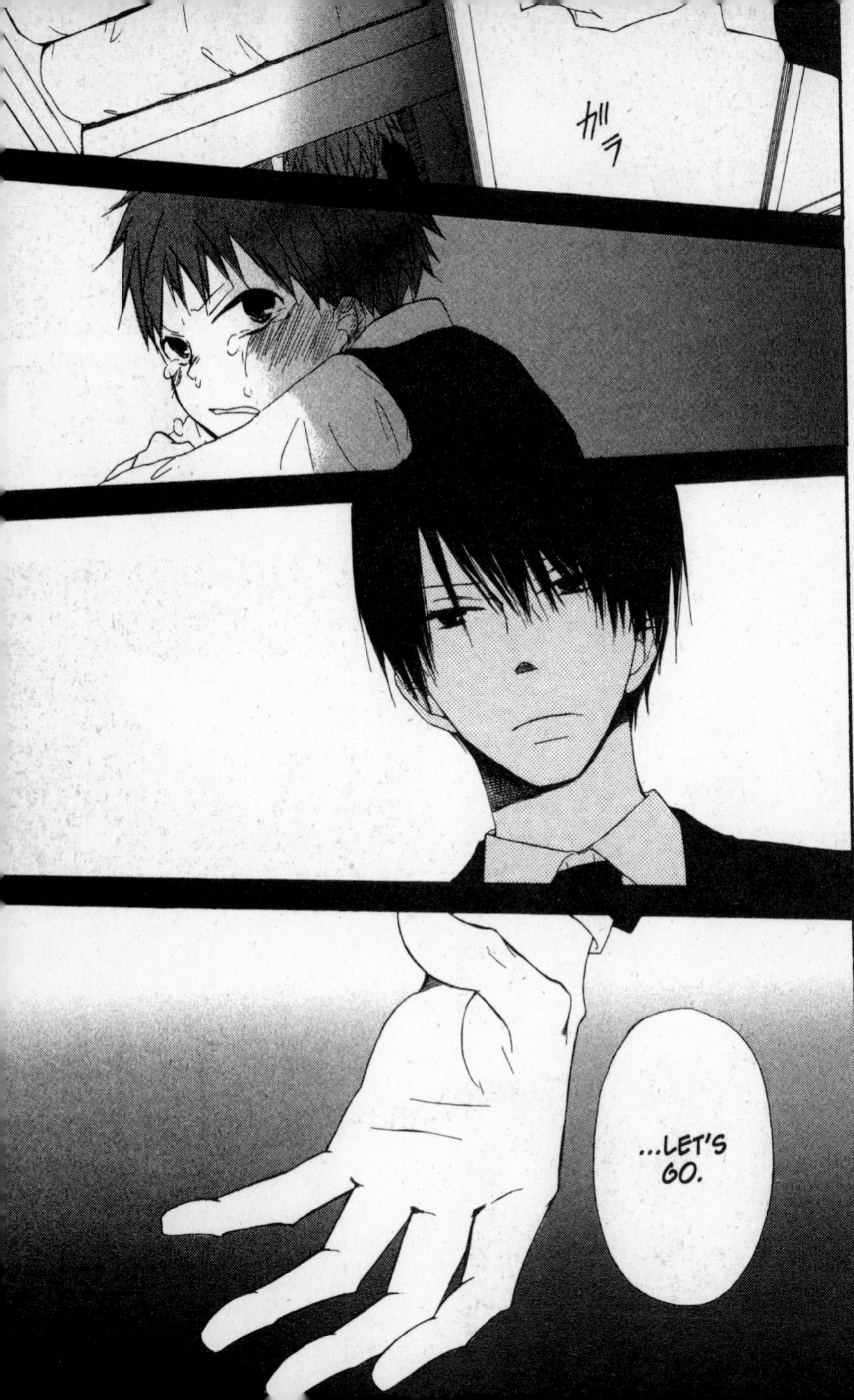
ガラ
...LET'S GO.

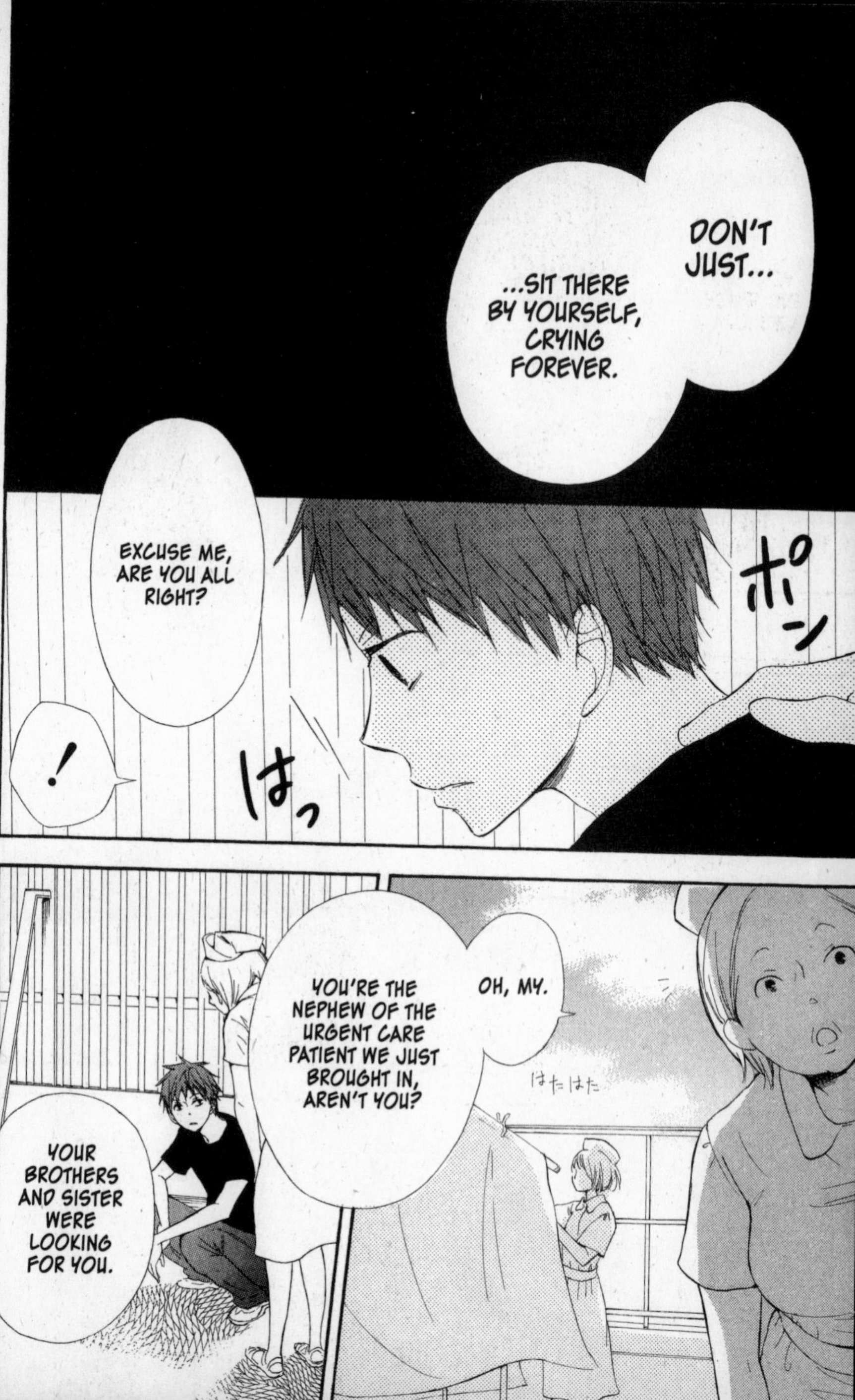
DON'T JUST...
...SIT THERE BY YOURSELF, CRYING FOREVER.
ポン
EXCUSE ME, ARE YOU ALL RIGHT?
はっ
!
OH, MY.
YOU'RE THE NEPHEW OF THE URGENT CARE PATIENT WE JUST BROUGHT IN, AREN'T YOU?
はたはた
YOUR BROTHERS AND SISTER WERE LOOKING FOR YOU.

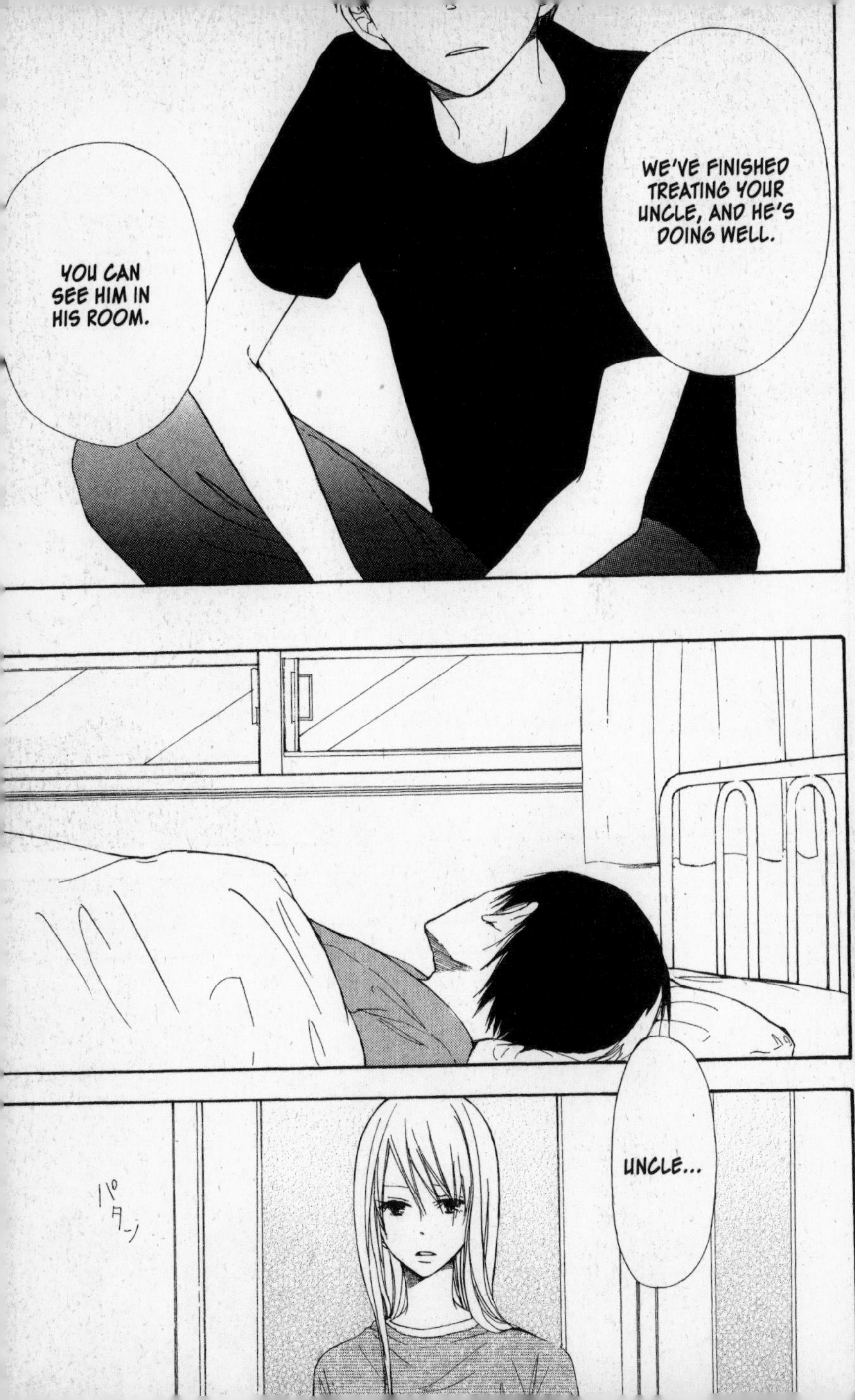
WE'VE FINISHED TREATING YOUR UNCLE, AND HE'S DOING WELL.
YOU CAN SEE HIM IN HIS ROOM.
UNCLE...
パタン

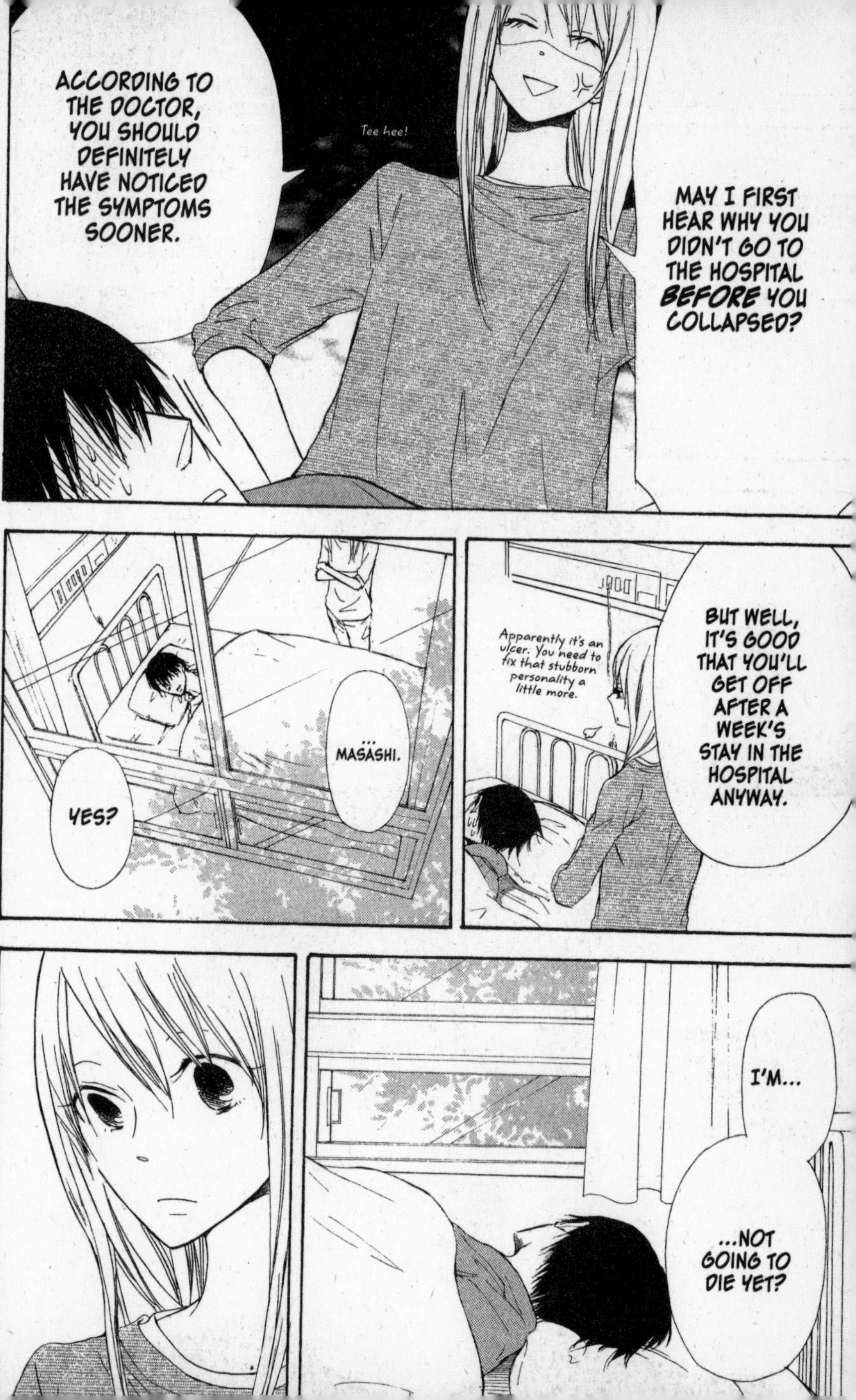
MAY I FIRST HEAR WHY YOU DIDN'T GO TO THE HOSPITAL BEFORE YOU COLLAPSED?
Tee hee!
ACCORDING TO THE DOCTOR, YOU SHOULD DEFINITELY HAVE NOTICED THE SYMPTOMS SOONER.
BUT WELL, IT'S GOOD THAT YOU'LL GET OFF AFTER A WEEK'S STAY IN THE HOSPITAL ANYWAY.
Apparently it's an ulcer. You need to fix that stubborn personality a little more.
...MASASHI.
YES?
I'M...
...NOT GOING TO DIE YET?

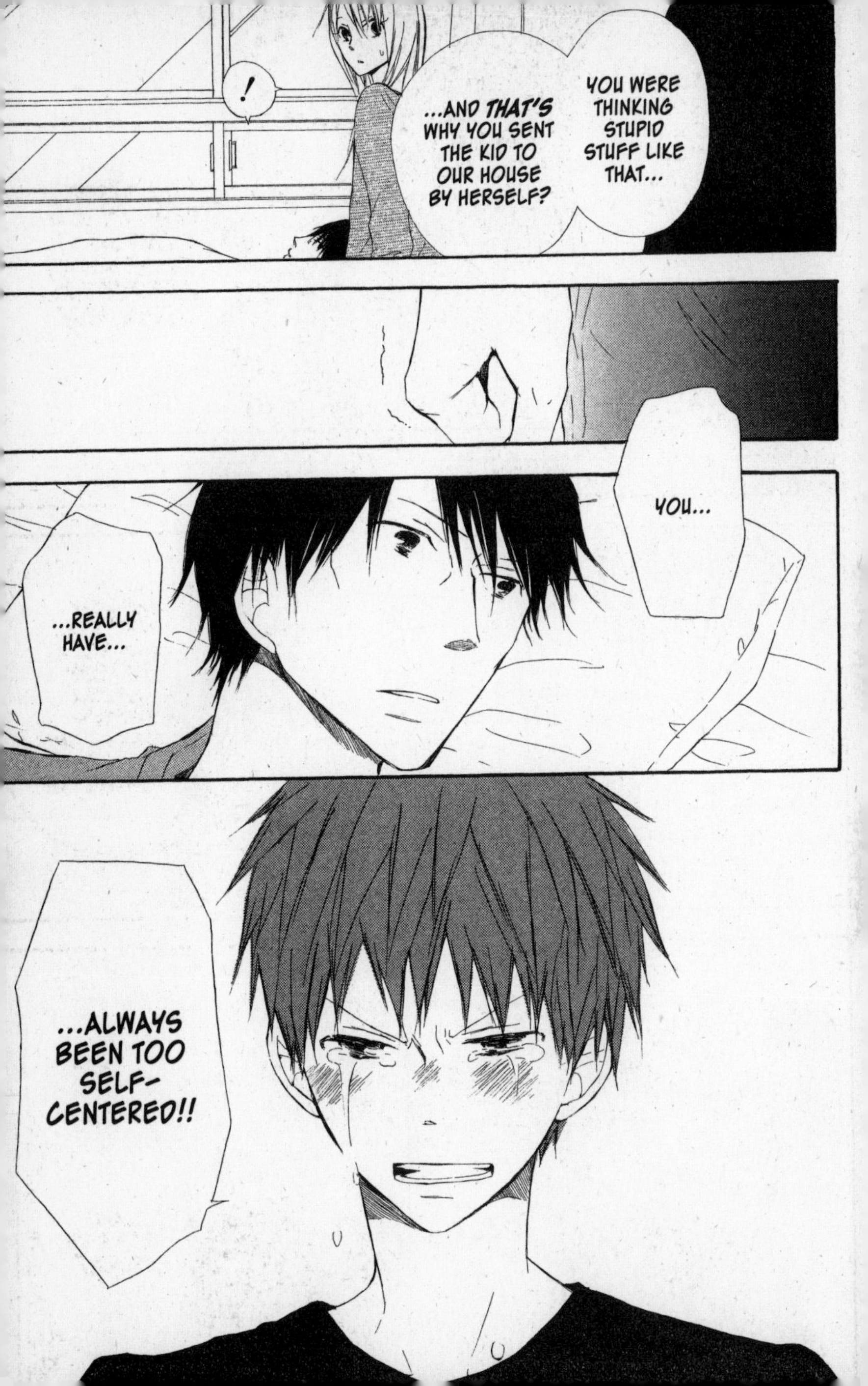
YOU WERE THINKING STUPID STUFF LIKE THAT...
...AND THAT'S WHY YOU SENT THE KID TO OUR HOUSE BY HERSELF?
!
YOU...
...REALLY HAVE...
...ALWAYS BEEN TOO SELF-CENTERED!!

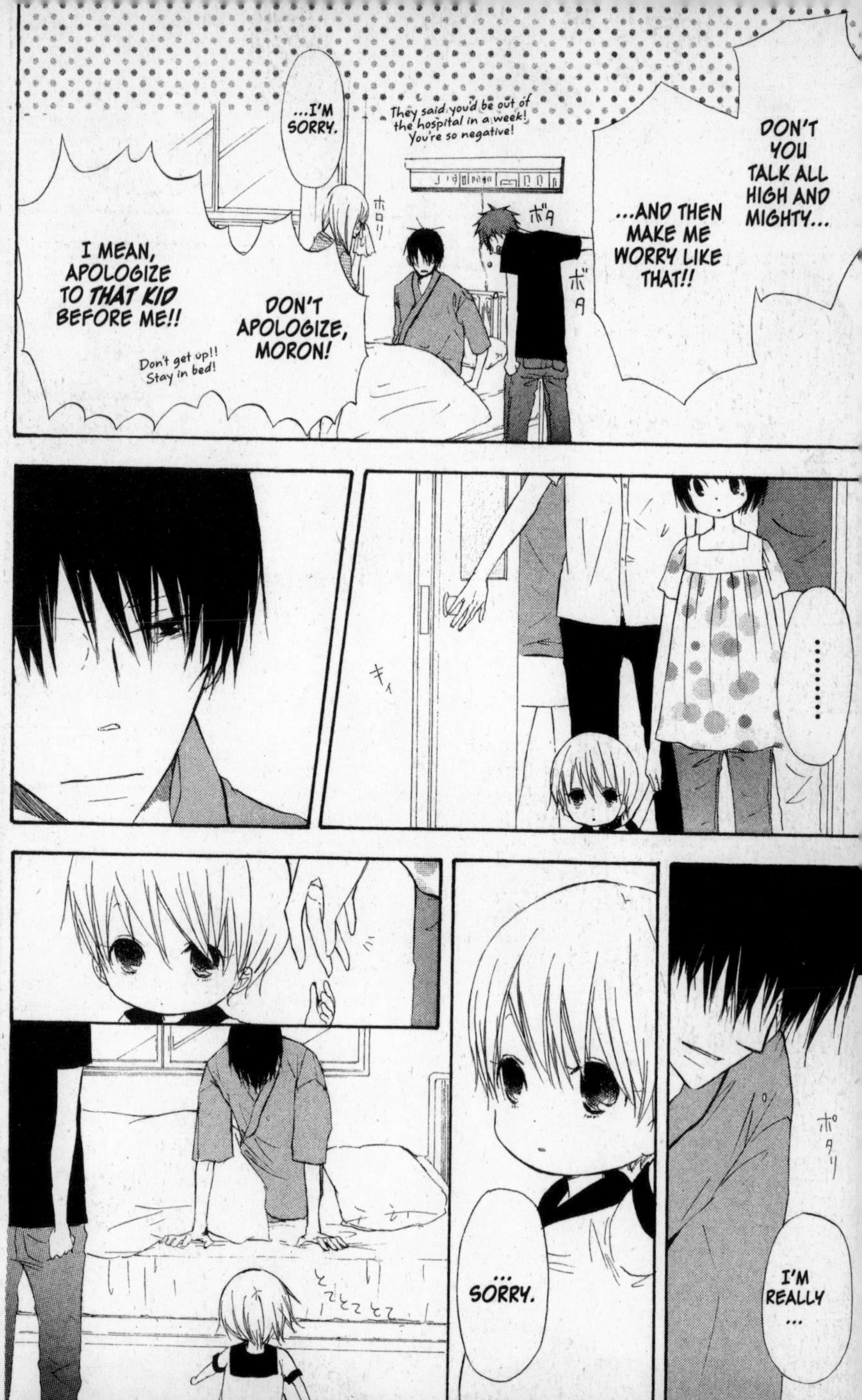
DON'T YOU TALK ALL HIGH AND MIGHTY...
...AND THEN MAKE ME WORRY LIKE THAT!!
ボタ
ボタ
They said you'd be out of the hospital in a week! You're so negative!
...I'M SORRY.
ホロリ
DON'T APOLOGIZE, MORON!
I MEAN, APOLOGIZE TO THAT KID BEFORE ME!!
Don't get up!! Stay in bed!
......
キィ
ポタリ
I'M REALLY ...
... SORRY.
とてとてとて

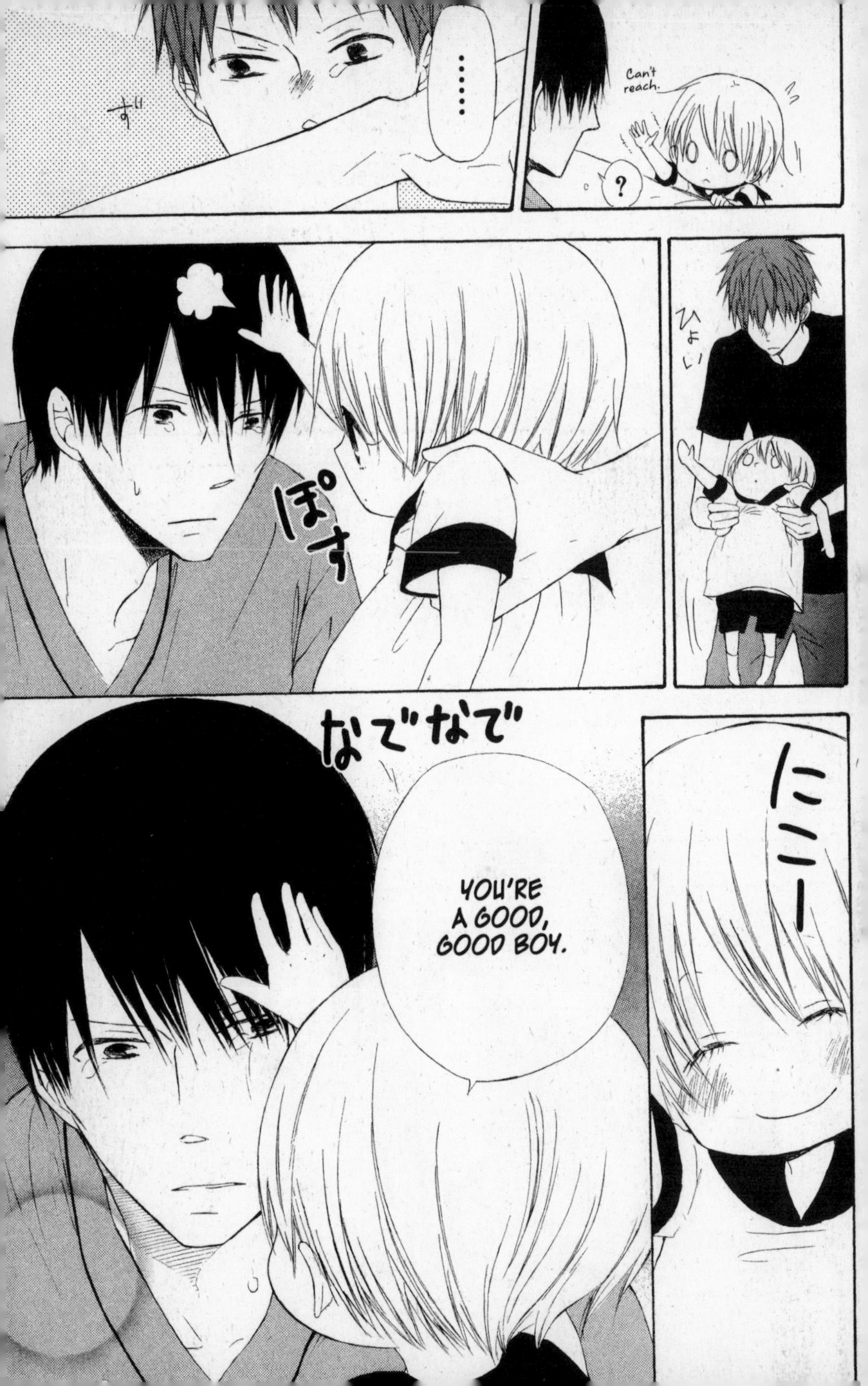
Can't reach.
?
......
すい
ひょい
ぽす
にこー
なでなで
YOU'RE A GOOD, GOOD BOY.

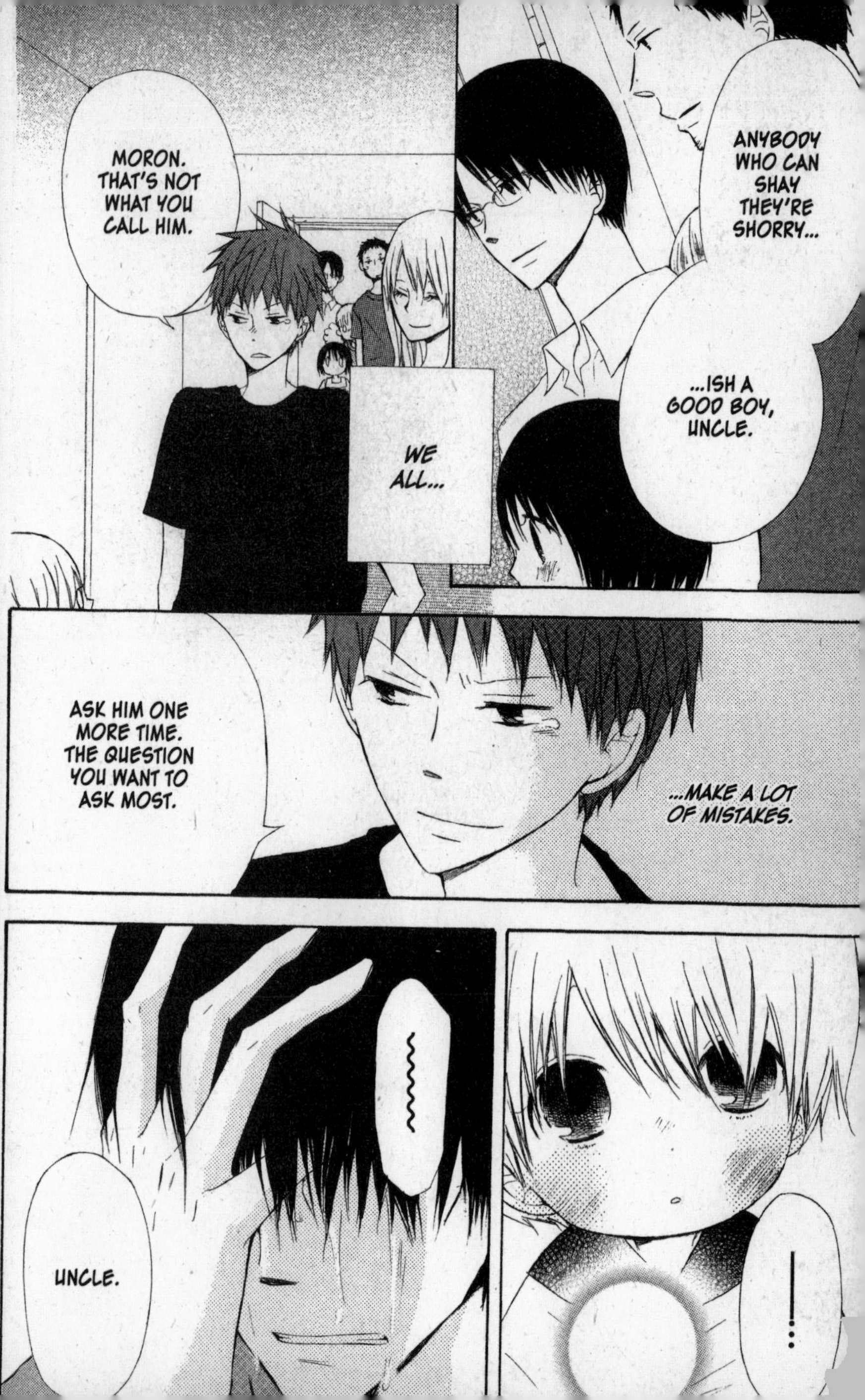
ANYBODY WHO CAN SHAY THEY'RE SHORRY...
...ISH A GOOD BOY, UNCLE.
WE ALL...
MORON. THAT'S NOT WHAT YOU CALL HIM.
...MAKE A LOT OF MISTAKES.
ASK HIM ONE MORE TIME. THE QUESTION YOU WANT TO ASK MOST.
UNCLE.

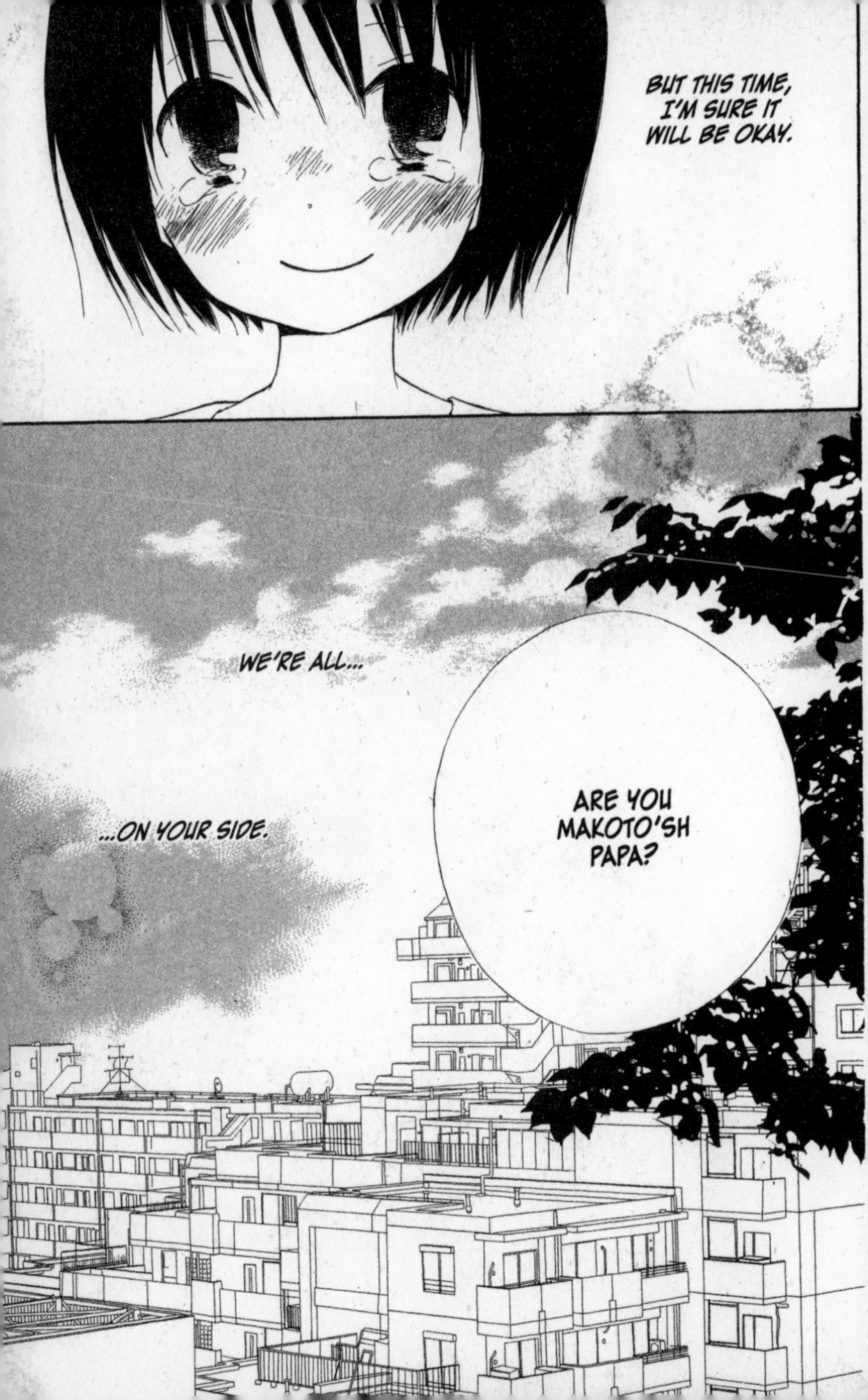
BUT THIS TIME, I'M SURE IT WILL BE OKAY.
ARE YOU MAKOTO'SH PAPA?
WE'RE ALL...
...ON YOUR SIDE.

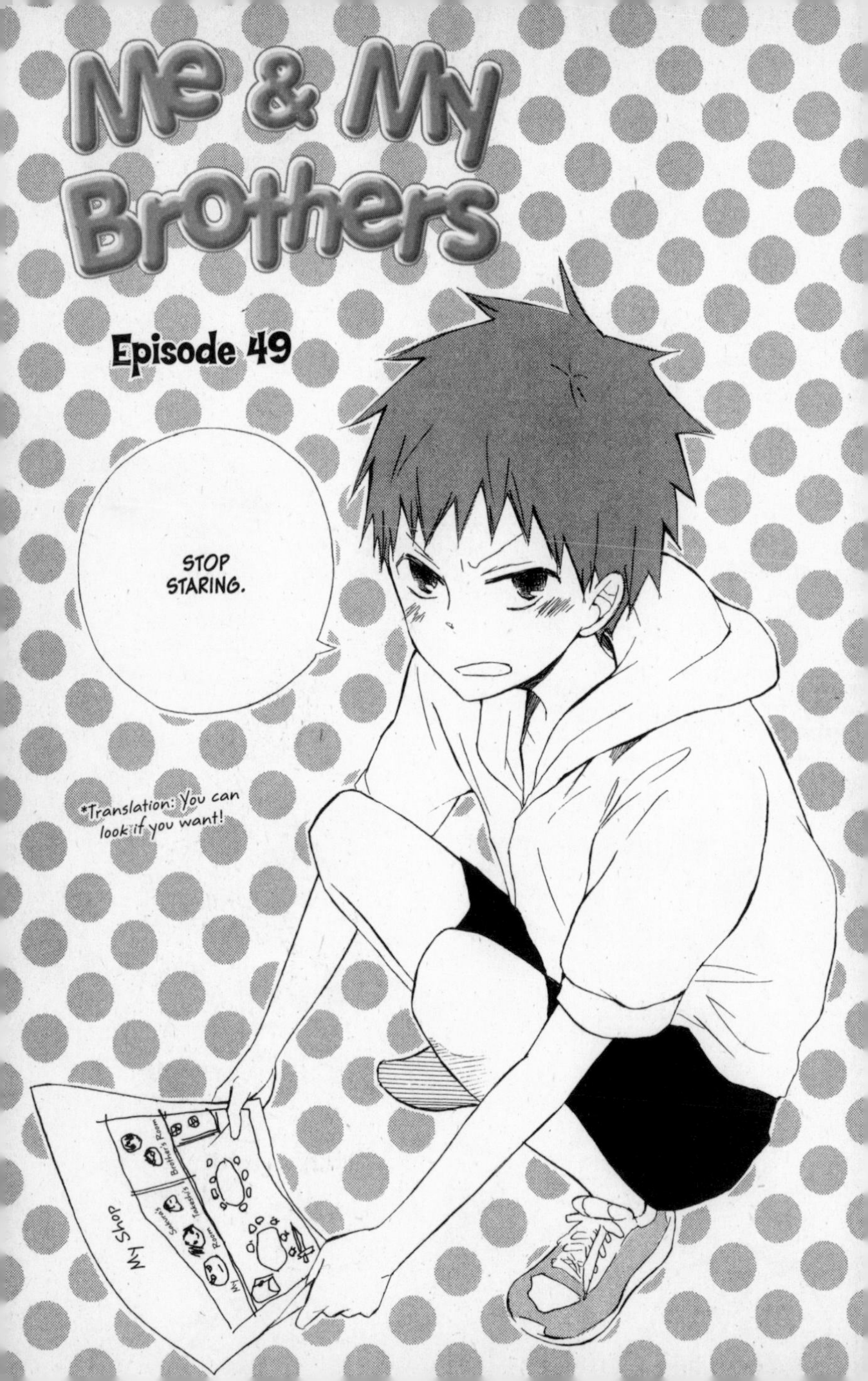
Me & My Brothers
Episode 49
STOP STARING.
*Translation: You can look if you want!
Brother's Room
Takeshi's
Room
My Shop
My

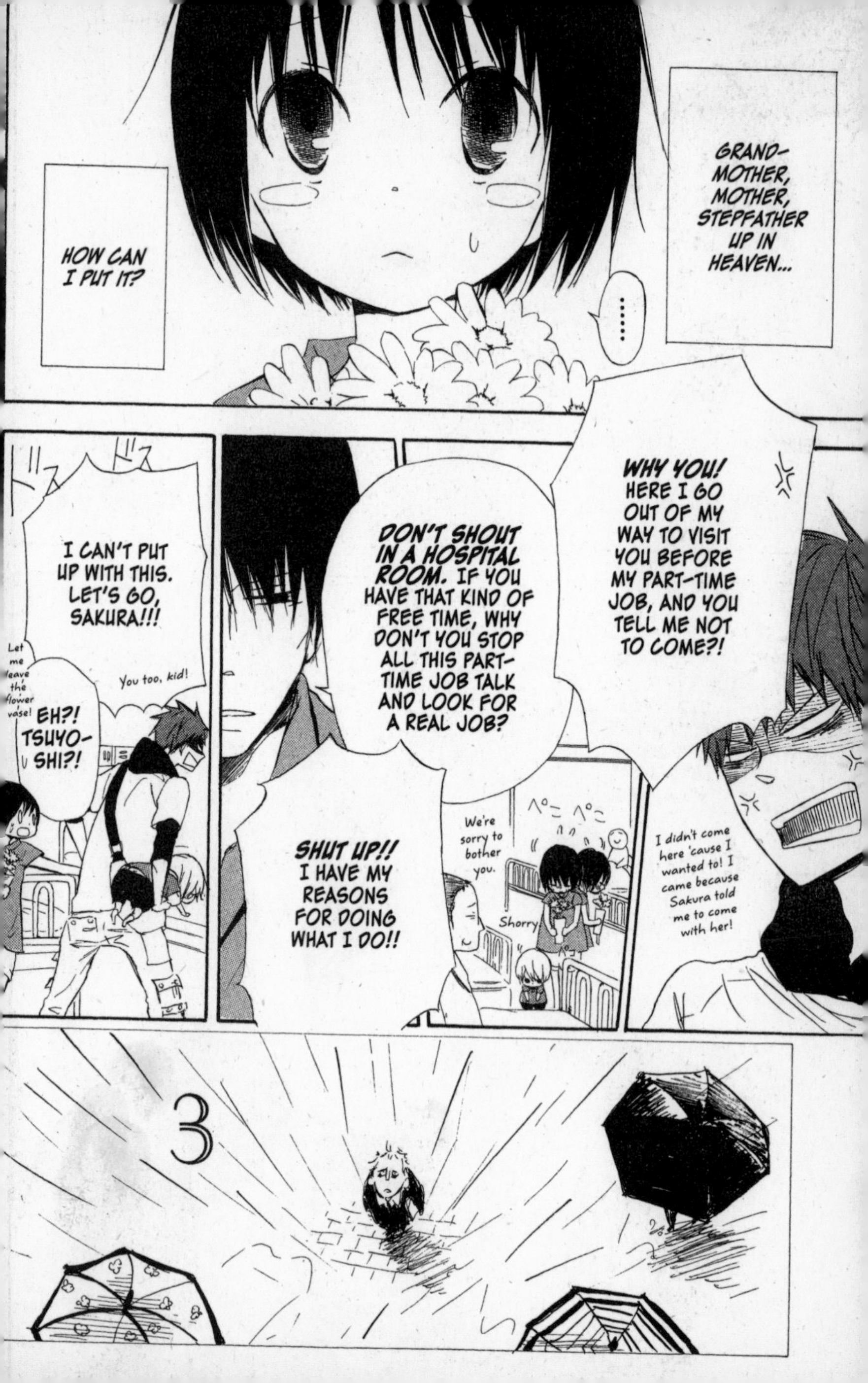
GRAND-MOTHER, MOTHER, STEPFATHER UP IN HEAVEN...
......
HOW CAN I PUT IT?
WHY YOU! HERE I GO OUT OF MY WAY TO VISIT YOU BEFORE MY PART-TIME JOB, AND YOU TELL ME NOT TO COME?!
I didn't come here 'cause I wanted to! I came because Sakura told me to come with her!
DON'T SHOUT IN A HOSPITAL ROOM. IF YOU HAVE THAT KIND OF FREE TIME, WHY DON'T YOU STOP ALL THIS PART-TIME JOB TALK AND LOOK FOR A REAL JOB?
SHUT UP!! I HAVE MY REASONS FOR DOING WHAT I DO!!
ぺこ ぺこ
We're sorry to bother you.
Shorry.
I CAN'T PUT UP WITH THIS. LET'S GO, SAKURA!!!
You too, kid!
EH?! TSUYO-SHI?!
Let me leave the flower vase!
3

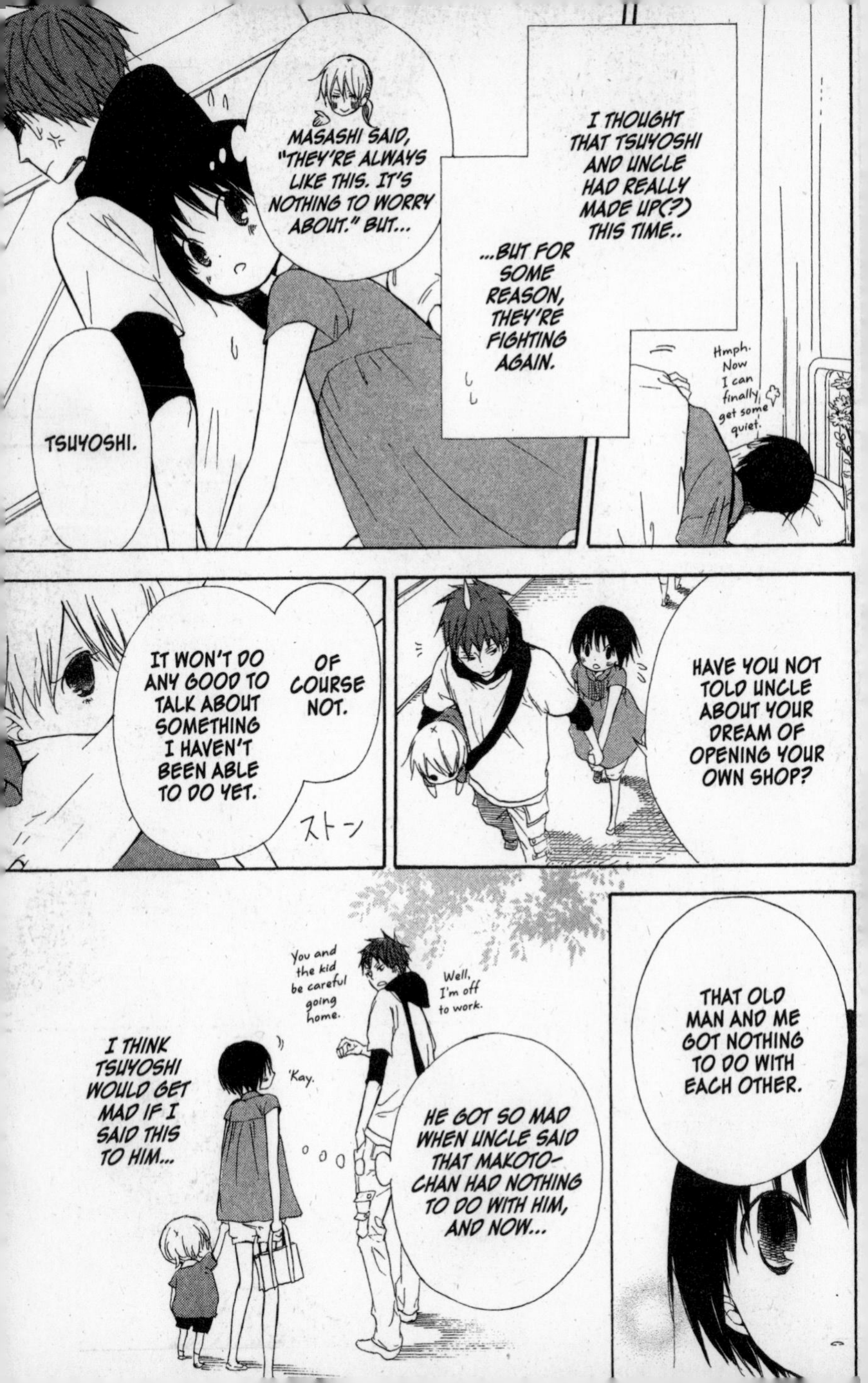
I THOUGHT THAT TSUYOSHI AND UNCLE HAD REALLY MADE UP(?) THIS TIME..
...BUT FOR SOME REASON, THEY'RE FIGHTING AGAIN.
Hmph. Now I can finally get some quiet.
MASASHI SAID, "THEY'RE ALWAYS LIKE THIS. IT'S NOTHING TO WORRY ABOUT." BUT...
TSUYOSHI.
HAVE YOU NOT TOLD UNCLE ABOUT YOUR DREAM OF OPENING YOUR OWN SHOP?
OF COURSE NOT.
IT WON'T DO ANY GOOD TO TALK ABOUT SOMETHING I HAVEN'T BEEN ABLE TO DO YET.
ストーン
THAT OLD MAN AND ME GOT NOTHING TO DO WITH EACH OTHER.
Well, I'm off to work.
You and the kid be careful going home.
HE GOT SO MAD WHEN UNCLE SAID THAT MAKOTO-CHAN HAD NOTHING TO DO WITH HIM, AND NOW...
'Kay.
I THINK TSUYOSHI WOULD GET MAD IF I SAID THIS TO HIM...

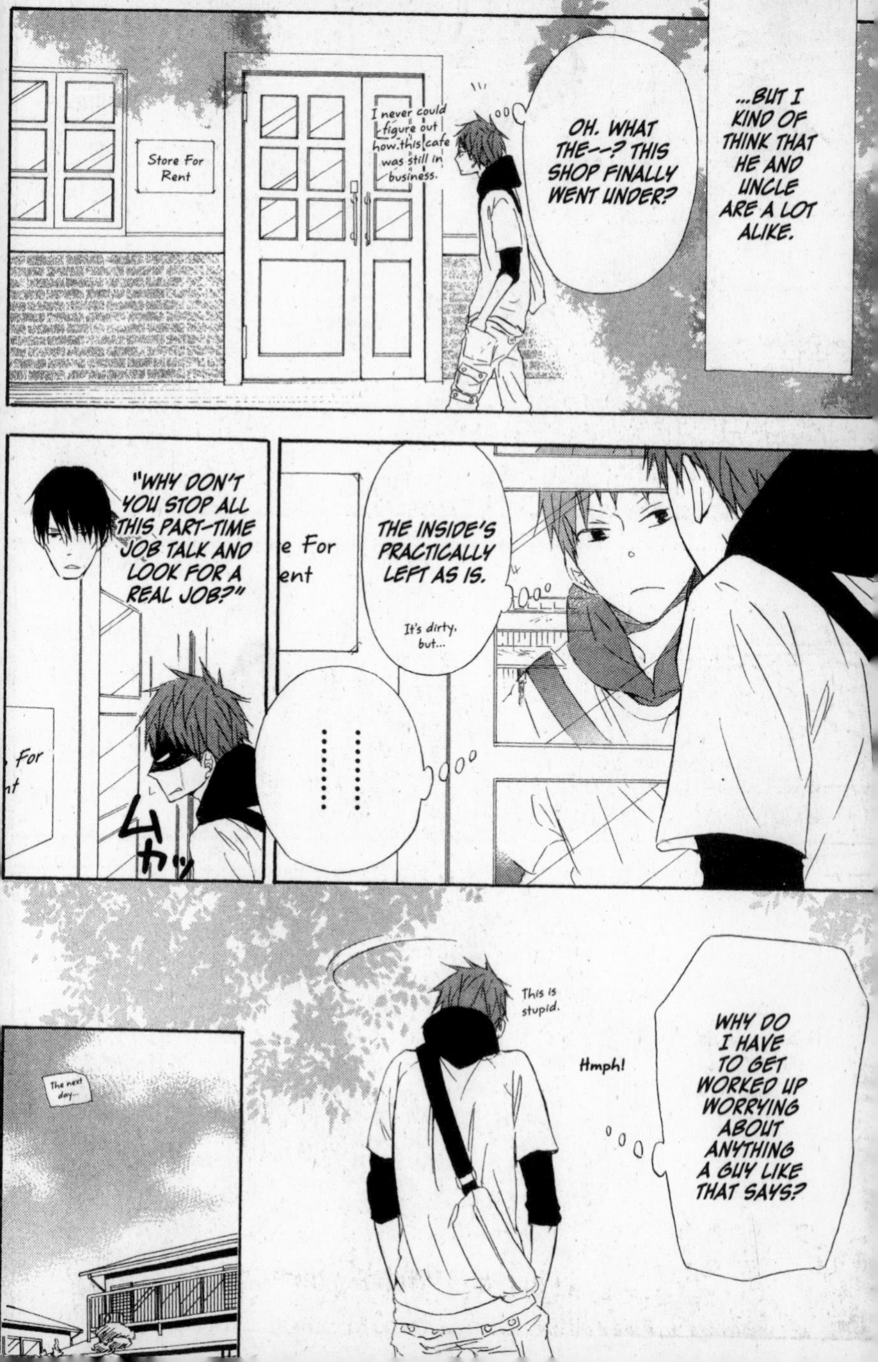
...BUT I KIND OF THINK THAT HE AND UNCLE ARE A LOT ALIKE.
OH. WHAT THE--? THIS SHOP FINALLY WENT UNDER?
I never could figure out how this cafe was still in business.
Store For Rent
THE INSIDE'S PRACTICALLY LEFT AS IS.
It's dirty, but...
......
"WHY DON'T YOU STOP ALL THIS PART-TIME JOB TALK AND LOOK FOR A REAL JOB?"
ムカッ
WHY DO I HAVE TO GET WORKED UP WORRYING ABOUT ANYTHING A GUY LIKE THAT SAYS?
Hmph!
This is stupid.
The next day...

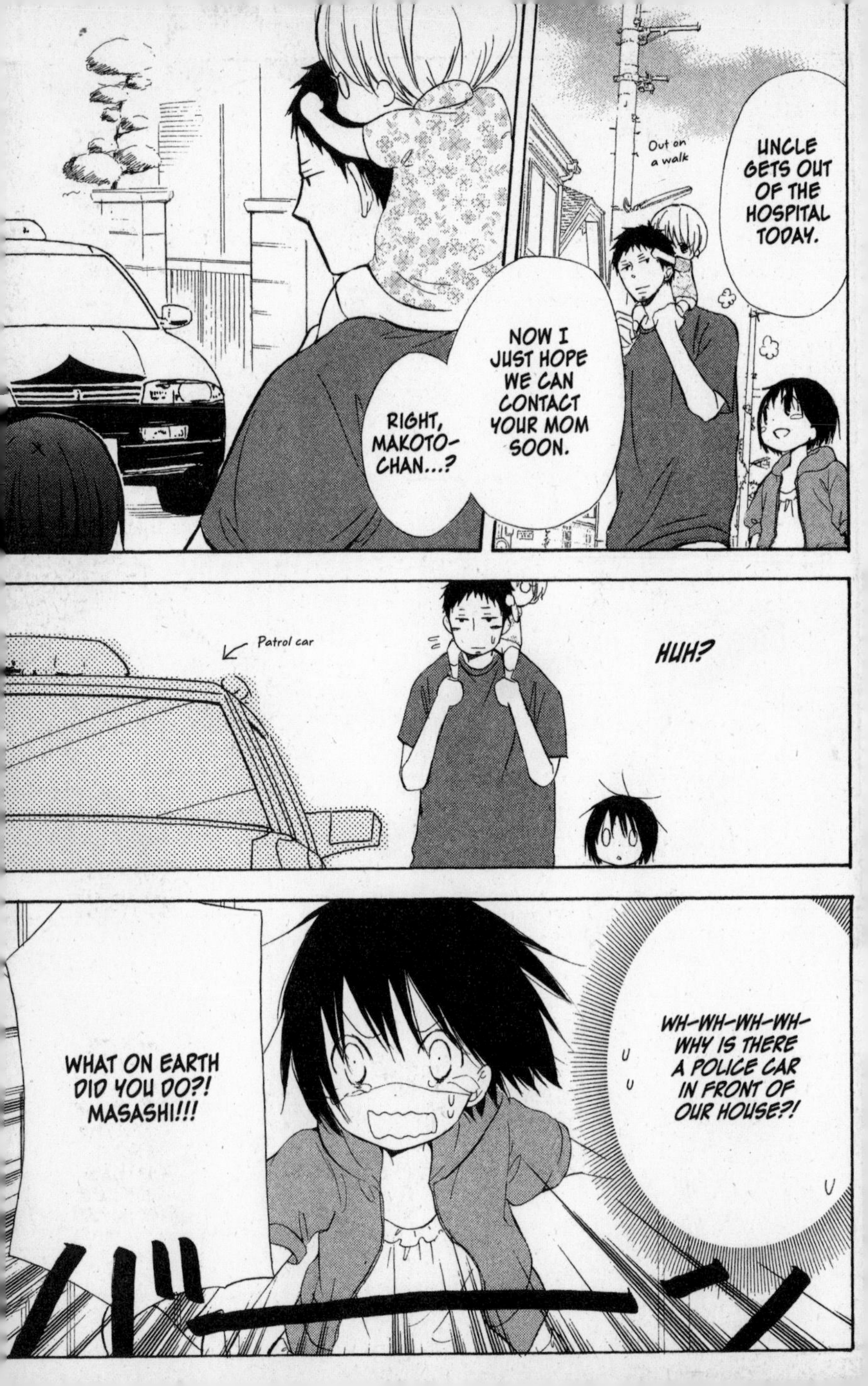
UNCLE GETS OUT OF THE HOSPITAL TODAY.
Out on a walk
NOW I JUST HOPE WE CAN CONTACT YOUR MOM SOON.
RIGHT, MAKOTO-CHAN...?
HUH?
Patrol car
WH-WH-WH-WH-WHY IS THERE A POLICE CAR IN FRONT OF OUR HOUSE?!
WHAT ON EARTH DID YOU DO?! MASASHI!!!

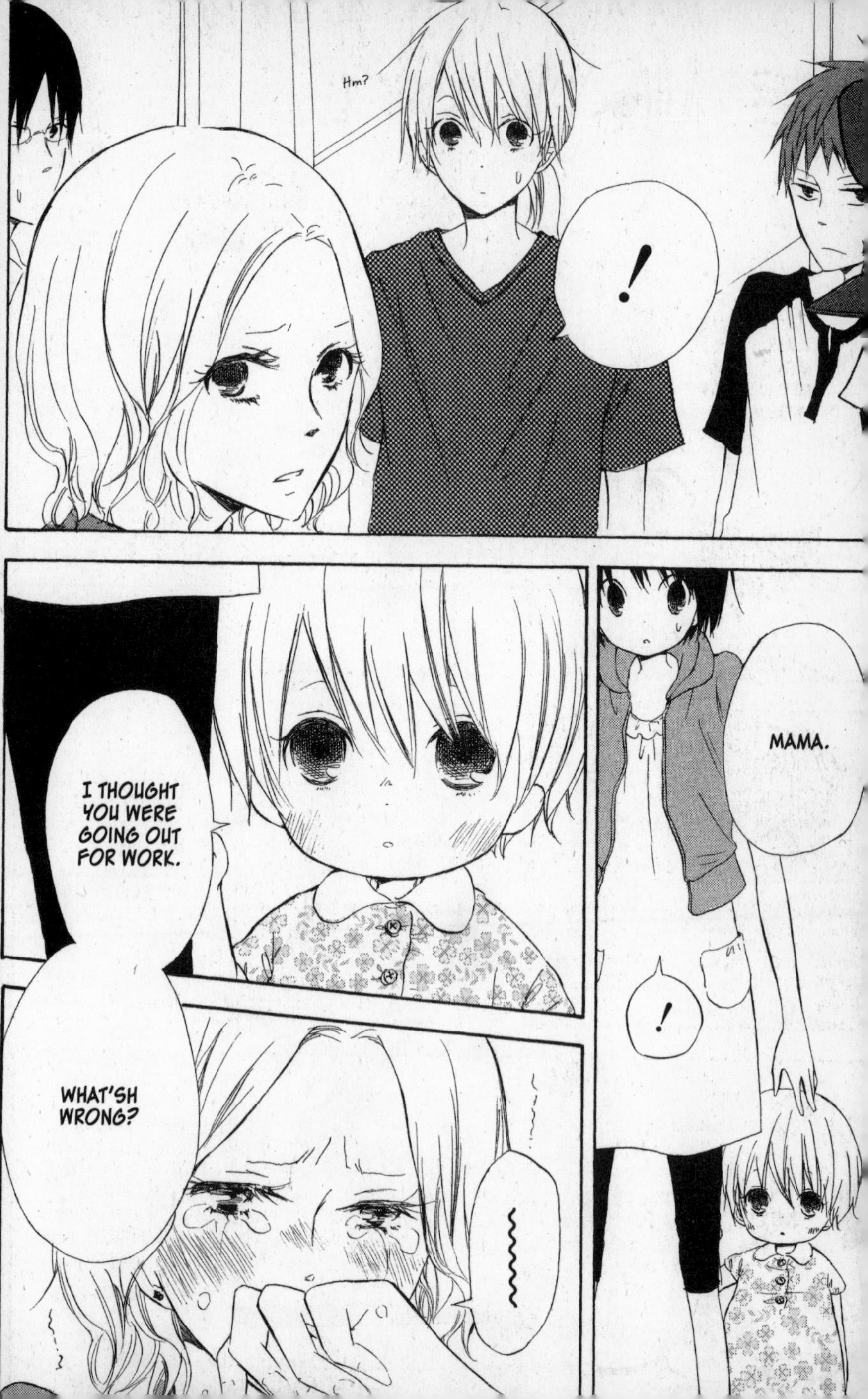
!
Hm?
MAMA.
!
I THOUGHT YOU WERE GOING OUT FOR WORK.
WHAT'SH WRONG?

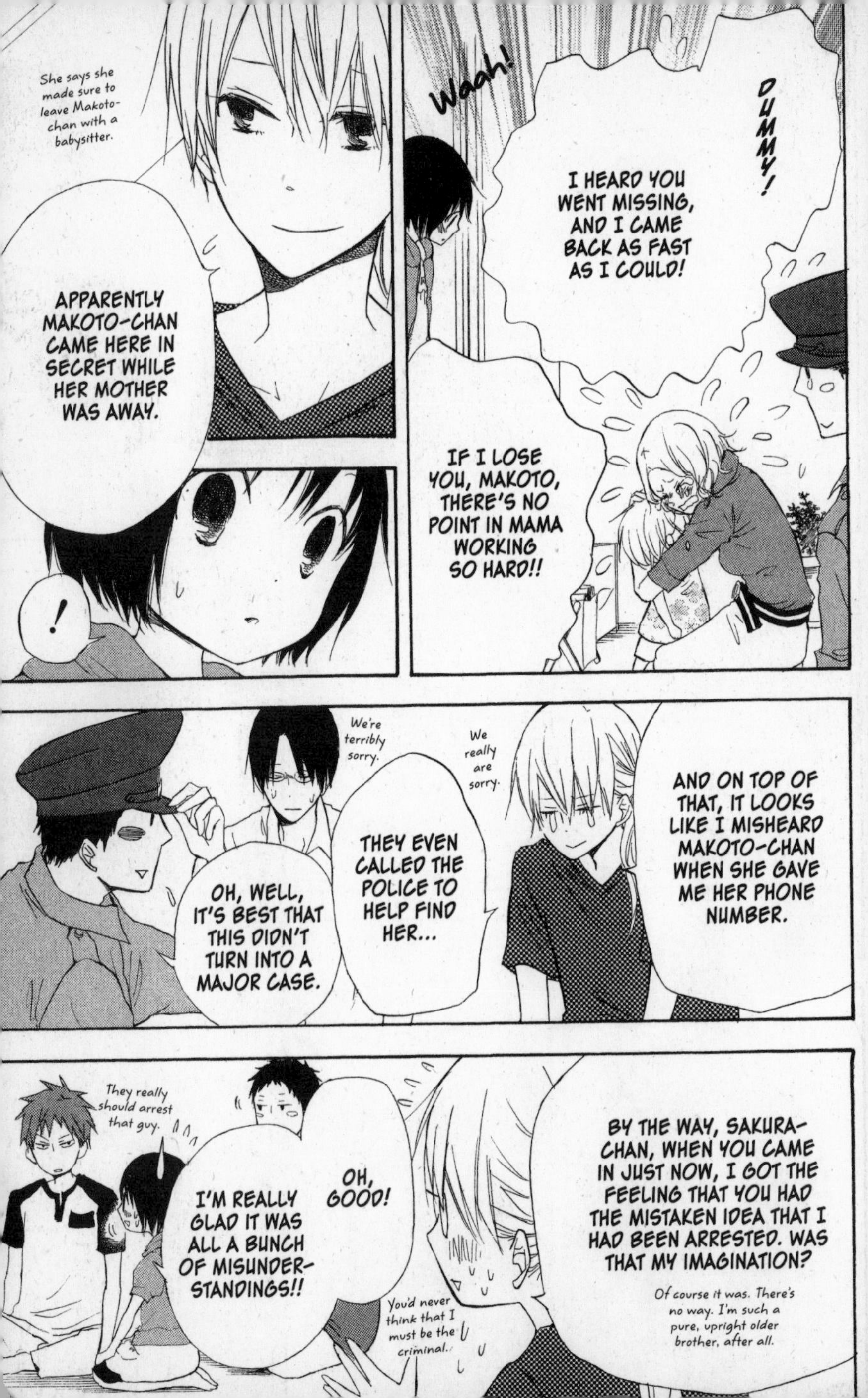
DUMMY!
I HEARD YOU WENT MISSING, AND I CAME BACK AS FAST AS I COULD!
Waah!
IF I LOSE YOU, MAKOTO, THERE'S NO POINT IN MAMA WORKING SO HARD!!
She says she made sure to leave Makoto-chan with a babysitter.
APPARENTLY MAKOTO-CHAN CAME HERE IN SECRET WHILE HER MOTHER WAS AWAY.
!
AND ON TOP OF THAT, IT LOOKS LIKE I MISHEARD MAKOTO-CHAN WHEN SHE GAVE ME HER PHONE NUMBER.
We really are sorry.
THEY EVEN CALLED THE POLICE TO HELP FIND HER...
We're terribly sorry.
OH, WELL, IT'S BEST THAT THIS DIDN'T TURN INTO A MAJOR CASE.
BY THE WAY, SAKURA-CHAN, WHEN YOU CAME IN JUST NOW, I GOT THE FEELING THAT YOU HAD THE MISTAKEN IDEA THAT I HAD BEEN ARRESTED. WAS THAT MY IMAGINATION?
Of course it was. There's no way. I'm such a pure, upright older brother, after all.
You'd never think that I must be the criminal.
OH, GOOD!
I'M REALLY GLAD IT WAS ALL A BUNCH OF MISUNDER-STANDINGS!!
They really should arrest that guy.

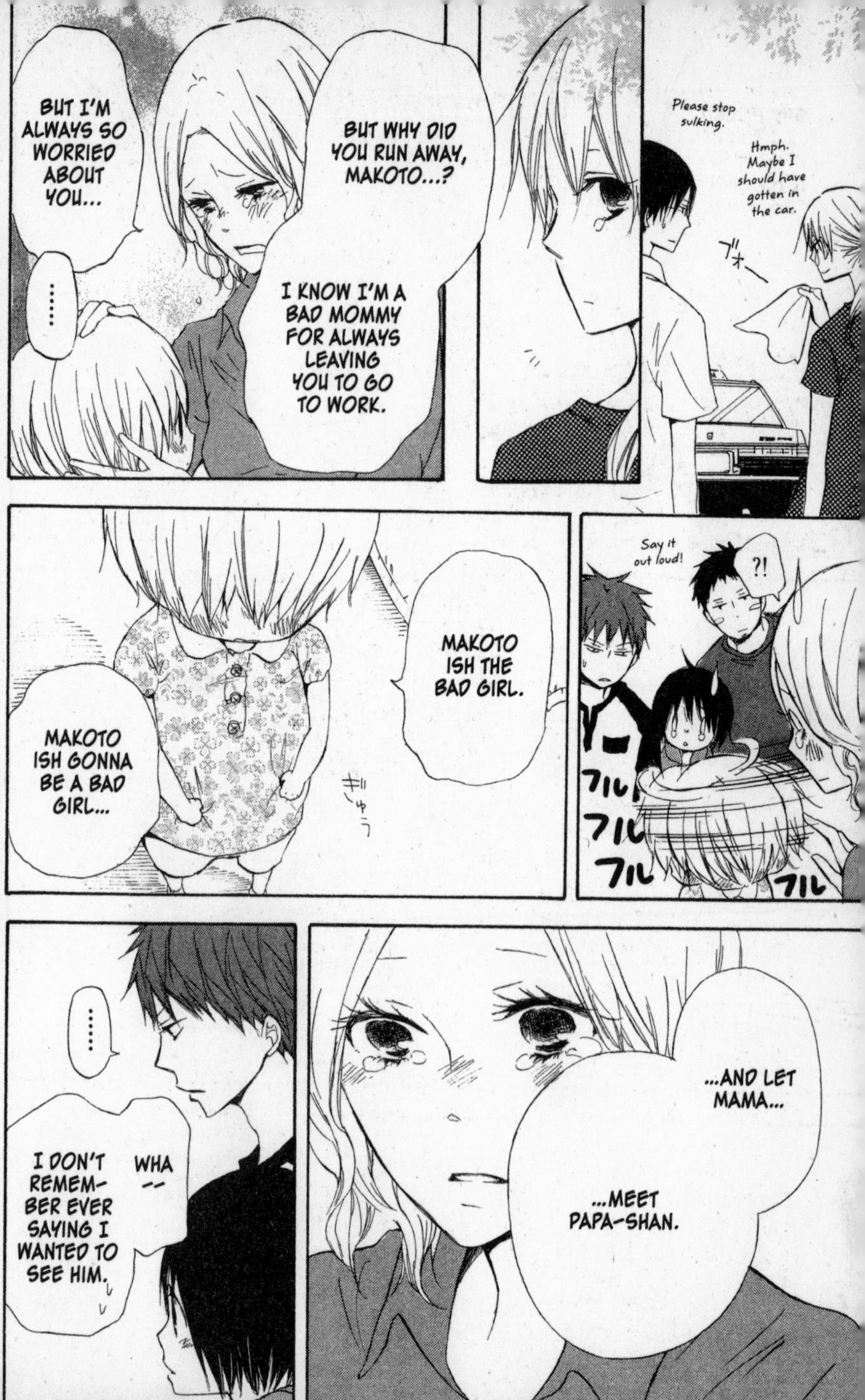
Please stop sulking.
Hmph. Maybe I should have gotten in the car.
ブオー
BUT WHY DID YOU RUN AWAY, MAKOTO...?
I KNOW I'M A BAD MOMMY FOR ALWAYS LEAVING YOU TO GO TO WORK.
BUT I'M ALWAYS SO WORRIED ABOUT YOU...
......
Say it out loud!
?!
フル
フル
フル
フル
MAKOTO ISH THE BAD GIRL.
MAKOTO ISH GONNA BE A BAD GIRL...
ぎゅう
...AND LET MAMA...
...MEET PAPA-SHAN.
......
WHA--
I DON'T REMEMBER EVER SAYING I WANTED TO SEE HIM.

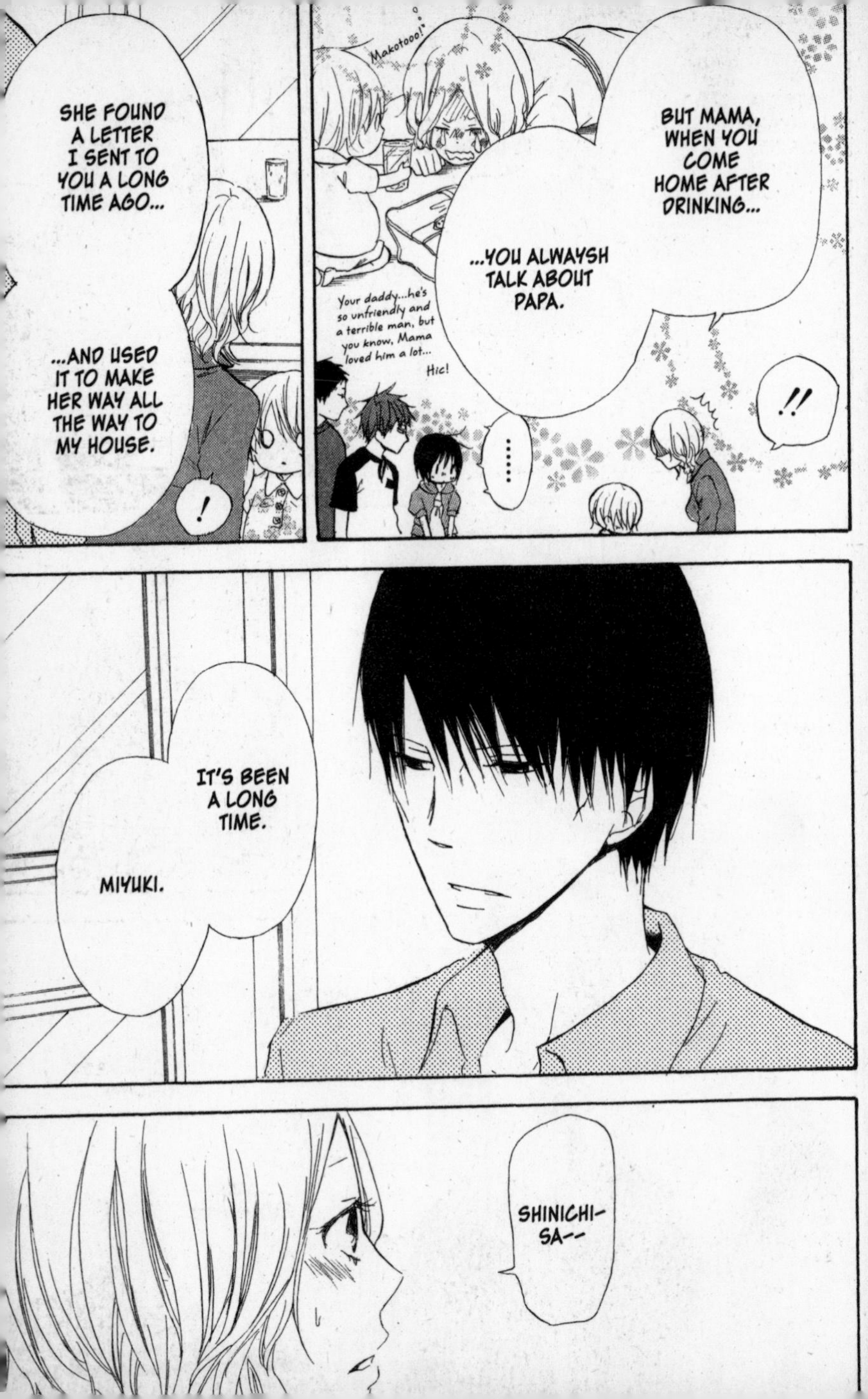
BUT MAMA, WHEN YOU COME HOME AFTER DRINKING...
Makotooo!
...YOU ALWAYSH TALK ABOUT PAPA.
Your daddy...he's so unfriendly and a terrible man, but you know, Mama loved him a lot...
Hic!
!!
......
SHE FOUND A LETTER I SENT TO YOU A LONG TIME AGO...
...AND USED IT TO MAKE HER WAY ALL THE WAY TO MY HOUSE.
!
IT'S BEEN A LONG TIME.
MIYUKI.
SHINICHI-SA--

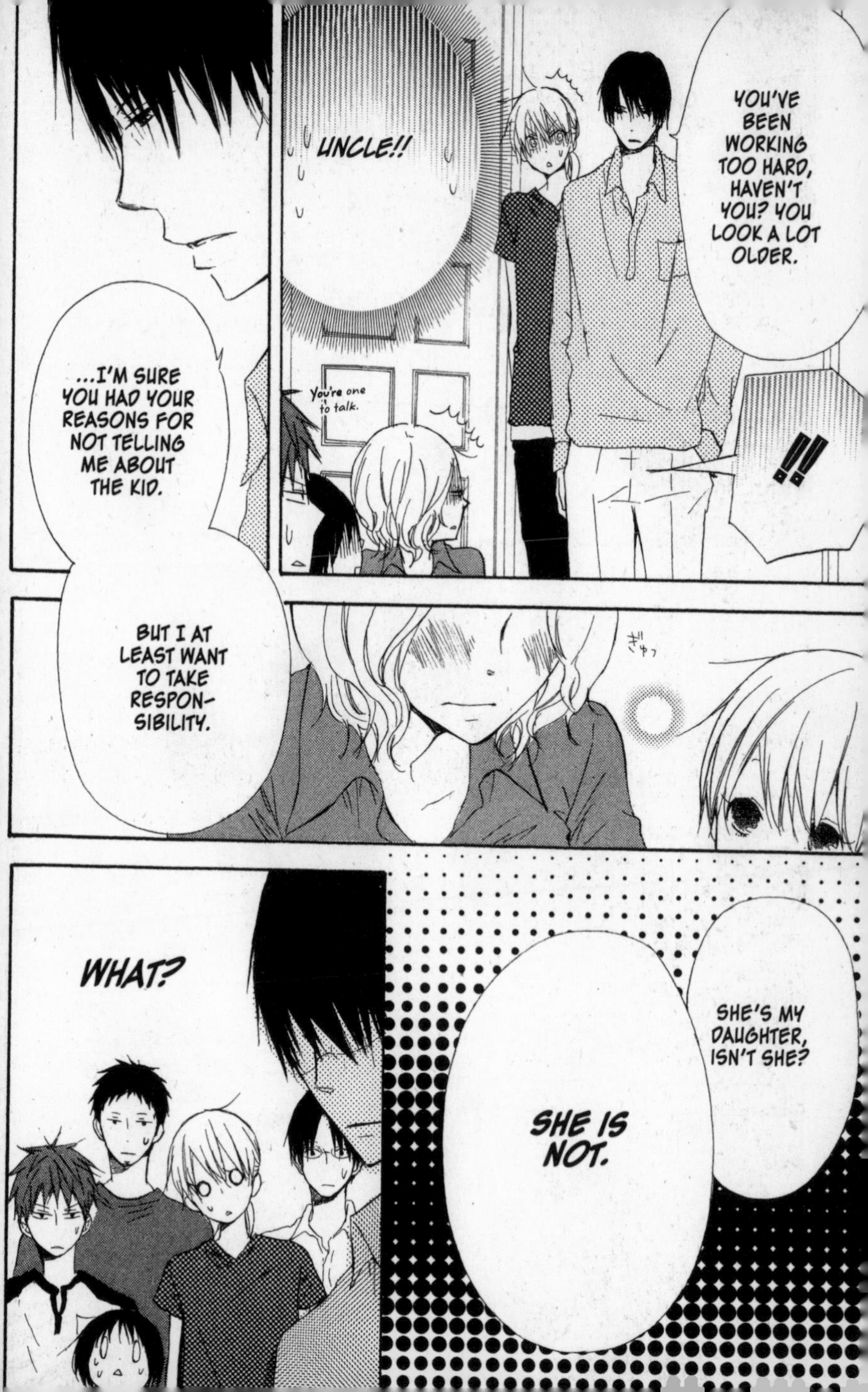
YOU'VE BEEN WORKING TOO HARD, HAVEN'T YOU? YOU LOOK A LOT OLDER.
!!
UNCLE!!
You're one to talk.
...I'M SURE YOU HAD YOUR REASONS FOR NOT TELLING ME ABOUT THE KID.
ぎゅっ
BUT I AT LEAST WANT TO TAKE RESPON-SIBILITY.
SHE'S MY DAUGHTER, ISN'T SHE?
SHE IS NOT.
WHAT?

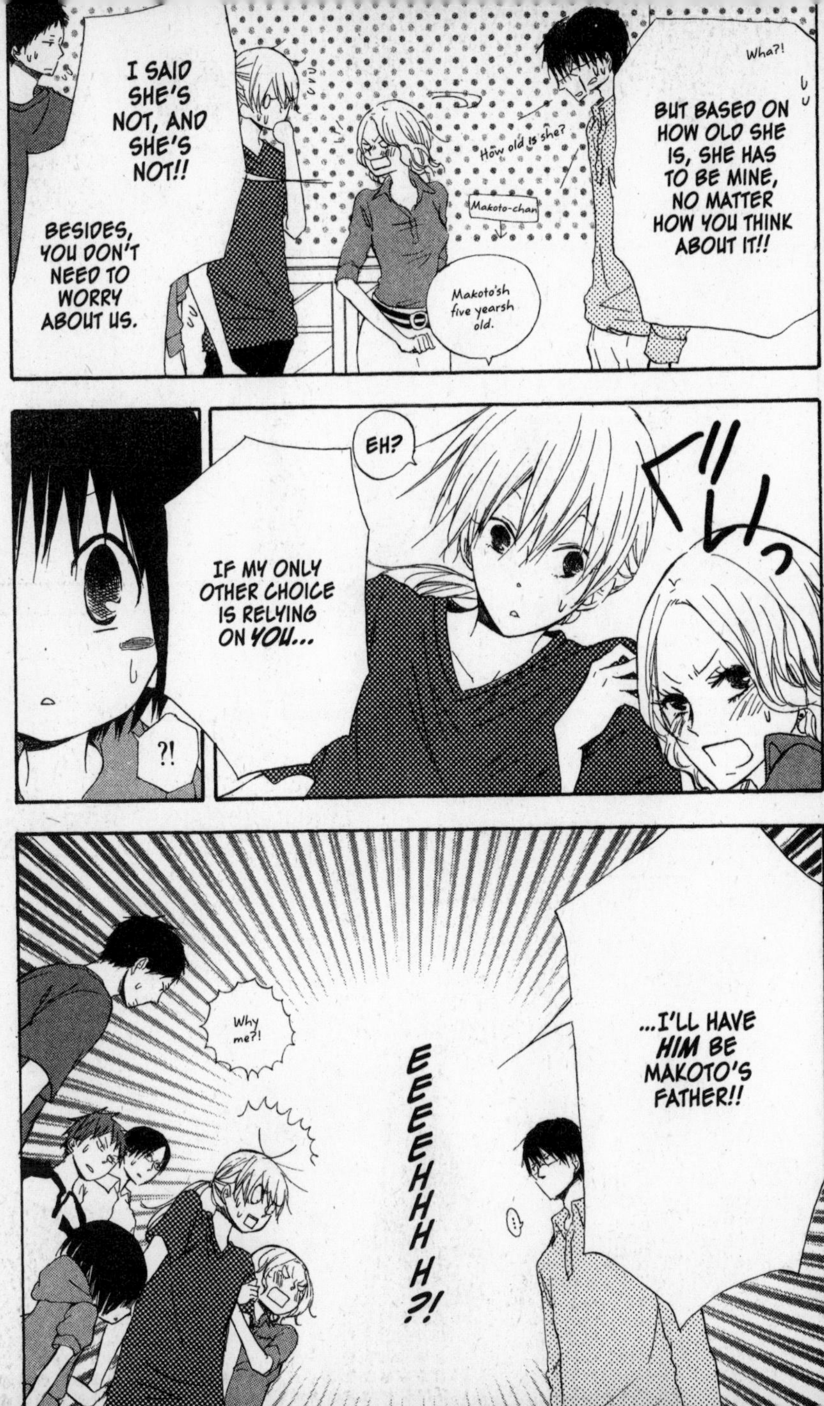
Wha?!
BUT BASED ON HOW OLD SHE IS, SHE HAS TO BE MINE, NO MATTER HOW YOU THINK ABOUT IT!!
How old is she?
Makoto-chan
Makoto'sh five yearsh old.
I SAID SHE'S NOT, AND SHE'S NOT!!
BESIDES, YOU DON'T NEED TO WORRY ABOUT US.
ぐいっ
EH?
IF MY ONLY OTHER CHOICE IS RELYING ON YOU...
?!
...I'LL HAVE HIM BE MAKOTO'S FATHER!!
EEEEHHHHH?!
...
Why me?!

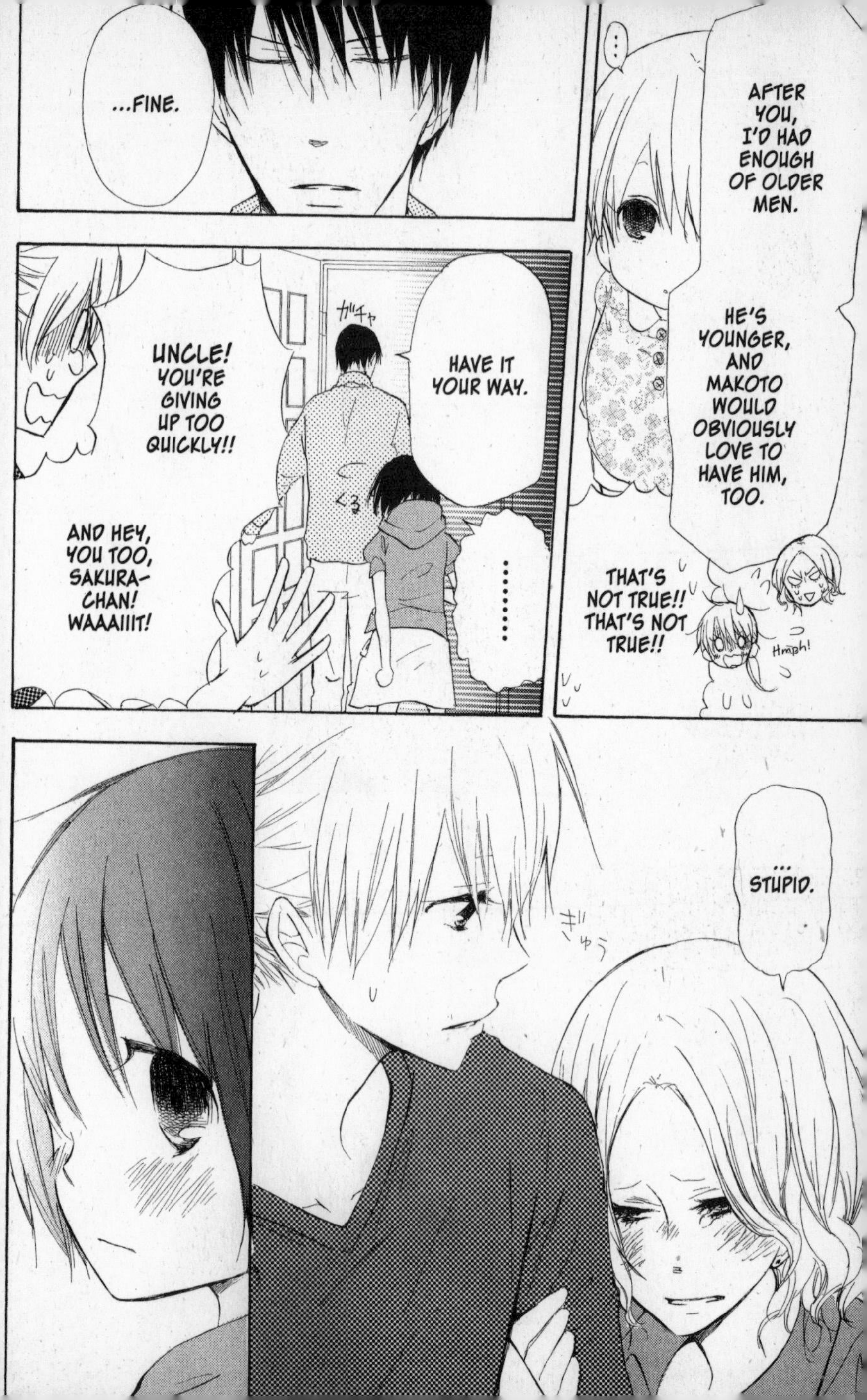
…
AFTER YOU, I'D HAD ENOUGH OF OLDER MEN.
HE'S YOUNGER, AND MAKOTO WOULD OBVIOUSLY LOVE TO HAVE HIM, TOO.
THAT'S NOT TRUE!! THAT'S NOT TRUE!!
Hmph!
...FINE.
HAVE IT YOUR WAY.
ガチャ
……
UNCLE! YOU'RE GIVING UP TOO QUICKLY!!
AND HEY, YOU TOO, SAKURA-CHAN! WAAAIIIT!
... STUPID.
ぎゅう

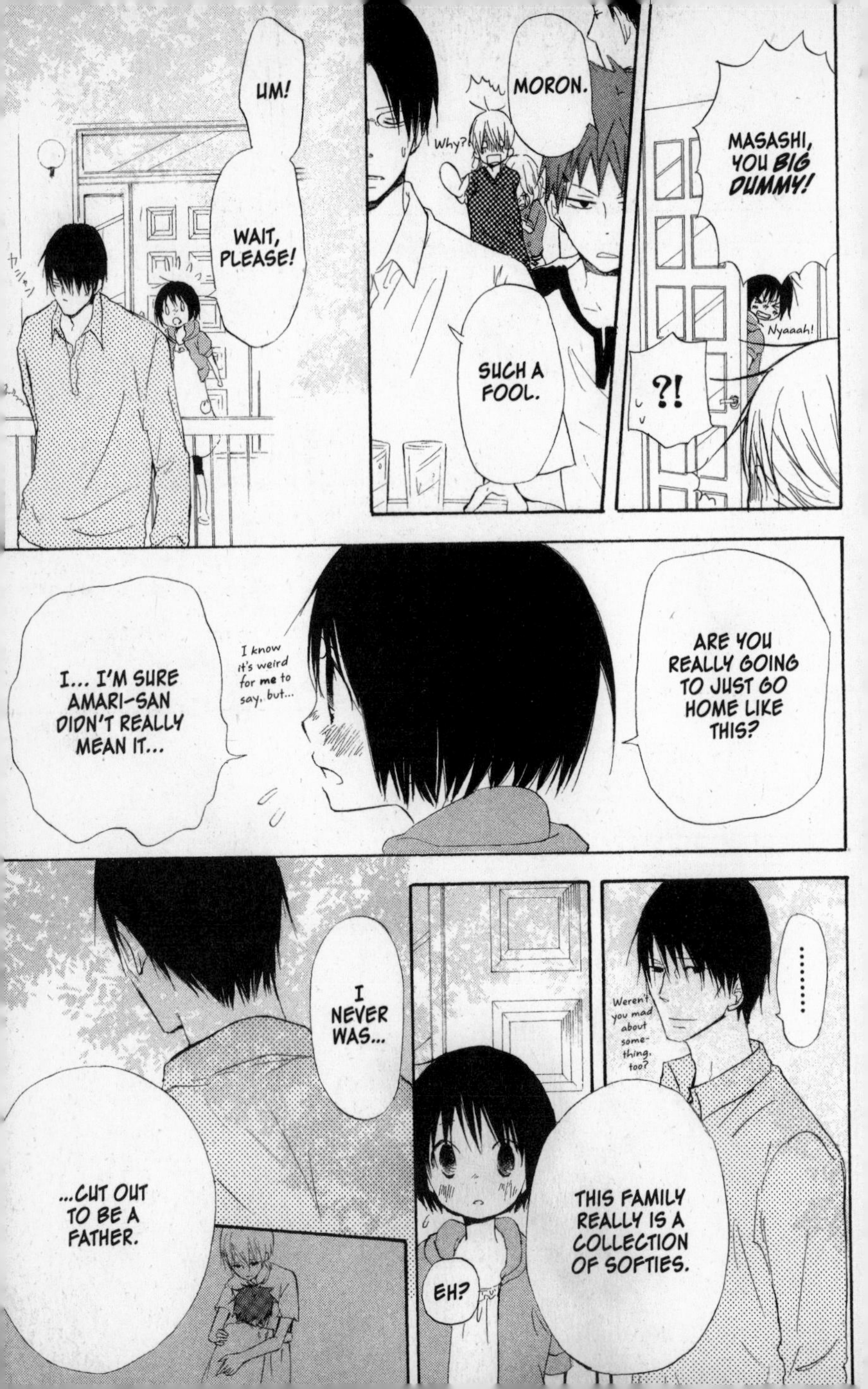
MASASHI, YOU BIG DUMMY!
Nyaaah!
?!
MORON.
Why?
SUCH A FOOL.
UM!
WAIT, PLEASE!
ARE YOU REALLY GOING TO JUST GO HOME LIKE THIS?
I know it's weird for me to say, but...
I... I'M SURE AMARI-SAN DIDN'T REALLY MEAN IT...
......
Weren't you mad about something, too?
THIS FAMILY REALLY IS A COLLECTION OF SOFTIES.
EH?
I NEVER WAS...
...CUT OUT TO BE A FATHER.

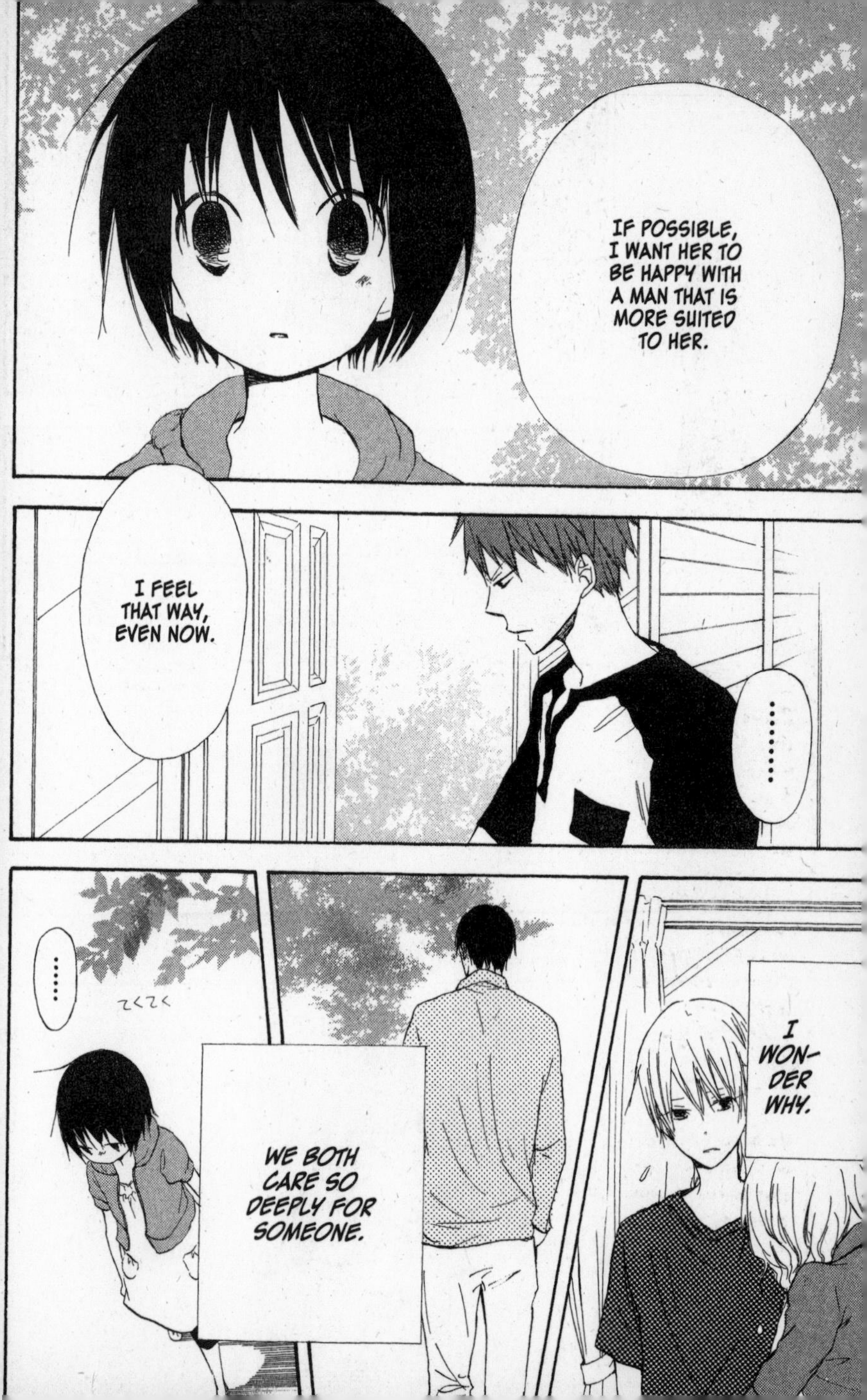
IF POSSIBLE, I WANT HER TO BE HAPPY WITH A MAN THAT IS MORE SUITED TO HER.
I FEEL THAT WAY, EVEN NOW.
......
I WONDER WHY.
WE BOTH CARE SO DEEPLY FOR SOMEONE.
......
てくてく

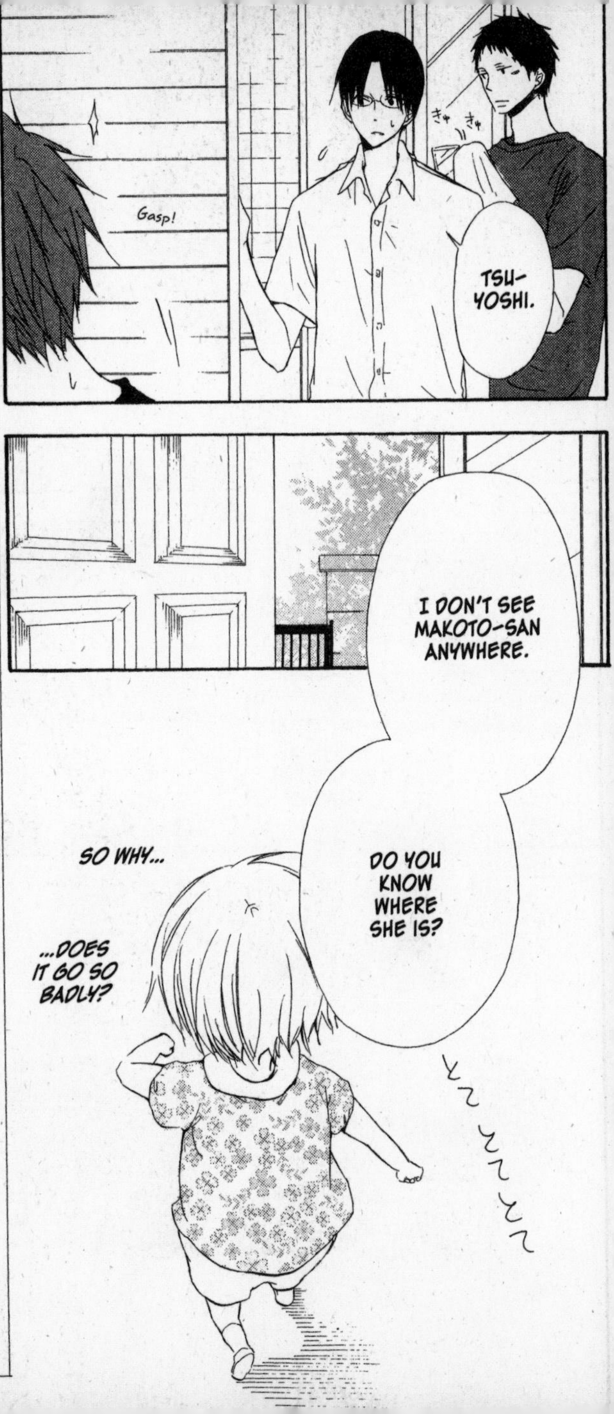
TSU-YOSHI.
きゅ きゅ
Gasp!
I DON'T SEE MAKOTO-SAN ANYWHERE.
DO YOU KNOW WHERE SHE IS?
SO WHY...
...DOES IT GO SO BADLY?
とてとてとて

3

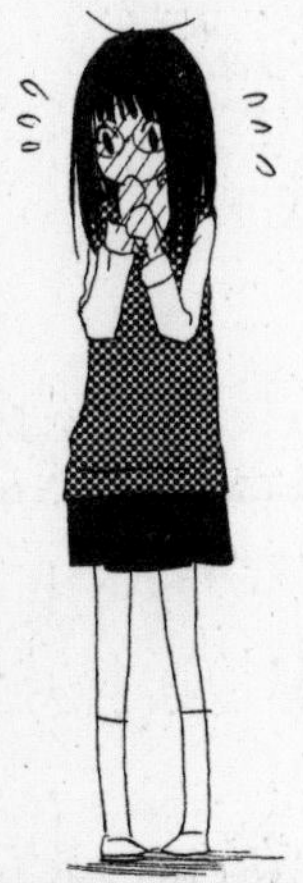

Come to think of it, this was a while ago, but T-san (male), who went to the same trade school as me, read the story about Sonomura-san and Katagiri-kun in volume eight, and said, "Katagiri-kun doesn't play fair!!"

To be more accurate, you got the name wrong and said "XX-kun doesn't play fair!!" but thank you so much for reading!!

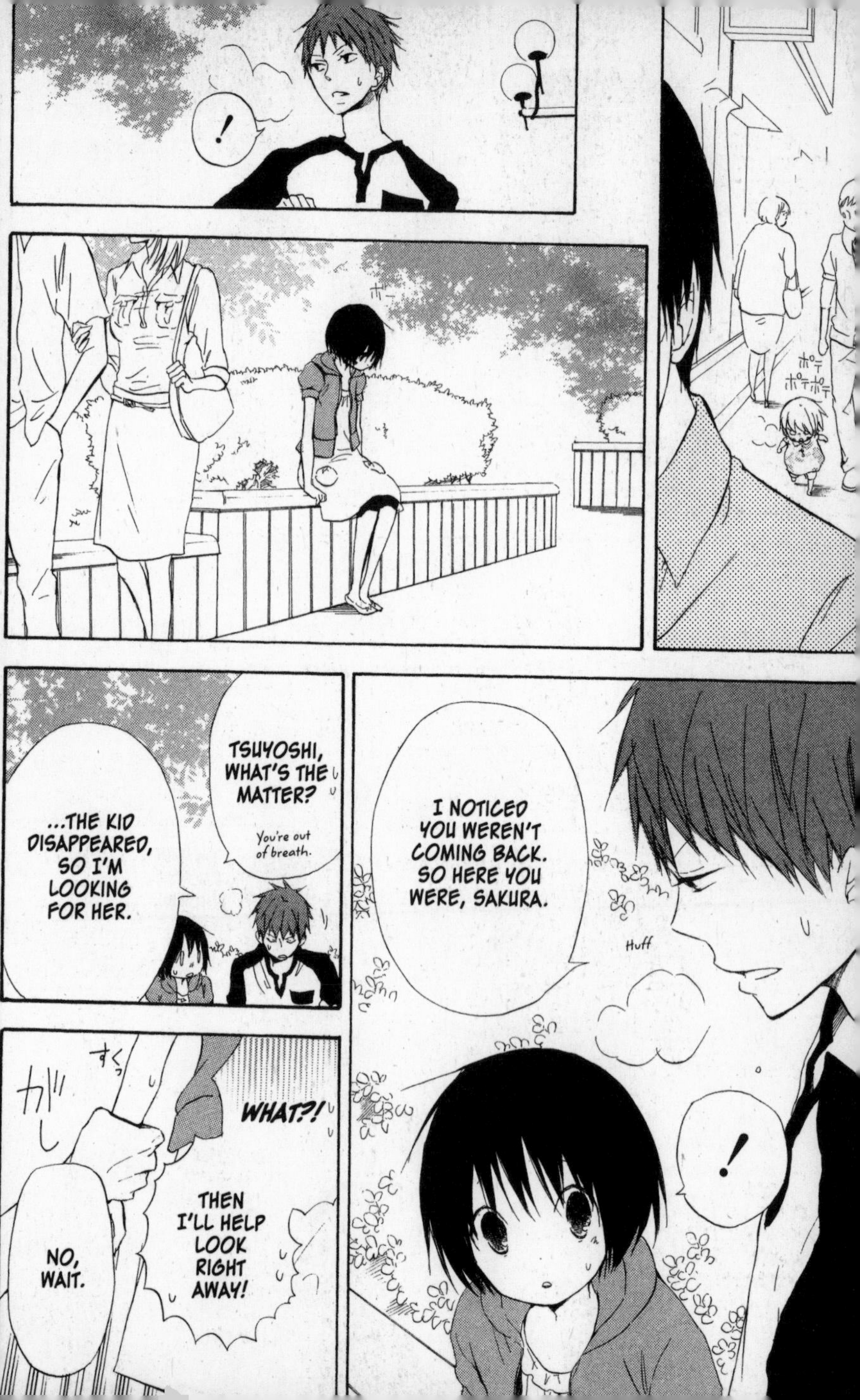

ポテ
ポテポテ
!
I NOTICED YOU WEREN'T COMING BACK. SO HERE YOU WERE, SAKURA.
Huff
!
TSUYOSHI, WHAT'S THE MATTER?
You're out of breath.
...THE KID DISAPPEARED, SO I'M LOOKING FOR HER.
すくっ
WHAT?!
THEN I'LL HELP LOOK RIGHT AWAY!
ガシ
NO, WAIT.

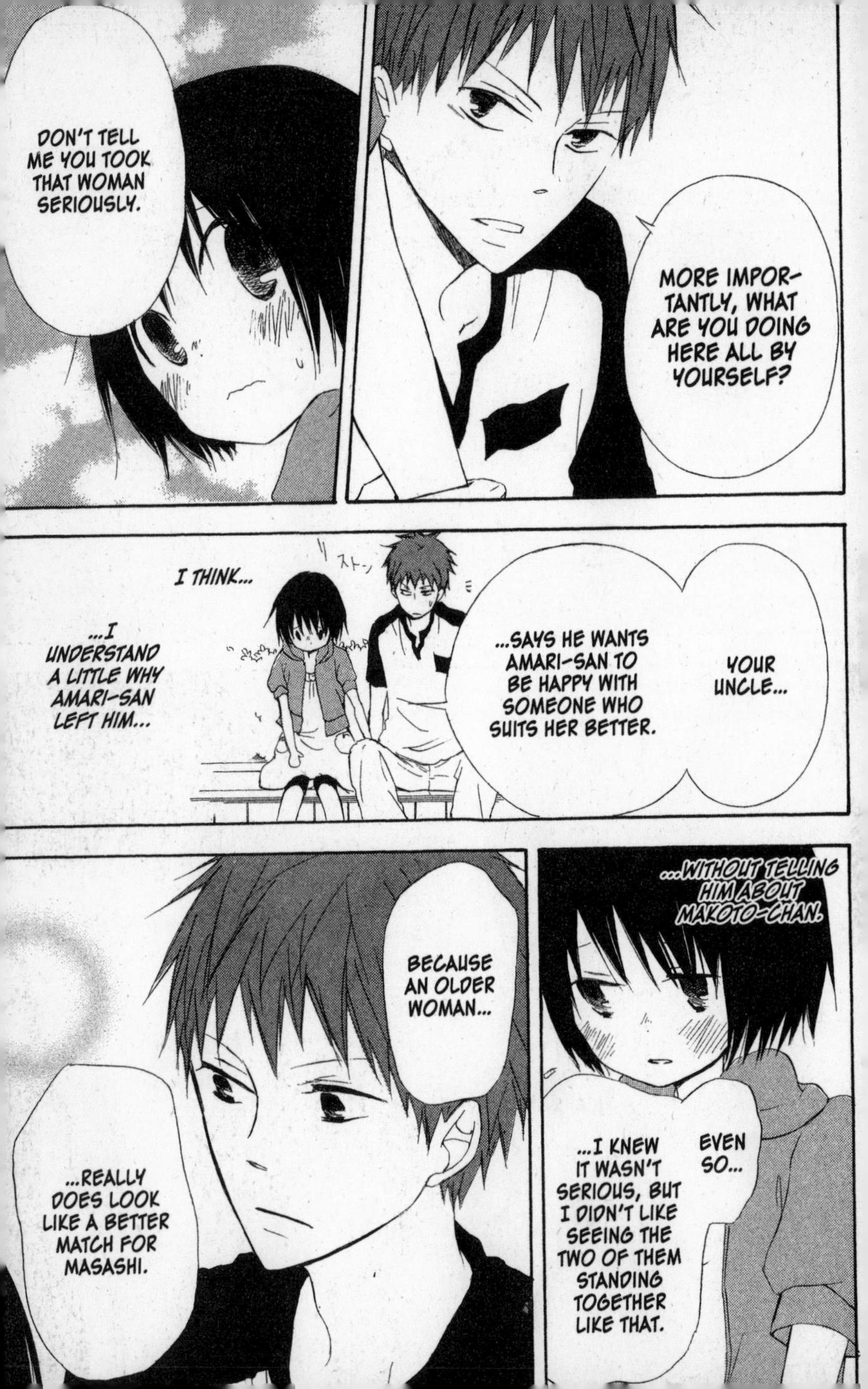
MORE IMPORTANTLY, WHAT ARE YOU DOING HERE ALL BY YOURSELF?
DON'T TELL ME YOU TOOK THAT WOMAN SERIOUSLY.
YOUR UNCLE...
...SAYS HE WANTS AMARI-SAN TO BE HAPPY WITH SOMEONE WHO SUITS HER BETTER.
I THINK...
...I UNDERSTAND A LITTLE WHY AMARI-SAN LEFT HIM...
...WITHOUT TELLING HIM ABOUT MAKOTO-CHAN.
EVEN SO...
...I KNEW IT WASN'T SERIOUS, BUT I DIDN'T LIKE SEEING THE TWO OF THEM STANDING TOGETHER LIKE THAT.
BECAUSE AN OLDER WOMAN...
...REALLY DOES LOOK LIKE A BETTER MATCH FOR MASASHI.

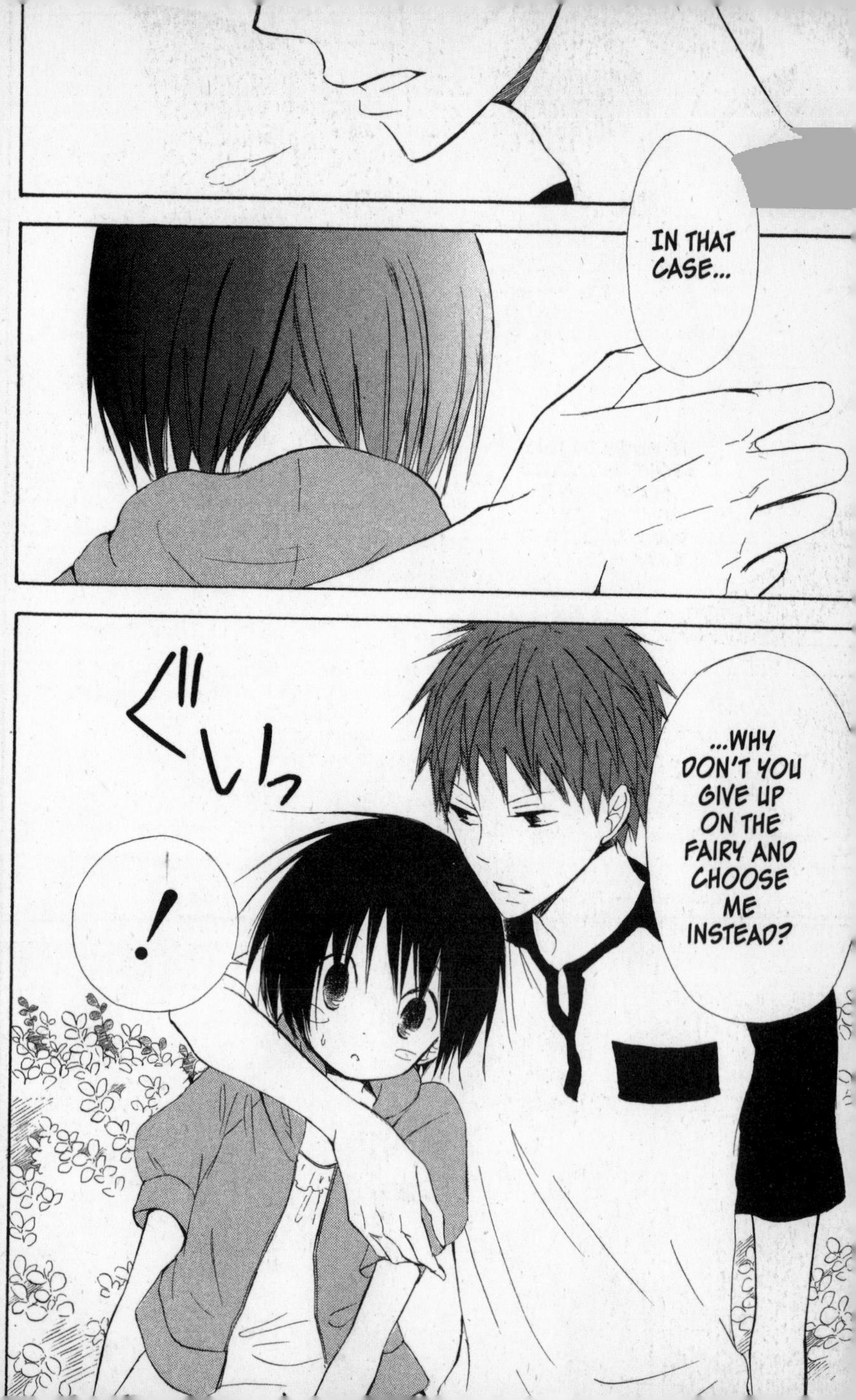
IN THAT CASE...
ぐいっ
...WHY DON'T YOU GIVE UP ON THE FAIRY AND CHOOSE ME INSTEAD?
!

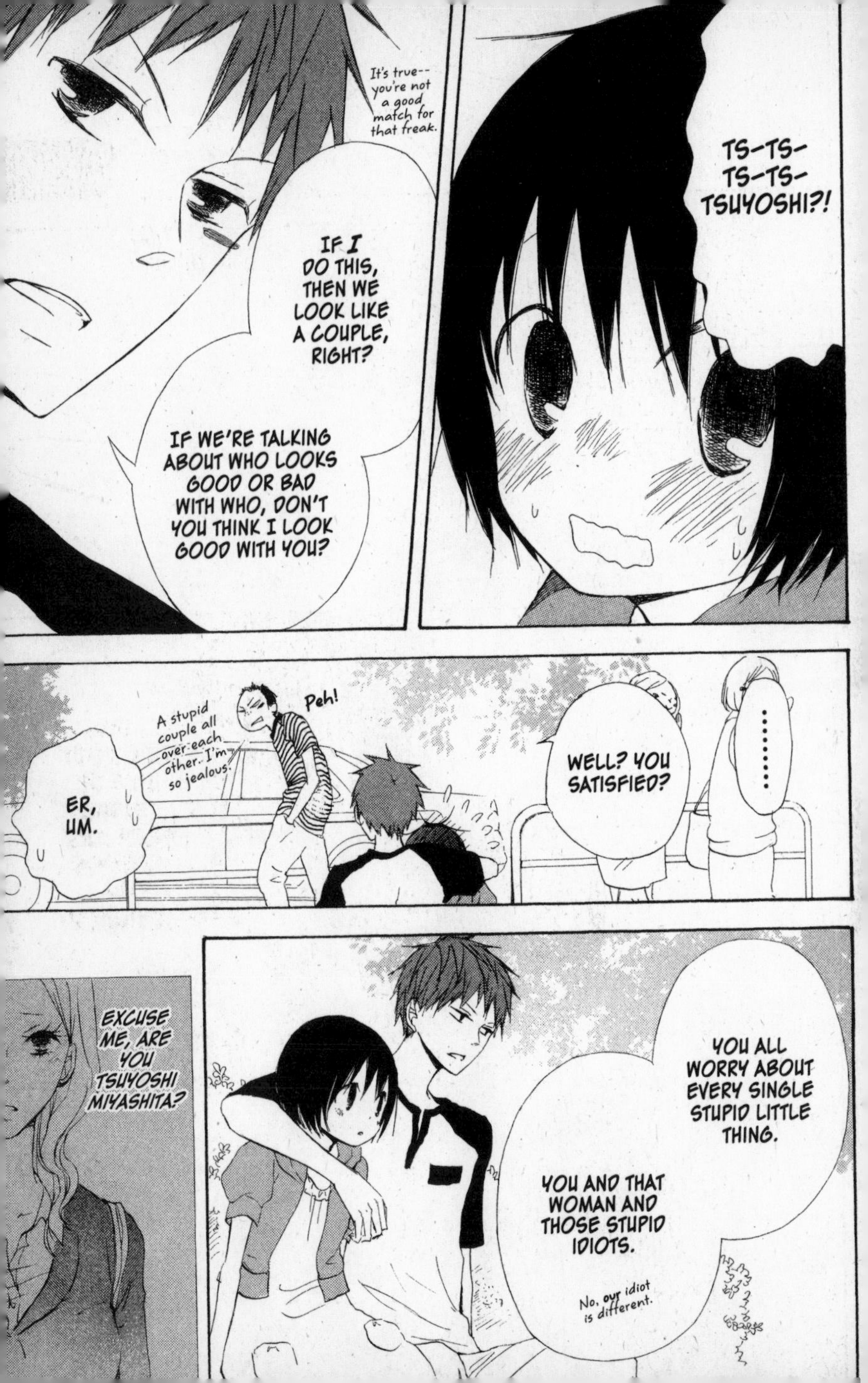
TS-TS-TS-TS-TSUYOSHI?!
IF I DO THIS, THEN WE LOOK LIKE A COUPLE, RIGHT?
It's true--you're not a good match for that freak.
IF WE'RE TALKING ABOUT WHO LOOKS GOOD OR BAD WITH WHO, DON'T YOU THINK I LOOK GOOD WITH YOU?
......
WELL? YOU SATISFIED?
Peh!
A stupid couple all over each other. I'm so jealous.
ER, UM.
YOU ALL WORRY ABOUT EVERY SINGLE STUPID LITTLE THING.
YOU AND THAT WOMAN AND THOSE STUPID IDIOTS.
No, our idiot is different.
EXCUSE ME, ARE YOU TSUYOSHI MIYASHITA?

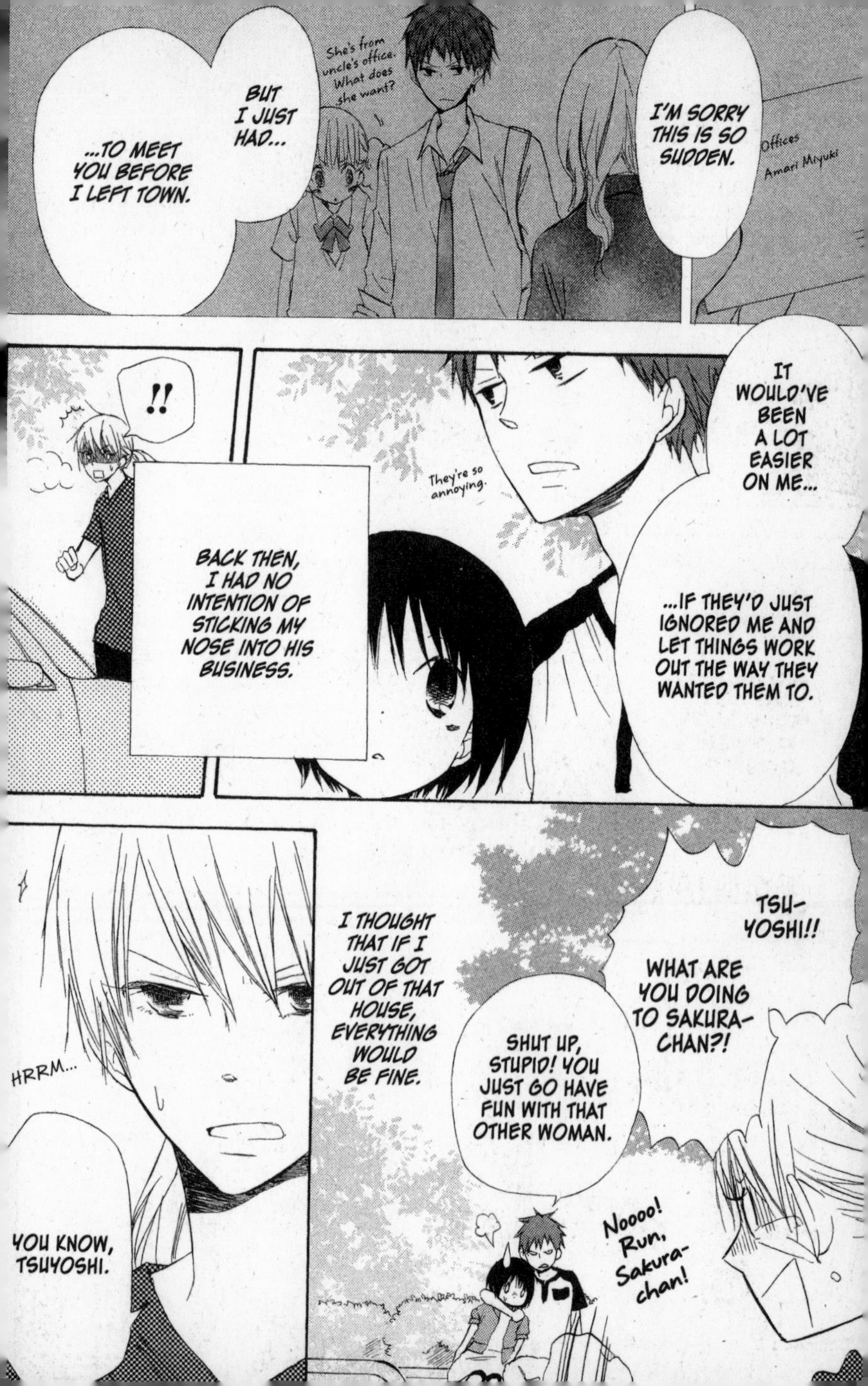
I'M SORRY THIS IS SO SUDDEN.
Offices
Amari Miyuki
She's from uncle's office. What does she want?
BUT I JUST HAD...
...TO MEET YOU BEFORE I LEFT TOWN.
IT WOULD'VE BEEN A LOT EASIER ON ME...
They're so annoying.
...IF THEY'D JUST IGNORED ME AND LET THINGS WORK OUT THE WAY THEY WANTED THEM TO.
BACK THEN, I HAD NO INTENTION OF STICKING MY NOSE INTO HIS BUSINESS.
!!
TSU-YOSHI!!
WHAT ARE YOU DOING TO SAKURA-CHAN?!
SHUT UP, STUPID! YOU JUST GO HAVE FUN WITH THAT OTHER WOMAN.
Noooo! Run, Sakura-chan!
I THOUGHT THAT IF I JUST GOT OUT OF THAT HOUSE, EVERYTHING WOULD BE FINE.
HRRM...
YOU KNOW, TSUYOSHI.

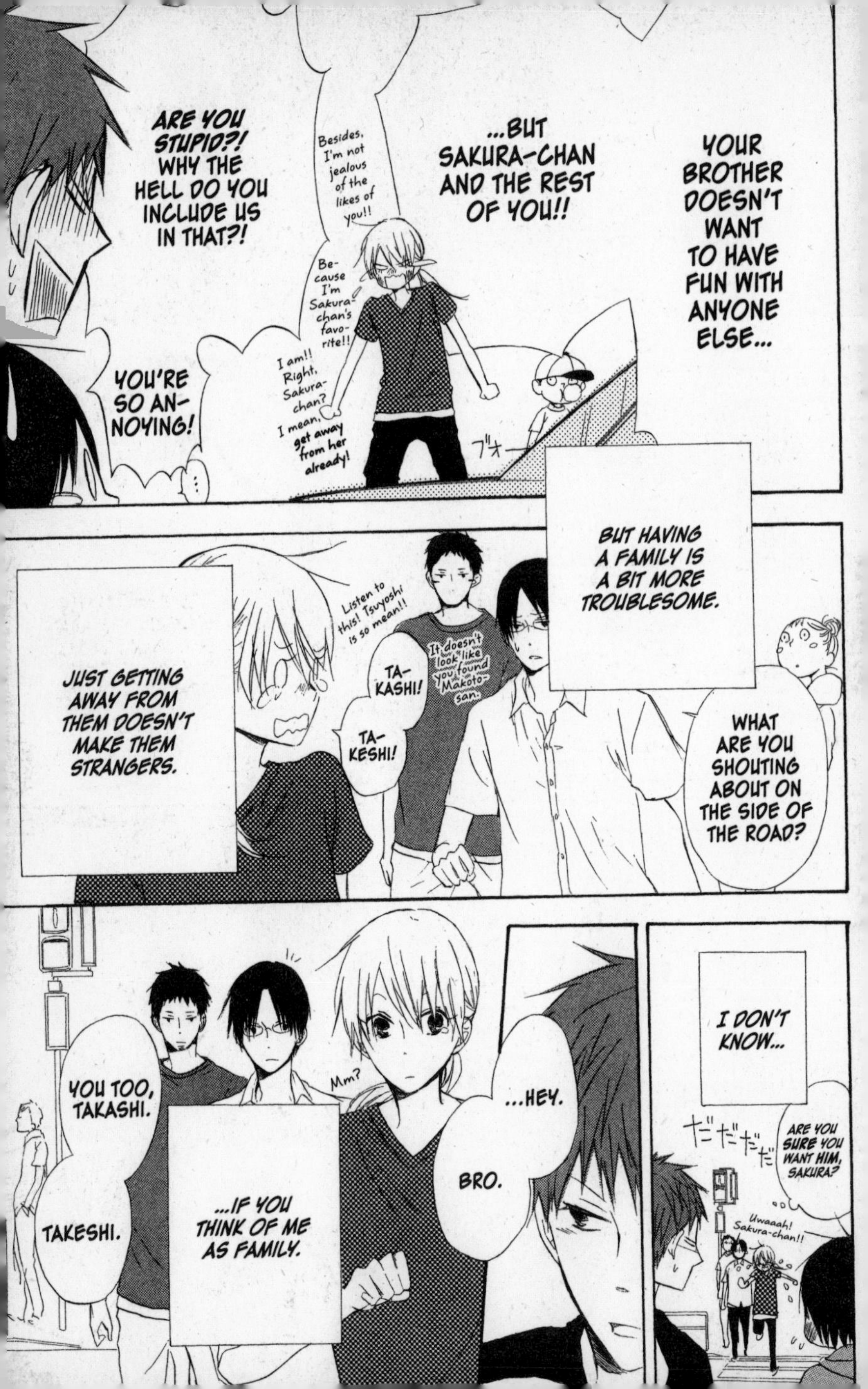
YOUR BROTHER DOESN'T WANT TO HAVE FUN WITH ANYONE ELSE...
...BUT SAKURA-CHAN AND THE REST OF YOU!!
Besides, I'm not jealous of the likes of you!!
Because I'm Sakura-chan's favorite!!
ARE YOU STUPID?! WHY THE HELL DO YOU INCLUDE US IN THAT?!
I am!! Right, Sakura-chan? I mean, get away from her already!
ブオー
YOU'RE SO ANNOYING!
...
BUT HAVING A FAMILY IS A BIT MORE TROUBLESOME.
WHAT ARE YOU SHOUTING ABOUT ON THE SIDE OF THE ROAD?
It doesn't look like you found Makoto-san.
Listen to this! Tsuyoshi is so mean!!
TAKASHI!
TAKESHI!
JUST GETTING AWAY FROM THEM DOESN'T MAKE THEM STRANGERS.
I DON'T KNOW...
ARE YOU SURE YOU WANT HIM, SAKURA?
だだだだ
Uwaaah! Sakura-chan!!
...HEY.
BRO.
Mm?
YOU TOO, TAKASHI.
...IF YOU THINK OF ME AS FAMILY.
TAKESHI.

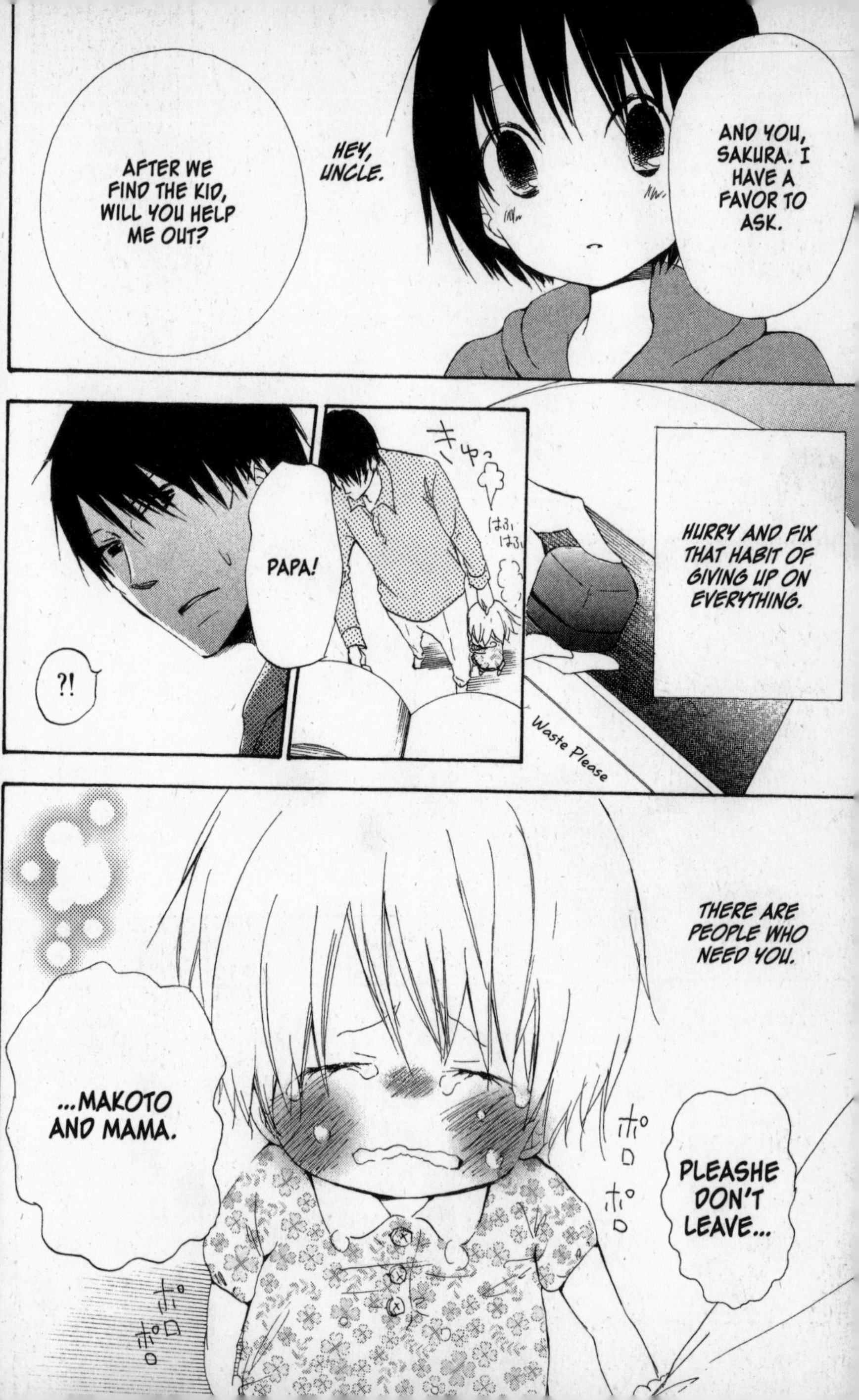
AND YOU, SAKURA. I HAVE A FAVOR TO ASK.
HEY, UNCLE.
AFTER WE FIND THE KID, WILL YOU HELP ME OUT?
HURRY AND FIX THAT HABIT OF GIVING UP ON EVERYTHING.
Waste Please
きゃっ
はふはふ
PAPA!
?!
THERE ARE PEOPLE WHO NEED YOU.
ポロポロ
PLEASHE DON'T LEAVE...
...MAKOTO AND MAMA.
ポロポロ

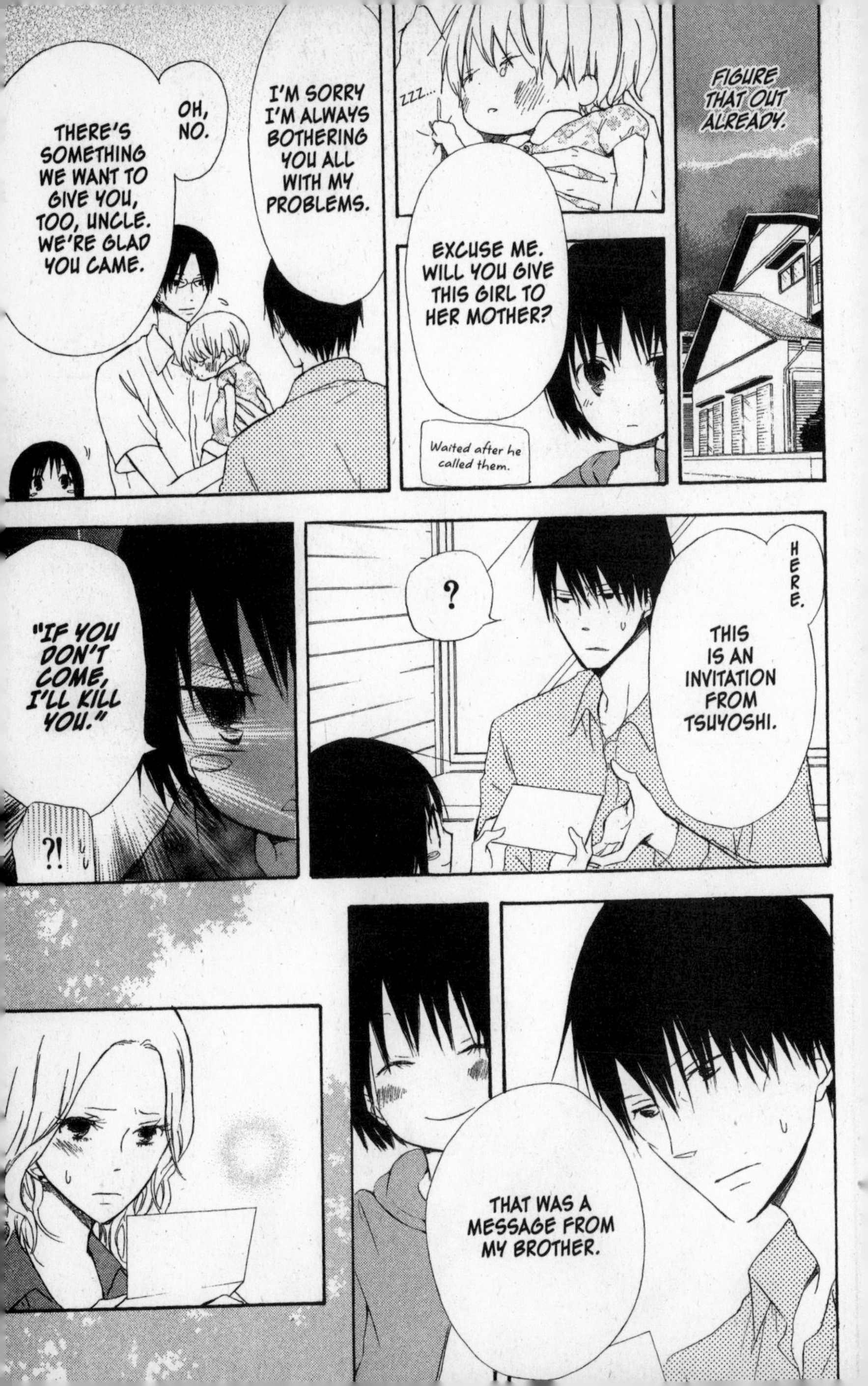
FIGURE THAT OUT ALREADY.
ZZZ...
EXCUSE ME. WILL YOU GIVE THIS GIRL TO HER MOTHER?
Waited after he called them.
I'M SORRY I'M ALWAYS BOTHERING YOU ALL WITH MY PROBLEMS.
OH, NO.
THERE'S SOMETHING WE WANT TO GIVE YOU, TOO, UNCLE. WE'RE GLAD YOU CAME.
HERE.
THIS IS AN INVITATION FROM TSUYOSHI.
?
"IF YOU DON'T COME, I'LL KILL YOU."
?!
THAT WAS A MESSAGE FROM MY BROTHER.

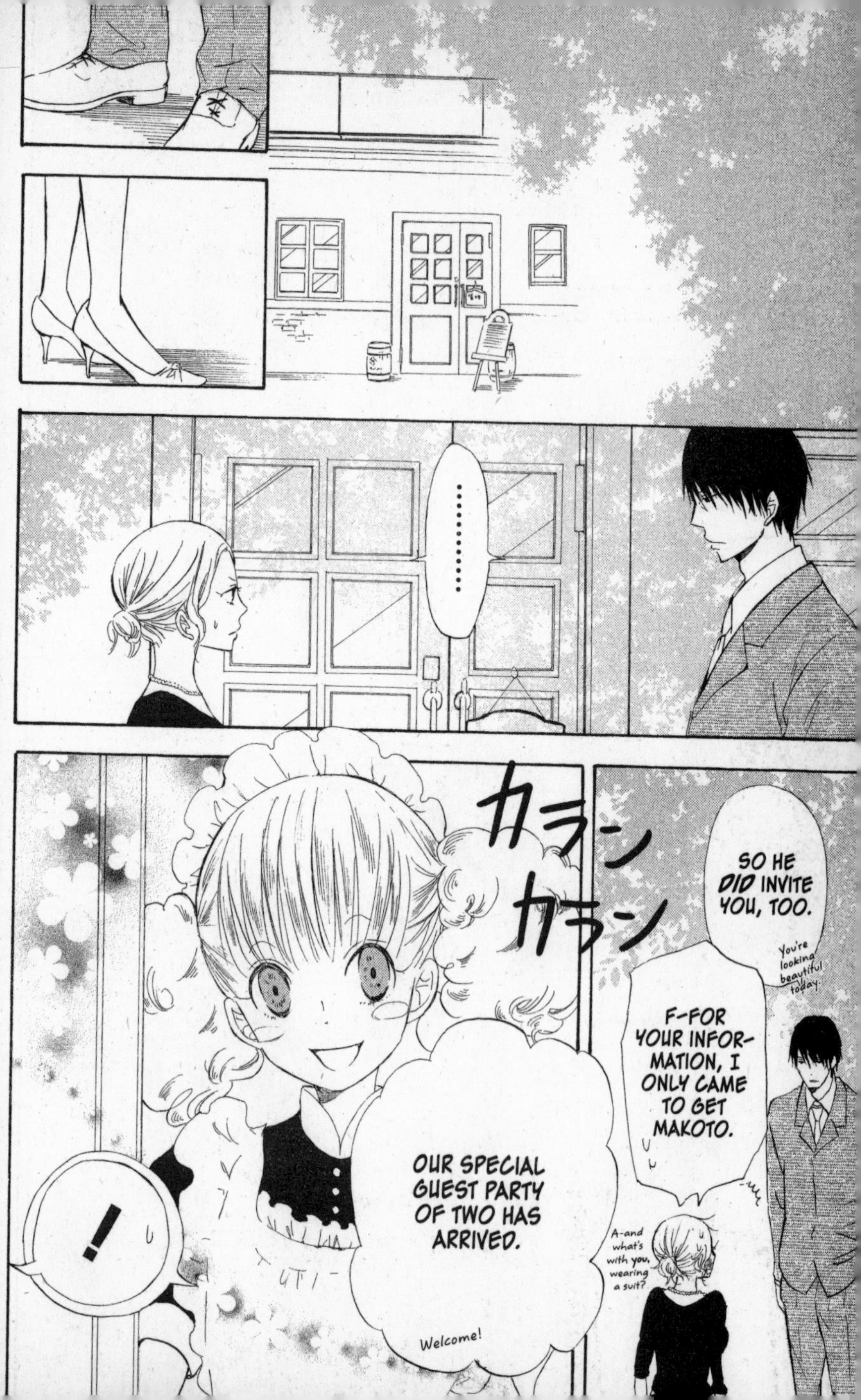

……
SO HE *DID* INVITE YOU, TOO.
You're looking beautiful today.
F-FOR YOUR INFORMATION, I ONLY CAME TO GET MAKOTO.
A-and what's with you, wearing a suit?
カラン カラン
OUR SPECIAL GUEST PARTY OF TWO HAS ARRIVED.
Welcome!
!

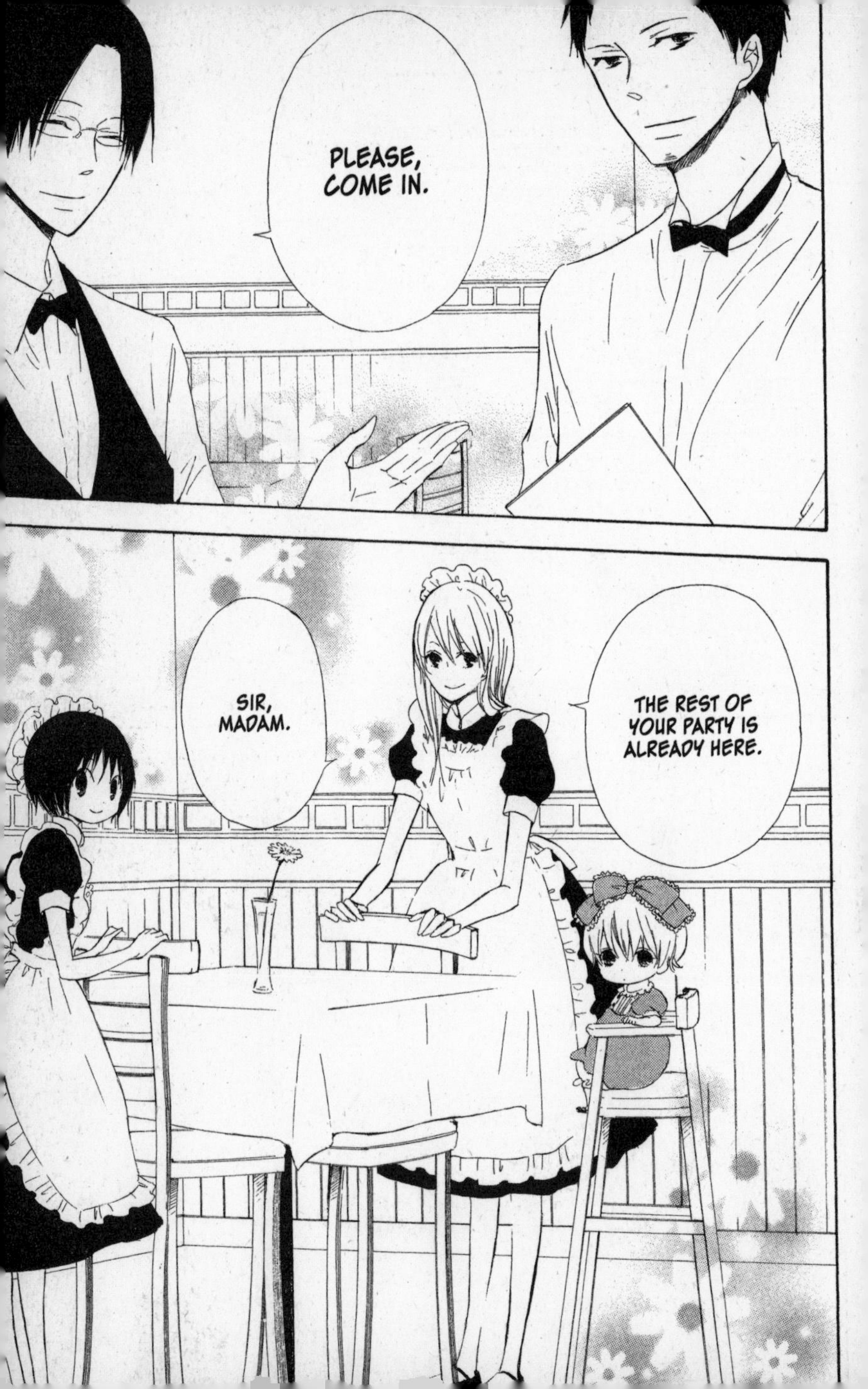
PLEASE, COME IN.
THE REST OF YOUR PARTY IS ALREADY HERE.
SIR, MADAM.

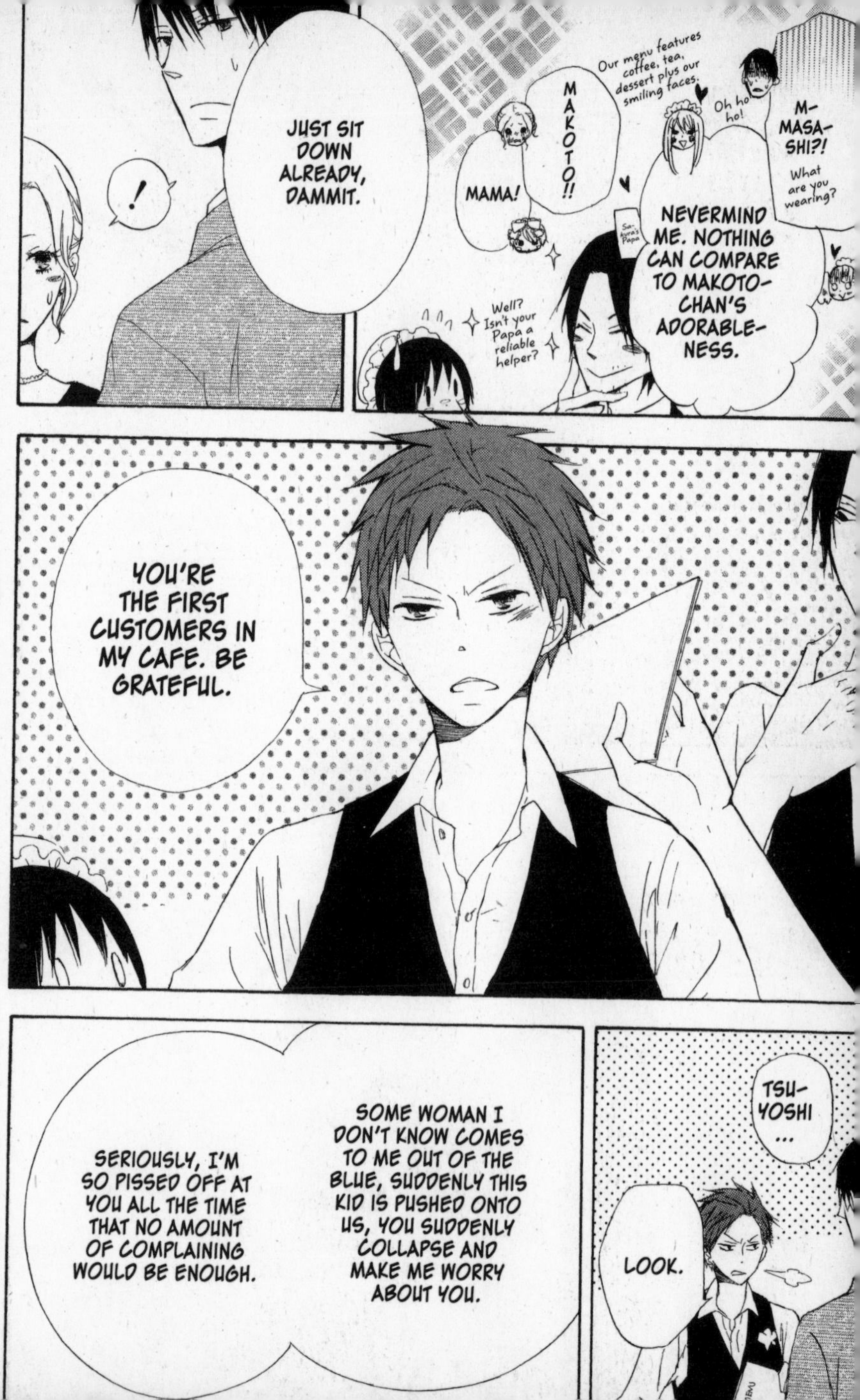
M-MASA-SHI?!
What are you wearing?
Our menu features coffee, tea, dessert plus our smiling faces.
Oh ho ho!
NEVERMIND ME. NOTHING CAN COMPARE TO MAKOTO-CHAN'S ADORABLE-NESS.
MAKOTO!!
Sa-kura's Papa
MAMA!
Well? Isn't your Papa a reliable helper?
JUST SIT DOWN ALREADY, DAMMIT.
!
YOU'RE THE FIRST CUSTOMERS IN MY CAFE. BE GRATEFUL.
TSU-YOSHI...
LOOK.
SOME WOMAN I DON'T KNOW COMES TO ME OUT OF THE BLUE, SUDDENLY THIS KID IS PUSHED ONTO US, YOU SUDDENLY COLLAPSE AND MAKE ME WORRY ABOUT YOU.
SERIOUSLY, I'M SO PISSED OFF AT YOU ALL THE TIME THAT NO AMOUNT OF COMPLAINING WOULD BE ENOUGH.

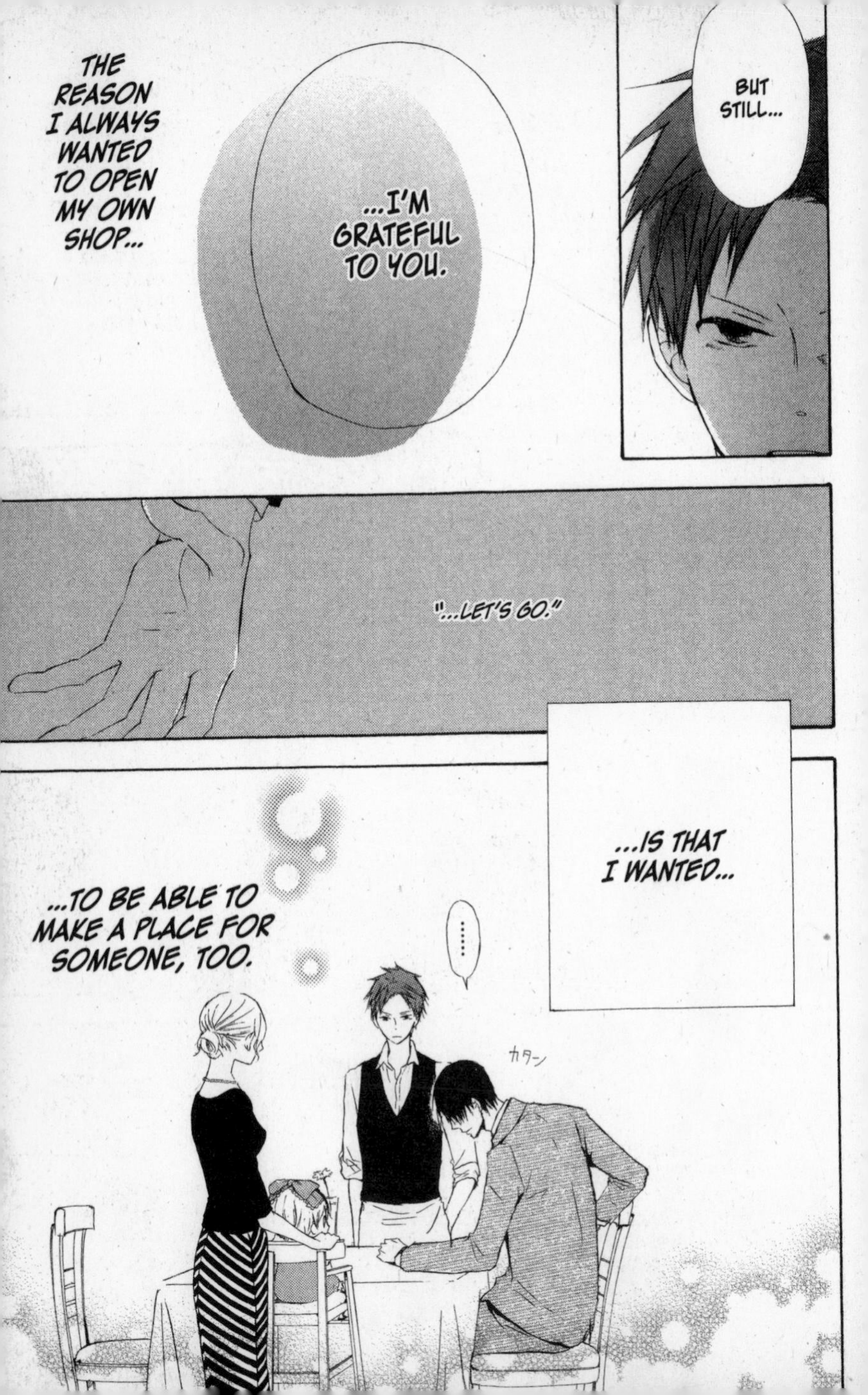
BUT STILL...
...I'M GRATEFUL TO YOU.
THE REASON I ALWAYS WANTED TO OPEN MY OWN SHOP...
"...LET'S GO."
...IS THAT I WANTED...
......
カターン
...TO BE ABLE TO MAKE A PLACE FOR SOMEONE, TOO.

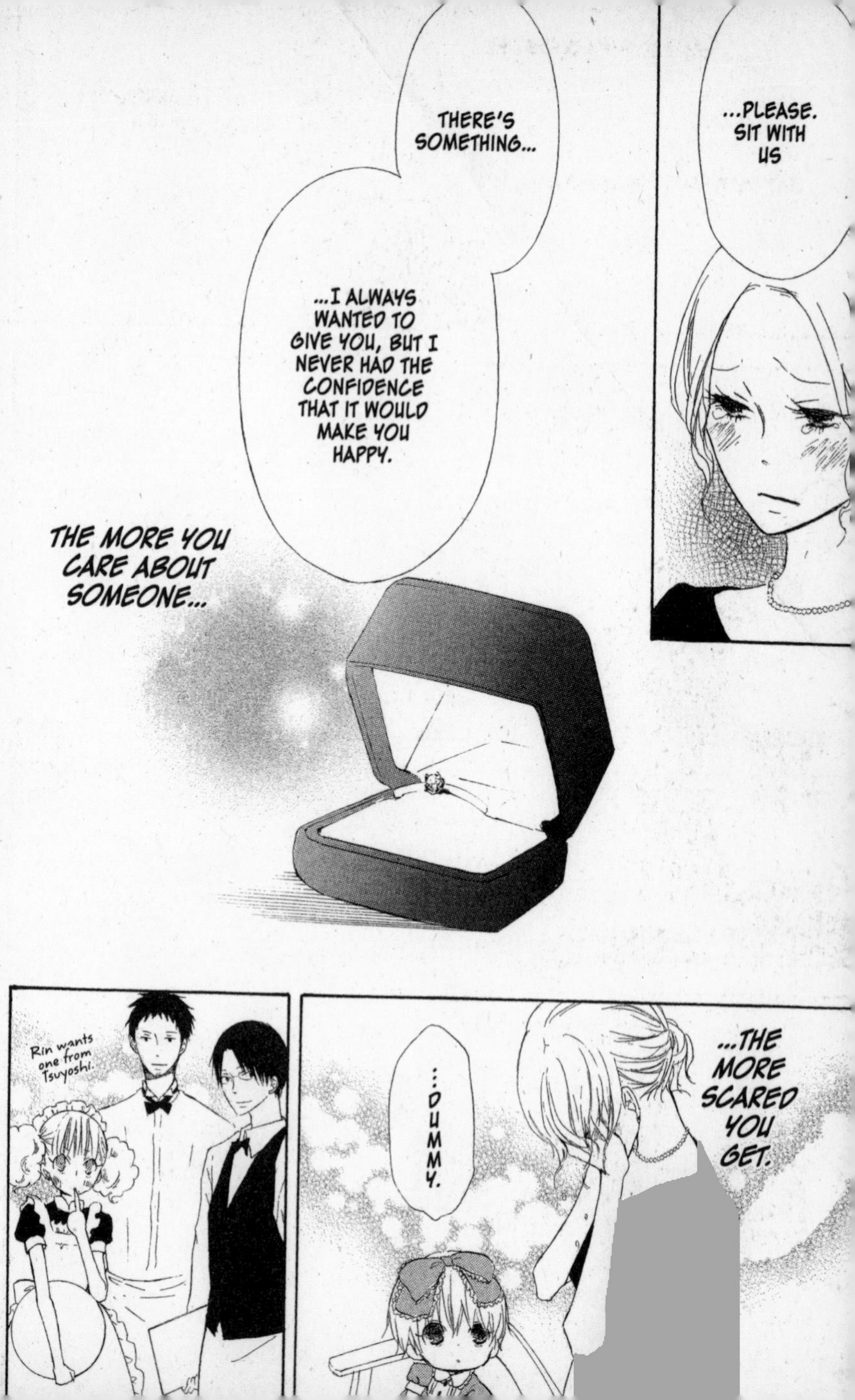
...PLEASE. SIT WITH US
THERE'S SOMETHING...
...I ALWAYS WANTED TO GIVE YOU, BUT I NEVER HAD THE CONFIDENCE THAT IT WOULD MAKE YOU HAPPY.
THE MORE YOU CARE ABOUT SOMEONE...
...THE MORE SCARED YOU GET.
...DUMMY.
Rin wants one from Tsuyoshi.

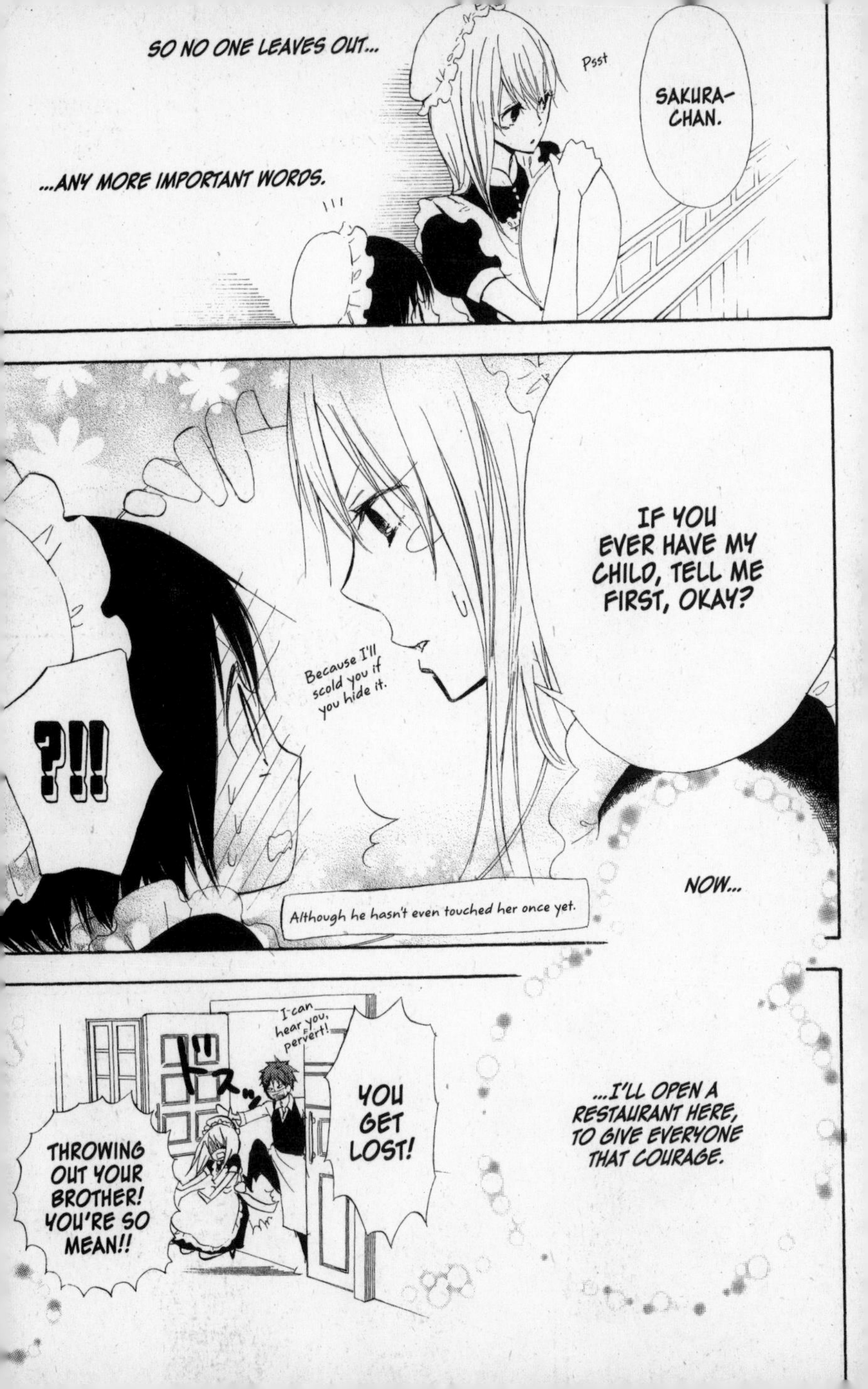
SAKURA-CHAN.
Psst
SO NO ONE LEAVES OUT...
...ANY MORE IMPORTANT WORDS.
IF YOU EVER HAVE MY CHILD, TELL ME FIRST, OKAY?
Because I'll scold you if you hide it.
?!!
NOW...
Although he hasn't even touched her once yet.
...I'LL OPEN A RESTAURANT HERE, TO GIVE EVERYONE THAT COURAGE.
YOU GET LOST!
I-can hear you, pervert!
ドスッ
THROWING OUT YOUR BROTHER! YOU'RE SO MEAN!!

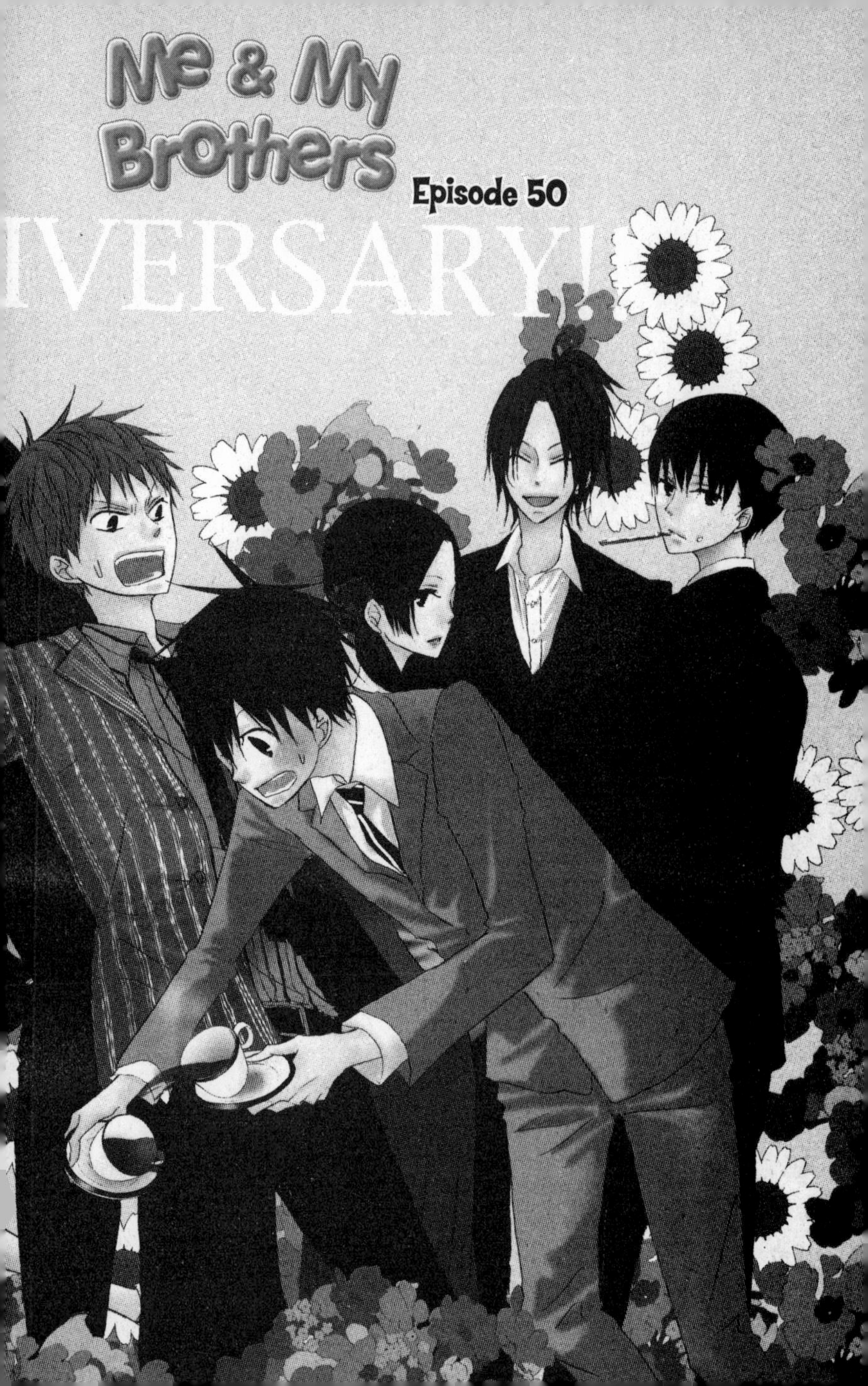
Me & My Brothers
Episode 50
IVERSARY!!

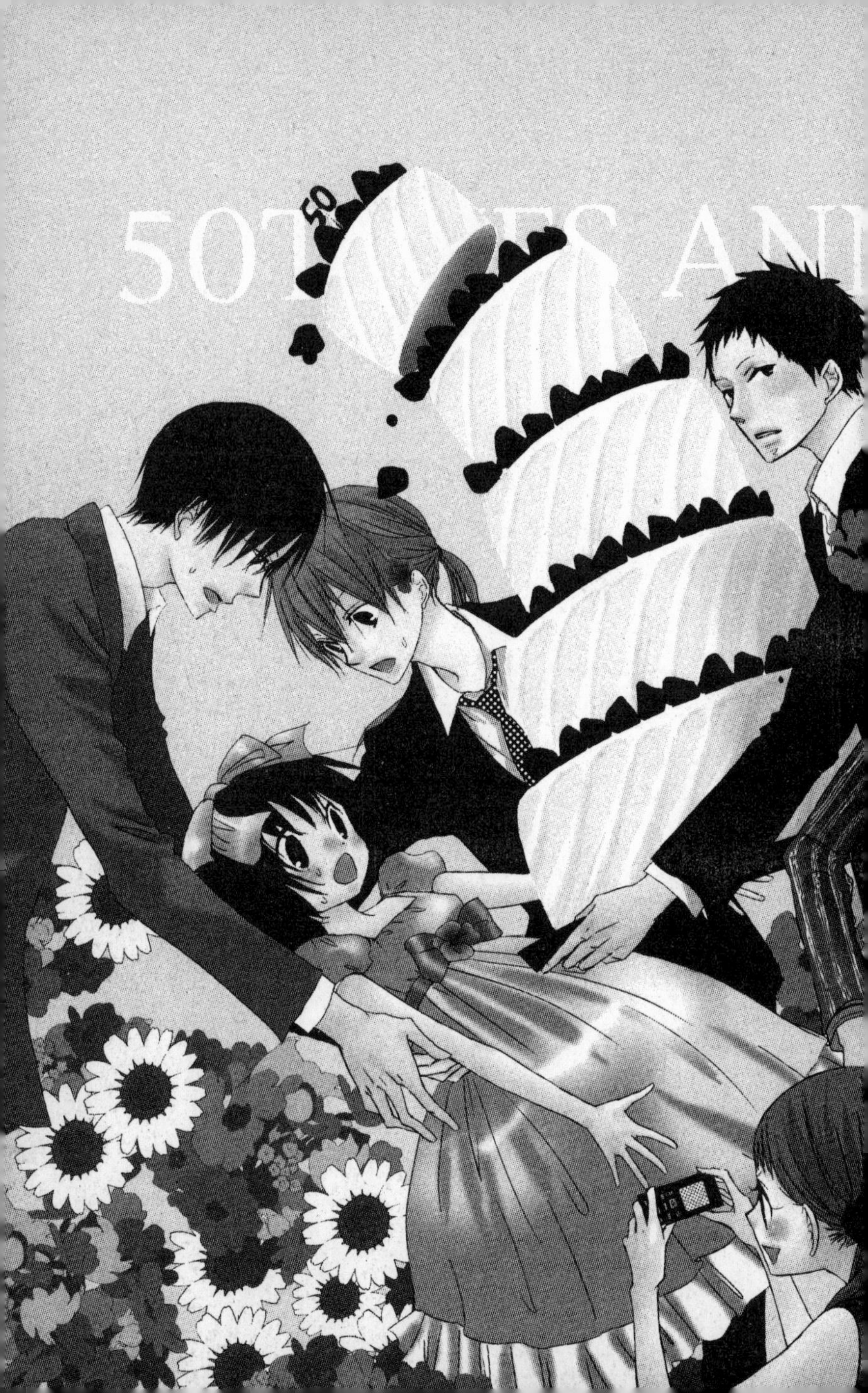
50T
ES AN

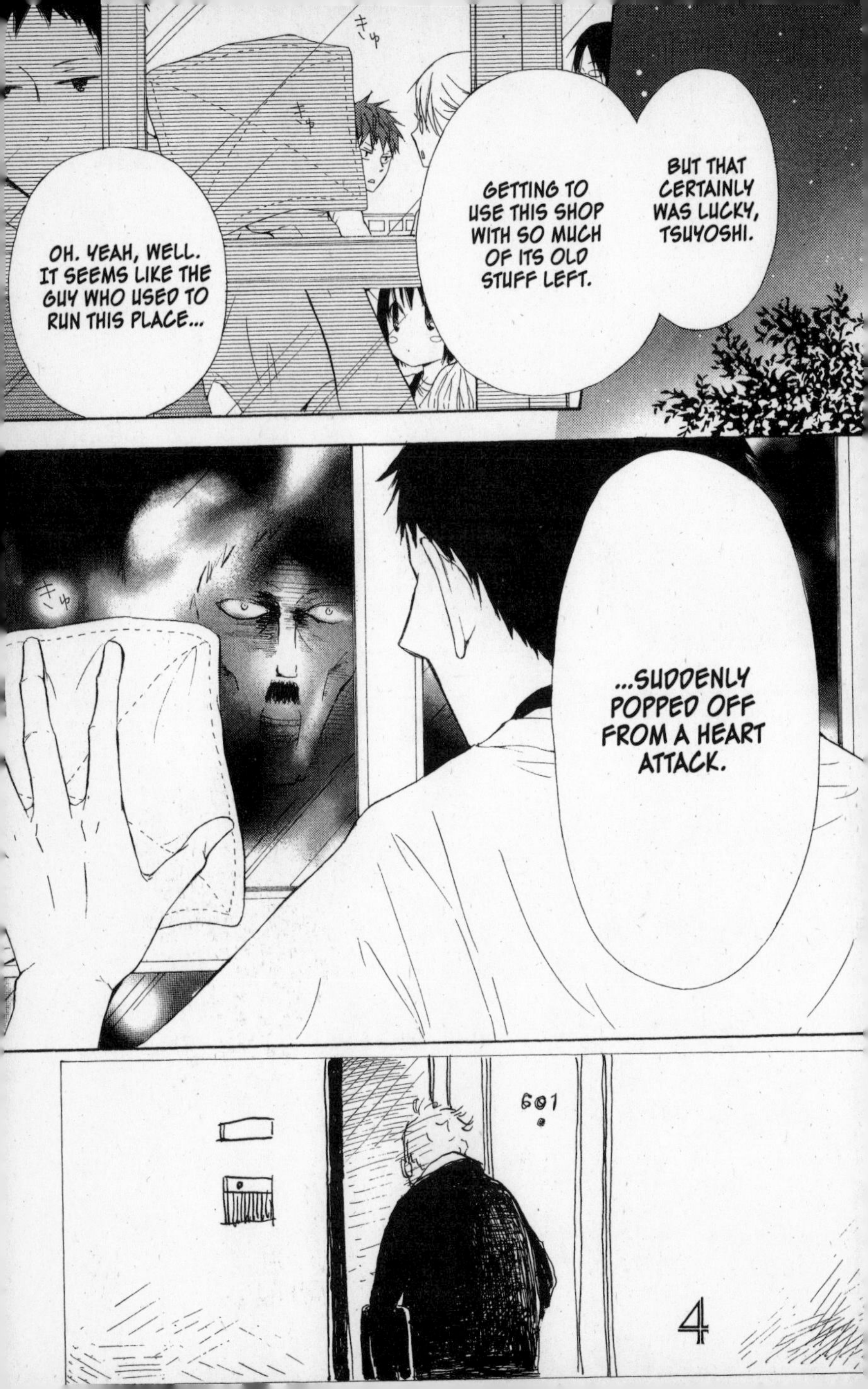
きゅ
きゅ
BUT THAT CERTAINLY WAS LUCKY, TSUYOSHI.
GETTING TO USE THIS SHOP WITH SO MUCH OF ITS OLD STUFF LEFT.
OH. YEAH, WELL. IT SEEMS LIKE THE GUY WHO USED TO RUN THIS PLACE...
...SUDDENLY POPPED OFF FROM A HEART ATTACK.
きゅ
601
4

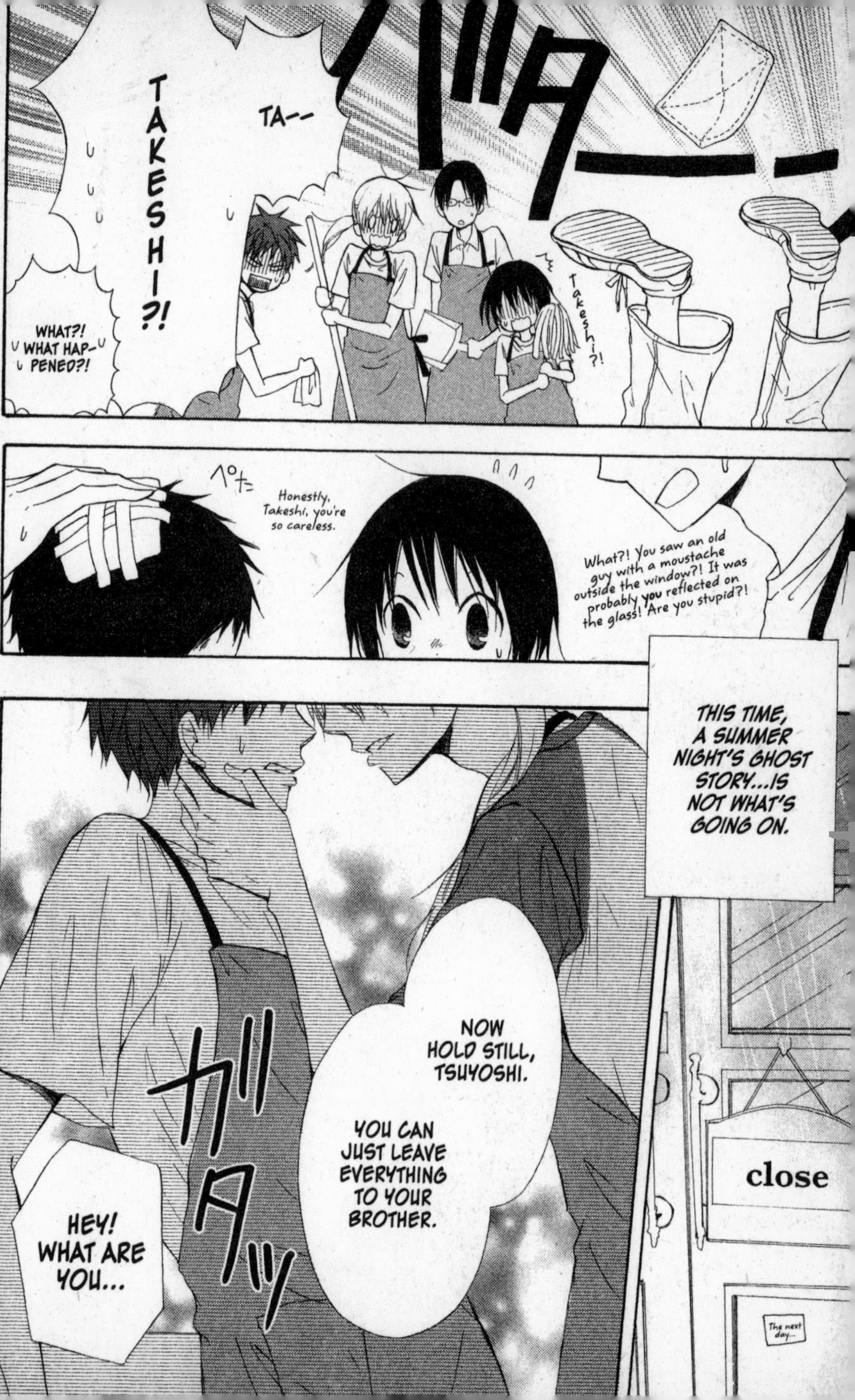
バターー
Takeshi?!
TA--
TAKESHI?!
WHAT?! WHAT HAP-PENED?!
What?! You saw an old guy with a moustache outside the window?! It was probably you reflected on the glass! Are you stupid?!
Honestly, Takeshi, you're so careless.
THIS TIME, A SUMMER NIGHT'S GHOST STORY...IS NOT WHAT'S GOING ON.
close
The next day...
NOW HOLD STILL, TSUYOSHI.
YOU CAN JUST LEAVE EVERYTHING TO YOUR BROTHER.
ガバッ
HEY! WHAT ARE YOU...

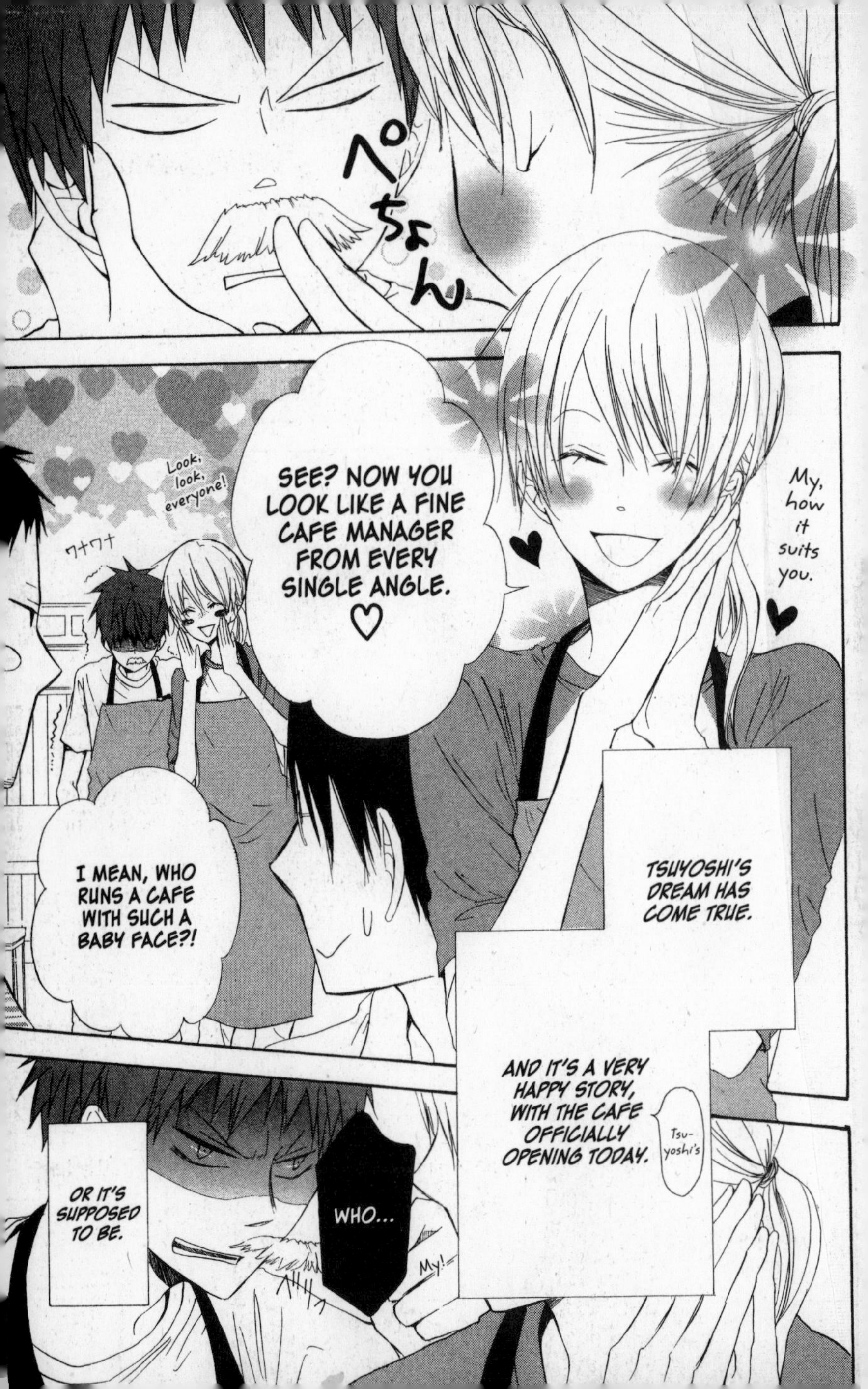
ぺちょん
My, how it suits you. ♥
SEE? NOW YOU LOOK LIKE A FINE CAFE MANAGER FROM EVERY SINGLE ANGLE. ♡
Look, look, everyone!
ワナワナ
I MEAN, WHO RUNS A CAFE WITH SUCH A BABY FACE?!
TSUYOSHI'S DREAM HAS COME TRUE.
AND IT'S A VERY HAPPY STORY, WITH THE CAFE OFFICIALLY OPENING TODAY.
Tsu-yoshi's
My!
WHO...
OR IT'S SUPPOSED TO BE.

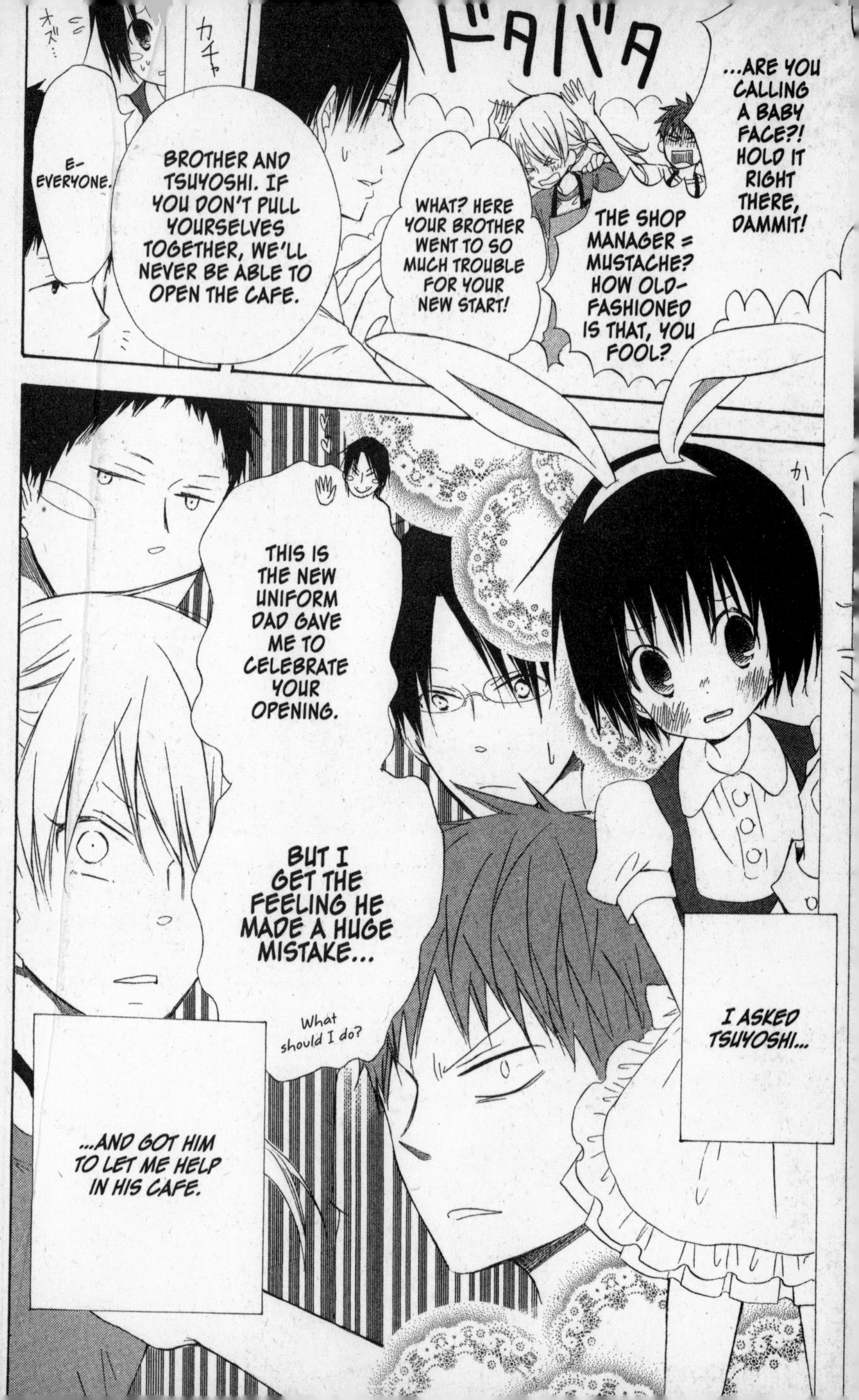
ドタバタ
...ARE YOU CALLING A BABY FACE?! HOLD IT RIGHT THERE, DAMMIT!
THE SHOP MANAGER = MUSTACHE? HOW OLD-FASHIONED IS THAT, YOU FOOL?
WHAT? HERE YOUR BROTHER WENT TO SO MUCH TROUBLE FOR YOUR NEW START!
BROTHER AND TSUYOSHI. IF YOU DON'T PULL YOURSELVES TOGETHER, WE'LL NEVER BE ABLE TO OPEN THE CAFE.
カチャ
E-EVERYONE.
オズ…
カー
THIS IS THE NEW UNIFORM DAD GAVE ME TO CELEBRATE YOUR OPENING.
BUT I GET THE FEELING HE MADE A HUGE MISTAKE...
What should I do?
I ASKED TSUYOSHI...
...AND GOT HIM TO LET ME HELP IN HIS CAFE.

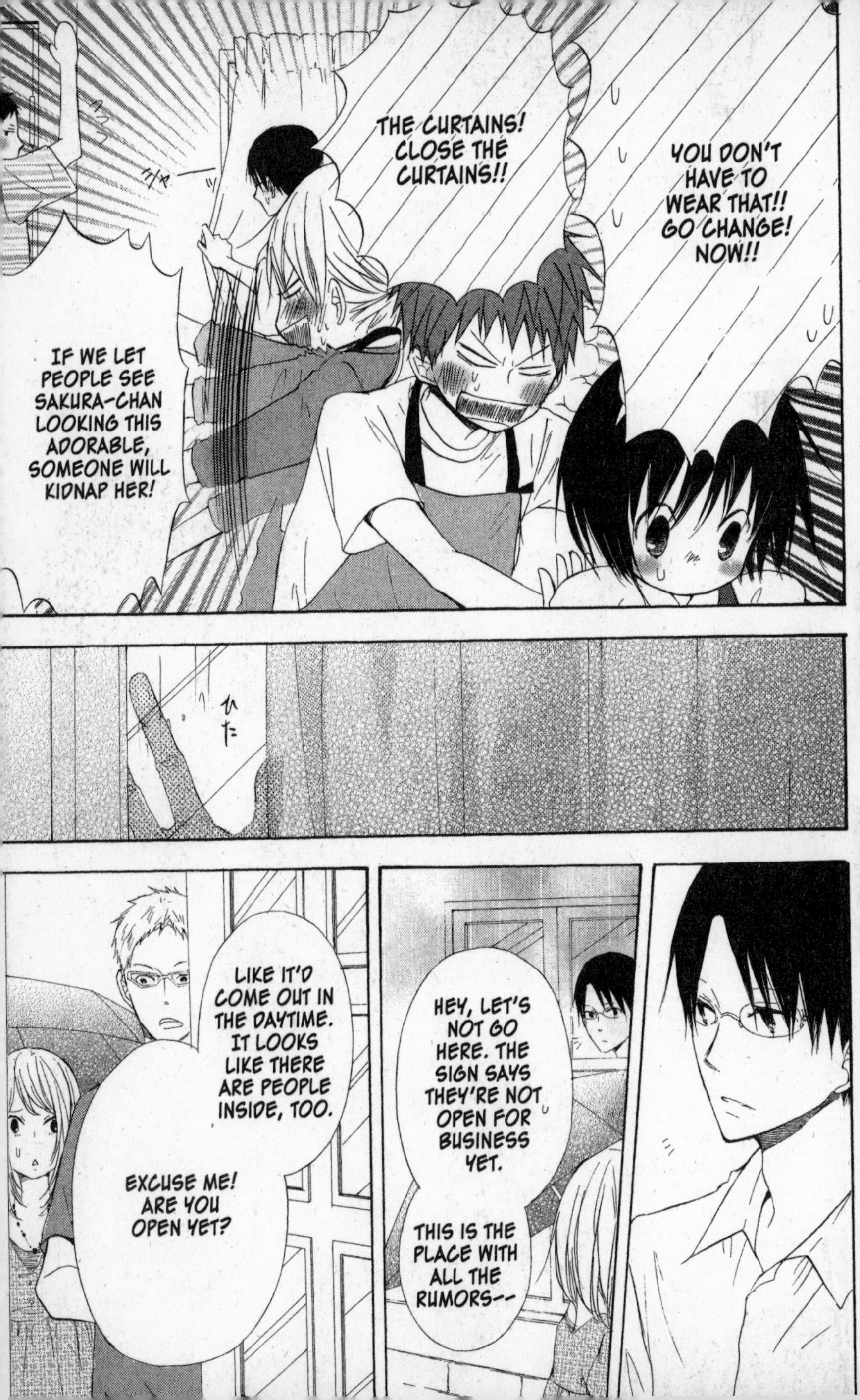
YOU DON'T HAVE TO WEAR THAT!! GO CHANGE! NOW!!
THE CURTAINS! CLOSE THE CURTAINS!!
IF WE LET PEOPLE SEE SAKURA-CHAN LOOKING THIS ADORABLE, SOMEONE WILL KIDNAP HER!
ひた
HEY, LET'S NOT GO HERE. THE SIGN SAYS THEY'RE NOT OPEN FOR BUSINESS YET.
THIS IS THE PLACE WITH ALL THE RUMORS--
LIKE IT'D COME OUT IN THE DAYTIME. IT LOOKS LIKE THERE ARE PEOPLE INSIDE, TOO.
EXCUSE ME! ARE YOU OPEN YET?

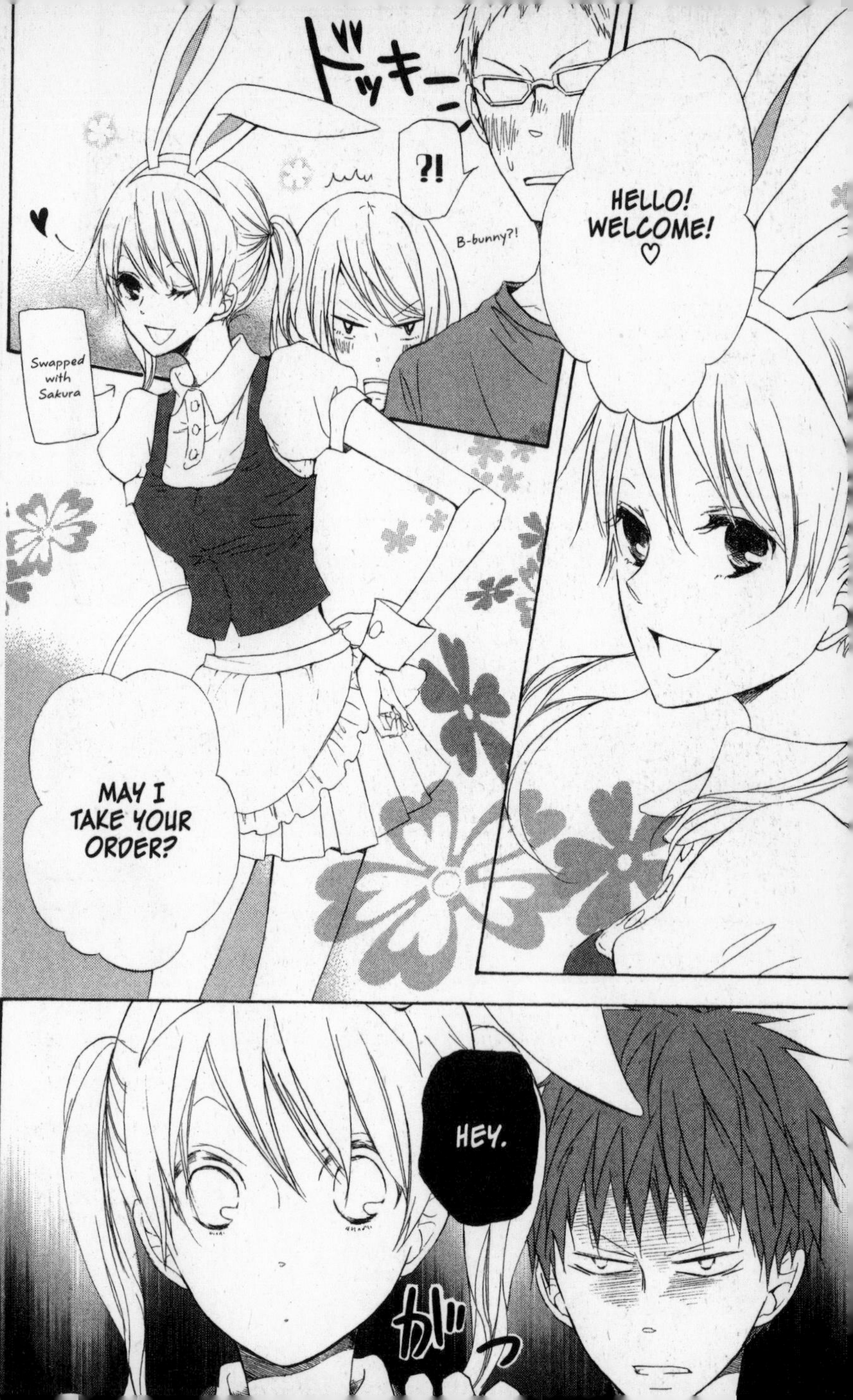
HELLO! WELCOME! ♡
ドッキー
?!
B-bunny?!
Swapped with Sakura
MAY I TAKE YOUR ORDER?
HEY.
がっ

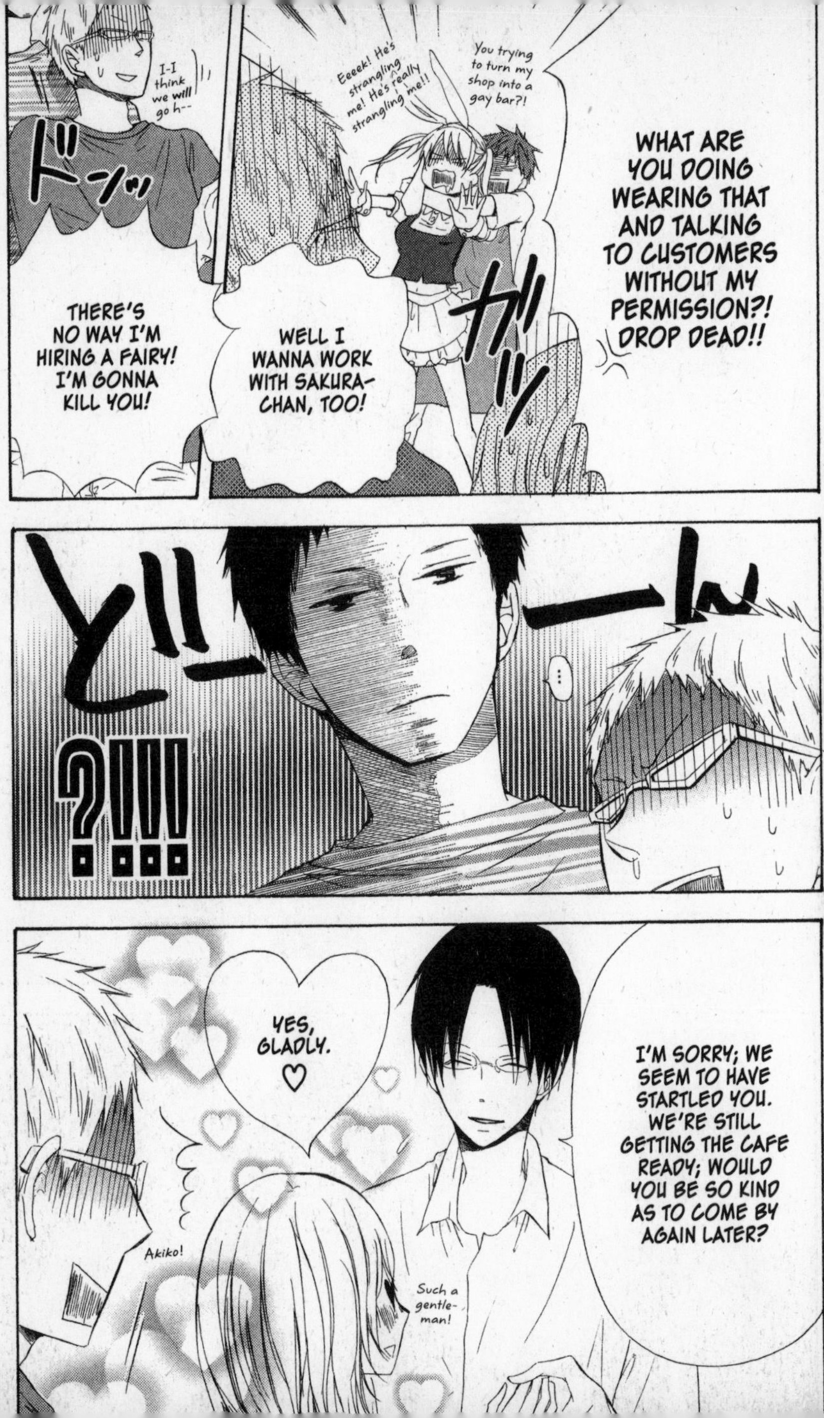
WHAT ARE YOU DOING WEARING THAT AND TALKING TO CUSTOMERS WITHOUT MY PERMISSION?! DROP DEAD!!
You trying to turn my shop into a gay bar?!
Eeeek! He's strangling me! He's really strangling me!!
WELL I WANNA WORK WITH SAKURA-CHAN, TOO!
I-I think we will go h--
THERE'S NO WAY I'M HIRING A FAIRY! I'M GONNA KILL YOU!
...
?!!!
I'M SORRY; WE SEEM TO HAVE STARTLED YOU. WE'RE STILL GETTING THE CAFE READY; WOULD YOU BE SO KIND AS TO COME BY AGAIN LATER?
YES, GLADLY. ♡
Such a gentle-man!
Akiko!

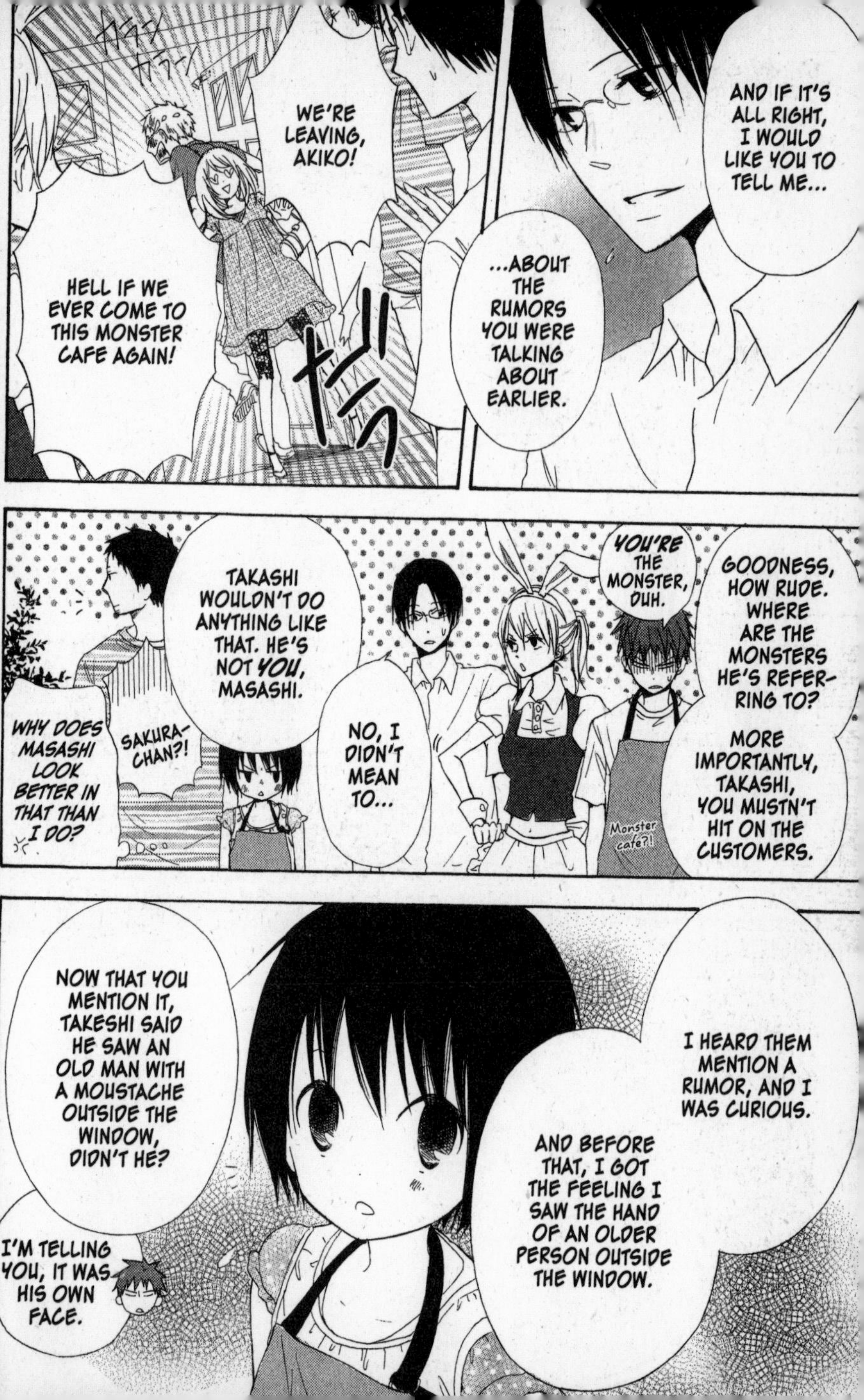
AND IF IT'S ALL RIGHT, I WOULD LIKE YOU TO TELL ME...
...ABOUT THE RUMORS YOU WERE TALKING ABOUT EARLIER.
WE'RE LEAVING, AKIKO!
HELL IF WE EVER COME TO THIS MONSTER CAFE AGAIN!
GOODNESS, HOW RUDE. WHERE ARE THE MONSTERS HE'S REFERRING TO?
MORE IMPORTANTLY, TAKASHI, YOU MUSTN'T HIT ON THE CUSTOMERS.
YOU'RE THE MONSTER, DUH.
Monster café?!
NO, I DIDN'T MEAN TO...
TAKASHI WOULDN'T DO ANYTHING LIKE THAT. HE'S NOT YOU, MASASHI.
SAKURA-CHAN?!
WHY DOES MASASHI LOOK BETTER IN THAT THAN I DO?
I HEARD THEM MENTION A RUMOR, AND I WAS CURIOUS.
AND BEFORE THAT, I GOT THE FEELING I SAW THE HAND OF AN OLDER PERSON OUTSIDE THE WINDOW.
NOW THAT YOU MENTION IT, TAKESHI SAID HE SAW AN OLD MAN WITH A MOUSTACHE OUTSIDE THE WINDOW, DIDN'T HE?
I'M TELLING YOU, IT WAS HIS OWN FACE.

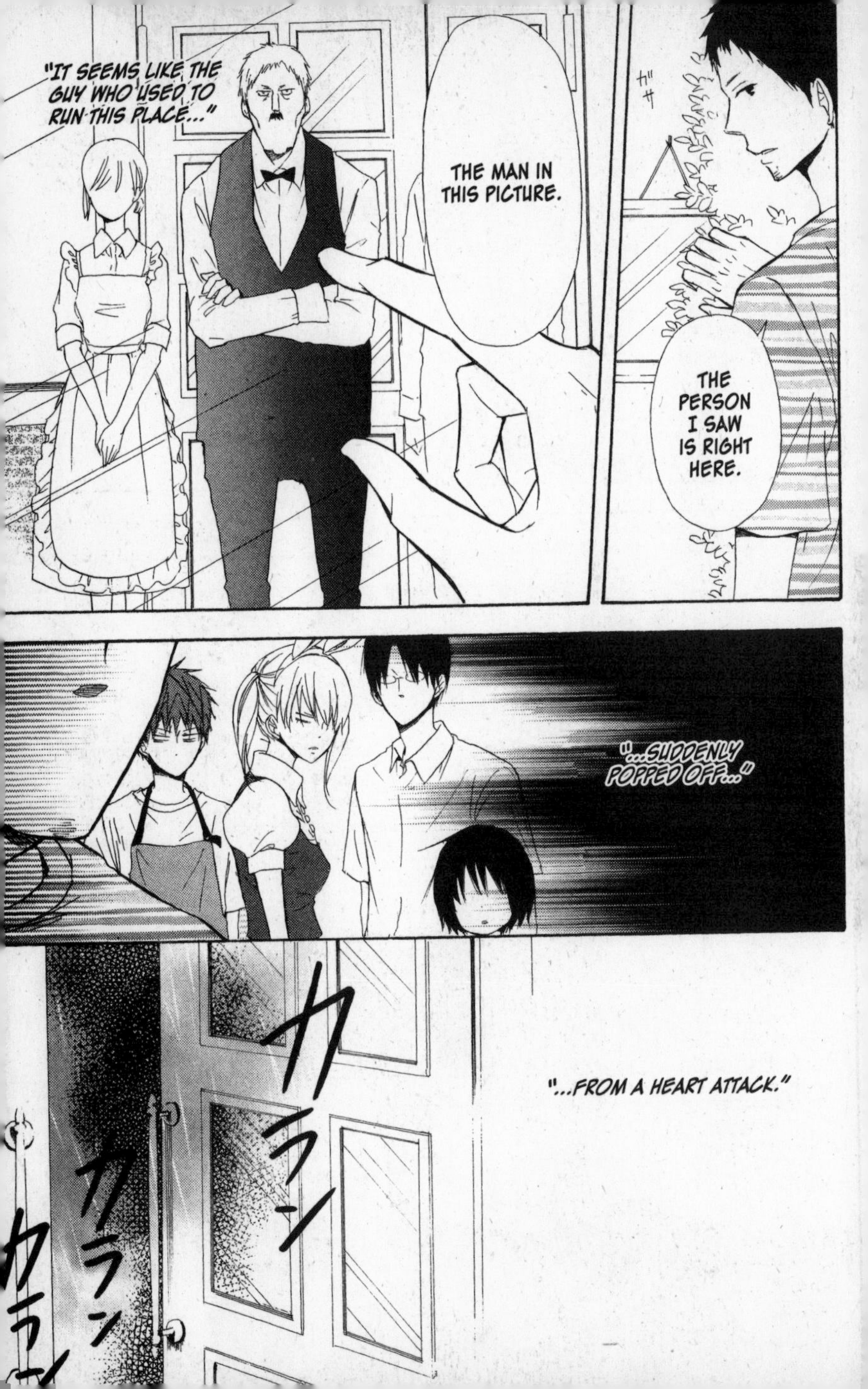
ガサ
THE PERSON I SAW IS RIGHT HERE.
THE MAN IN THIS PICTURE.
"IT SEEMS LIKE THE GUY WHO USED TO RUN THIS PLACE..."
"...SUDDENLY POPPED OFF..."
カラーン
カラン
"...FROM A HEART ATTACK."

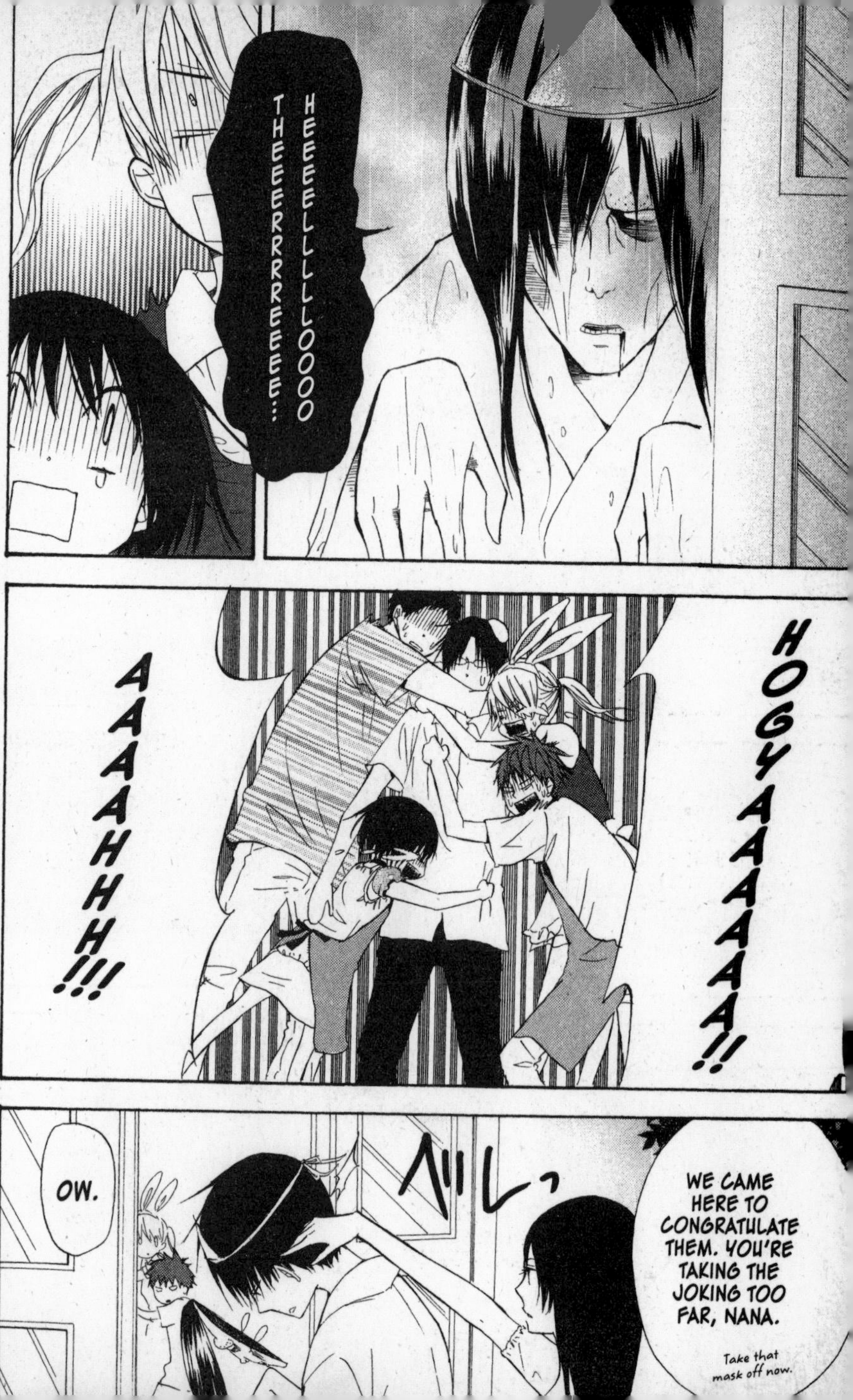
HEEEELLLLLOOOO THEEERRRREEEE...
HOGYAAAAAAAAA!!
AAAAAHHHH!!!
WE CAME HERE TO CONGRATULATE THEM. YOU'RE TAKING THE JOKING TOO FAR, NANA.
Take that mask off now.
ベリっ
OW.

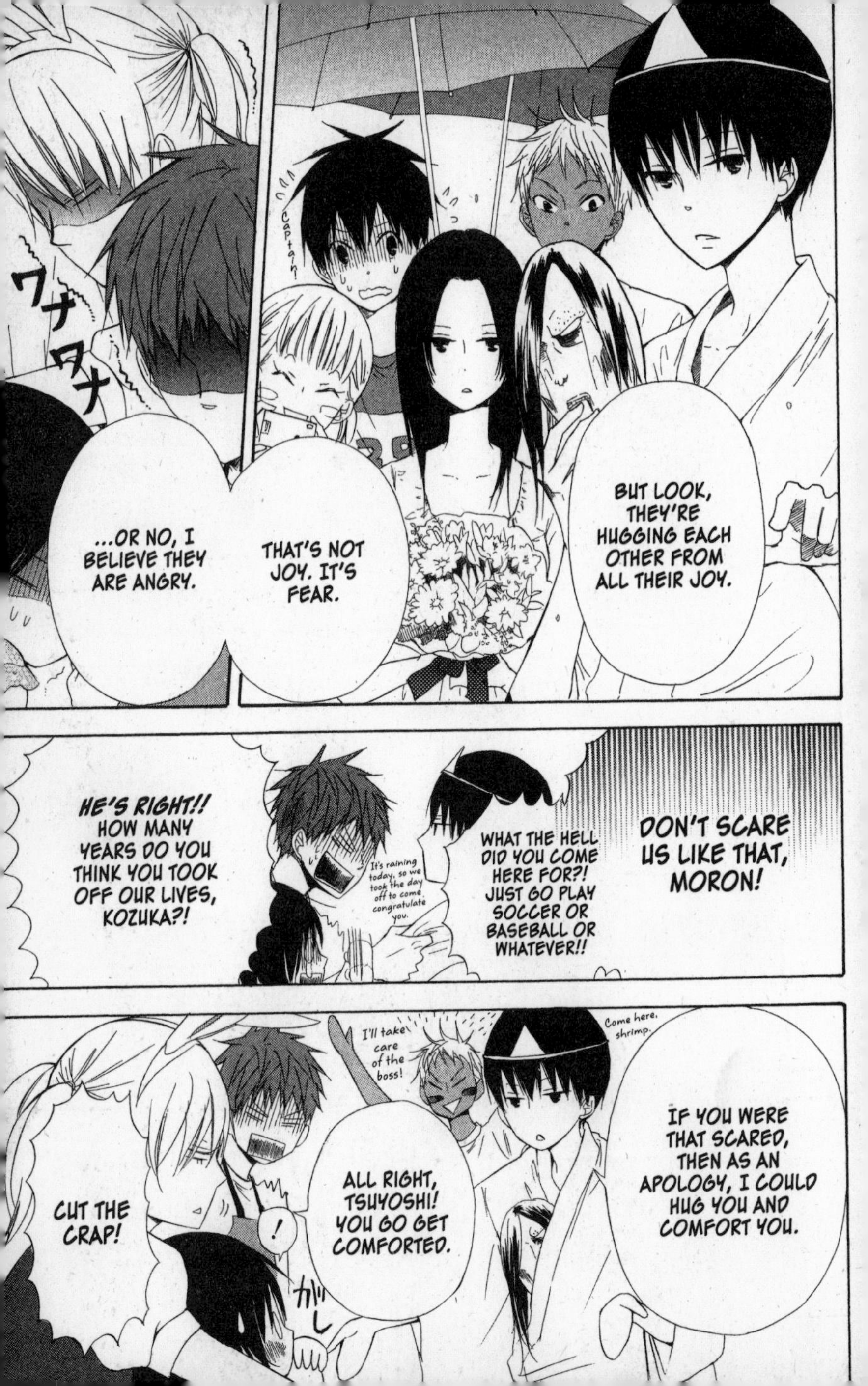
Captain!
BUT LOOK, THEY'RE HUGGING EACH OTHER FROM ALL THEIR JOY.
THAT'S NOT JOY. IT'S FEAR.
...OR NO, I BELIEVE THEY ARE ANGRY.
ワナワナ
DON'T SCARE US LIKE THAT, MORON!
WHAT THE HELL DID YOU COME HERE FOR?! JUST GO PLAY SOCCER OR BASEBALL OR WHATEVER!!
It's raining today, so we took the day off to come congratulate you.
HE'S RIGHT!! HOW MANY YEARS DO YOU THINK YOU TOOK OFF OUR LIVES, KOZUKA?!
Come here, shrimp.
IF YOU WERE THAT SCARED, THEN AS AN APOLOGY, I COULD HUG YOU AND COMFORT YOU.
I'll take care of the boss!
ALL RIGHT, TSUYOSHI! YOU GO GET COMFORTED.
!
ガシ
CUT THE CRAP!

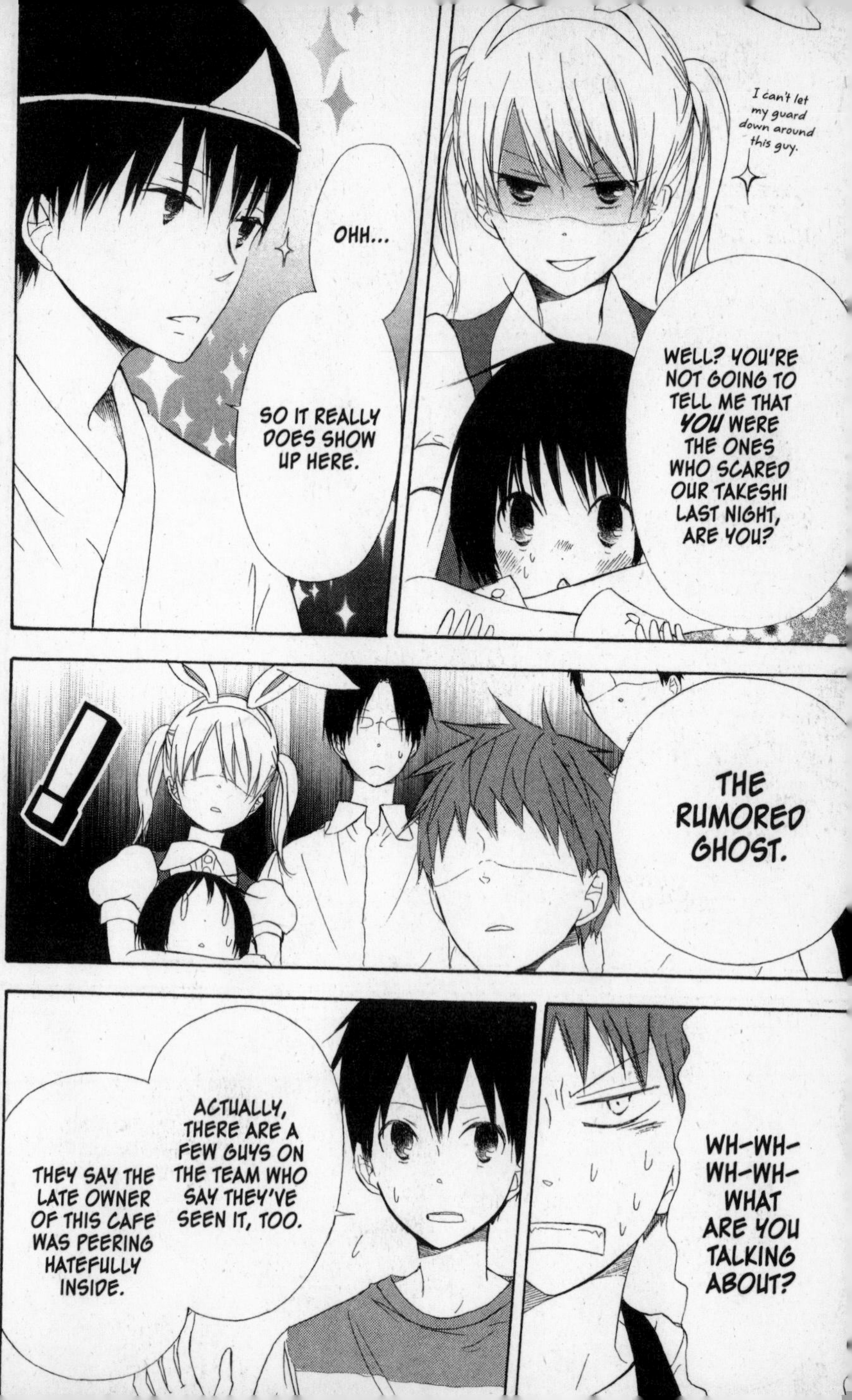
I can't let my guard down around this guy.
WELL? YOU'RE NOT GOING TO TELL ME THAT YOU WERE THE ONES WHO SCARED OUR TAKESHI LAST NIGHT, ARE YOU?
OHH...
SO IT REALLY DOES SHOW UP HERE.
THE RUMORED GHOST.
WH-WH-WH-WH-WHAT ARE YOU TALKING ABOUT?
ACTUALLY, THERE ARE A FEW GUYS ON THE TEAM WHO SAY THEY'VE SEEN IT, TOO.
THEY SAY THE LATE OWNER OF THIS CAFE WAS PEERING HATEFULLY INSIDE.

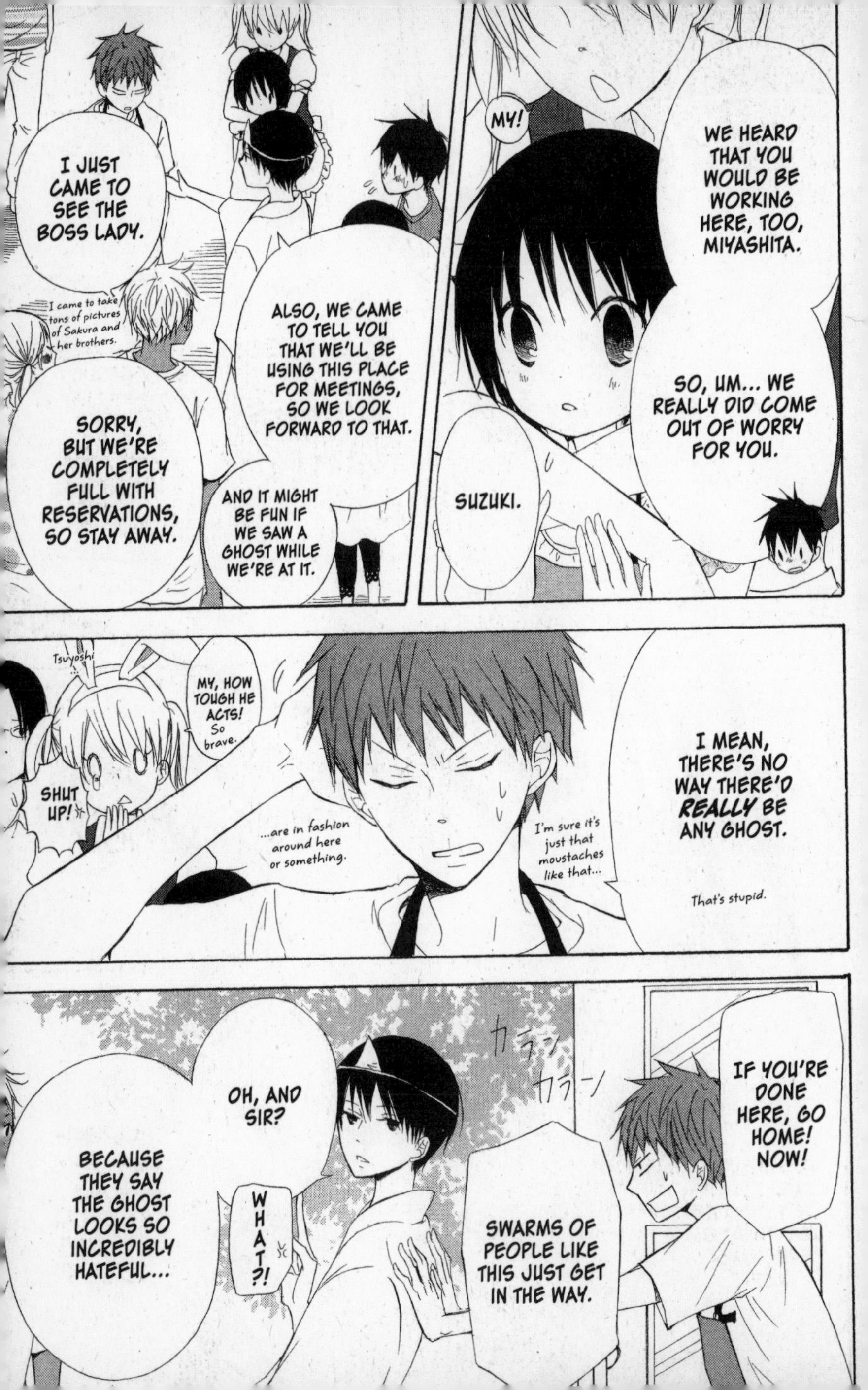
MY!
WE HEARD THAT YOU WOULD BE WORKING HERE, TOO, MIYASHITA.
SO, UM... WE REALLY DID COME OUT OF WORRY FOR YOU.
SUZUKI.
I JUST CAME TO SEE THE BOSS LADY.
I came to take tons of pictures of Sakura and her brothers.
ALSO, WE CAME TO TELL YOU THAT WE'LL BE USING THIS PLACE FOR MEETINGS, SO WE LOOK FORWARD TO THAT.
AND IT MIGHT BE FUN IF WE SAW A GHOST WHILE WE'RE AT IT.
SORRY, BUT WE'RE COMPLETELY FULL WITH RESERVATIONS, SO STAY AWAY.
I MEAN, THERE'S NO WAY THERE'D REALLY BE ANY GHOST.
That's stupid.
I'm sure it's just that moustaches like that...
...are in fashion around here or something.
MY, HOW TOUGH HE ACTS!
So brave.
Tsuyoshi
SHUT UP!
IF YOU'RE DONE HERE, GO HOME! NOW!
SWARMS OF PEOPLE LIKE THIS JUST GET IN THE WAY.
カラン
カラーン
OH, AND SIR?
BECAUSE THEY SAY THE GHOST LOOKS SO INCREDIBLY HATEFUL...
WHAT?!

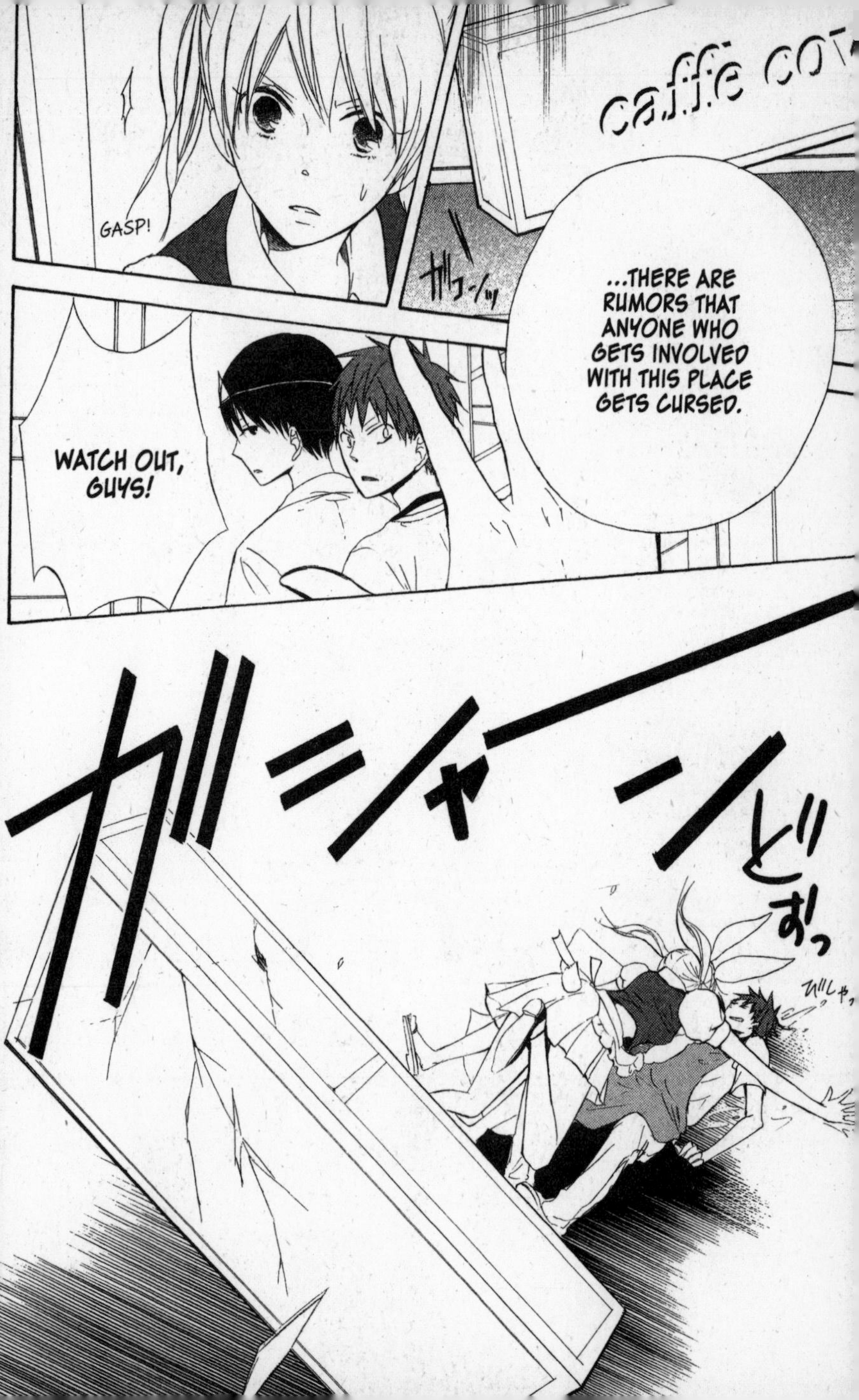
caffe co
...THERE ARE RUMORS THAT ANYONE WHO GETS INVOLVED WITH THIS PLACE GETS CURSED.
GASP!
WATCH OUT, GUYS!
ガシャーン
どすっ

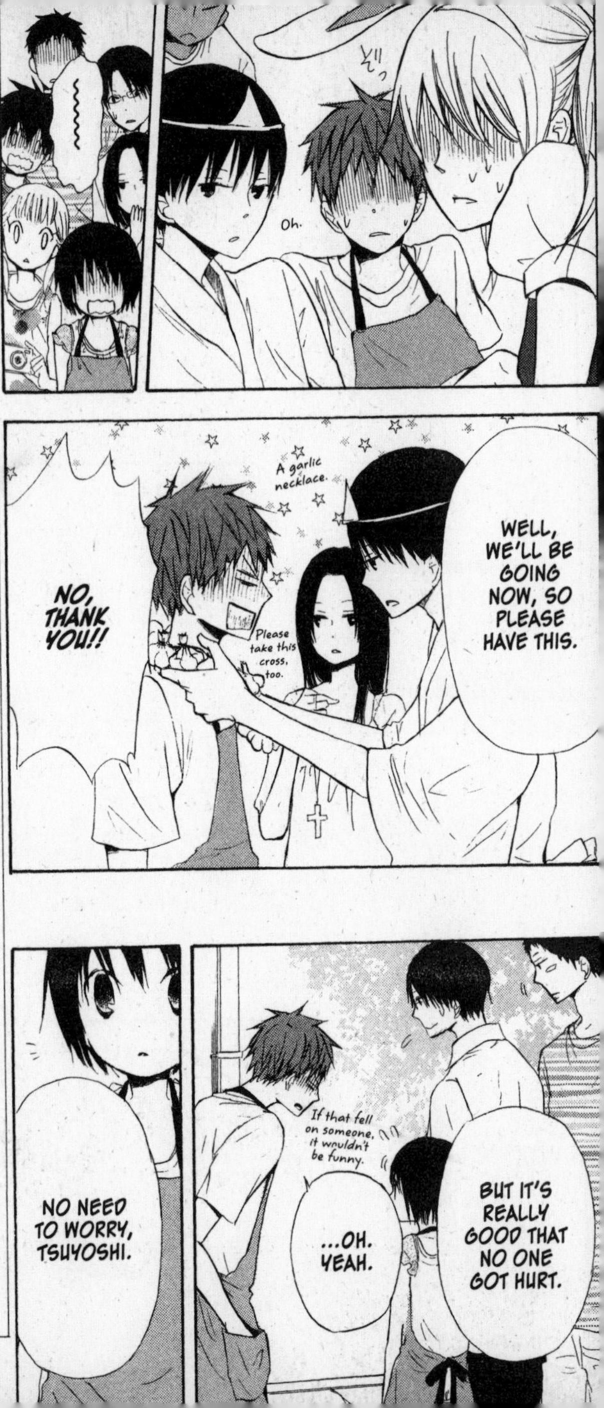
ぞくっ
Oh.
WELL, WE'LL BE GOING NOW, SO PLEASE HAVE THIS.
A garlic necklace.
Please take this cross, too.
NO, THANK YOU!!
BUT IT'S REALLY GOOD THAT NO ONE GOT HURT.
...OH. YEAH.
If that fell on someone, it wouldn't be funny.
NO NEED TO WORRY, TSUYOSHI.

4

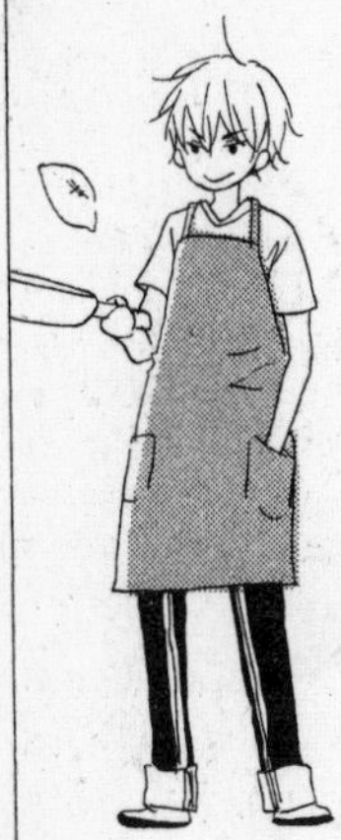

And so(?) the bonus manga this time, partially at the suggestion of my editor, is about Katagiri-kun, who apparently doesn't play fair, and Sonomura-san, after that episode.

I hope you enjoy it even a little.

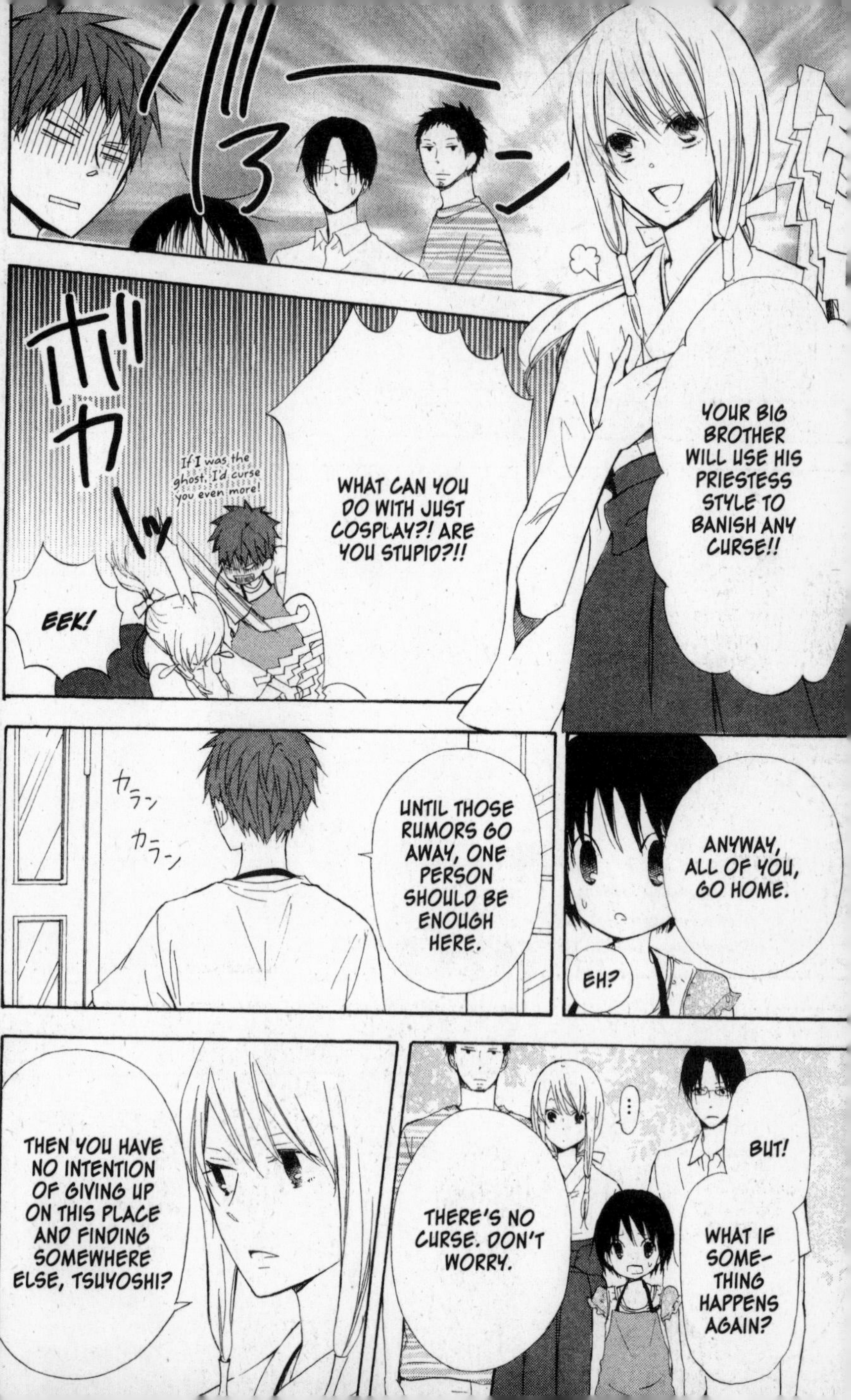
YOUR BIG BROTHER WILL USE HIS PRIESTESS STYLE TO BANISH ANY CURSE!!
WHAT CAN YOU DO WITH JUST COSPLAY?! ARE YOU STUPID?!!
ボカーッ
If I was the ghost, I'd curse you even more!
EEK!
ANYWAY, ALL OF YOU, GO HOME.
EH?
UNTIL THOSE RUMORS GO AWAY, ONE PERSON SHOULD BE ENOUGH HERE.
カラン
カラン
...
BUT!
WHAT IF SOME-THING HAPPENS AGAIN?
THERE'S NO CURSE. DON'T WORRY.
THEN YOU HAVE NO INTENTION OF GIVING UP ON THIS PLACE AND FINDING SOMEWHERE ELSE, TSUYOSHI?

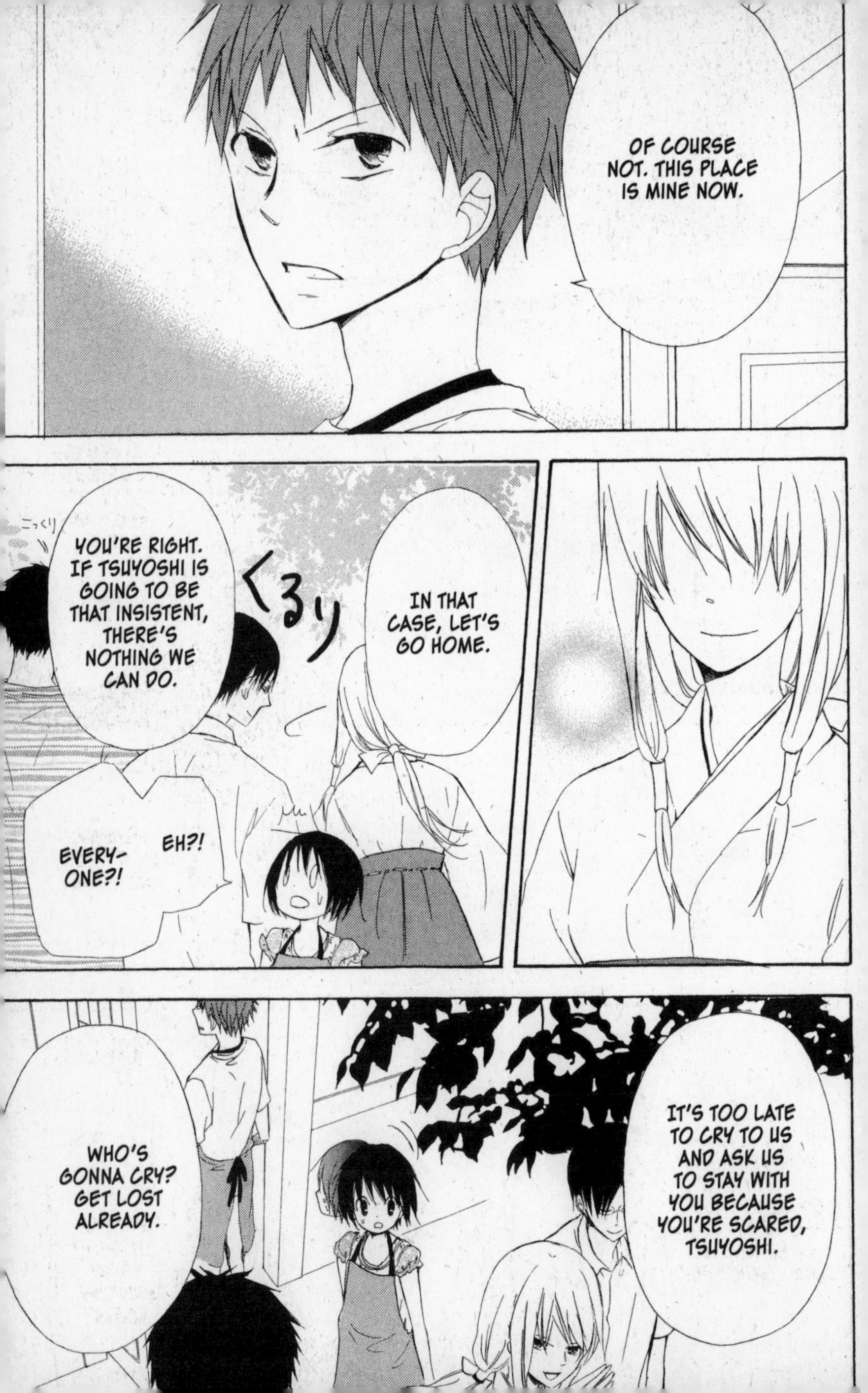
OF COURSE NOT. THIS PLACE IS MINE NOW.
IN THAT CASE, LET'S GO HOME.
くるり
YOU'RE RIGHT. IF TSUYOSHI IS GOING TO BE THAT INSISTENT, THERE'S NOTHING WE CAN DO.
こっくり
EH?!
EVERY-ONE?!
IT'S TOO LATE TO CRY TO US AND ASK US TO STAY WITH YOU BECAUSE YOU'RE SCARED, TSUYOSHI.
WHO'S GONNA CRY? GET LOST ALREADY.

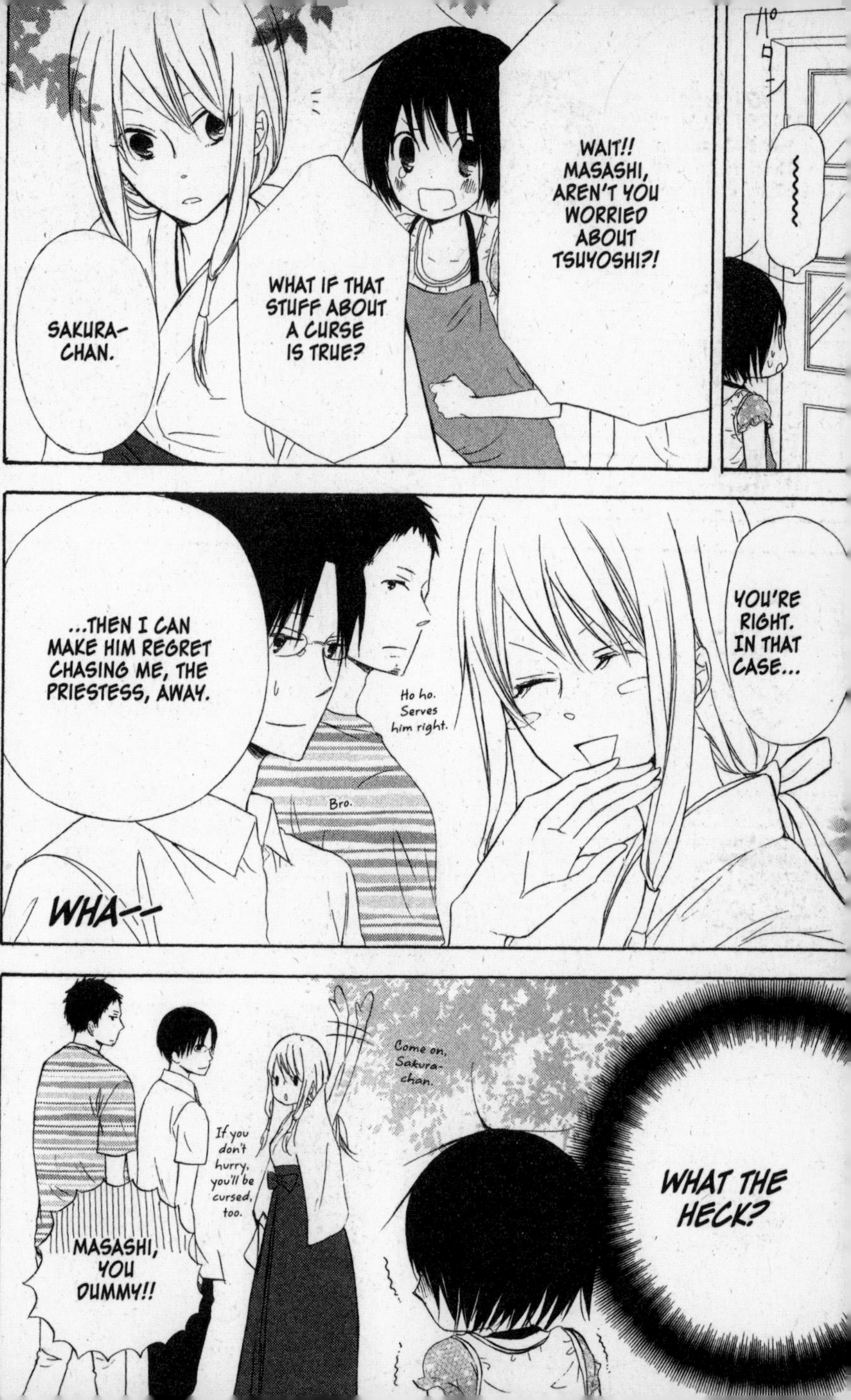
WAIT!! MASASHI, AREN'T YOU WORRIED ABOUT TSUYOSHI?!
WHAT IF THAT STUFF ABOUT A CURSE IS TRUE?
SAKURA-CHAN.
YOU'RE RIGHT. IN THAT CASE...
...THEN I CAN MAKE HIM REGRET CHASING ME, THE PRIESTESS, AWAY.
Ho ho. Serves him right.
Bro.
WHA--
WHAT THE HECK?
Come on, Sakura-chan.
If you don't hurry, you'll be cursed, too.
MASASHI, YOU DUMMY!!

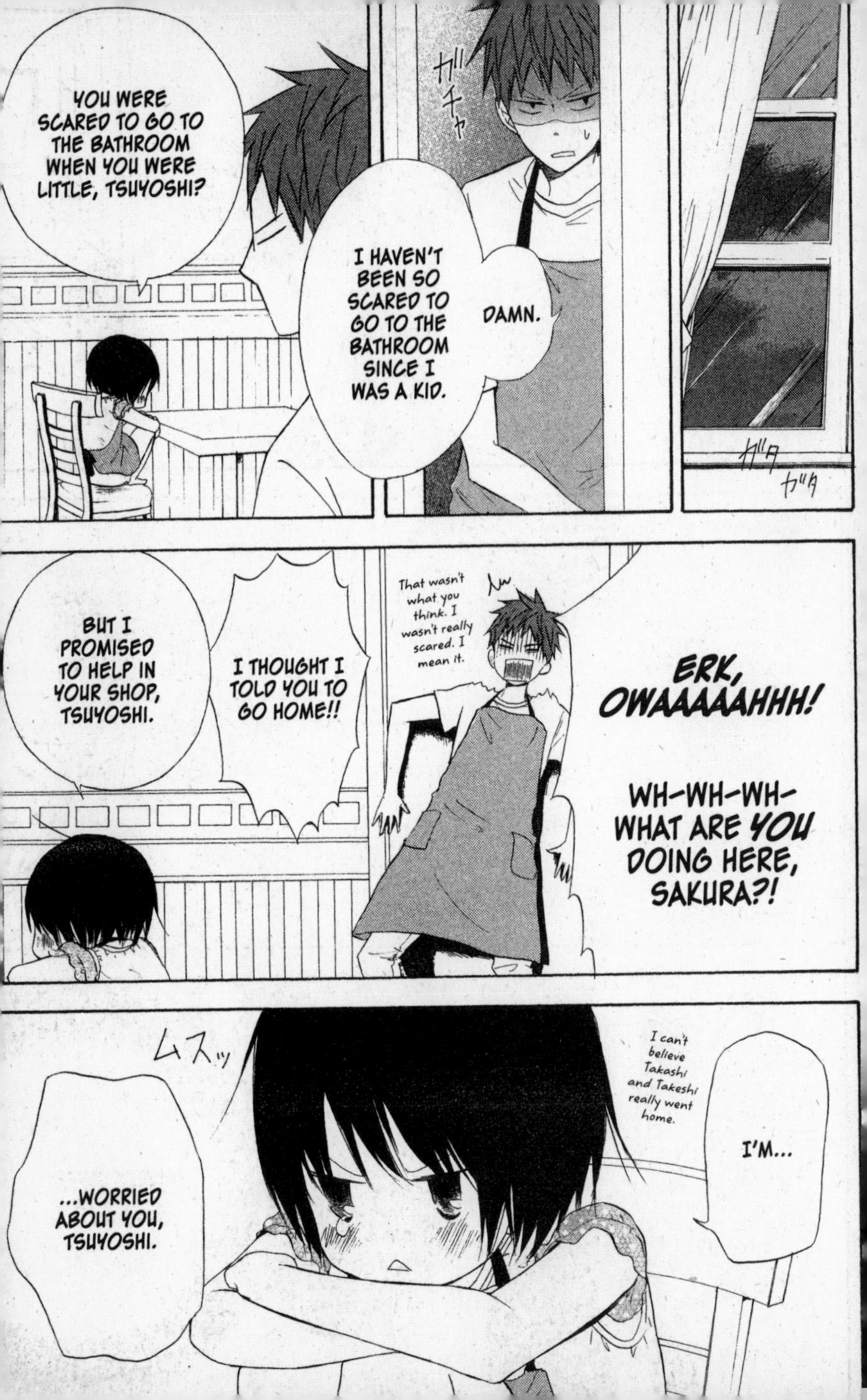
ガタ
ガタ
ガチャ
DAMN.
I HAVEN'T BEEN SO SCARED TO GO TO THE BATHROOM SINCE I WAS A KID.
YOU WERE SCARED TO GO TO THE BATHROOM WHEN YOU WERE LITTLE, TSUYOSHI?
ERK, OWAAAAAHHH!
WH-WH-WH-WHAT ARE YOU DOING HERE, SAKURA?!
That wasn't what you think. I wasn't really scared. I mean it.
I THOUGHT I TOLD YOU TO GO HOME!!
BUT I PROMISED TO HELP IN YOUR SHOP, TSUYOSHI.
I can't believe Takashi and Takeshi really went home.
I'M...
ムスッ
...WORRIED ABOUT YOU, TSUYOSHI.

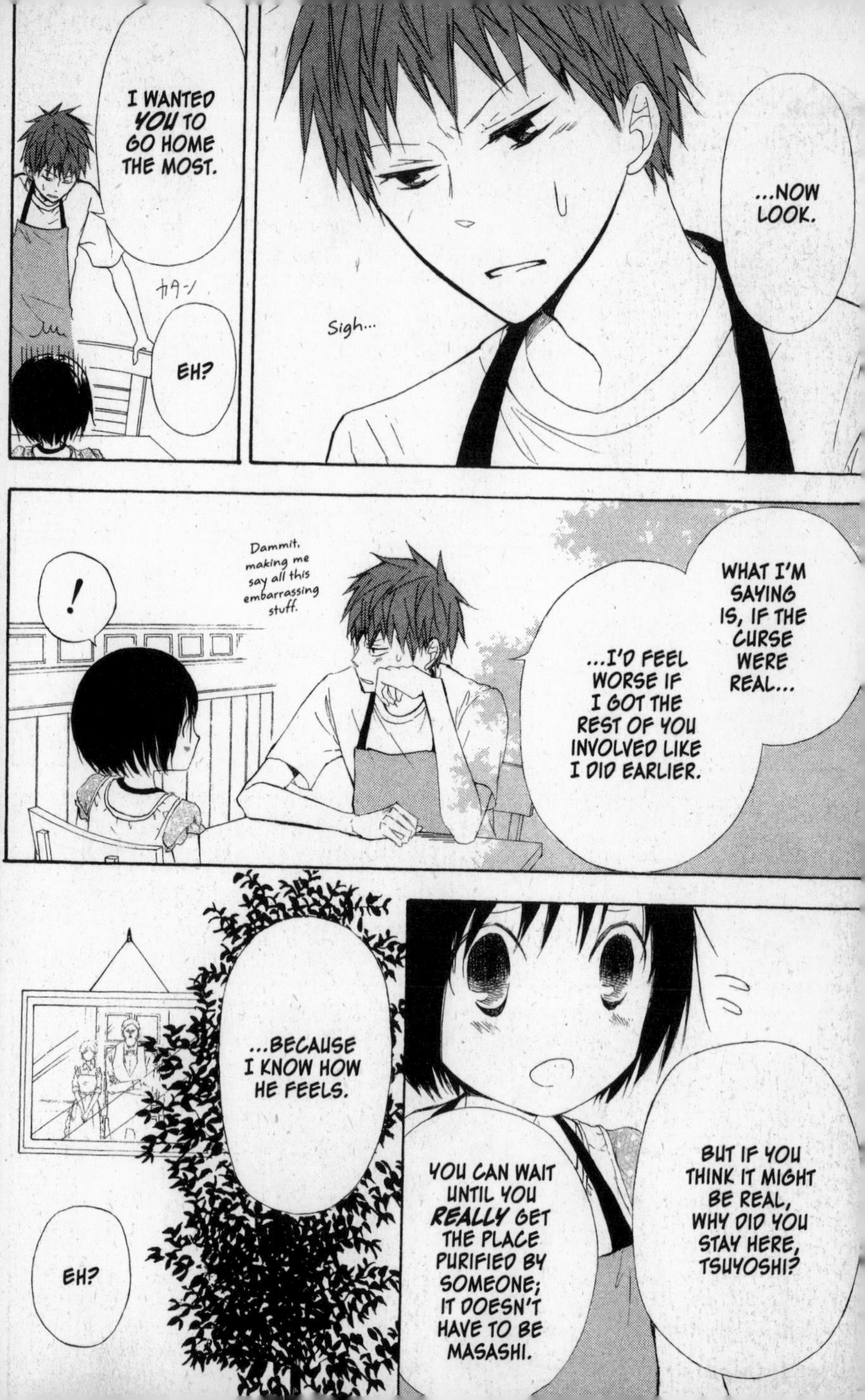
...NOW LOOK.
Sigh...
I WANTED YOU TO GO HOME THE MOST.
カターン
EH?
WHAT I'M SAYING IS, IF THE CURSE WERE REAL...
...I'D FEEL WORSE IF I GOT THE REST OF YOU INVOLVED LIKE I DID EARLIER.
Dammit, making me say all this embarrassing stuff.
!
BUT IF YOU THINK IT MIGHT BE REAL, WHY DID YOU STAY HERE, TSUYOSHI?
YOU CAN WAIT UNTIL YOU REALLY GET THE PLACE PURIFIED BY SOMEONE; IT DOESN'T HAVE TO BE MASASHI.
...BECAUSE I KNOW HOW HE FEELS.
EH?

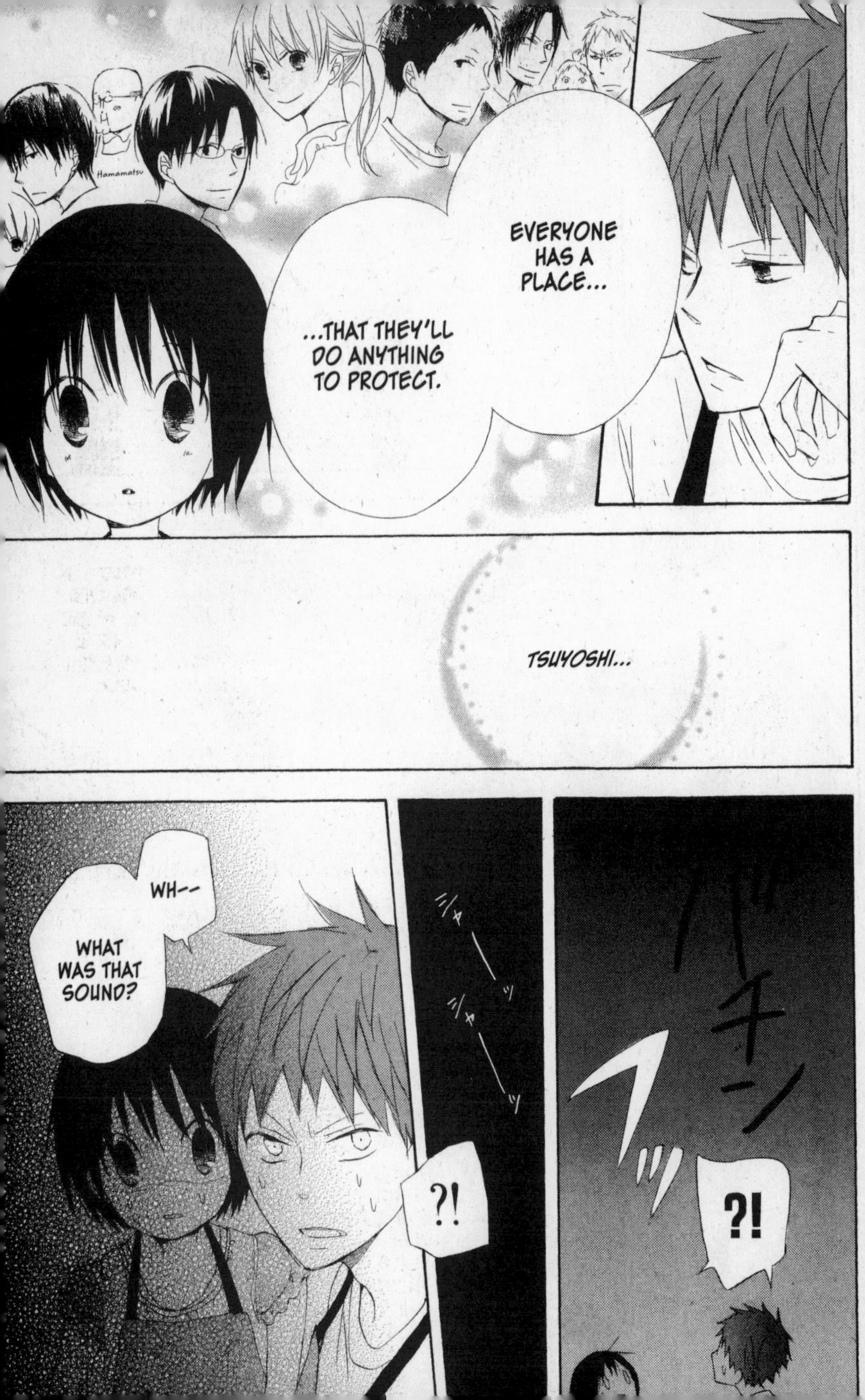
EVERYONE HAS A PLACE...
...THAT THEY'LL DO ANYTHING TO PROTECT.
Hamamatsu
TSUYOSHI...
?!
シャーッ
シャーッ
?!
WH--
WHAT WAS THAT SOUND?

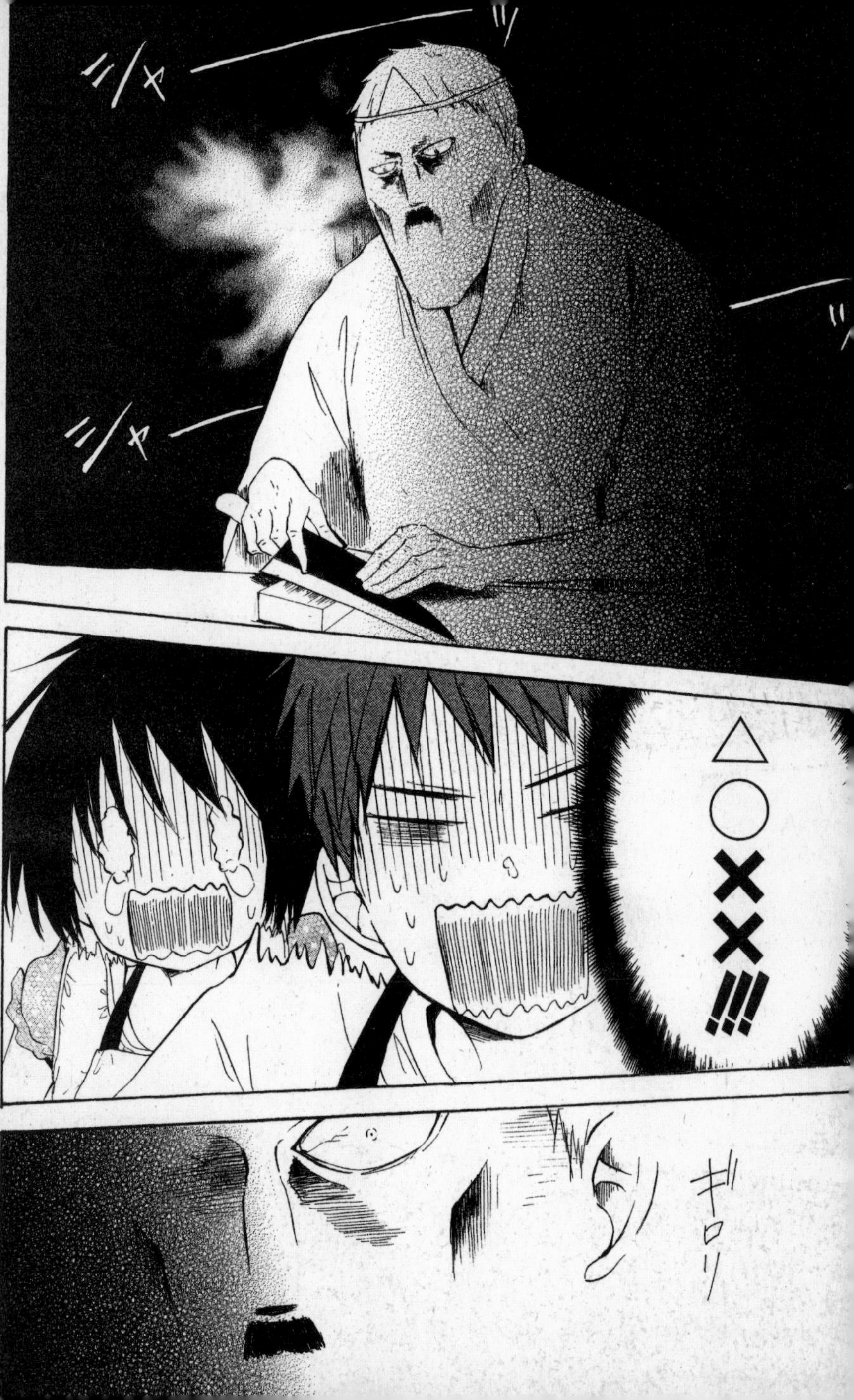
シャーーッ
シャーーッ
△○××!!!
ギロリ

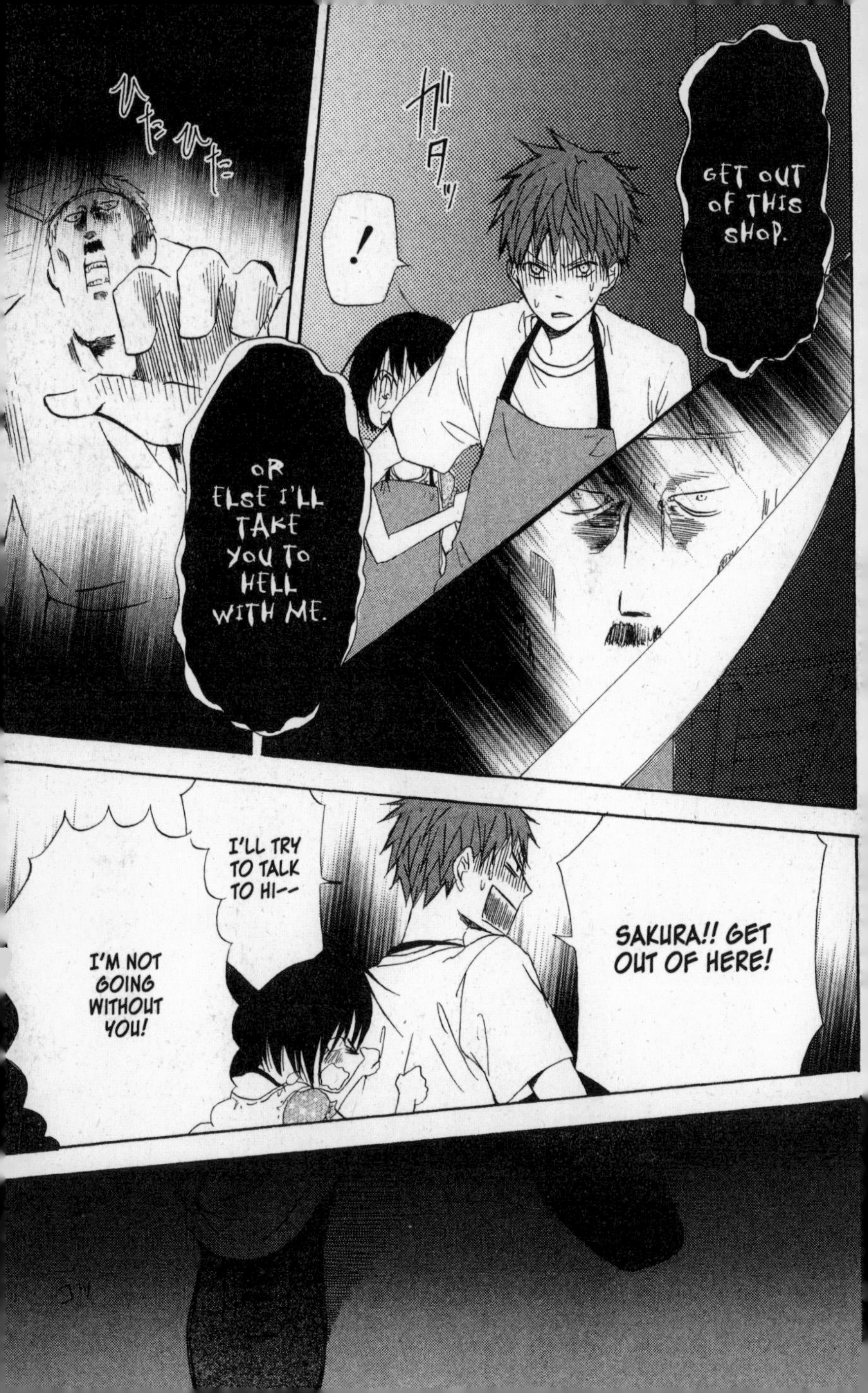
GET OUT OF THIS SHOP.
ガタッ
!
OR ELSE I'LL TAKE YOU TO HELL WITH ME.
ひたひた
SAKURA!! GET OUT OF HERE!
I'LL TRY TO TALK TO HI--
I'M NOT GOING WITHOUT YOU!

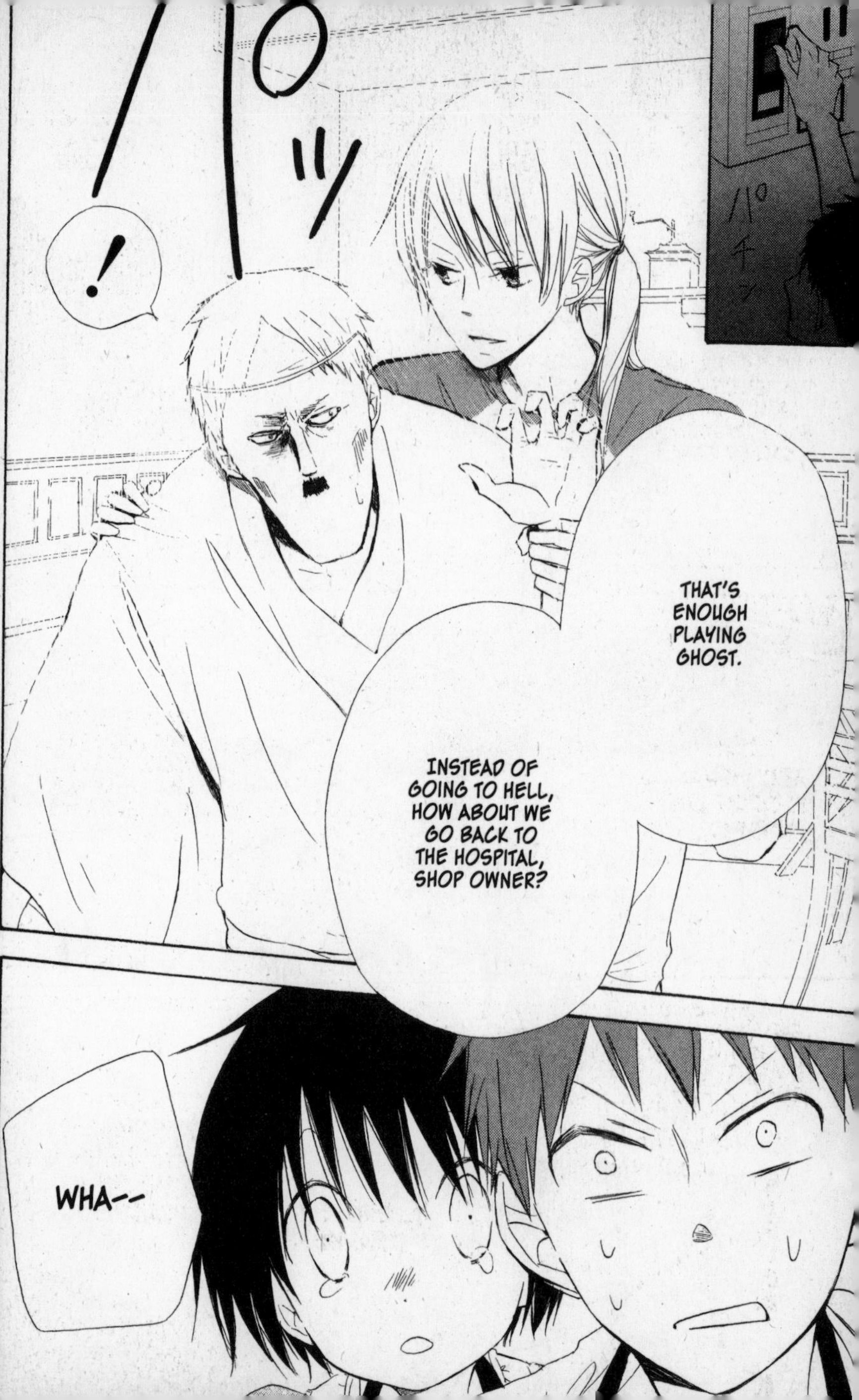
!
THAT'S ENOUGH PLAYING GHOST.
INSTEAD OF GOING TO HELL, HOW ABOUT WE GO BACK TO THE HOSPITAL, SHOP OWNER?
WHA--

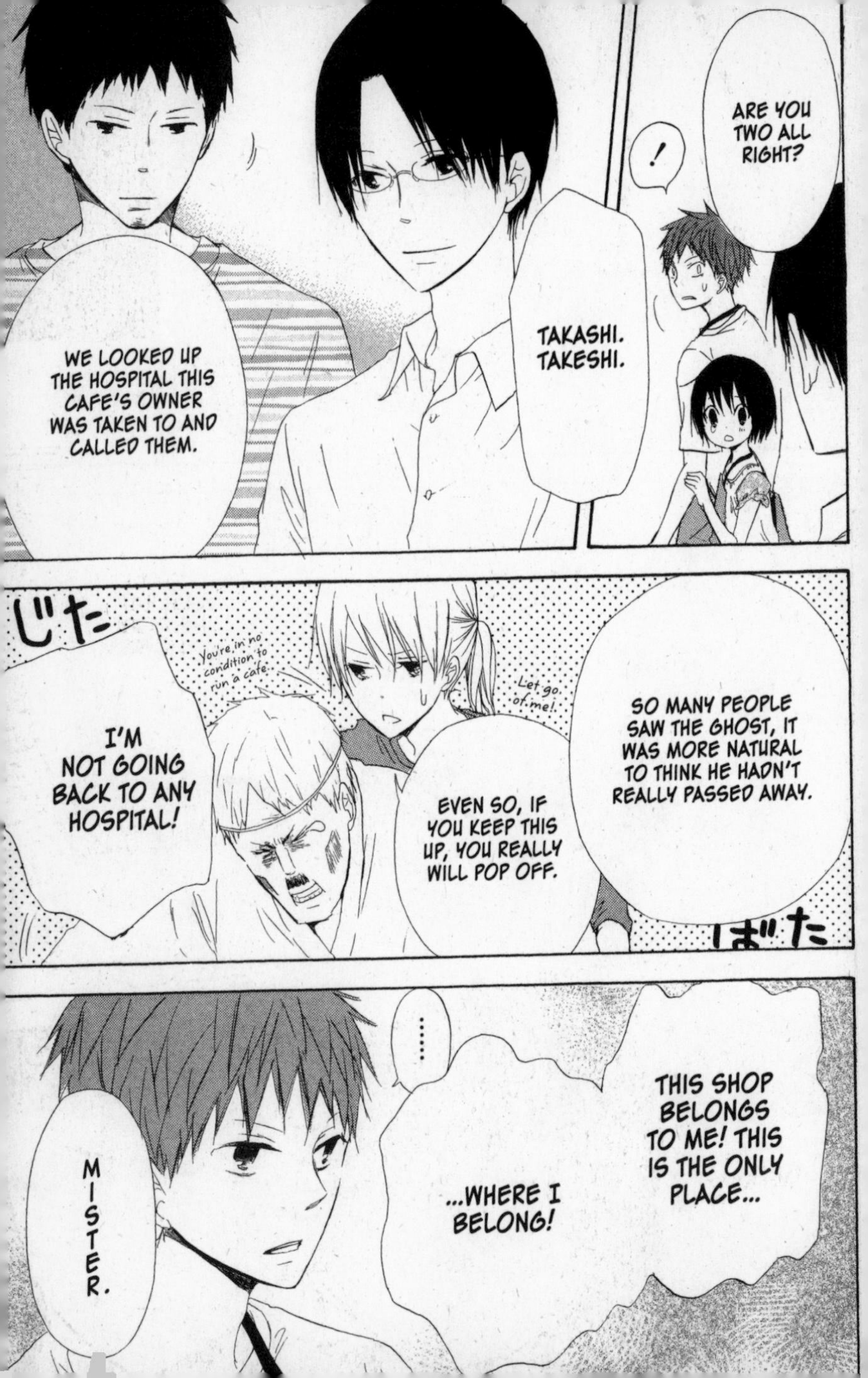
ARE YOU TWO ALL RIGHT?
!
TAKASHI. TAKESHI.
WE LOOKED UP THE HOSPITAL THIS CAFE'S OWNER WAS TAKEN TO AND CALLED THEM.
SO MANY PEOPLE SAW THE GHOST, IT WAS MORE NATURAL TO THINK HE HADN'T REALLY PASSED AWAY.
ばた
Let go of me!
EVEN SO, IF YOU KEEP THIS UP, YOU REALLY WILL POP OFF.
You're in no condition to run a cafe..
じた
I'M NOT GOING BACK TO ANY HOSPITAL!
THIS SHOP BELONGS TO ME! THIS IS THE ONLY PLACE...
...WHERE I BELONG!
......
MISTER.

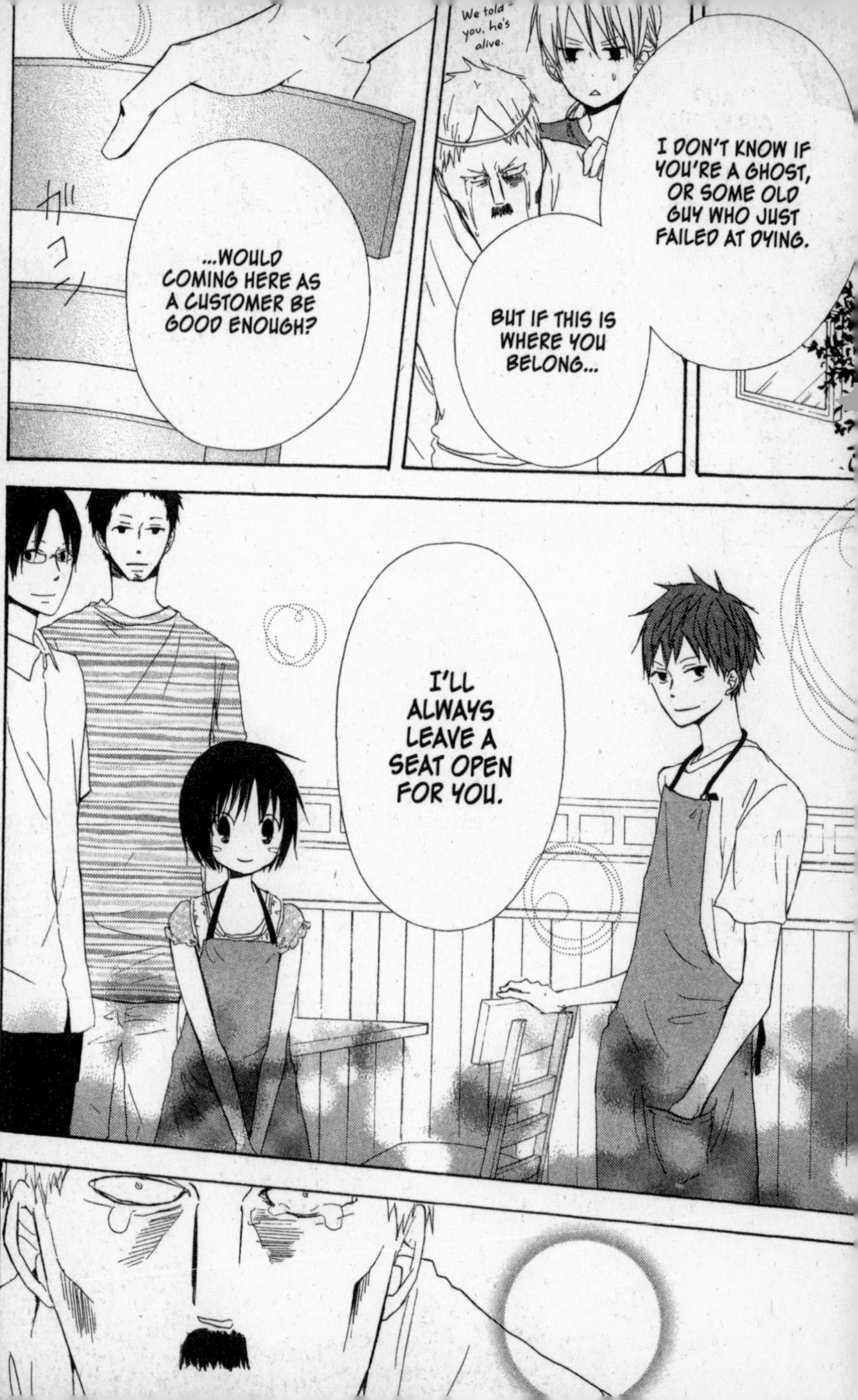
We told you, he's alive.
I DON'T KNOW IF YOU'RE A GHOST, OR SOME OLD GUY WHO JUST FAILED AT DYING.
BUT IF THIS IS WHERE YOU BELONG...
...WOULD COMING HERE AS A CUSTOMER BE GOOD ENOUGH?
I'LL ALWAYS LEAVE A SEAT OPEN FOR YOU.

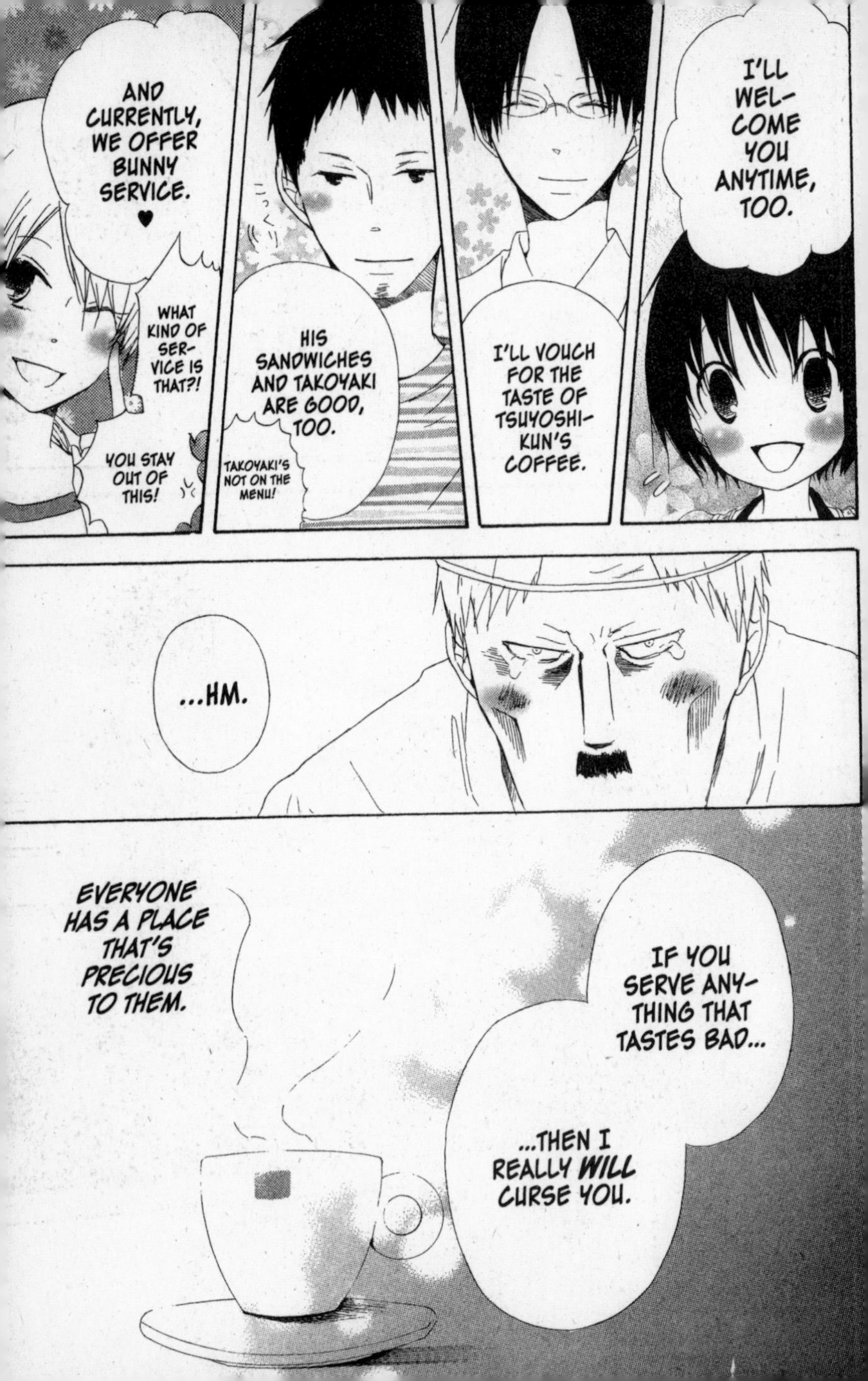
I'LL WEL-COME YOU ANYTIME, TOO.
I'LL VOUCH FOR THE TASTE OF TSUYOSHI-KUN'S COFFEE.
HIS SANDWICHES AND TAKOYAKI ARE GOOD, TOO.
TAKOYAKI'S NOT ON THE MENU!
AND CURRENTLY, WE OFFER BUNNY SERVICE. ♥
WHAT KIND OF SER-VICE IS THAT?!
YOU STAY OUT OF THIS!
...HM.
IF YOU SERVE ANY-THING THAT TASTES BAD...
...THEN I REALLY *WILL* CURSE YOU.
EVERYONE HAS A PLACE THAT'S PRECIOUS TO THEM.

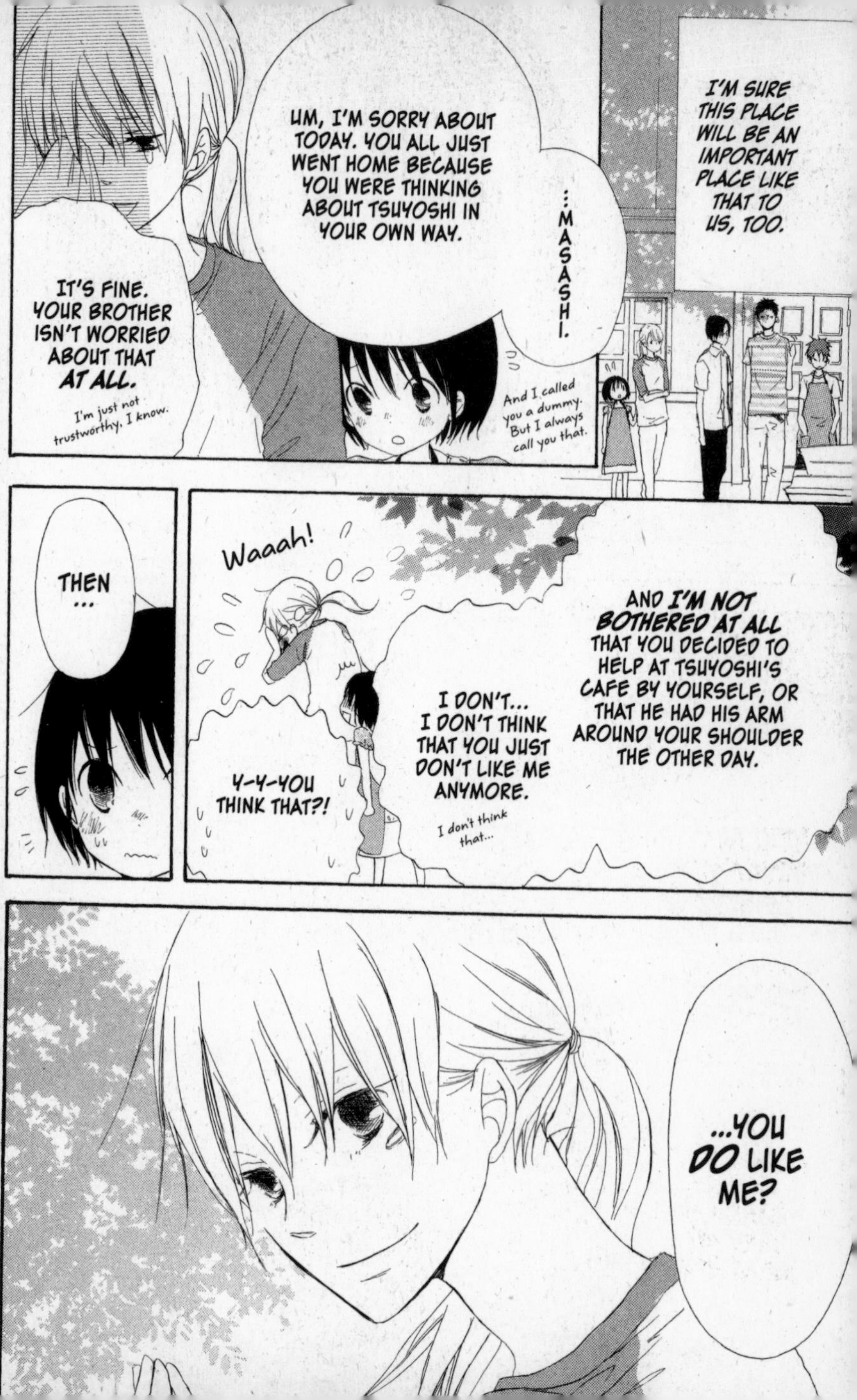
I'M SURE THIS PLACE WILL BE AN IMPORTANT PLACE LIKE THAT TO US, TOO.
...MASASHI.
UM, I'M SORRY ABOUT TODAY. YOU ALL JUST WENT HOME BECAUSE YOU WERE THINKING ABOUT TSUYOSHI IN YOUR OWN WAY.
And I called you a dummy. But I always call you that.
IT'S FINE. YOUR BROTHER ISN'T WORRIED ABOUT THAT AT ALL.
I'm just not trustworthy, I know.
AND I'M NOT BOTHERED AT ALL THAT YOU DECIDED TO HELP AT TSUYOSHI'S CAFE BY YOURSELF, OR THAT HE HAD HIS ARM AROUND YOUR SHOULDER THE OTHER DAY.
Waaah!
I DON'T... I DON'T THINK THAT YOU JUST DON'T LIKE ME ANYMORE.
I don't think that...
Y-Y-YOU THINK THAT?!
THEN ...
...YOU DO LIKE ME?

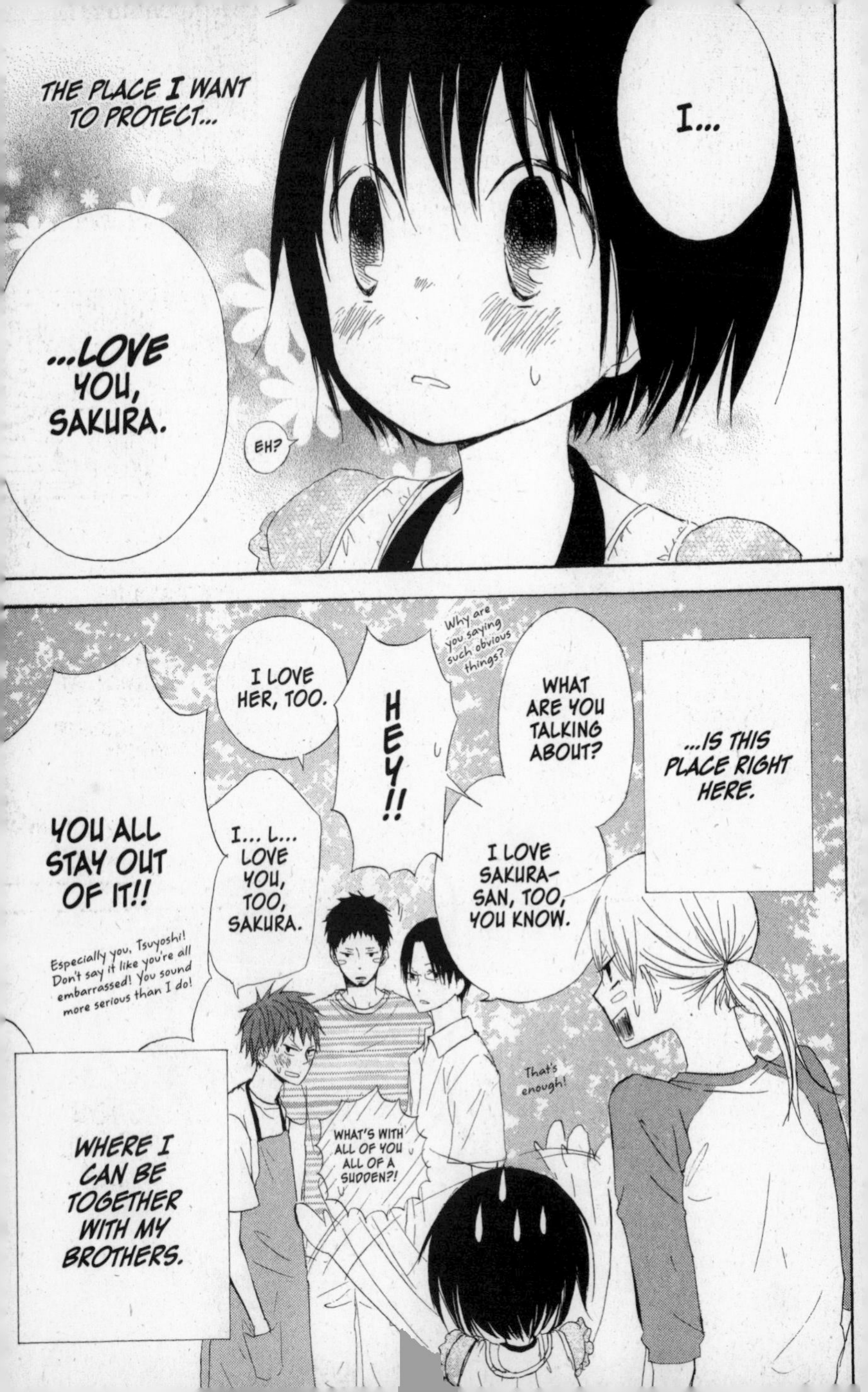
I...
THE PLACE I WANT TO PROTECT...
...LOVE YOU, SAKURA.
EH?
...IS THIS PLACE RIGHT HERE.
WHAT ARE YOU TALKING ABOUT?
Why are you saying such obvious things?
HEY!!
I LOVE HER, TOO.
I LOVE SAKURA-SAN, TOO, YOU KNOW.
I... L... LOVE YOU, TOO, SAKURA.
YOU ALL STAY OUT OF IT!!
Especially you, Tsuyoshi! Don't say it like you're all embarrassed! You sound more serious than I do!
That's enough!
WHAT'S WITH ALL OF YOU ALL OF A SUDDEN?!
WHERE I CAN BE TOGETHER WITH MY BROTHERS.

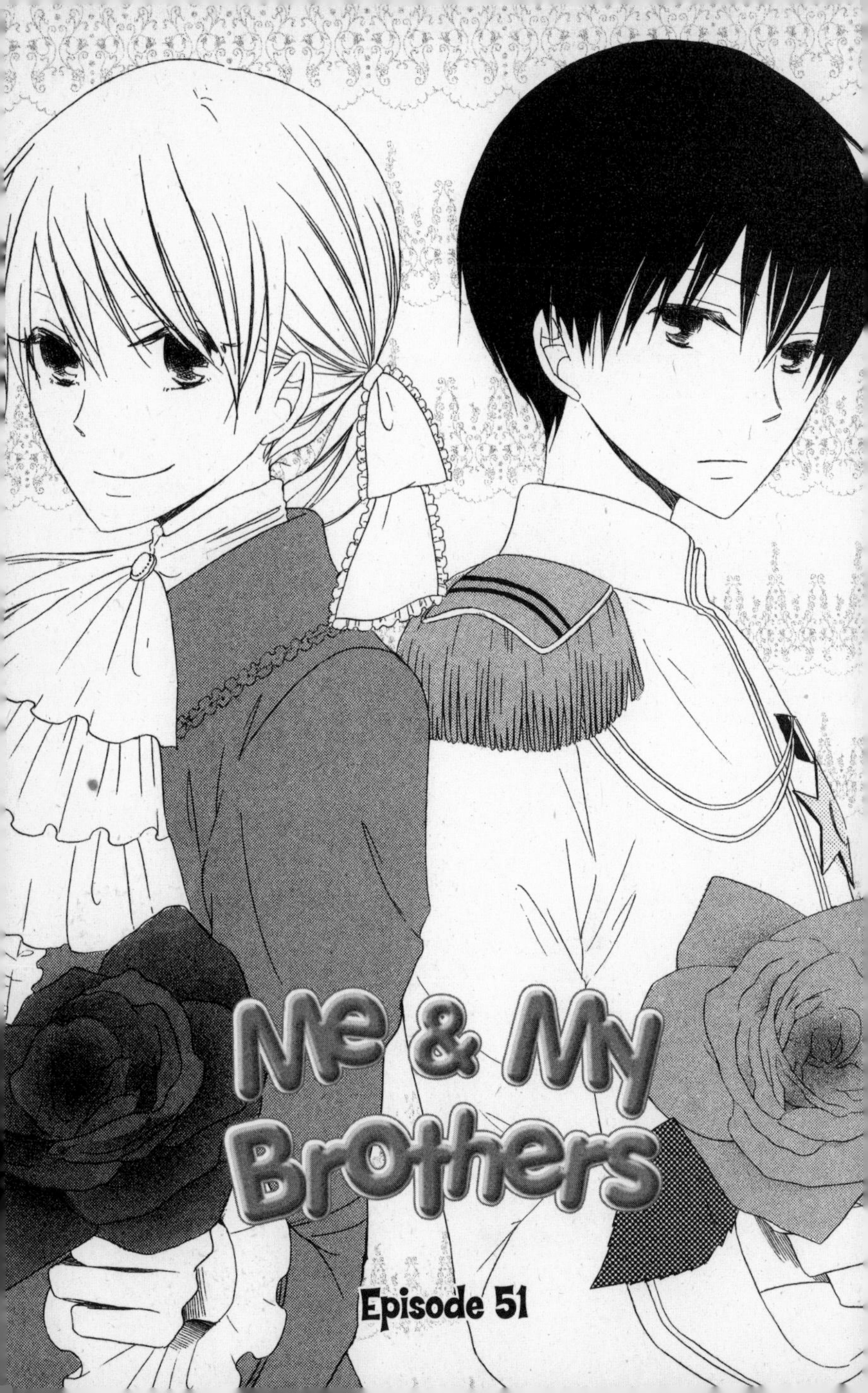
Me & My Brothers
Episode 51

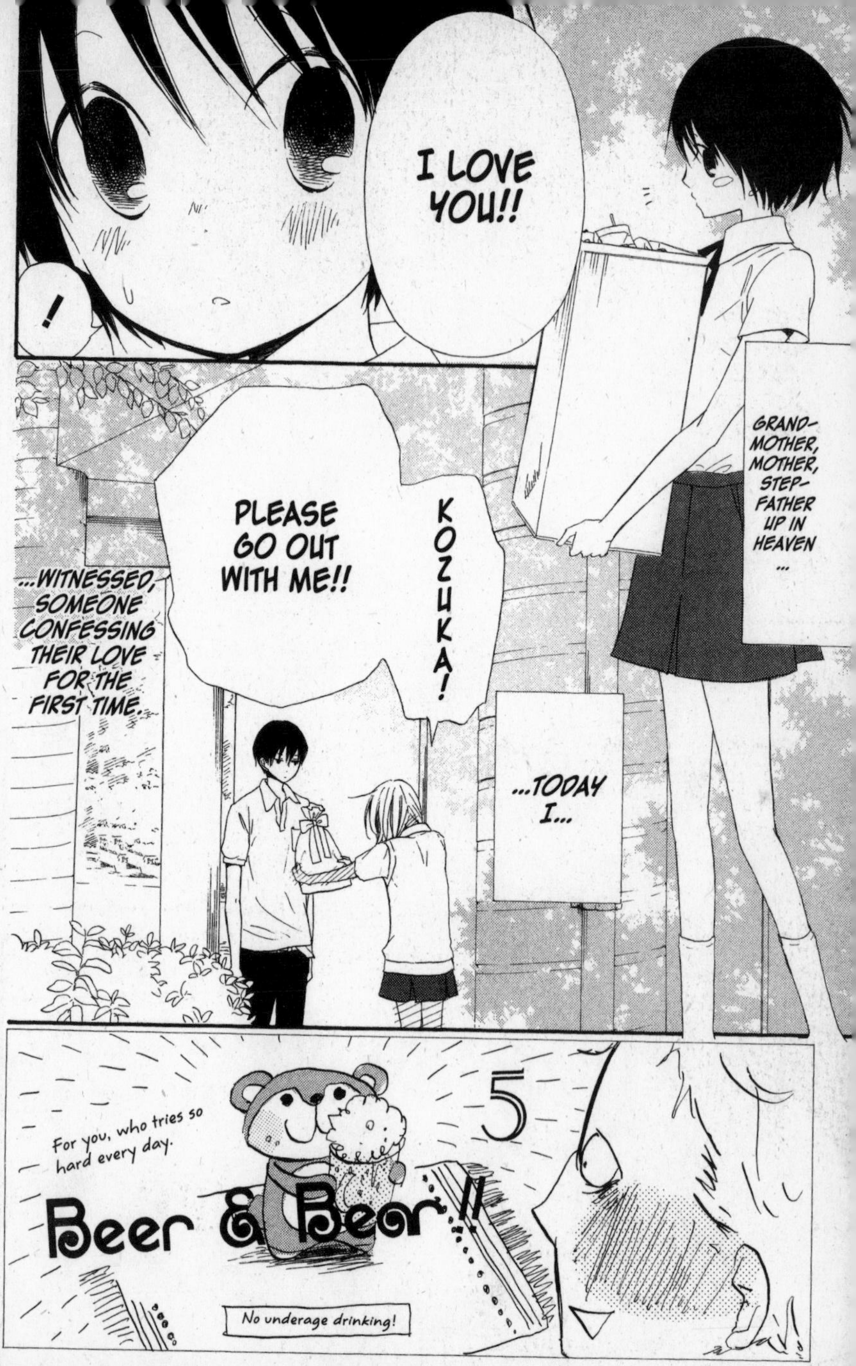
GRAND-MOTHER, MOTHER, STEP-FATHER UP IN HEAVEN ...
I LOVE YOU!!
!
...TODAY I...
KOZUKA!
PLEASE GO OUT WITH ME!!
...WITNESSED, SOMEONE CONFESSING THEIR LOVE FOR THE FIRST TIME.
5
Beer & Bear!!
For you, who tries so hard every day.
No underage drinking!

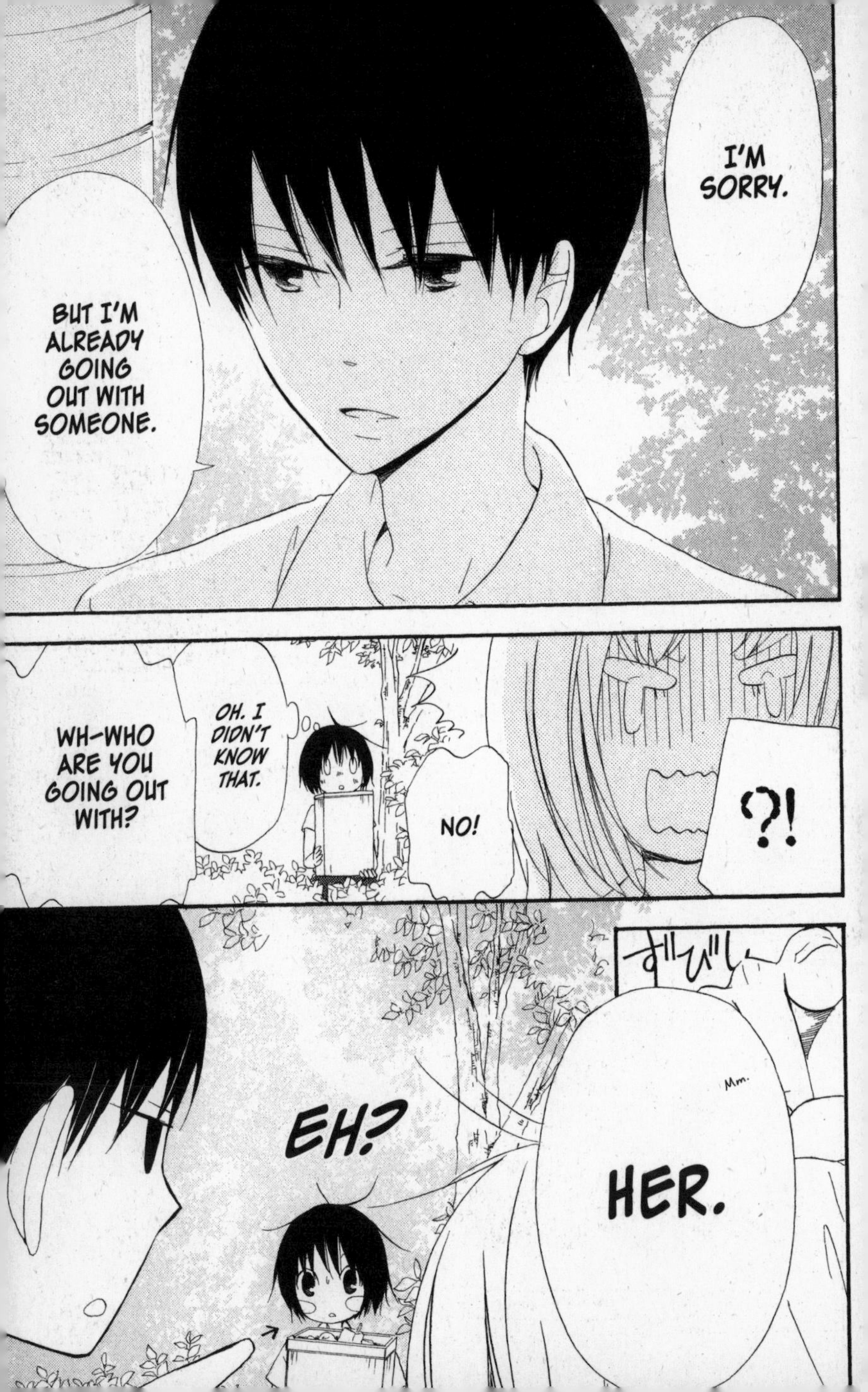
I'M SORRY.
BUT I'M ALREADY GOING OUT WITH SOMEONE.
?!
NO!
OH. I DIDN'T KNOW THAT.
WH-WHO ARE YOU GOING OUT WITH?
ずびし
Mm.
HER.
EH?

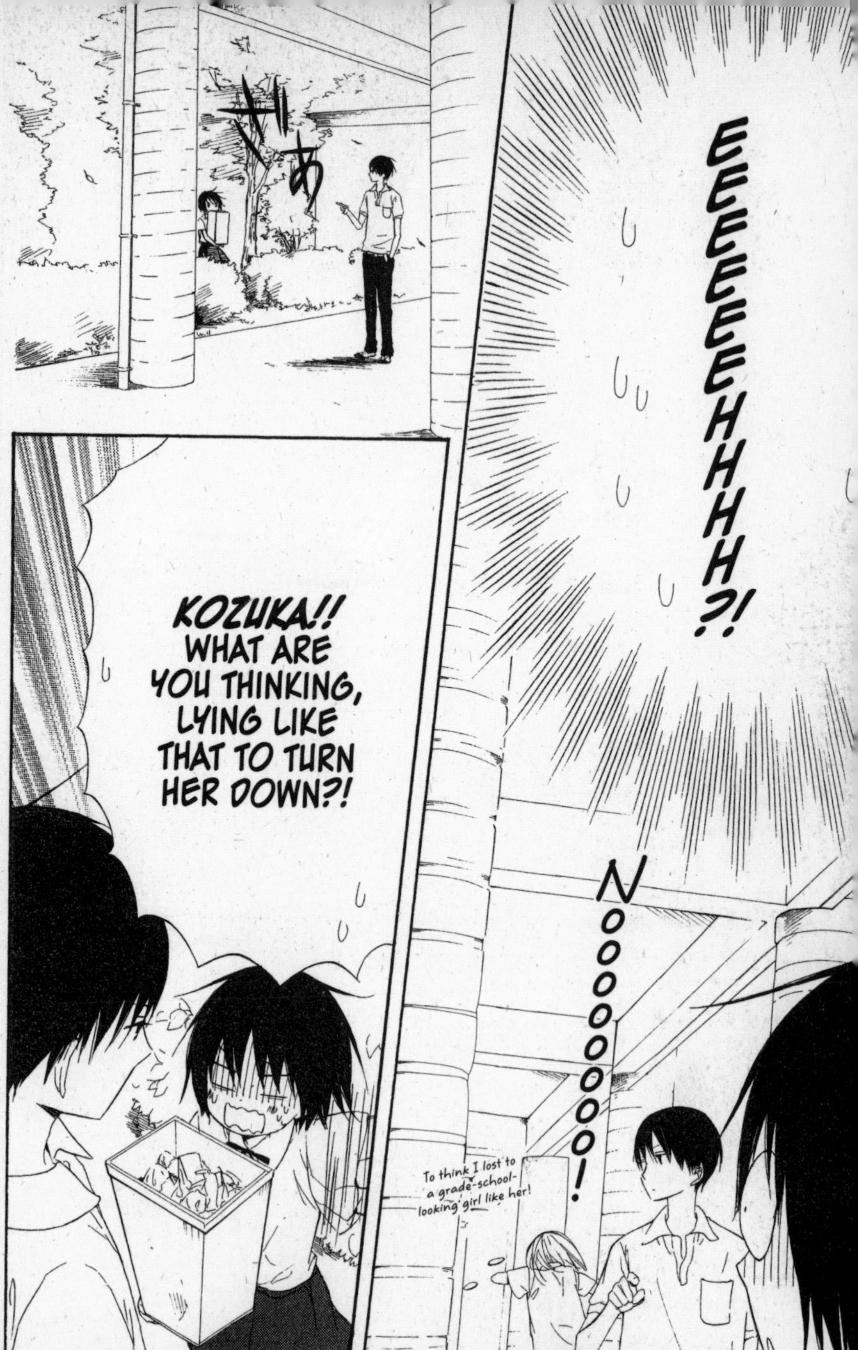
EEEEEEEHHHHH?!
NOOOOOOOOOO!
To think I lost to a grade-school-looking girl like her!
ざあ
KOZUKA!! WHAT ARE YOU THINKING, LYING LIKE THAT TO TURN HER DOWN?!

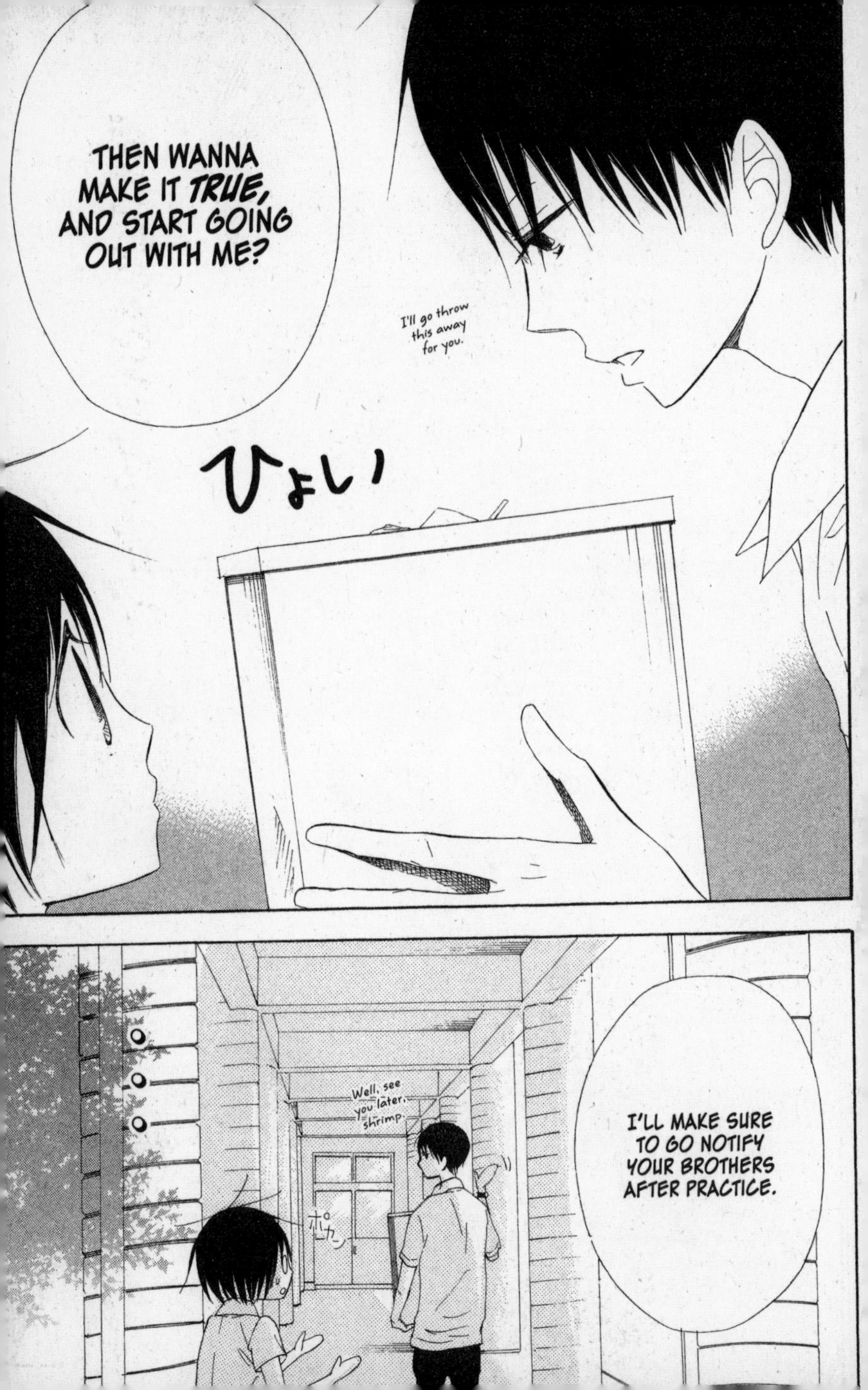
THEN WANNA MAKE IT TRUE, AND START GOING OUT WITH ME?
ひょい
I'll go throw this away for you.
I'LL MAKE SURE TO GO NOTIFY YOUR BROTHERS AFTER PRACTICE.
Well, see you later, shrimp.
ポカン

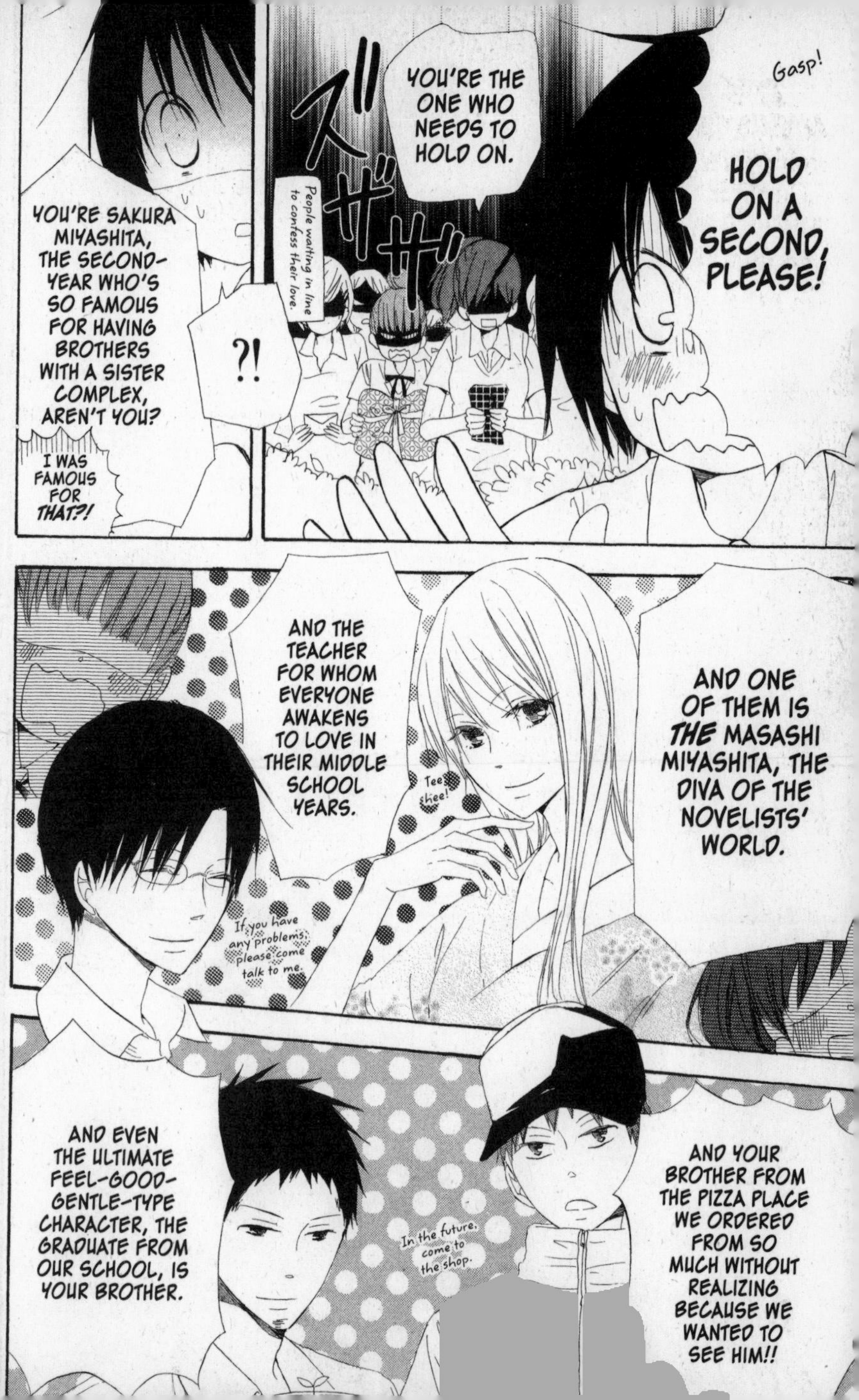
Gasp!
HOLD ON A SECOND, PLEASE!
YOU'RE THE ONE WHO NEEDS TO HOLD ON.
People waiting in line to confess their love.
?!
YOU'RE SAKURA MIYASHITA, THE SECOND-YEAR WHO'S SO FAMOUS FOR HAVING BROTHERS WITH A SISTER COMPLEX, AREN'T YOU?
I WAS FAMOUS FOR THAT?!
AND ONE OF THEM IS THE MASASHI MIYASHITA, THE DIVA OF THE NOVELISTS' WORLD.
Tee hee!
AND THE TEACHER FOR WHOM EVERYONE AWAKENS TO LOVE IN THEIR MIDDLE SCHOOL YEARS.
If you have any problems, please come talk to me.
AND YOUR BROTHER FROM THE PIZZA PLACE WE ORDERED FROM SO MUCH WITHOUT REALIZING BECAUSE WE WANTED TO SEE HIM!!
In the future, come to the shop.
AND EVEN THE ULTIMATE FEEL-GOOD-GENTLE-TYPE CHARACTER, THE GRADUATE FROM OUR SCHOOL, IS YOUR BROTHER.

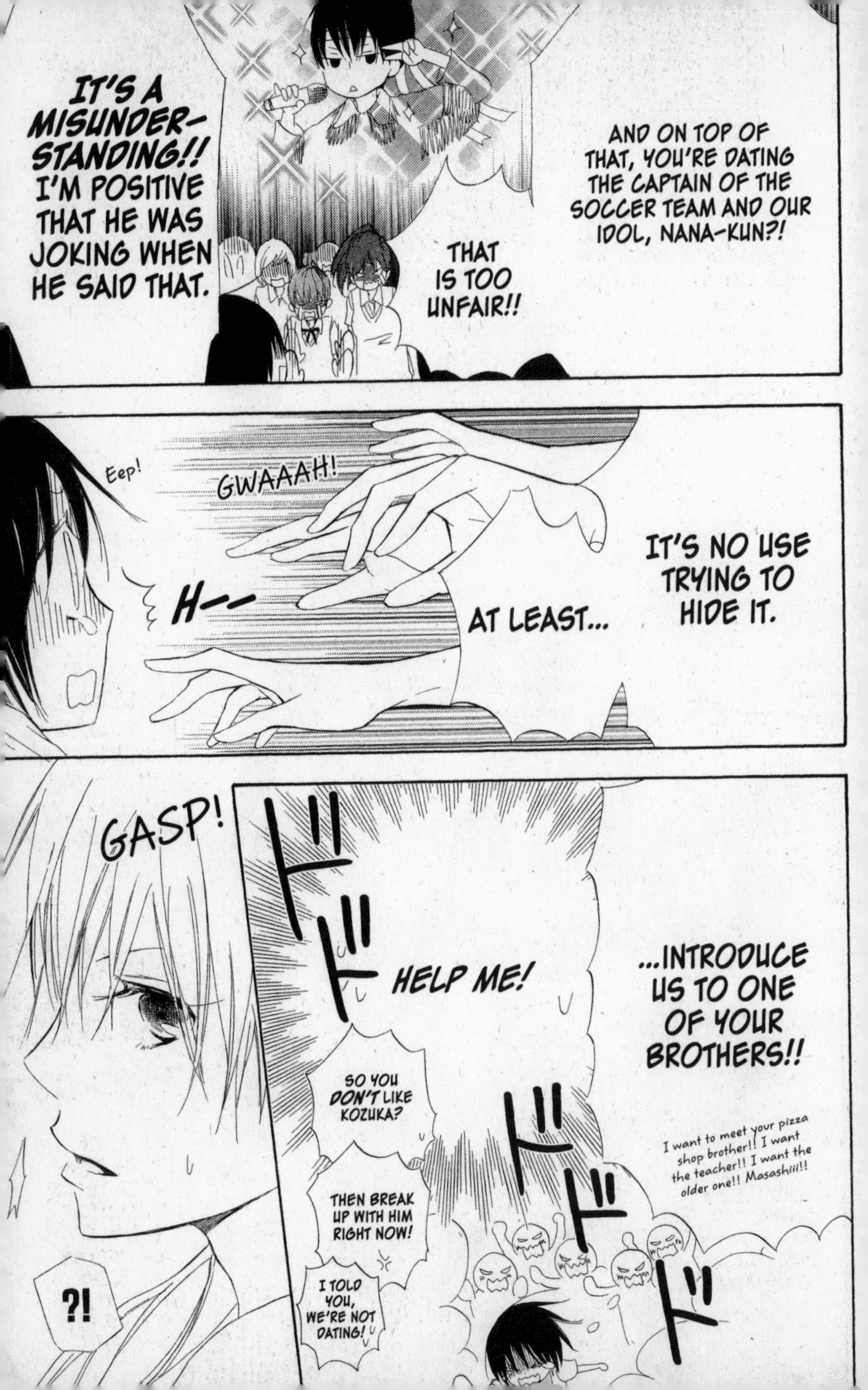

AND ON TOP OF THAT, YOU'RE DATING THE CAPTAIN OF THE SOCCER TEAM AND OUR IDOL, NANA-KUN?!
THAT IS TOO UNFAIR!!
IT'S A MISUNDERSTANDING!! I'M POSITIVE THAT HE WAS JOKING WHEN HE SAID THAT.
IT'S NO USE TRYING TO HIDE IT.
AT LEAST...
GWAAAH!
Eep!
H--
...INTRODUCE US TO ONE OF YOUR BROTHERS!!
I want to meet your pizza shop brother!! I want the teacher!! I want the older one!! Masashiiii!!
ドド
ドド
HELP ME!
SO YOU DON'T LIKE KOZUKA?
THEN BREAK UP WITH HIM RIGHT NOW!
I TOLD YOU, WE'RE NOT DATING!
GASP!
?!

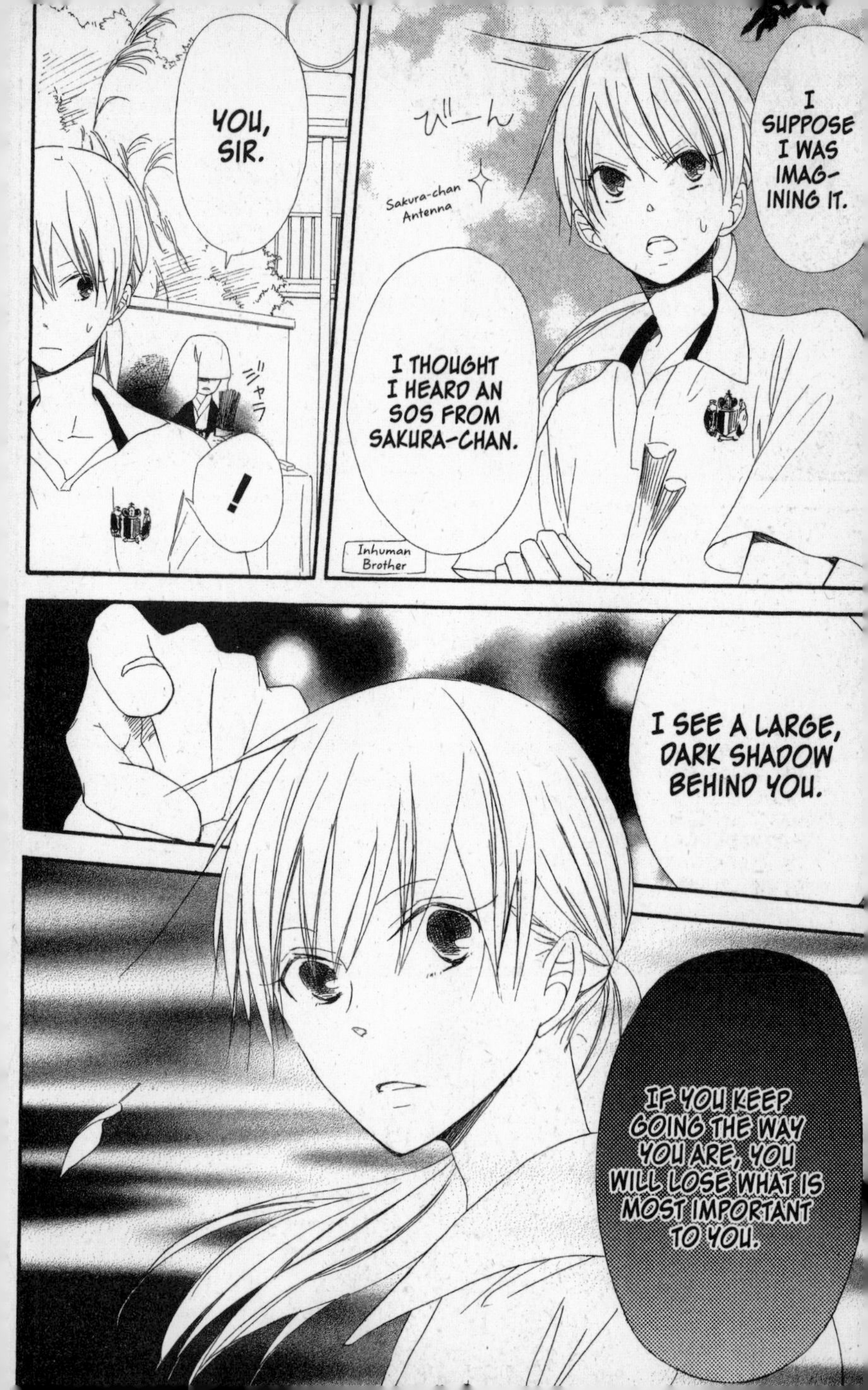
I SUPPOSE I WAS IMAGINING IT.
びーん
Sakura-chan Antenna
I THOUGHT I HEARD AN SOS FROM SAKURA-CHAN.
Inhuman Brother
YOU, SIR.
ジャラ
!
I SEE A LARGE, DARK SHADOW BEHIND YOU.
IF YOU KEEP GOING THE WAY YOU ARE, YOU WILL LOSE WHAT IS MOST IMPORTANT TO YOU.

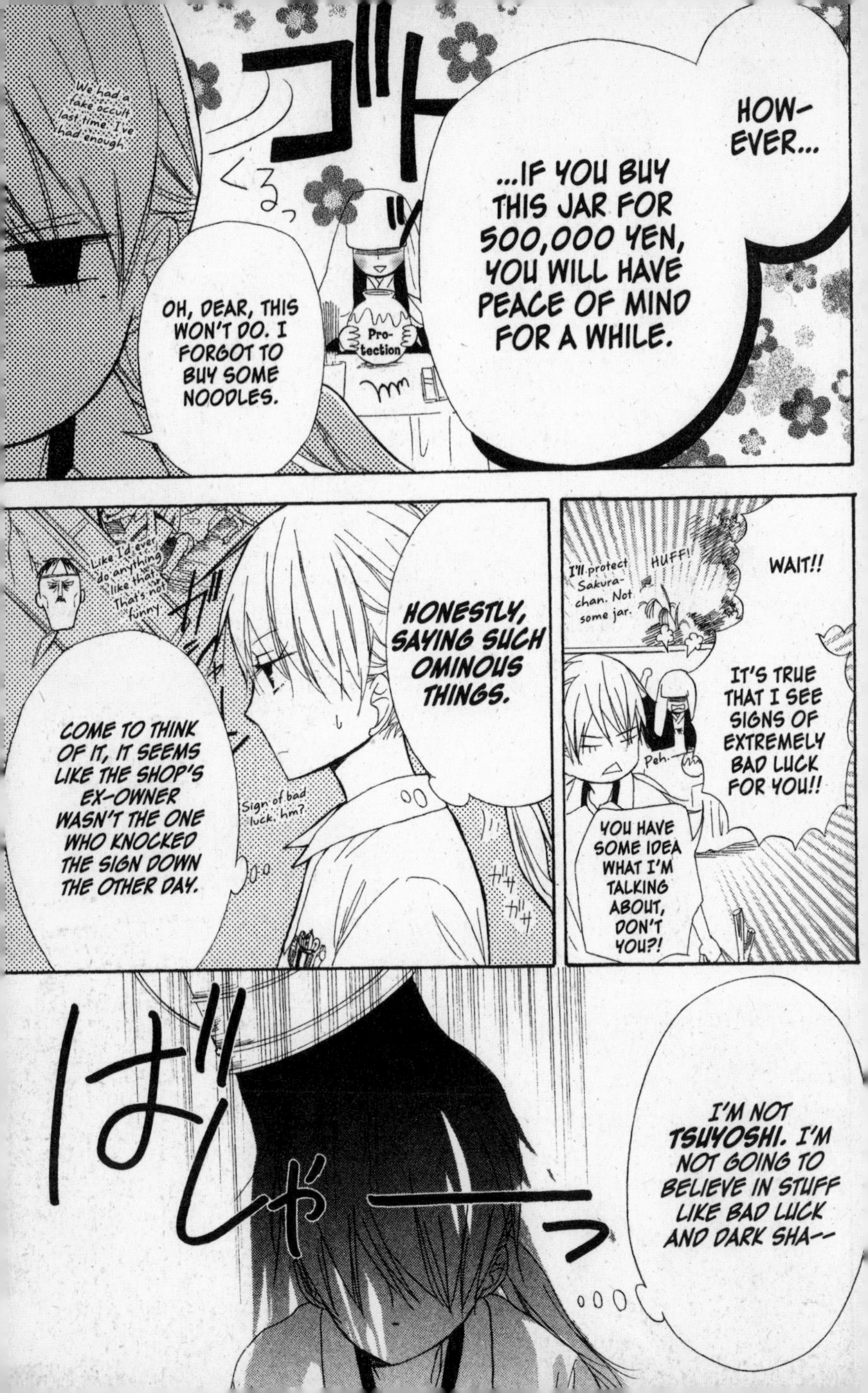
HOW-EVER...
...IF YOU BUY THIS JAR FOR 500,000 YEN, YOU WILL HAVE PEACE OF MIND FOR A WHILE.
ゴト
Pro-tection
くるっ
OH, DEAR, THIS WON'T DO. I FORGOT TO BUY SOME NOODLES.
We had a fake occult last time. I've had enough.
WAIT!!
IT'S TRUE THAT I SEE SIGNS OF EXTREMELY BAD LUCK FOR YOU!!
HUFF!
I'll protect Sakura-chan. Not some jar.
Peh.
YOU HAVE SOME IDEA WHAT I'M TALKING ABOUT, DON'T YOU?!
HONESTLY, SAYING SUCH OMINOUS THINGS.
Like I'd ever do anything like that. That's not funny.
Sign of bad luck, hm?
COME TO THINK OF IT, IT SEEMS LIKE THE SHOP'S EX-OWNER WASN'T THE ONE WHO KNOCKED THE SIGN DOWN THE OTHER DAY.
I'M NOT TSUYOSHI. I'M NOT GOING TO BELIEVE IN STUFF LIKE BAD LUCK AND DARK SHA--
はじゃーっ

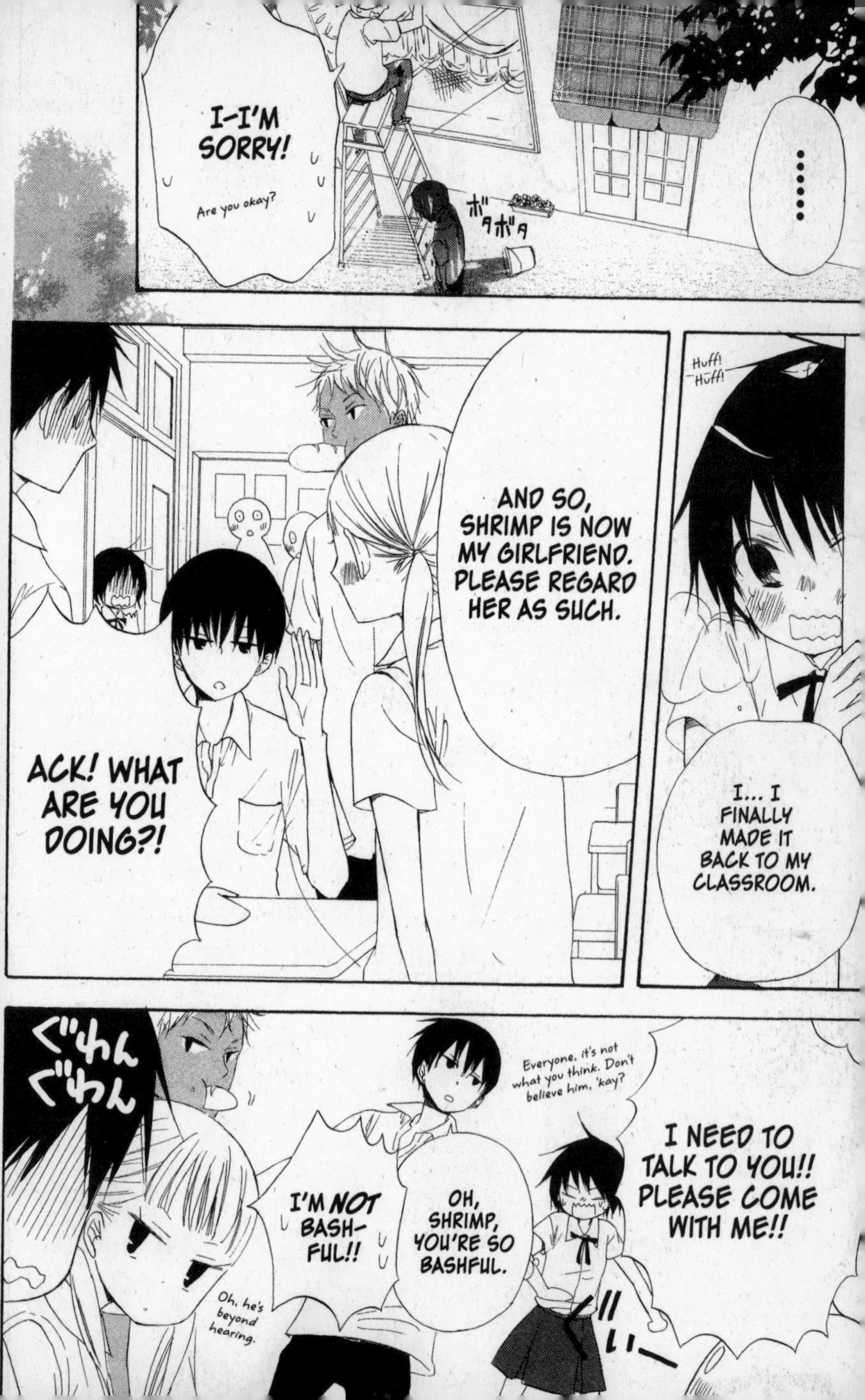
……
ボタボタ
I-I'M SORRY!
Are you okay?
Huff! Huff!
I... I FINALLY MADE IT BACK TO MY CLASSROOM.
AND SO, SHRIMP IS NOW MY GIRLFRIEND. PLEASE REGARD HER AS SUCH.
ACK! WHAT ARE YOU DOING?!
I NEED TO TALK TO YOU!! PLEASE COME WITH ME!!
Everyone, it's not what you think. Don't believe him, 'kay?
OH, SHRIMP, YOU'RE SO BASHFUL.
I'M NOT BASHFUL!!
ぐわんぐわん
Oh, he's beyond hearing.

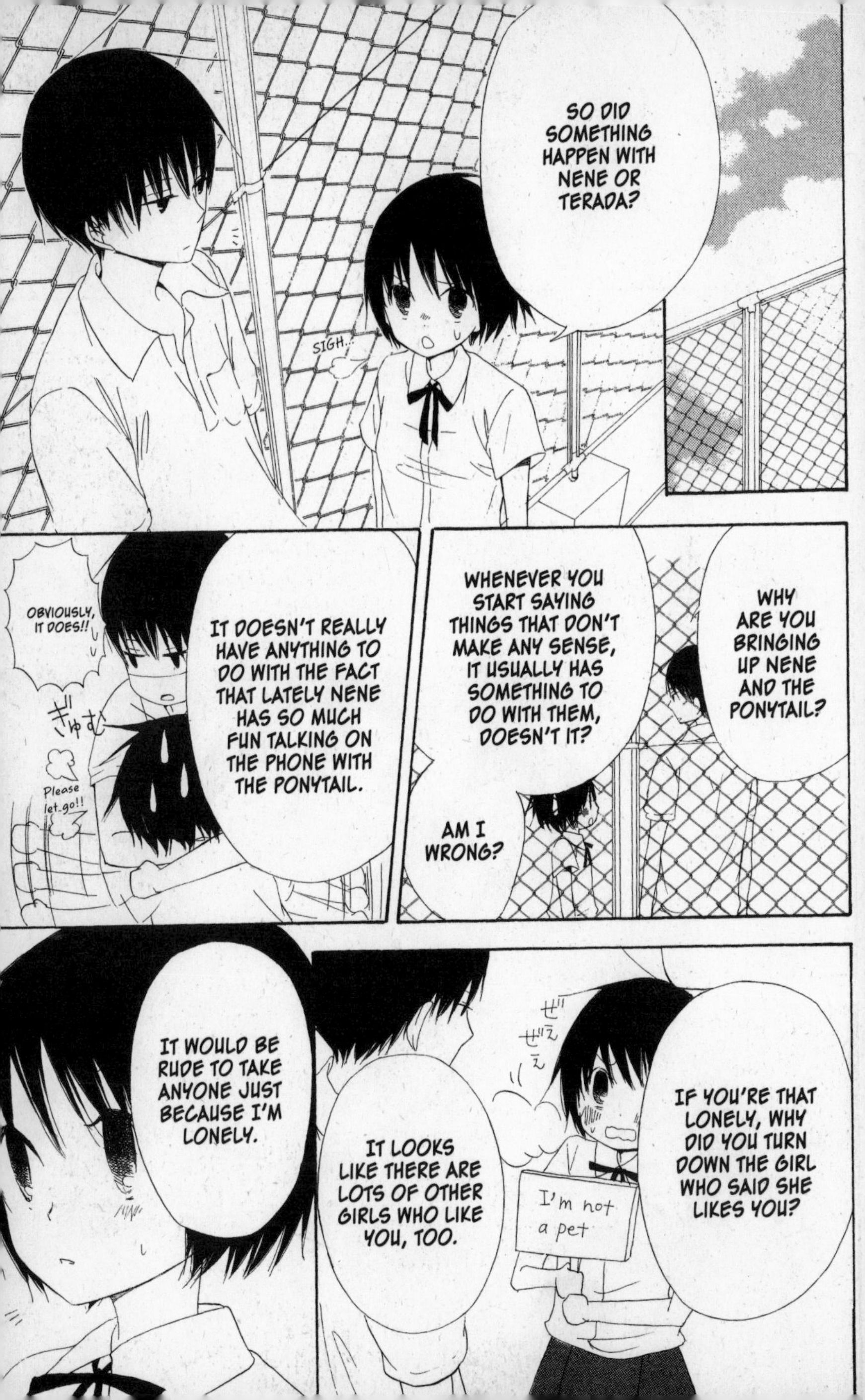
SO DID SOMETHING HAPPEN WITH NENE OR TERADA?
SIGH...
WHY ARE YOU BRINGING UP NENE AND THE PONYTAIL?
WHENEVER YOU START SAYING THINGS THAT DON'T MAKE ANY SENSE, IT USUALLY HAS SOMETHING TO DO WITH THEM, DOESN'T IT?
AM I WRONG?
IT DOESN'T REALLY HAVE ANYTHING TO DO WITH THE FACT THAT LATELY NENE HAS SO MUCH FUN TALKING ON THE PHONE WITH THE PONYTAIL.
OBVIOUSLY, IT DOES!!
ぎゅむ
Please let go!!
IF YOU'RE THAT LONELY, WHY DID YOU TURN DOWN THE GIRL WHO SAID SHE LIKES YOU?
ぜぇ ぜぇ
I'm not a pet
IT LOOKS LIKE THERE ARE LOTS OF OTHER GIRLS WHO LIKE YOU, TOO.
IT WOULD BE RUDE TO TAKE ANYONE JUST BECAUSE I'M LONELY.

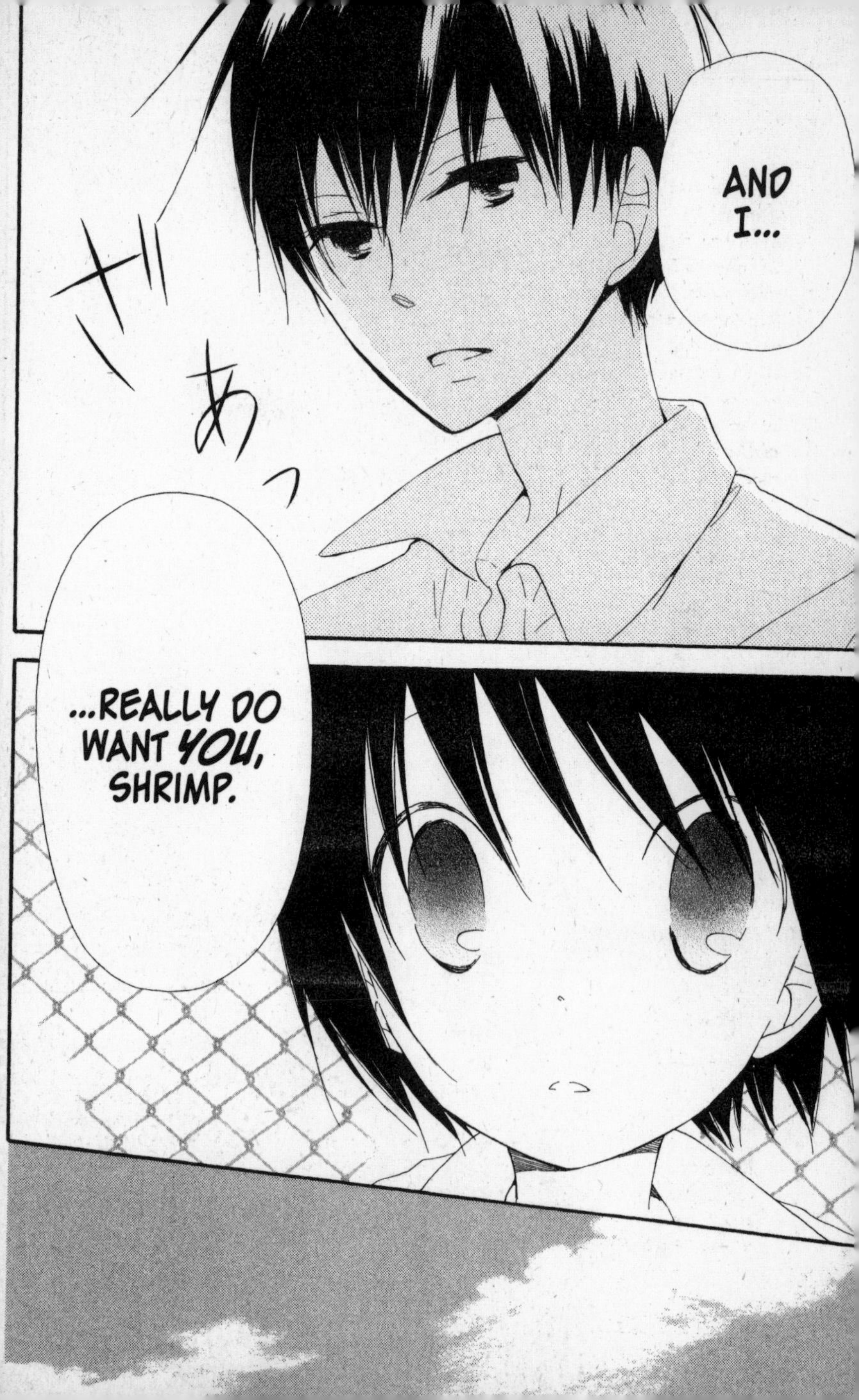
AND I...
あっ
...REALLY DO WANT YOU, SHRIMP.

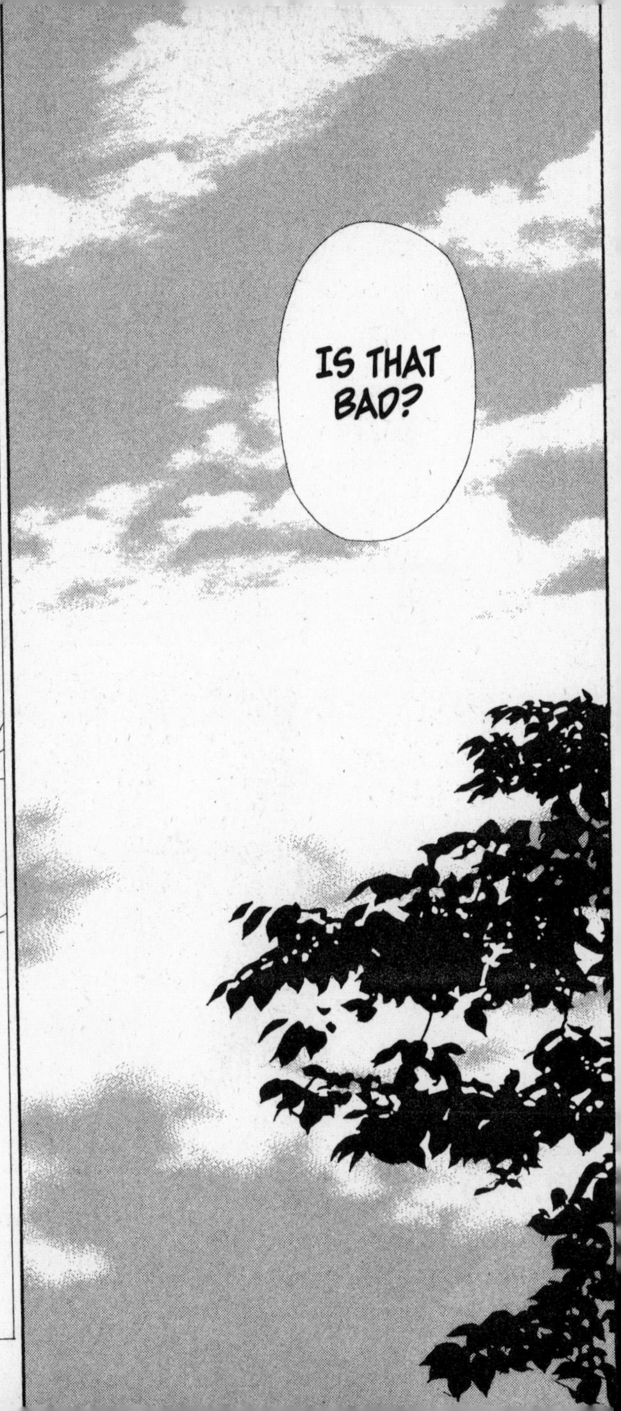
IS THAT BAD?

5

When I was drawing Masashi in Chapter 52, sometimes I felt like something was off, but when I drew him again in women's clothes, it all really worked.

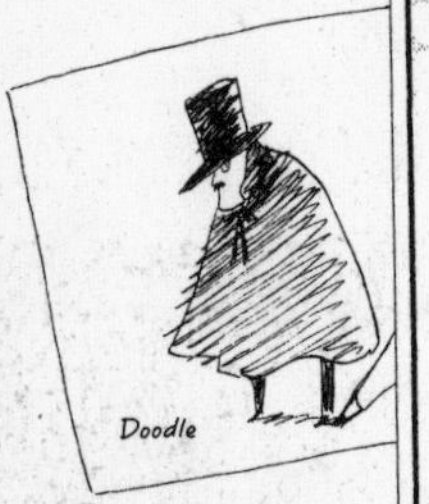
Doodle

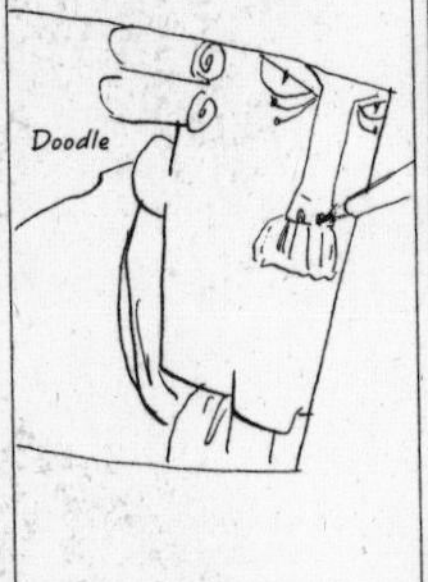
Doodle

He really is very much a drag queen in my head.

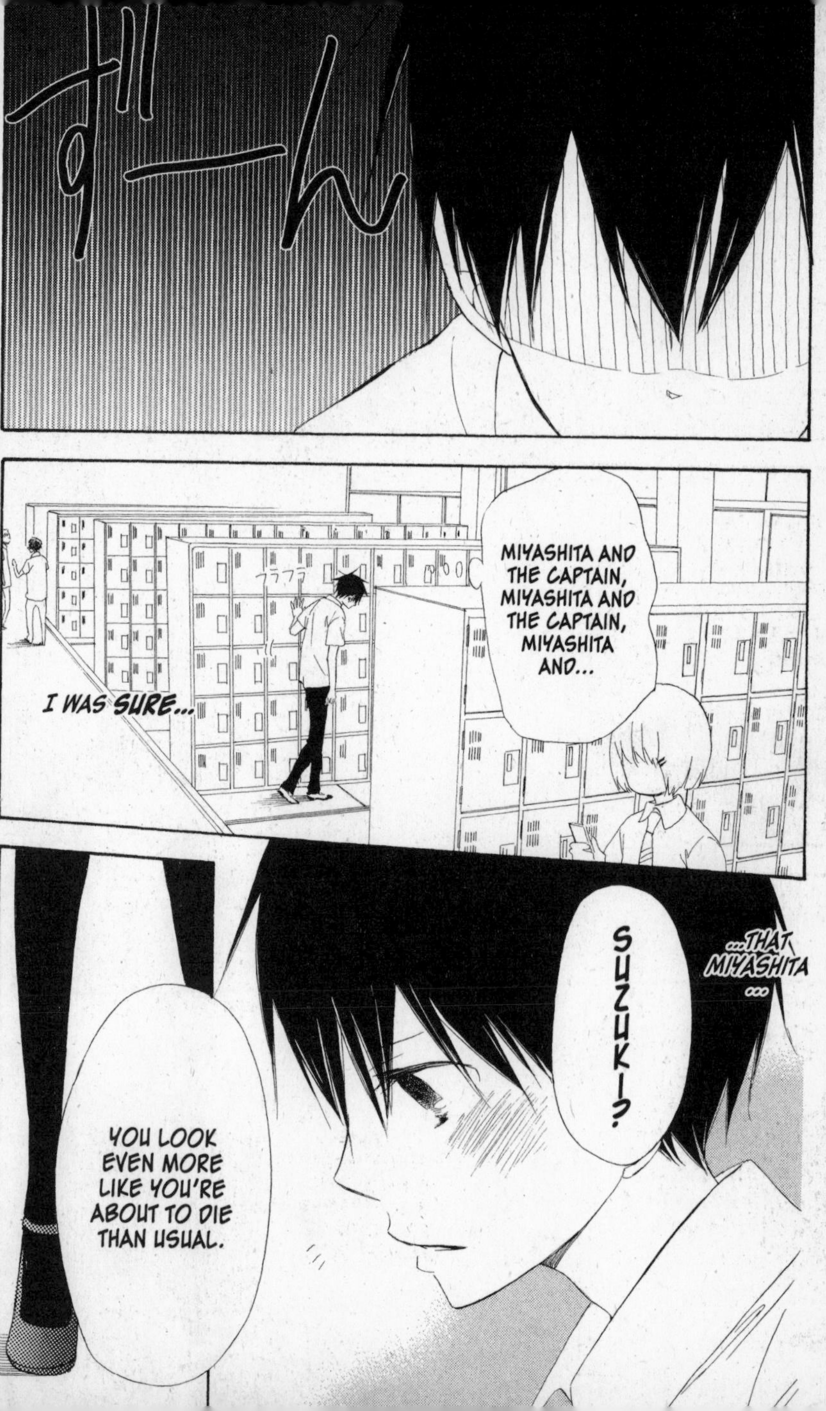
ずーん
MIYASHITA AND THE CAPTAIN, MIYASHITA AND THE CAPTAIN, MIYASHITA AND...
フラフラ
I WAS SURE...
...THAT MIYASHITA ...
SUZUKI?
YOU LOOK EVEN MORE LIKE YOU'RE ABOUT TO DIE THAN USUAL.

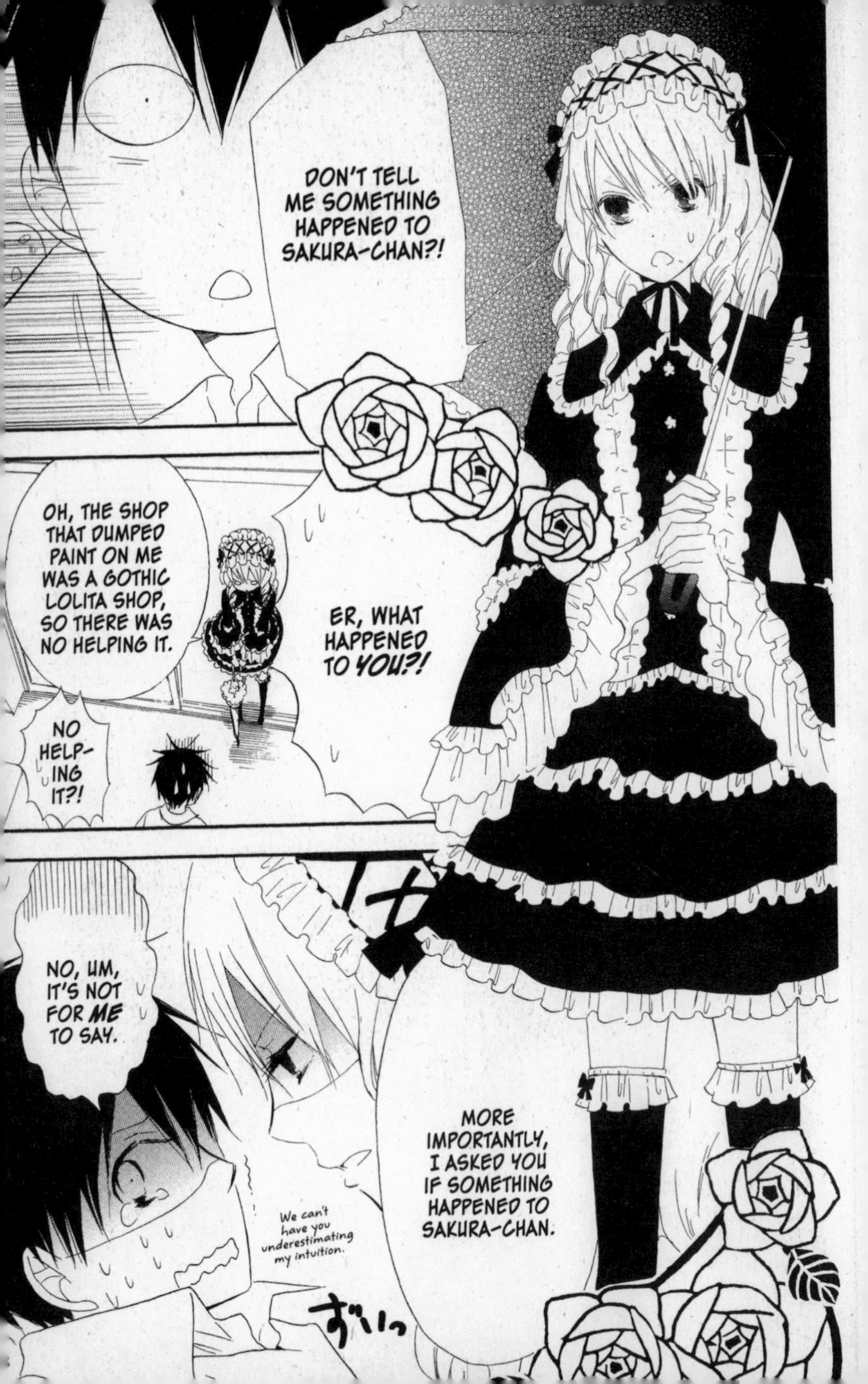
DON'T TELL ME SOMETHING HAPPENED TO SAKURA-CHAN?!
ER, WHAT HAPPENED TO *YOU*?!
OH, THE SHOP THAT DUMPED PAINT ON ME WAS A GOTHIC LOLITA SHOP, SO THERE WAS NO HELPING IT.
NO HELPING IT?!
NO, UM, IT'S NOT FOR *ME* TO SAY.
MORE IMPORTANTLY, I ASKED YOU IF SOMETHING HAPPENED TO SAKURA-CHAN.
We can't have you underestimating my intuition.
ずいっ

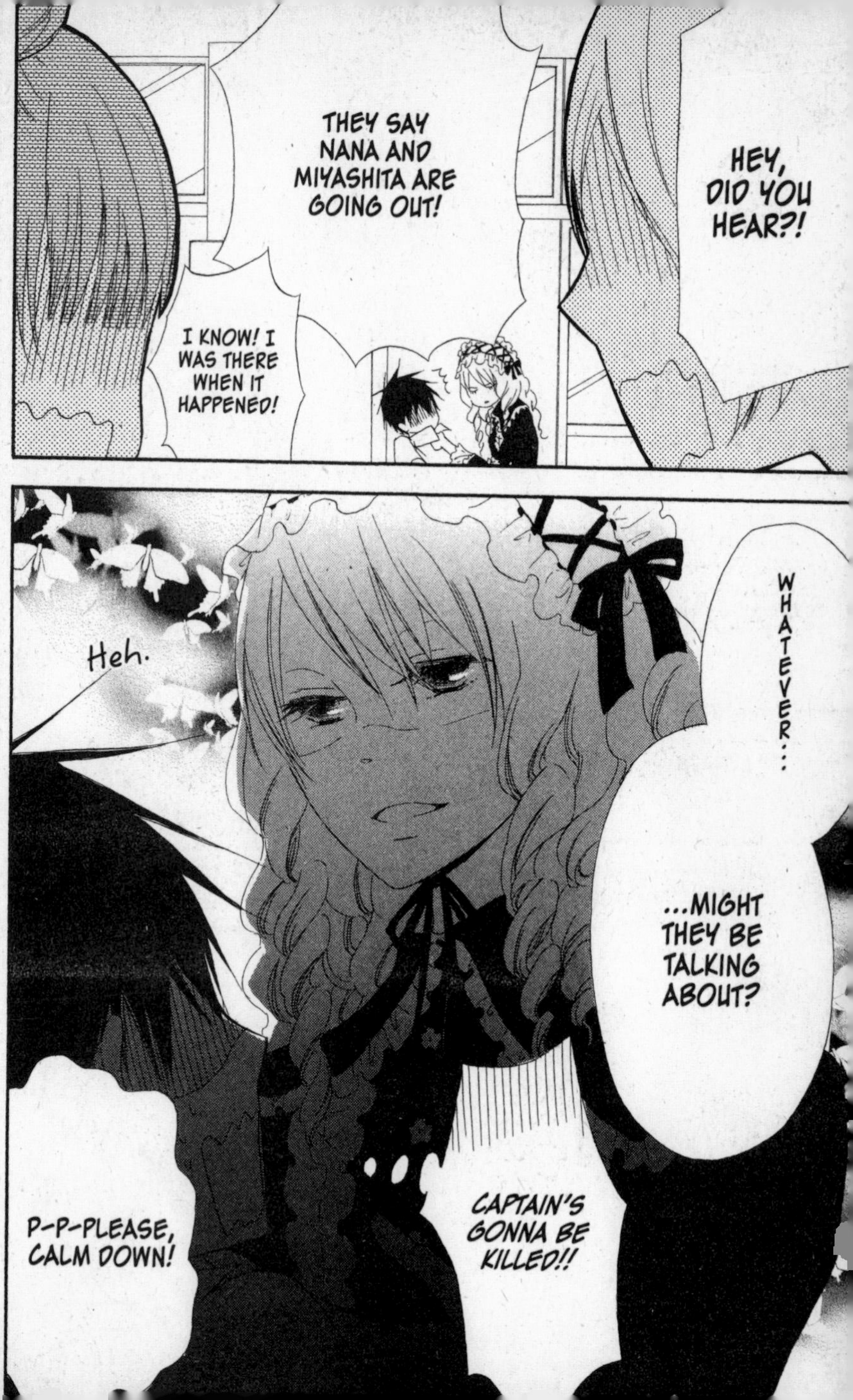
HEY, DID YOU HEAR?!
THEY SAY NANA AND MIYASHITA ARE GOING OUT!
I KNOW! I WAS THERE WHEN IT HAPPENED!
WHATEVER...
...MIGHT THEY BE TALKING ABOUT?
Heh.
CAPTAIN'S GONNA BE KILLED!!
P-P-PLEASE, CALM DOWN!

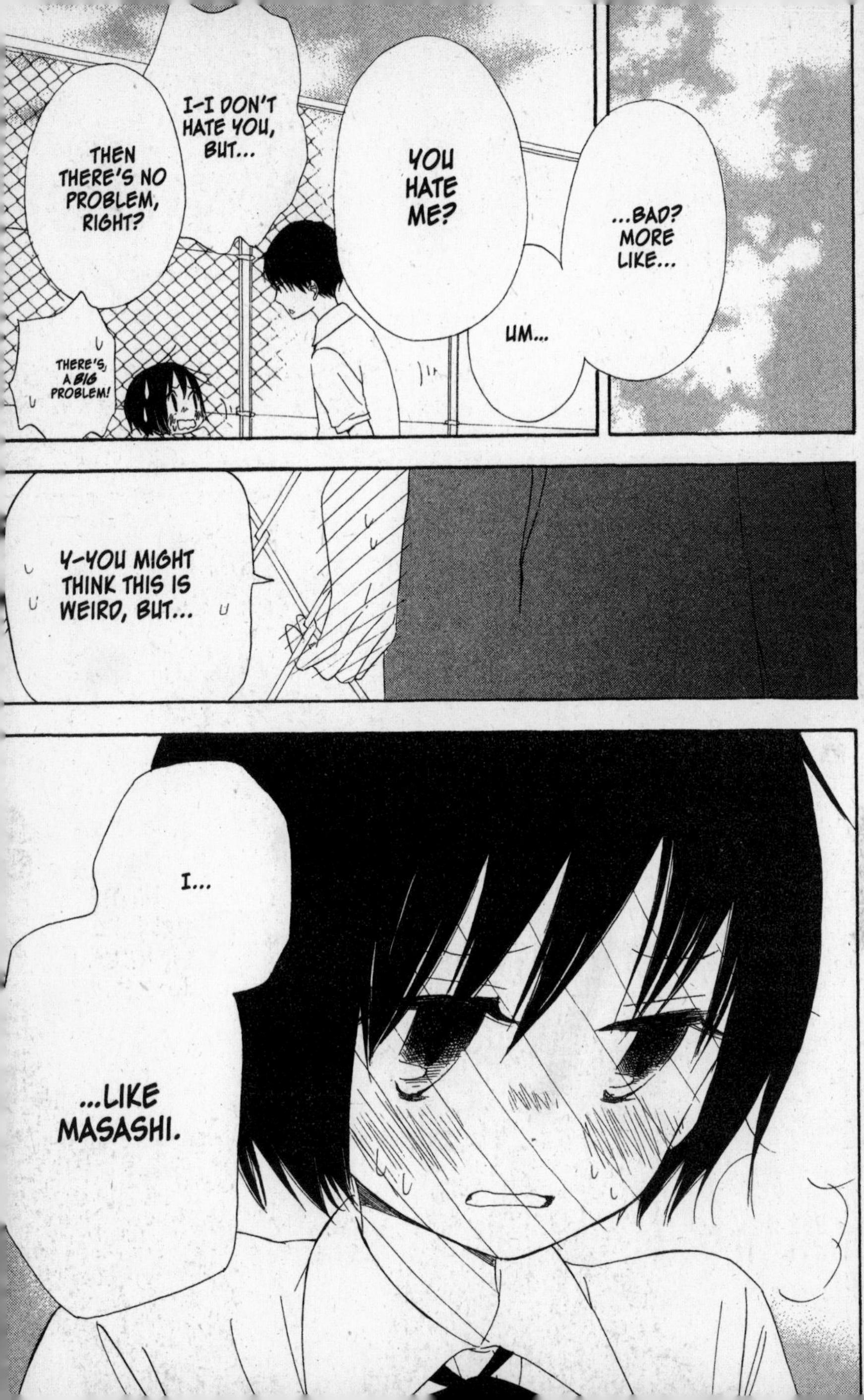

...BAD? MORE LIKE...
UM...
YOU HATE ME?
I-I DON'T HATE YOU, BUT...
THEN THERE'S NO PROBLEM, RIGHT?
THERE'S, A BIG PROBLEM!
Y-YOU MIGHT THINK THIS IS WEIRD, BUT...
I...
...LIKE MASASHI.

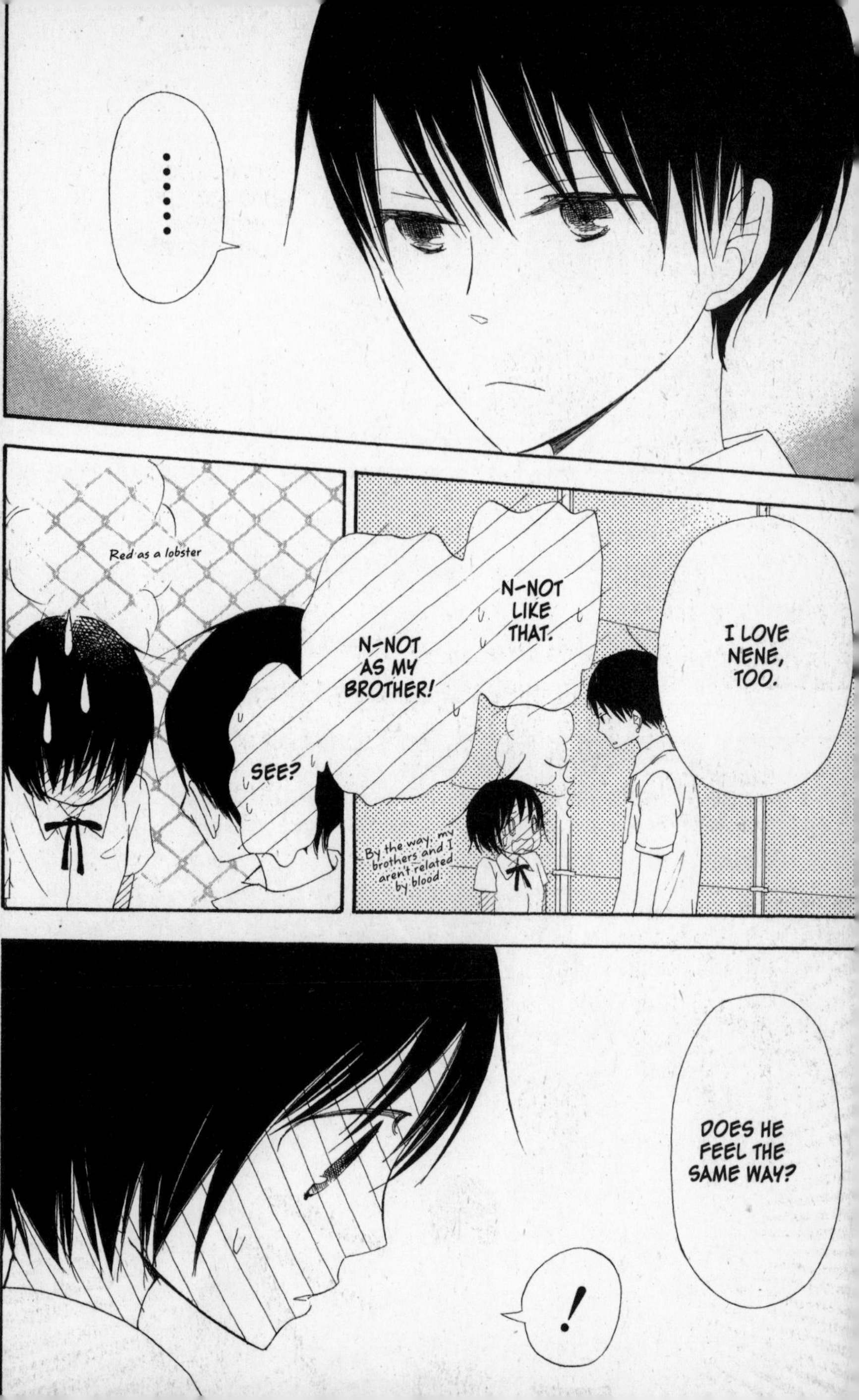
……
I LOVE NENE, TOO.
N-NOT LIKE THAT.
N-NOT AS MY BROTHER!
By the way, my brothers and I aren't related by blood.
SEE?
Red as a lobster
DOES HE FEEL THE SAME WAY?
!

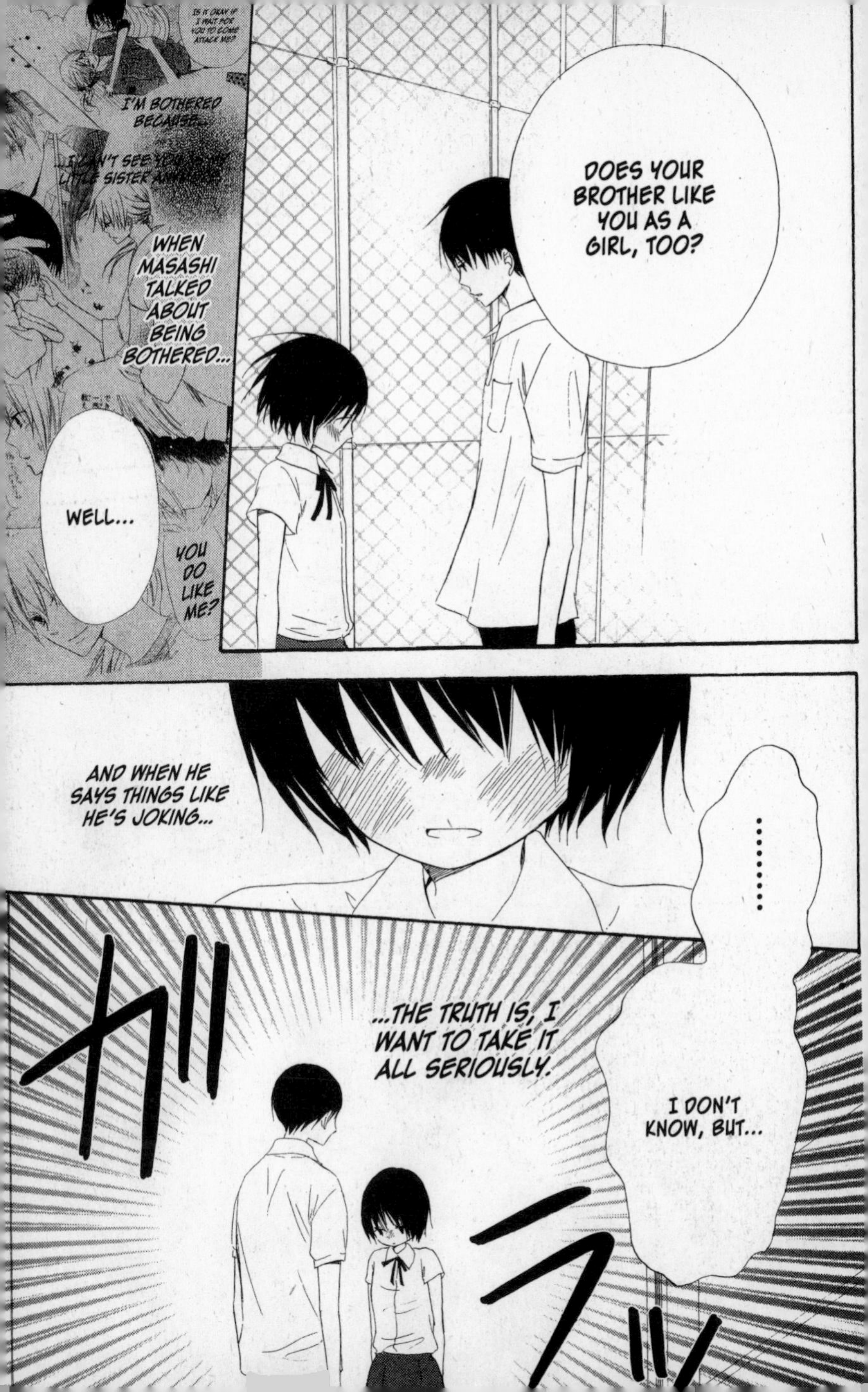
DOES YOUR BROTHER LIKE YOU AS A GIRL, TOO?
IS IT OKAY IF I WAIT FOR YOU TO COME ATTACK ME?
I'M BOTHERED BECAUSE...
...I CAN'T SEE YOU AS MY LITTLE SISTER ANYMORE
WHEN MASASHI TALKED ABOUT BEING BOTHERED...
WELL...
YOU DO LIKE ME?
......
AND WHEN HE SAYS THINGS LIKE HE'S JOKING...
I DON'T KNOW, BUT...
...THE TRUTH IS, I WANT TO TAKE IT ALL SERIOUSLY.

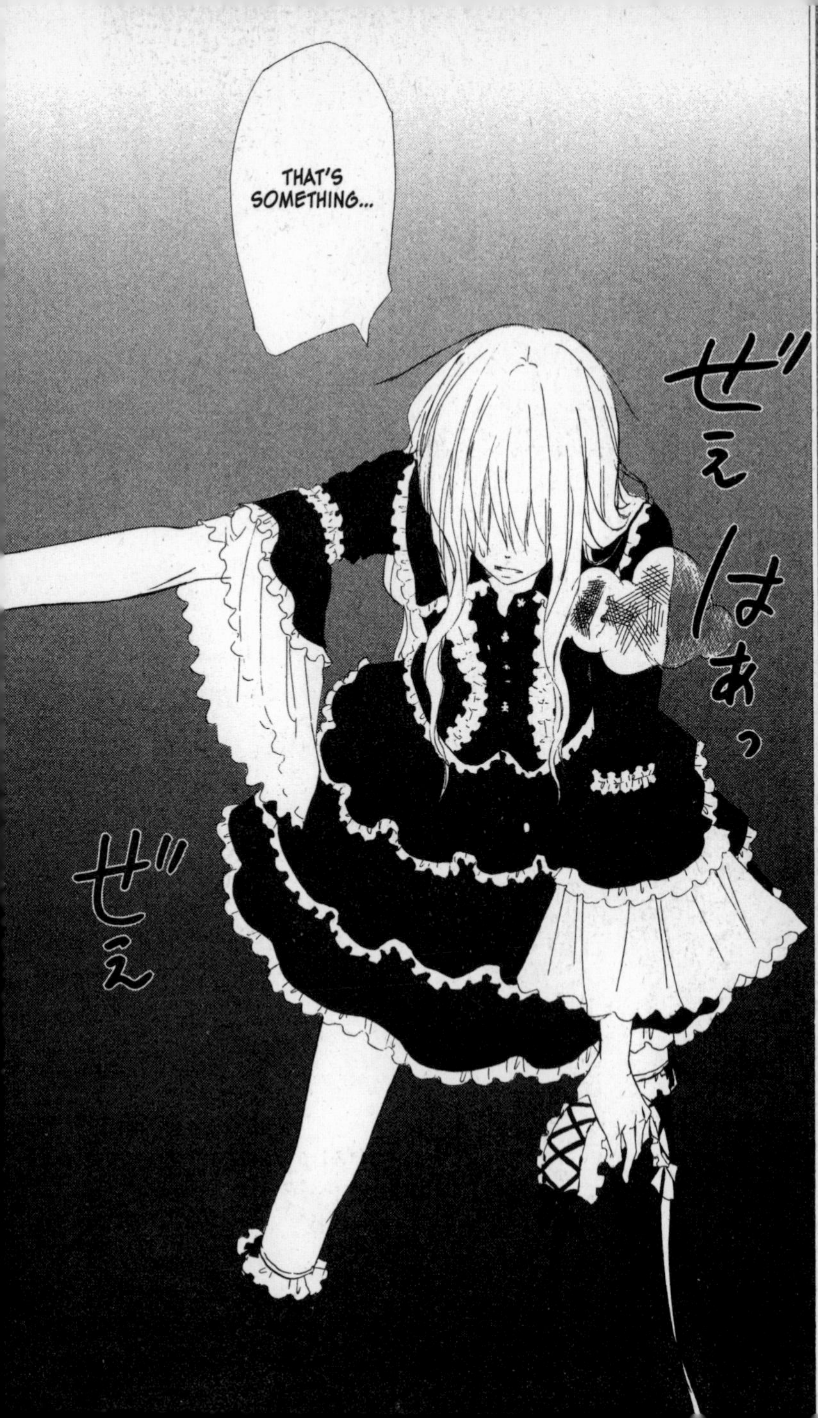

THAT'S SOMETHING...
ぜぇはぁっ
ぜぇ

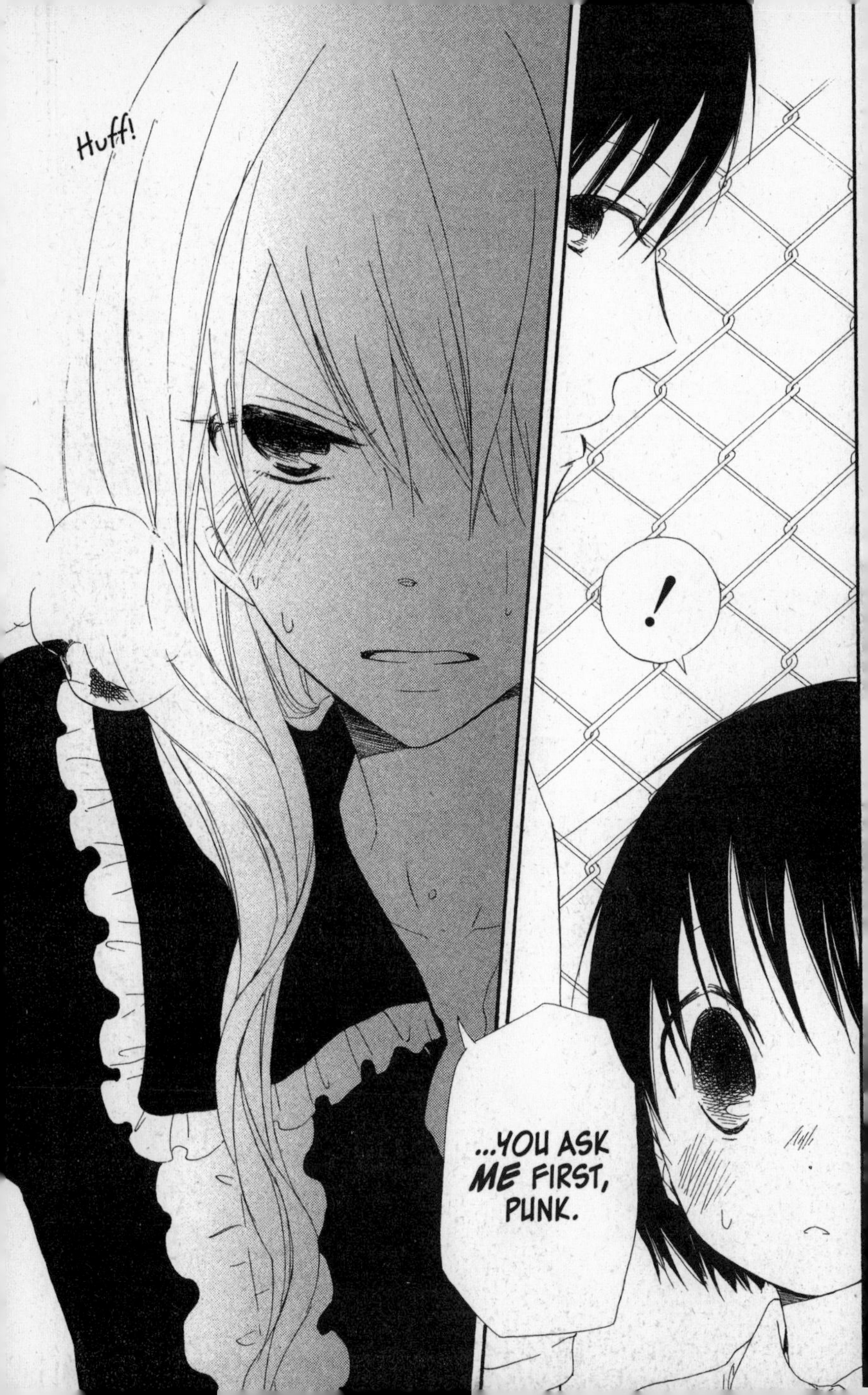
!
Huff!
...YOU ASK ME FIRST, PUNK.

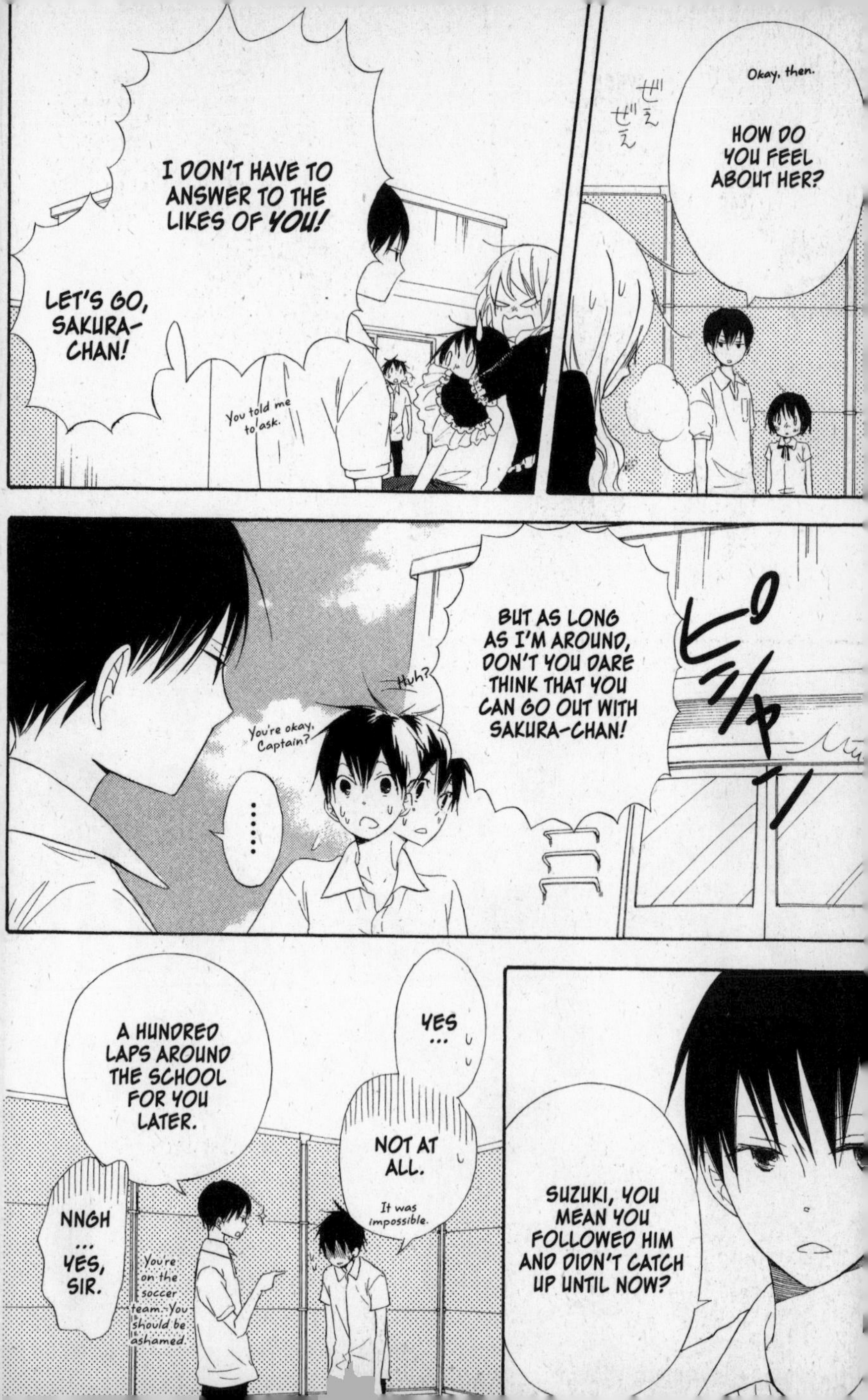

Okay, then.
HOW DO YOU FEEL ABOUT HER?
ぜぇ ぜぇ
I DON'T HAVE TO ANSWER TO THE LIKES OF YOU!
LET'S GO, SAKURA-CHAN!
You told me to ask.
ピシャーン
BUT AS LONG AS I'M AROUND, DON'T YOU DARE THINK THAT YOU CAN GO OUT WITH SAKURA-CHAN!
Huh?
You're okay, Captain?
......
SUZUKI, YOU MEAN YOU FOLLOWED HIM AND DIDN'T CATCH UP UNTIL NOW?
NOT AT ALL.
It was impossible.
You're on the soccer team. You should be ashamed.
A HUNDRED LAPS AROUND THE SCHOOL FOR YOU LATER.
NNGH ... YES, SIR.
YES ...

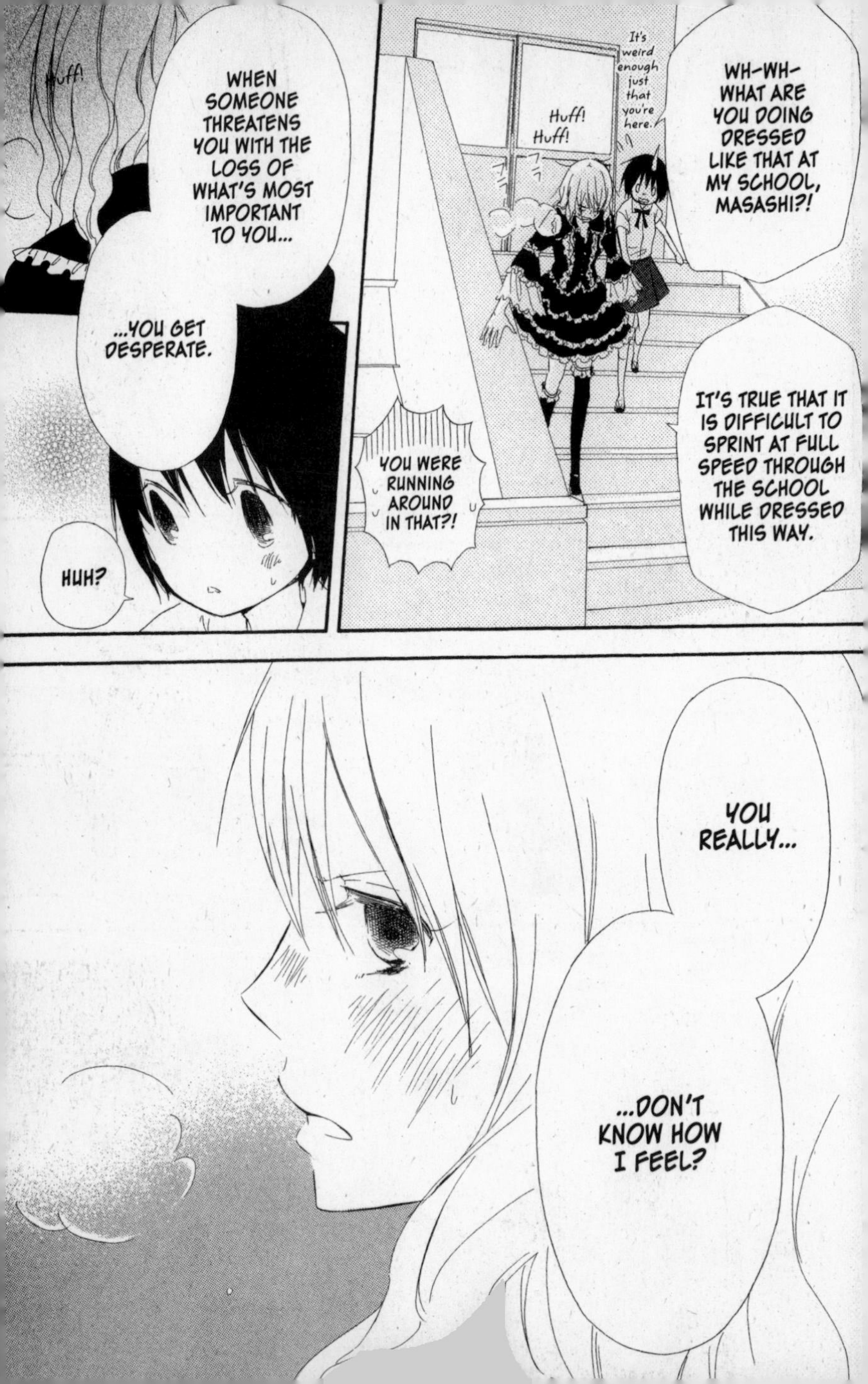
WH-WH-WHAT ARE YOU DOING DRESSED LIKE THAT AT MY SCHOOL, MASASHI?!
It's weird enough just that you're here.
Huff! Huff!
IT'S TRUE THAT IT IS DIFFICULT TO SPRINT AT FULL SPEED THROUGH THE SCHOOL WHILE DRESSED THIS WAY.
YOU WERE RUNNING AROUND IN THAT?!
Huff!
WHEN SOMEONE THREATENS YOU WITH THE LOSS OF WHAT'S MOST IMPORTANT TO YOU...
...YOU GET DESPERATE.
HUH?
YOU REALLY...
...DON'T KNOW HOW I FEEL?

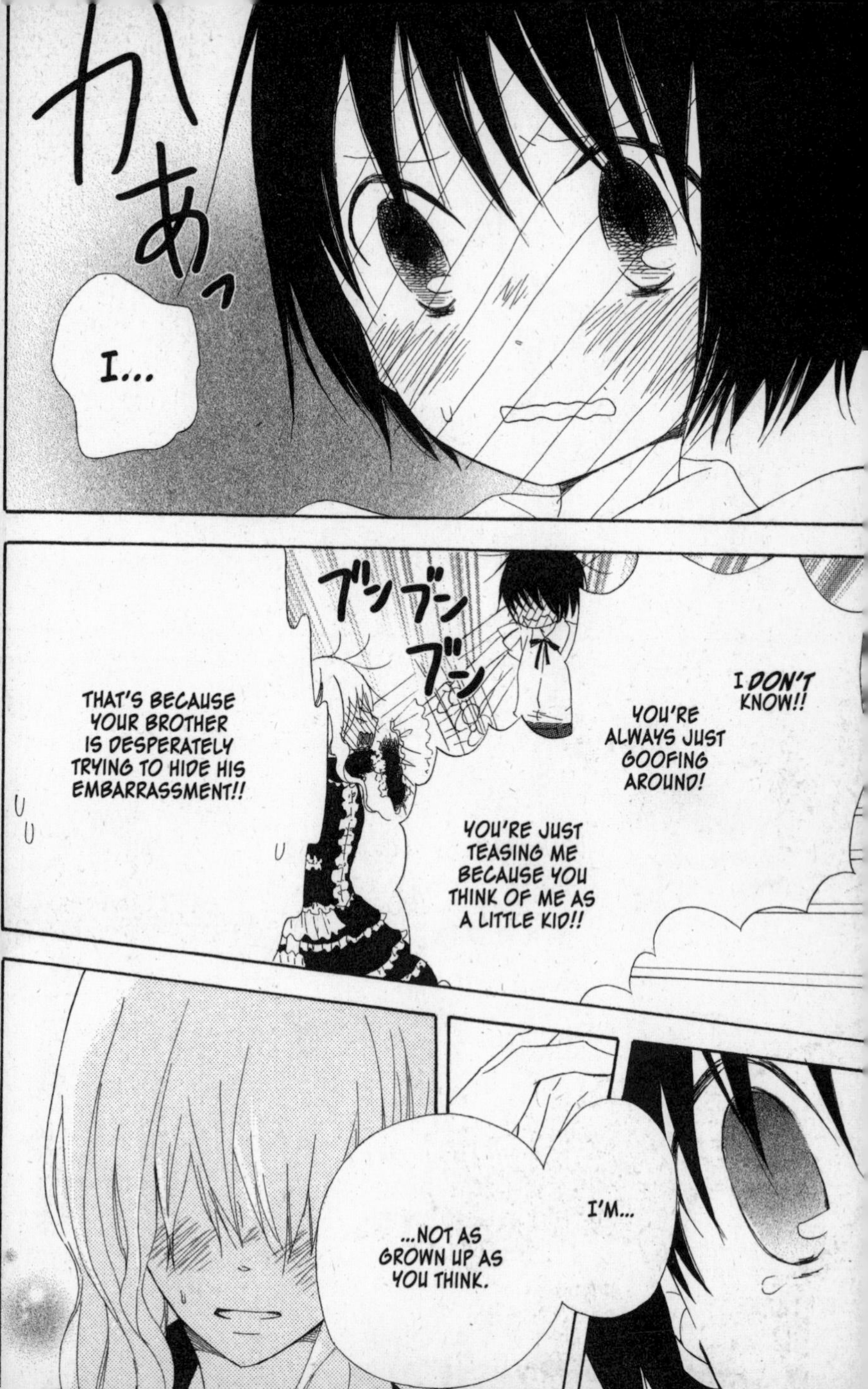
かぁっ
I...
I DON'T KNOW!!
YOU'RE ALWAYS JUST GOOFING AROUND!
YOU'RE JUST TEASING ME BECAUSE YOU THINK OF ME AS A LITTLE KID!!
ブンブンブン
THAT'S BECAUSE YOUR BROTHER IS DESPERATELY TRYING TO HIDE HIS EMBARRASSMENT!!
I'M...
...NOT AS GROWN UP AS YOU THINK.

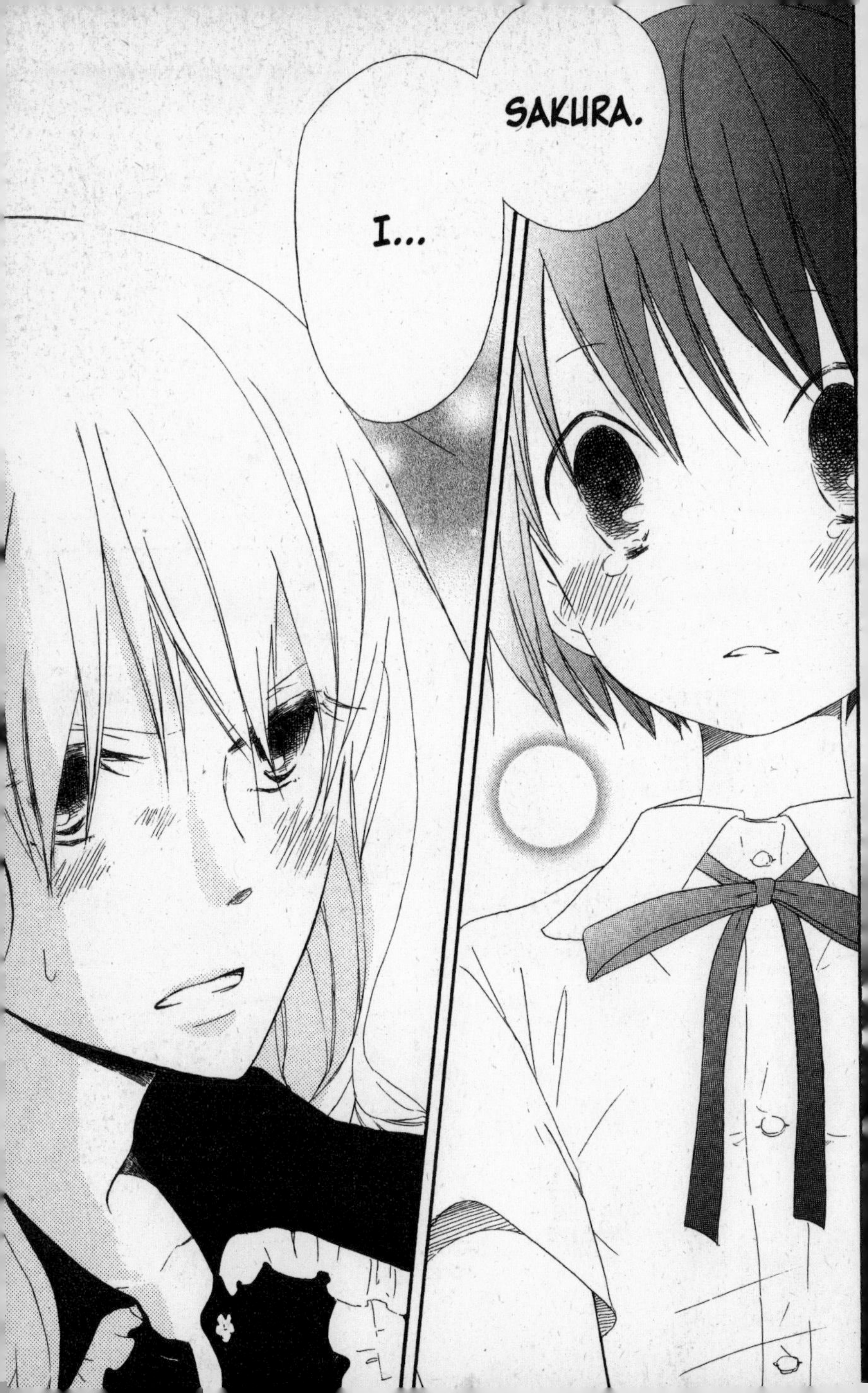
SAKURA.
I...

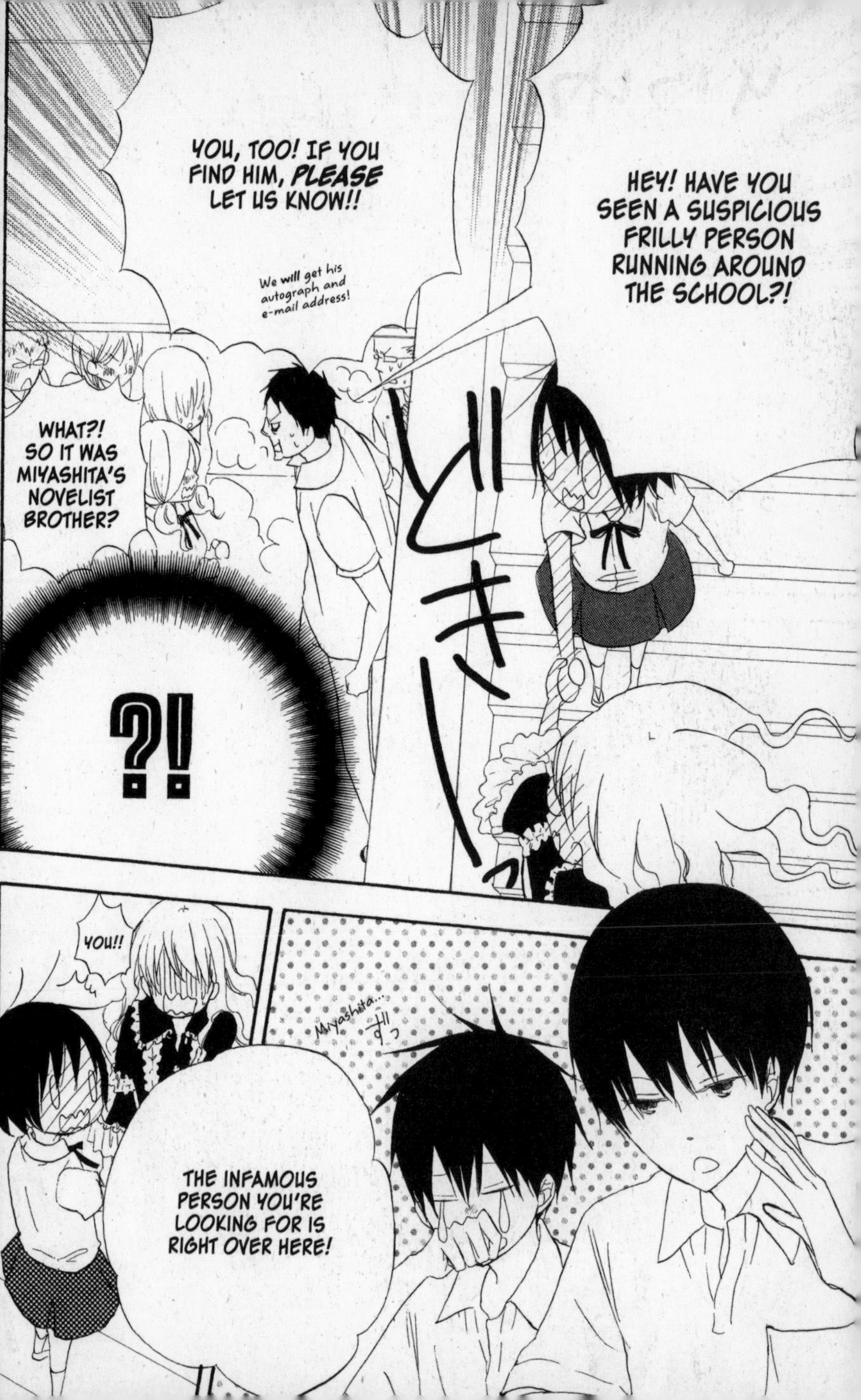
HEY! HAVE YOU SEEN A SUSPICIOUS FRILLY PERSON RUNNING AROUND THE SCHOOL?!
YOU, TOO! IF YOU FIND HIM, *PLEASE* LET US KNOW!!
We will get his autograph and e-mail address!
WHAT?! SO IT WAS MIYASHITA'S NOVELIST BROTHER?
どきーっ
?!
Miyashita...
すっ
YOU!!
THE INFAMOUS PERSON YOU'RE LOOKING FOR IS RIGHT OVER HERE!

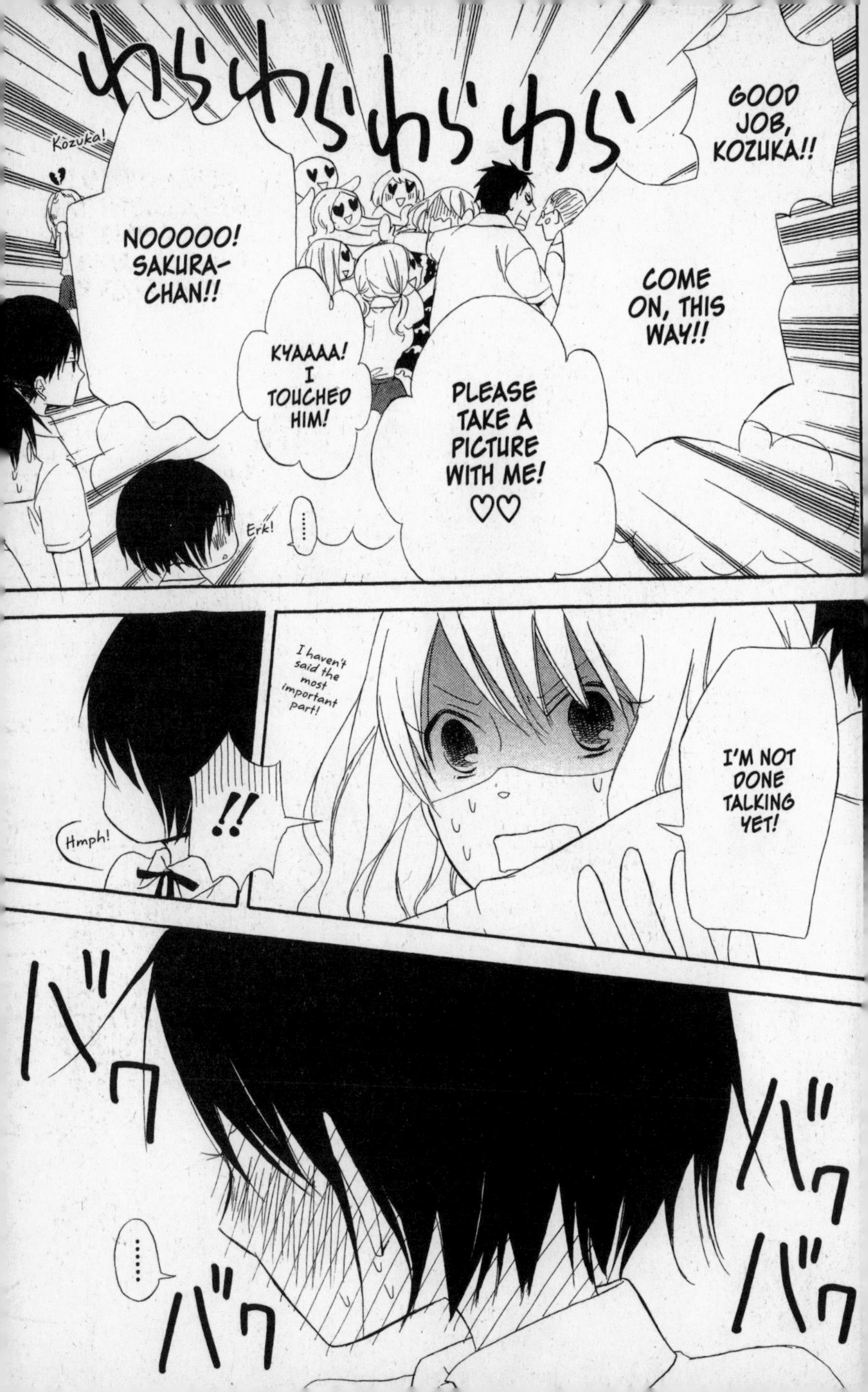
わらわらわらわら
GOOD JOB, KOZUKA!!
COME ON, THIS WAY!!
PLEASE TAKE A PICTURE WITH ME! ♡♡
KYAAAA! I TOUCHED HIM!
NOOOOO! SAKURA-CHAN!!
Kozuka!
……
Erk!
I'M NOT DONE TALKING YET!
I haven't said the most important part!
!!
Hmph!
バクバク
バク
……
バク

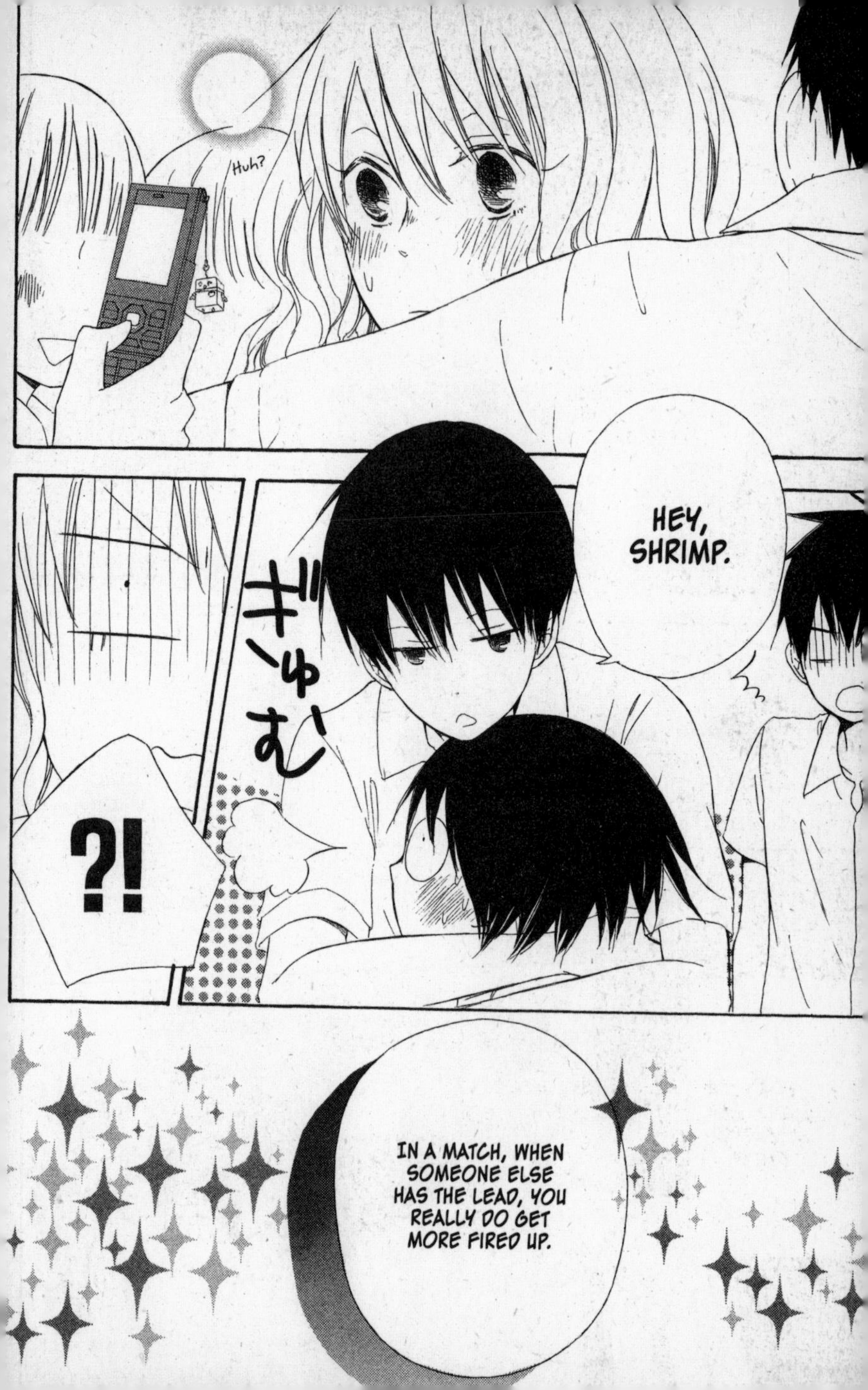
Huh?
HEY, SHRIMP.
ぎゅむ
?!
IN A MATCH, WHEN SOMEONE ELSE HAS THE LEAD, YOU REALLY DO GET MORE FIRED UP.

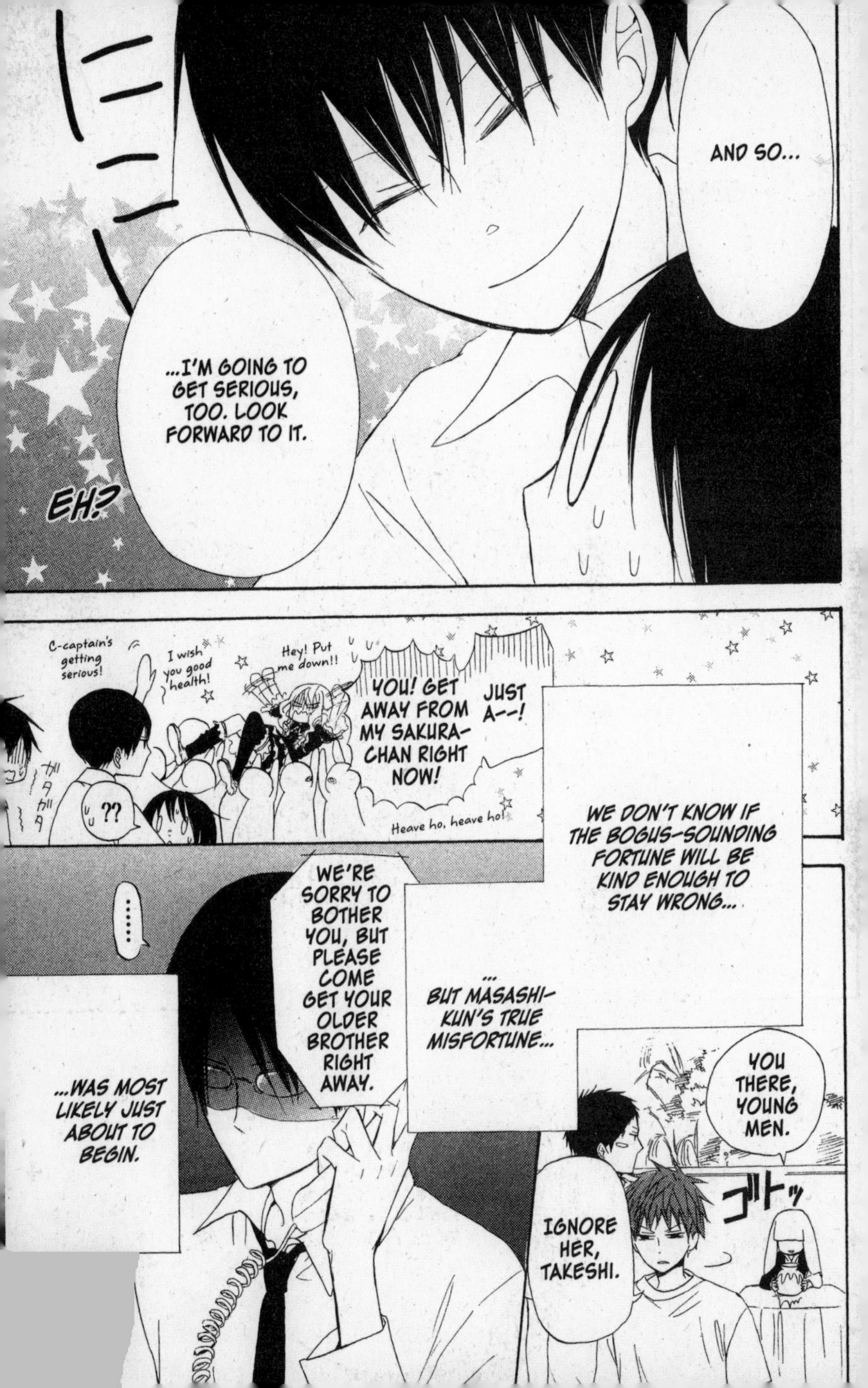
AND SO...
...I'M GOING TO GET SERIOUS, TOO. LOOK FORWARD TO IT.
EH?
JUST A--!
YOU! GET AWAY FROM MY SAKURA-CHAN RIGHT NOW!
Hey! Put me down!!
I wish you good health!
C-captain's getting serious!
ガタガタ
??
Heave ho, heave ho!
WE DON'T KNOW IF THE BOGUS-SOUNDING FORTUNE WILL BE KIND ENOUGH TO STAY WRONG...
...BUT MASASHI-KUN'S TRUE MISFORTUNE...
YOU THERE, YOUNG MEN.
ゴトッ
IGNORE HER, TAKESHI.
WE'RE SORRY TO BOTHER YOU, BUT PLEASE COME GET YOUR OLDER BROTHER RIGHT AWAY.
......
...WAS MOST LIKELY JUST ABOUT TO BEGIN.

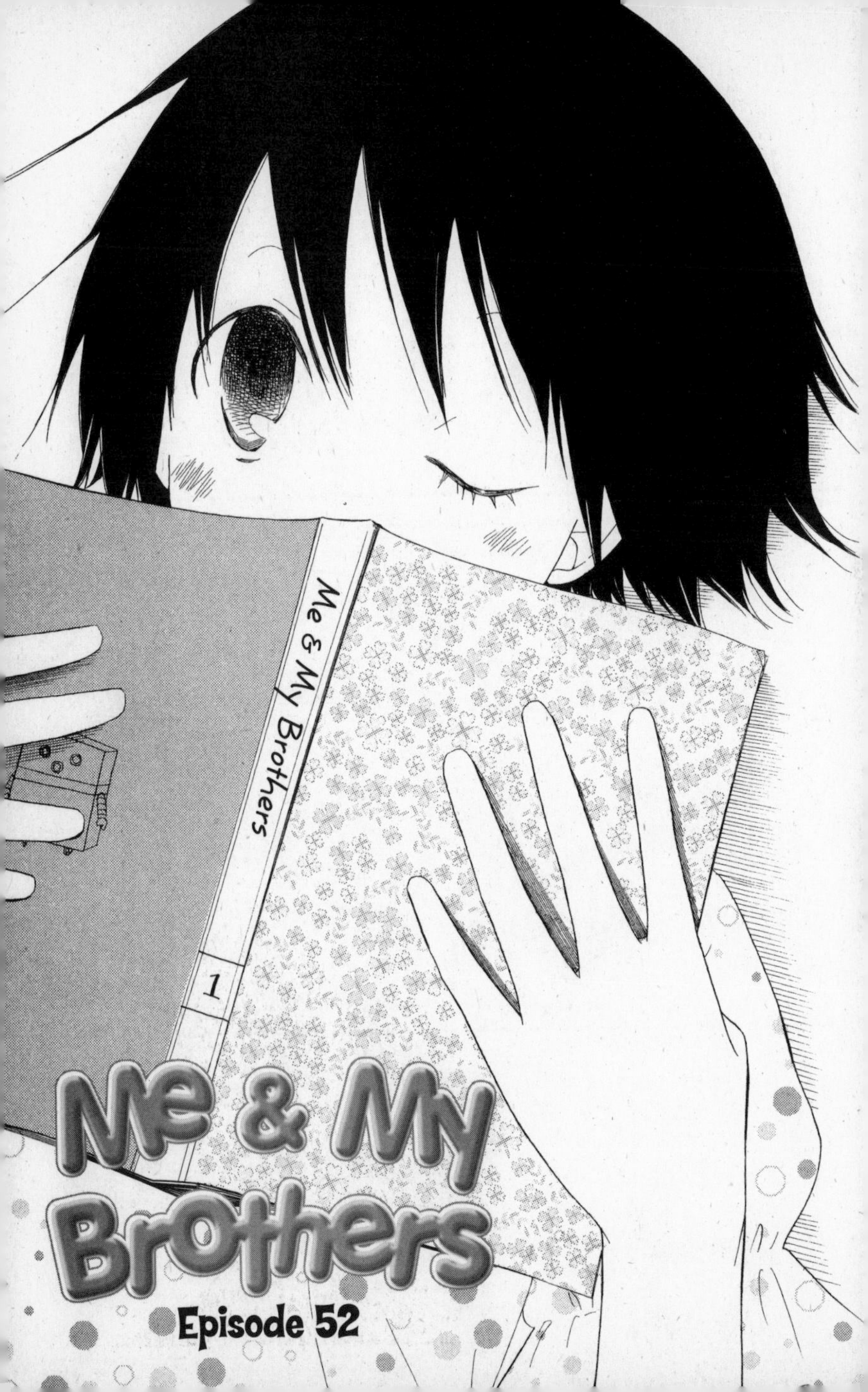
Me & My Brothers
1
Me & My Brothers
Episode 52

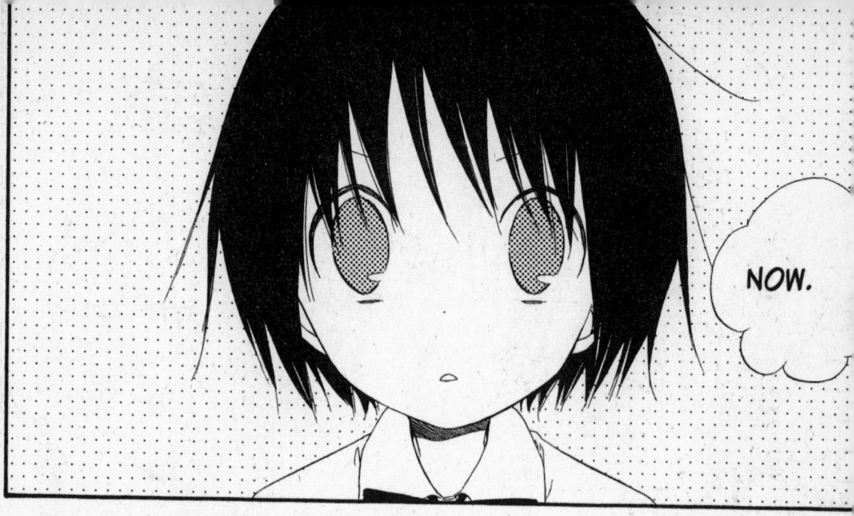
NOW.

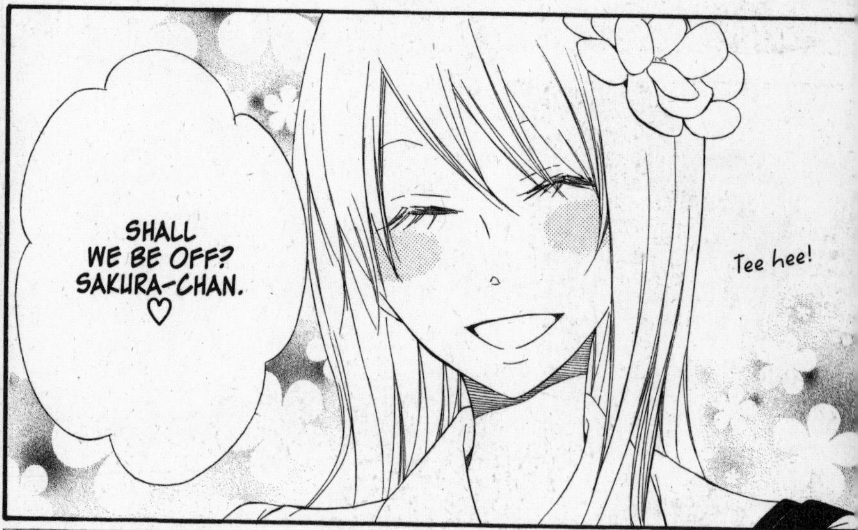
Tee hee!
SHALL WE BE OFF? SAKURA-CHAN. ♡

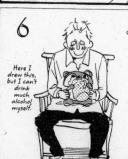

6

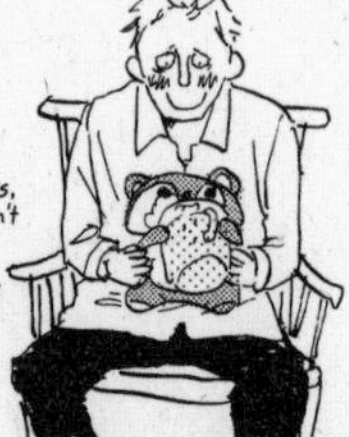

Here I drew this, but I can't drink much alcohol myself.

Chito Mikami-sama

Emiko Nakano-sama

Shinobu Amano-sama

Kondou-sama & you!!

Thanks!!

Anyone who would like to tell me what you think, please send letters here. →

TOKYOPOP
c/o Me & My Brothers Fanmail
5900 Wilshire Blvd, #2000
Los Angeles, CA 90036

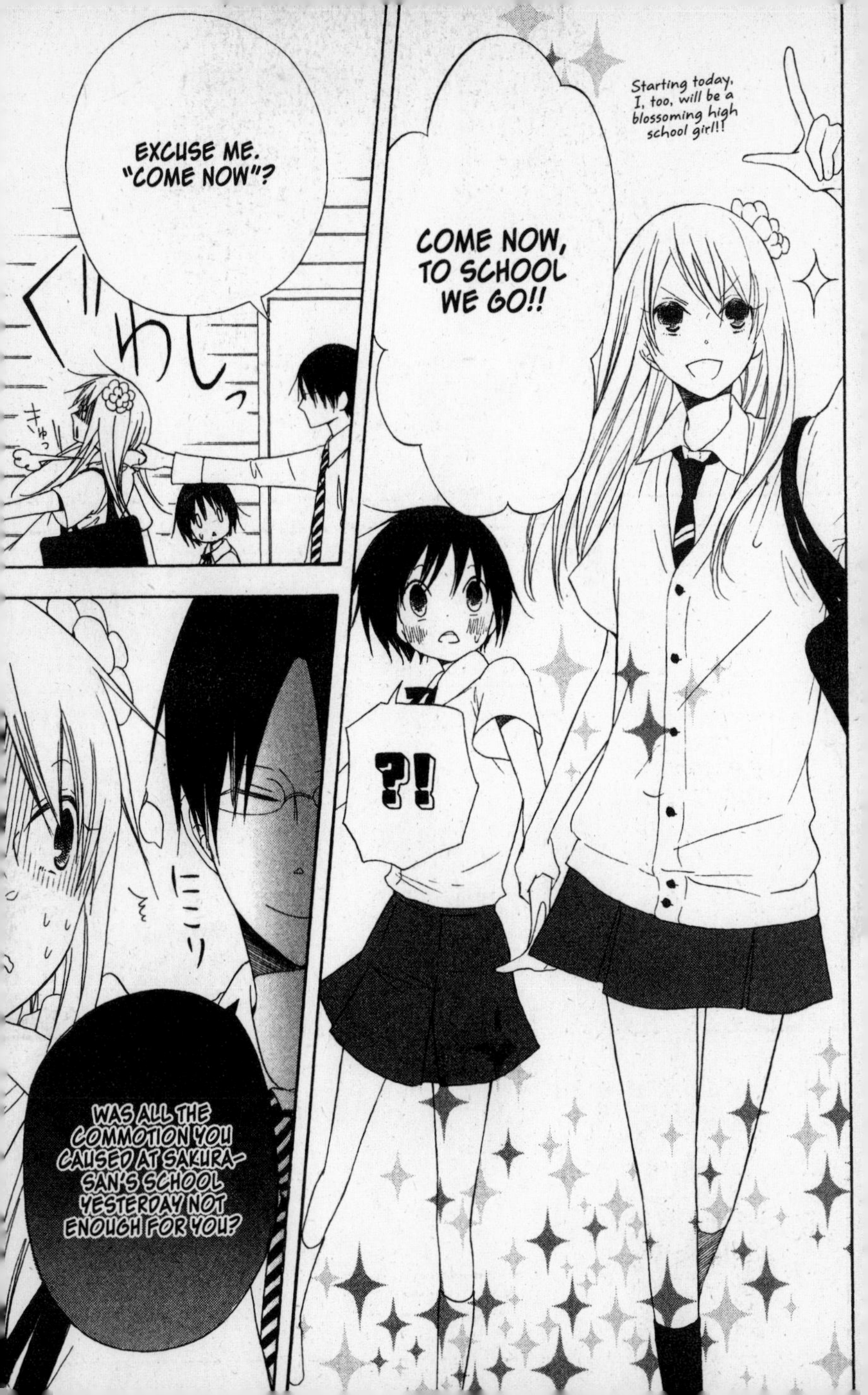
Starting today, I, too, will be a blossoming high school girl!!
COME NOW, TO SCHOOL WE GO!!
?!
EXCUSE ME. "COME NOW"?
きゅっ
WAS ALL THE COMMOTION YOU CAUSED AT SAKURA-SAN'S SCHOOL YESTERDAY NOT ENOUGH FOR YOU?
にこり

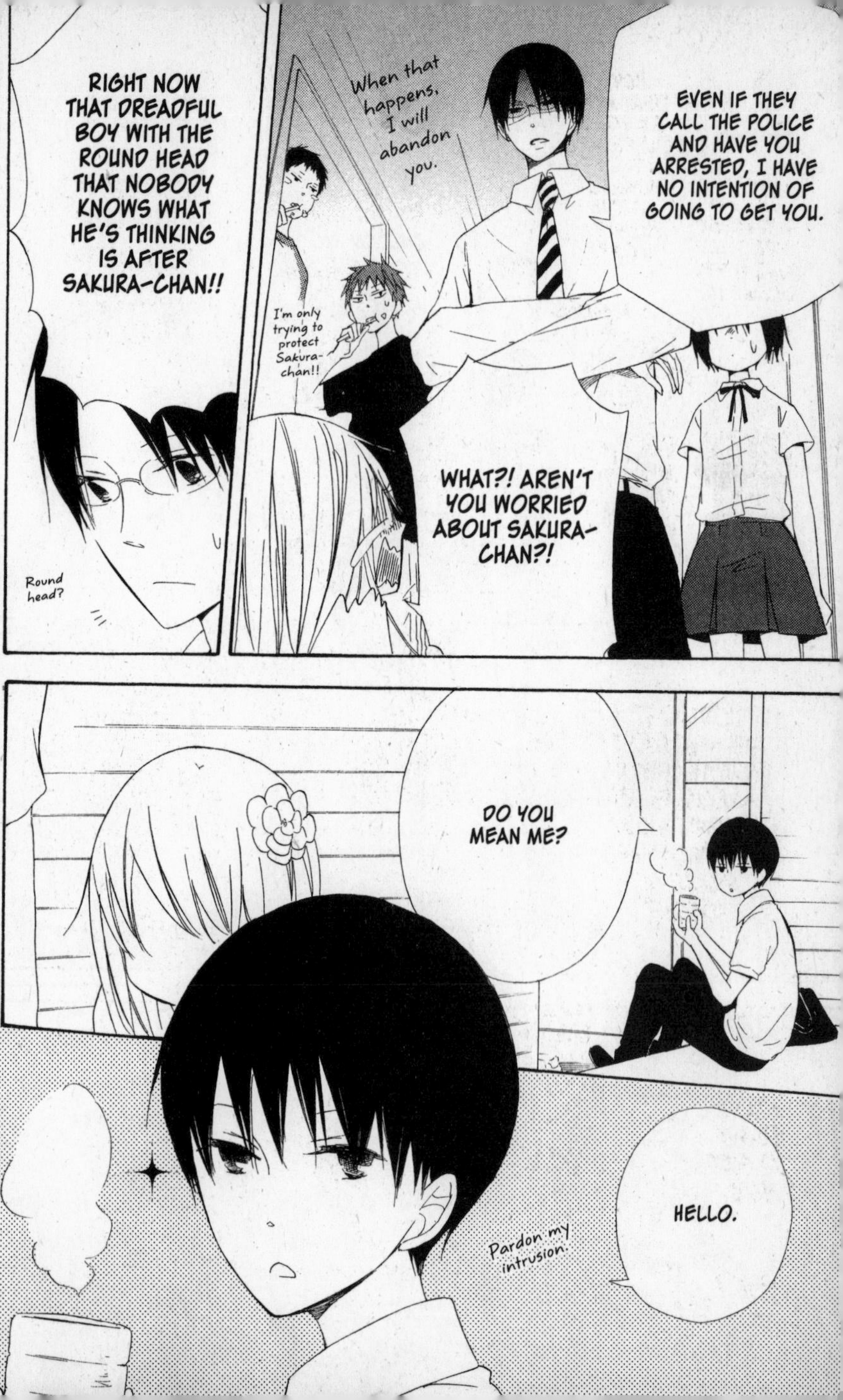
EVEN IF THEY CALL THE POLICE AND HAVE YOU ARRESTED, I HAVE NO INTENTION OF GOING TO GET YOU.
When that happens, I will abandon you.
I'm only trying to protect Sakura-chan!!
WHAT?! AREN'T YOU WORRIED ABOUT SAKURA-CHAN?!
RIGHT NOW THAT DREADFUL BOY WITH THE ROUND HEAD THAT NOBODY KNOWS WHAT HE'S THINKING IS AFTER SAKURA-CHAN!!
Round head?
DO YOU MEAN ME?
HELLO.
Pardon my intrusion.

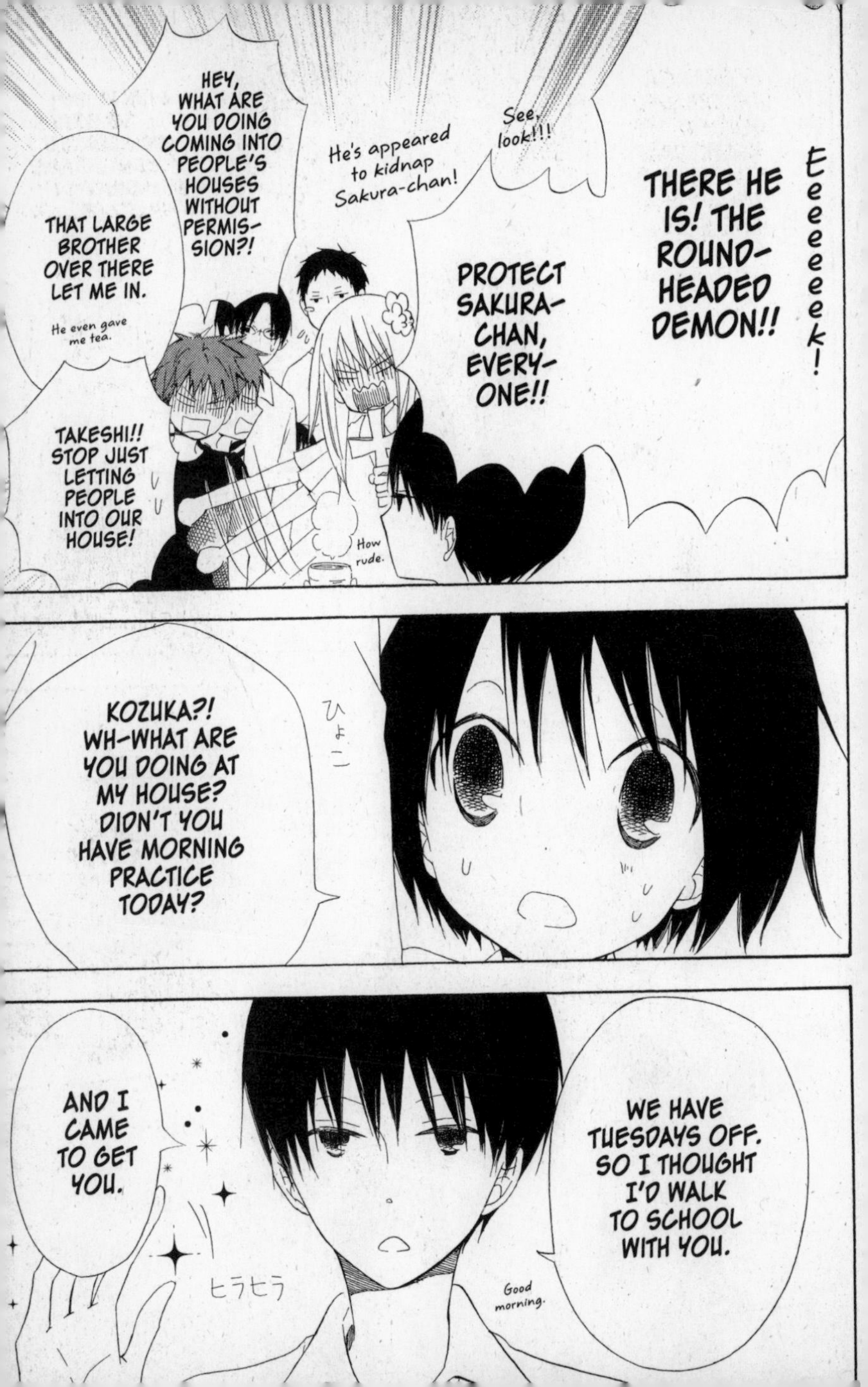
Eeeeeeek!
THERE HE IS! THE ROUND-HEADED DEMON!!
PROTECT SAKURA-CHAN, EVERYONE!!
See, look!!!
He's appeared to kidnap Sakura-chan!
HEY, WHAT ARE YOU DOING COMING INTO PEOPLE'S HOUSES WITHOUT PERMISSION?!
THAT LARGE BROTHER OVER THERE LET ME IN.
He even gave me tea.
How rude.
TAKESHI!! STOP JUST LETTING PEOPLE INTO OUR HOUSE!
ひょこ
KOZUKA?! WH-WHAT ARE YOU DOING AT MY HOUSE? DIDN'T YOU HAVE MORNING PRACTICE TODAY?
WE HAVE TUESDAYS OFF. SO I THOUGHT I'D WALK TO SCHOOL WITH YOU.
Good morning.
ヒラヒラ
AND I CAME TO GET YOU.

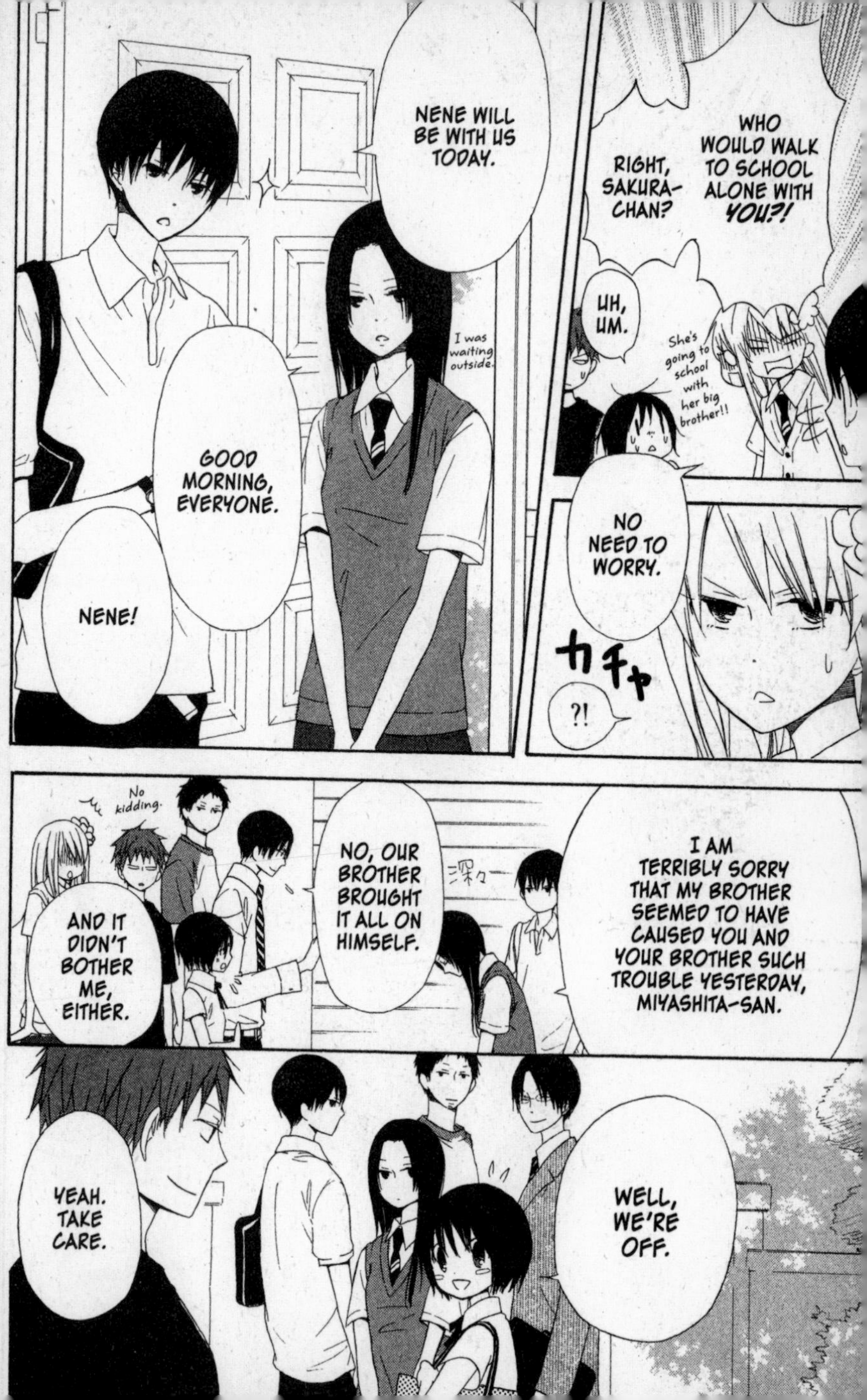
WHO WOULD WALK TO SCHOOL ALONE WITH YOU?!
RIGHT, SAKURA-CHAN?
UH, UM.
She's going to school with her big brother!!
NO NEED TO WORRY.
カチャ
?!
NENE WILL BE WITH US TODAY.
I was waiting outside.
GOOD MORNING, EVERYONE.
NENE!
I AM TERRIBLY SORRY THAT MY BROTHER SEEMED TO HAVE CAUSED YOU AND YOUR BROTHER SUCH TROUBLE YESTERDAY, MIYASHITA-SAN.
深々ー
NO, OUR BROTHER BROUGHT IT ALL ON HIMSELF.
No kidding.
AND IT DIDN'T BOTHER ME, EITHER.
WELL, WE'RE OFF.
YEAH. TAKE CARE.

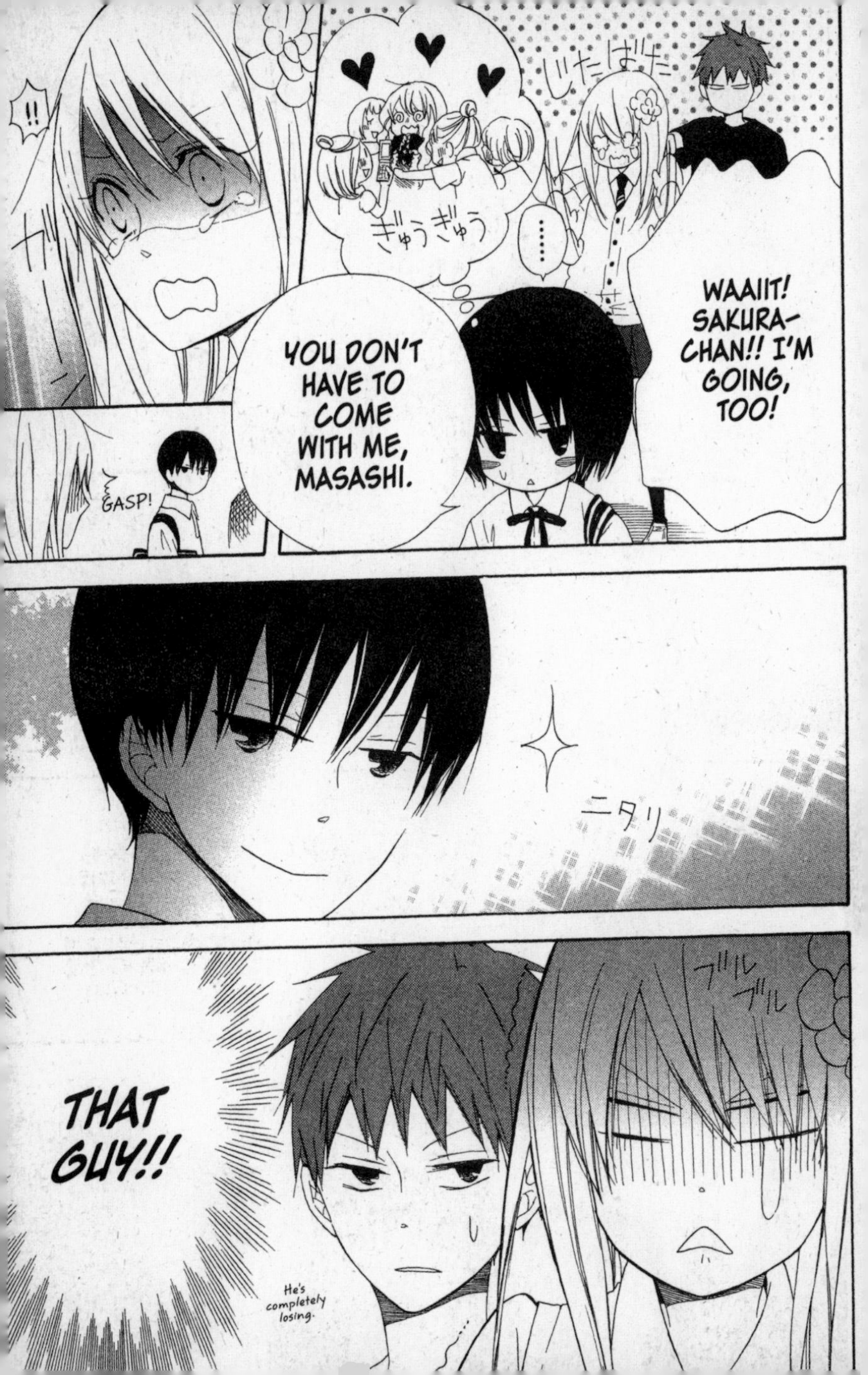
じたばた
ぎゅうぎゅう
……
WAAIIT! SAKURA-CHAN!! I'M GOING, TOO!
!!
YOU DON'T HAVE TO COME WITH ME, MASASHI.
GASP!
ニタリ
ブルブル
THAT GUY!!
He's completely losing.

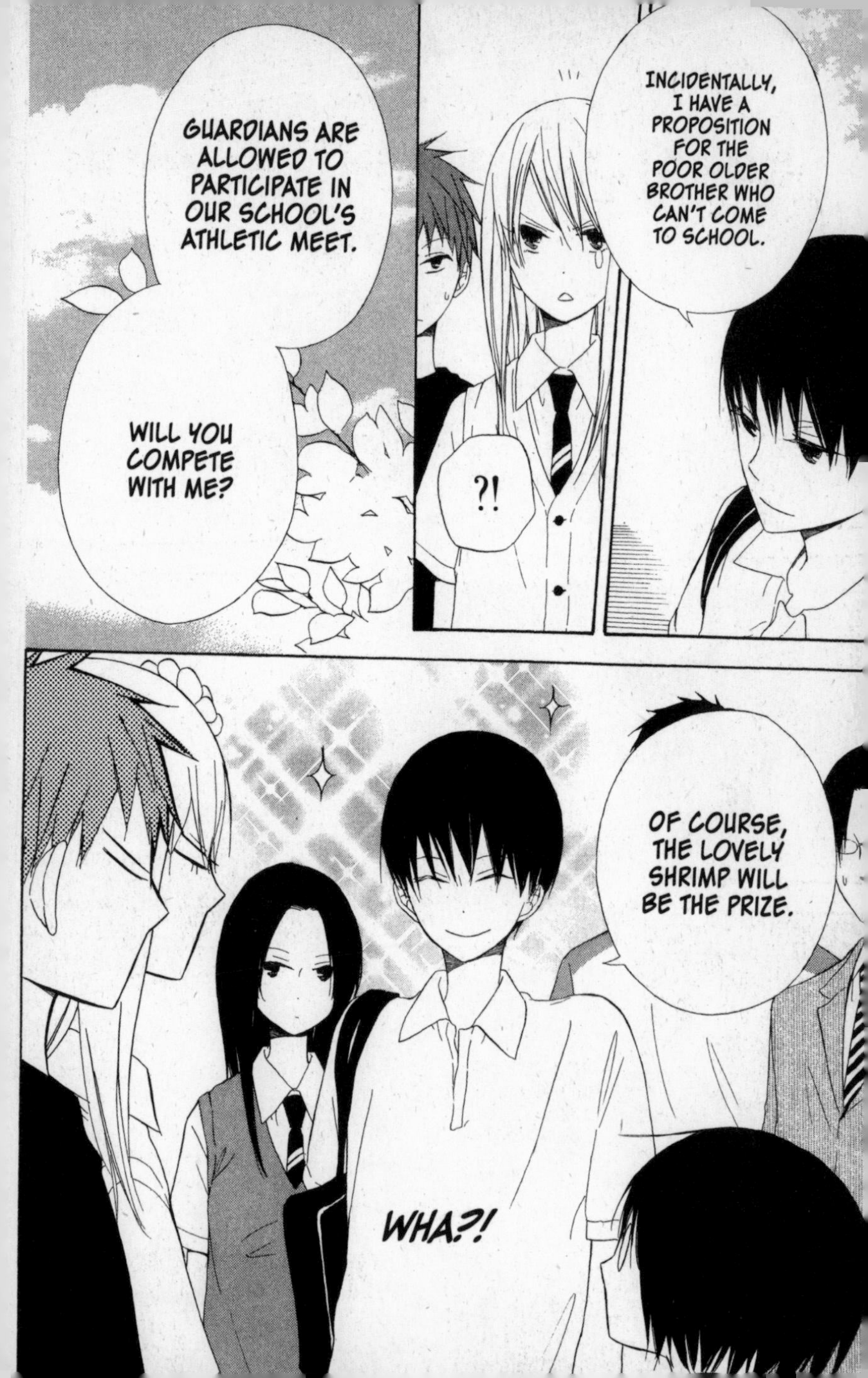
INCIDENTALLY, I HAVE A PROPOSITION FOR THE POOR OLDER BROTHER WHO CAN'T COME TO SCHOOL.
?!
GUARDIANS ARE ALLOWED TO PARTICIPATE IN OUR SCHOOL'S ATHLETIC MEET.
WILL YOU COMPETE WITH ME?
OF COURSE, THE LOVELY SHRIMP WILL BE THE PRIZE.
WHA?!

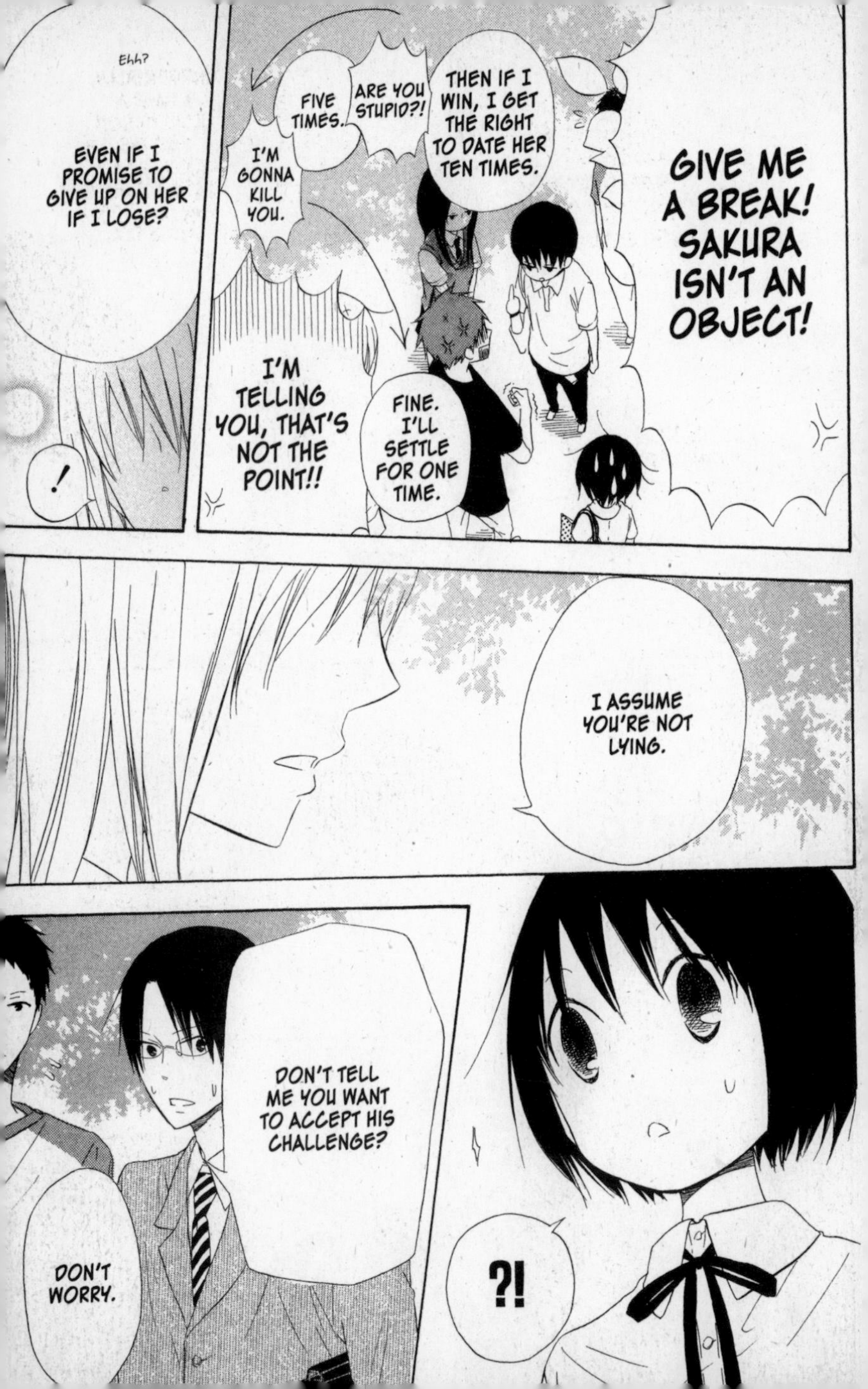
GIVE ME A BREAK! SAKURA ISN'T AN OBJECT!
THEN IF I WIN, I GET THE RIGHT TO DATE HER TEN TIMES.
ARE YOU STUPID?!
FIVE TIMES.
I'M GONNA KILL YOU.
FINE. I'LL SETTLE FOR ONE TIME.
I'M TELLING YOU, THAT'S NOT THE POINT!!
Ehh?
EVEN IF I PROMISE TO GIVE UP ON HER IF I LOSE?
!
I ASSUME YOU'RE NOT LYING.
?!
DON'T TELL ME YOU WANT TO ACCEPT HIS CHALLENGE?
DON'T WORRY.

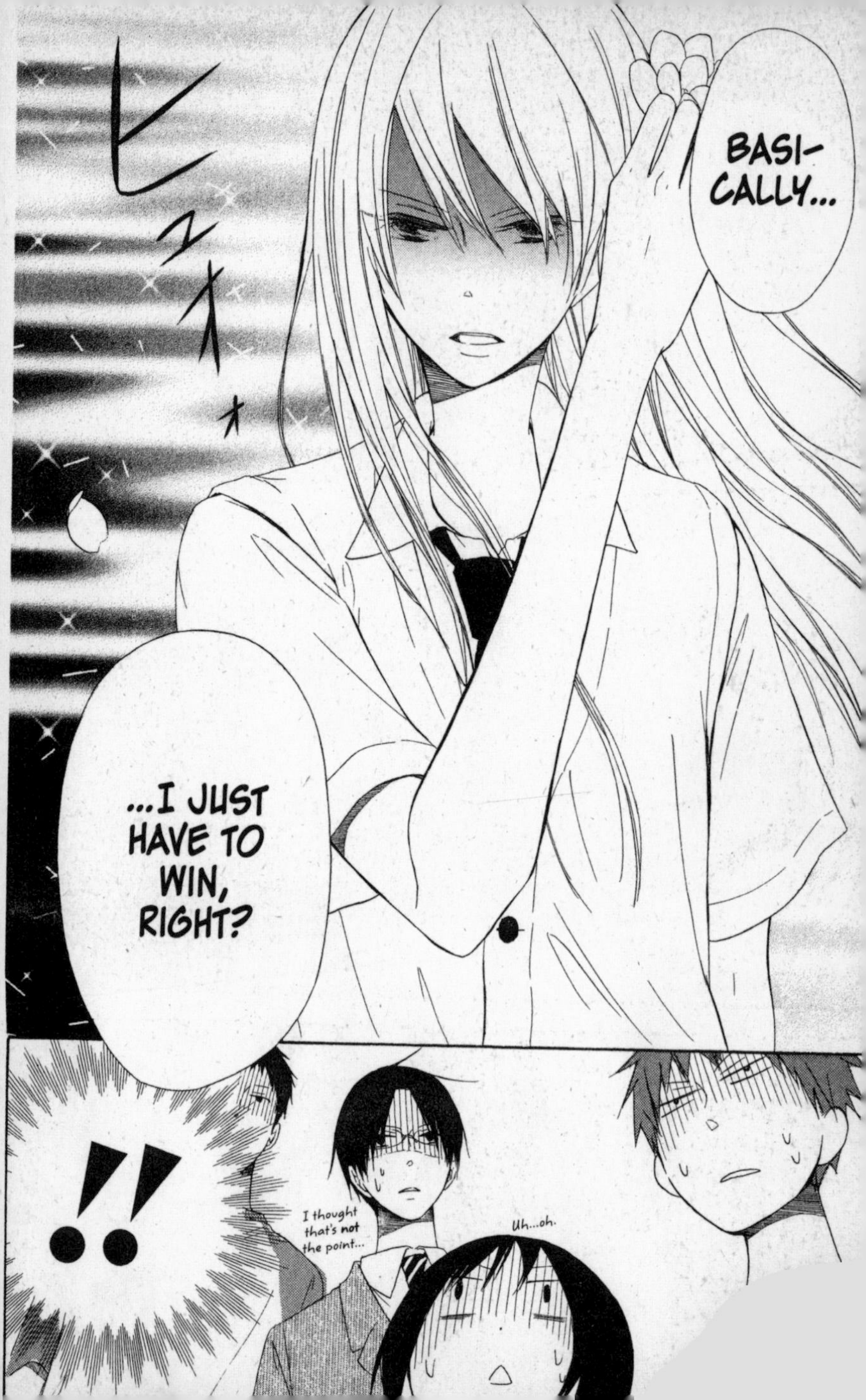

BASI-CALLY...
ヒュオォ
...I JUST HAVE TO WIN, RIGHT?
Uh...oh.
I thought that's not the point...
!!

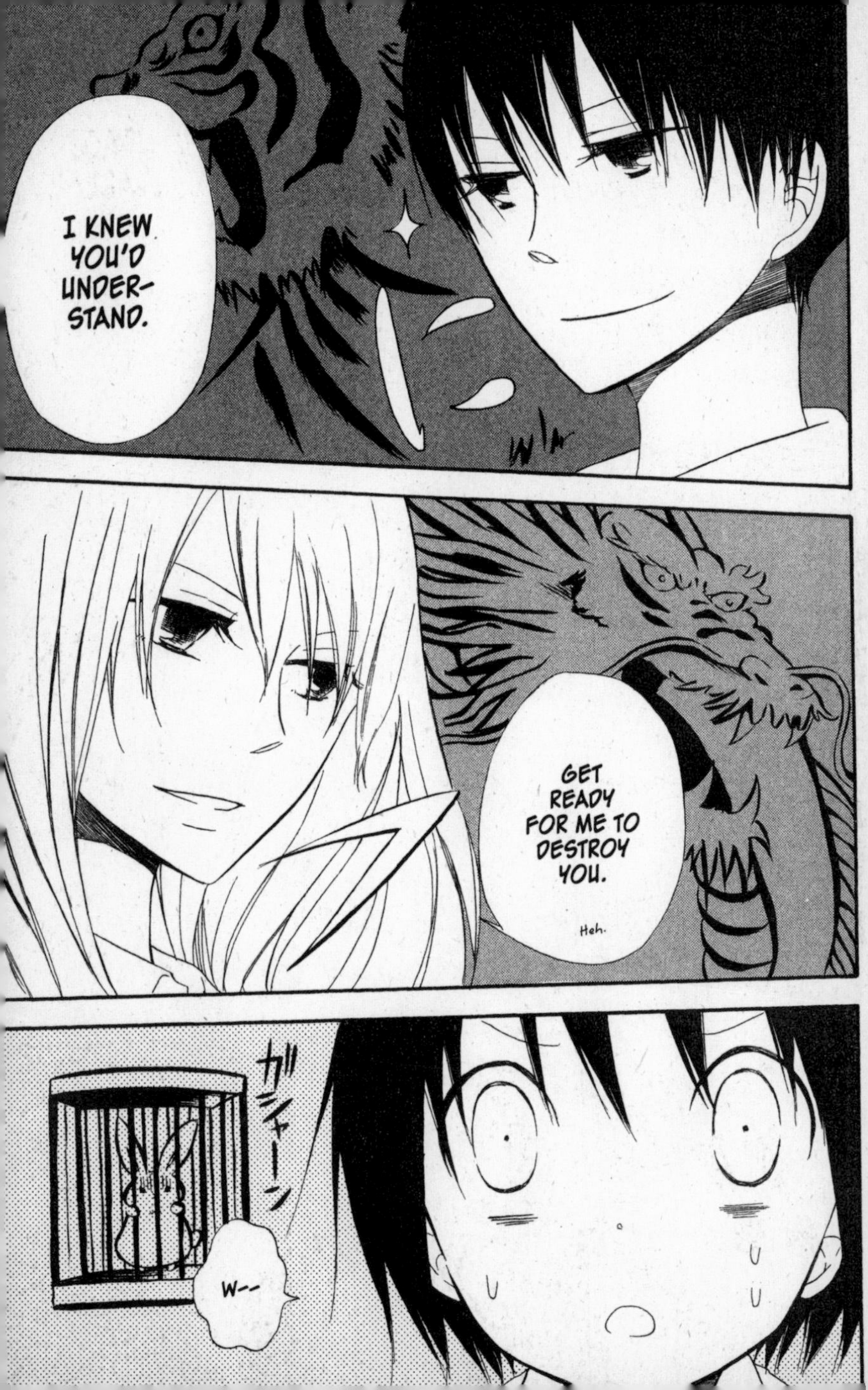
I KNEW YOU'D UNDER-STAND.
GET READY FOR ME TO DESTROY YOU.
Heh.
ガシャーン
W--

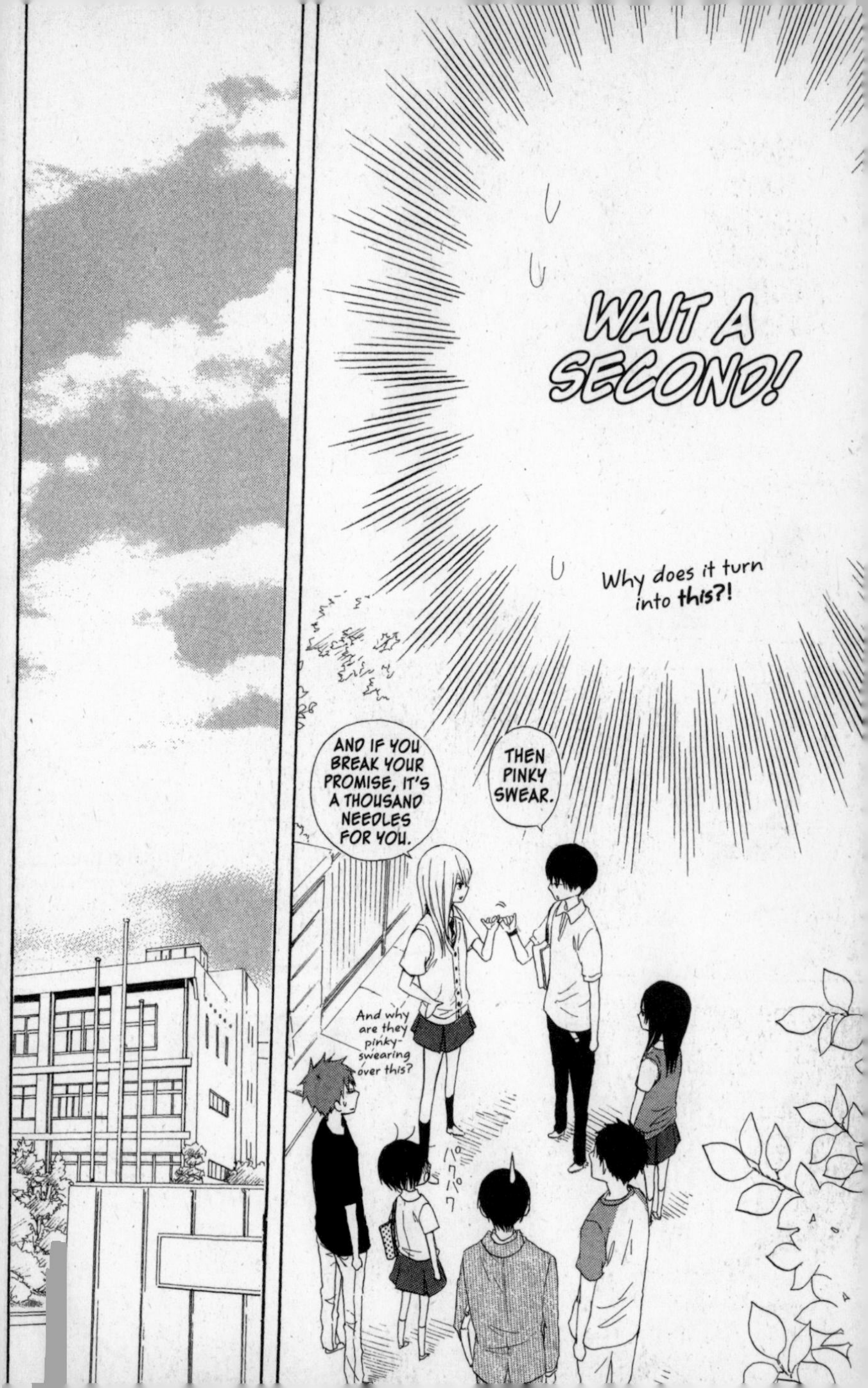
WAIT A SECOND!
Why does it turn into this?!
THEN PINKY SWEAR.
AND IF YOU BREAK YOUR PROMISE, IT'S A THOUSAND NEEDLES FOR YOU.
And why are they pinky-swearing over this?
パクパク

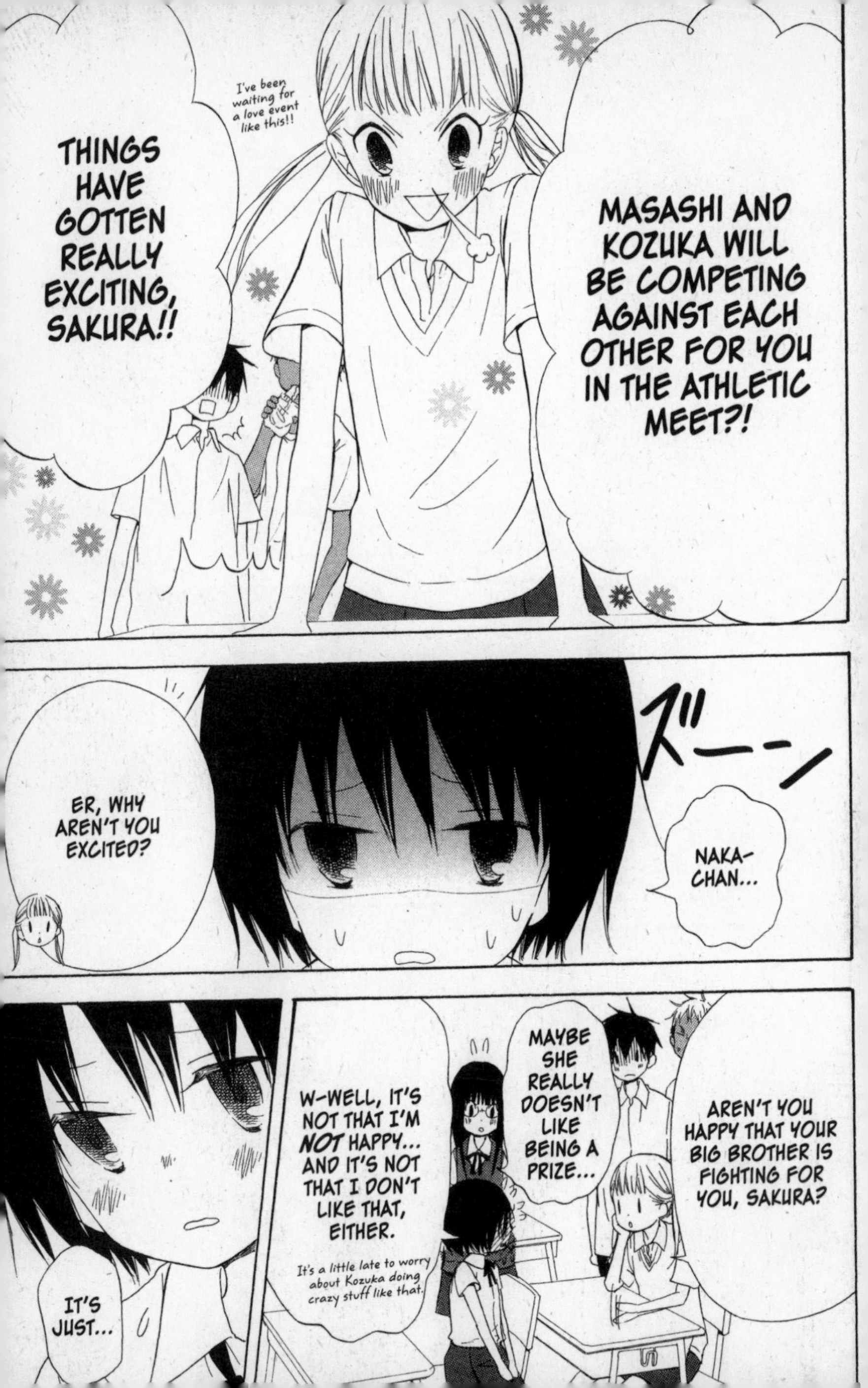
MASASHI AND KOZUKA WILL BE COMPETING AGAINST EACH OTHER FOR YOU IN THE ATHLETIC MEET?!
I've been waiting for a love event like this!!
THINGS HAVE GOTTEN REALLY EXCITING, SAKURA!!
ズーーン
NAKA-CHAN...
ER, WHY AREN'T YOU EXCITED?
AREN'T YOU HAPPY THAT YOUR BIG BROTHER IS FIGHTING FOR YOU, SAKURA?
MAYBE SHE REALLY DOESN'T LIKE BEING A PRIZE...
W-WELL, IT'S NOT THAT I'M *NOT* HAPPY... AND IT'S NOT THAT I DON'T LIKE THAT, EITHER.
It's a little late to worry about Kozuka doing crazy stuff like that.
IT'S JUST...

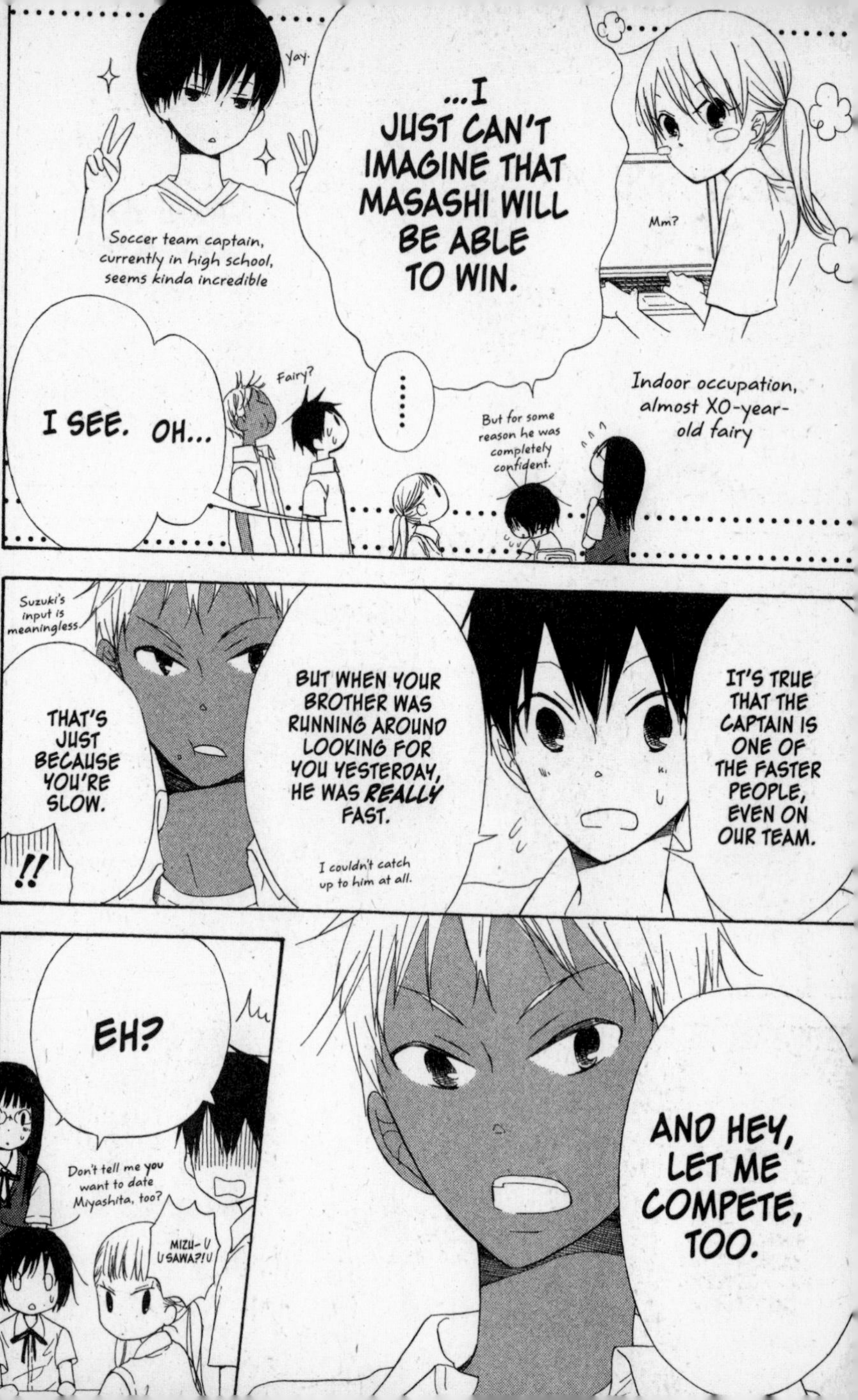
Mm?
Indoor occupation, almost XO-year-old fairy
...I JUST CAN'T IMAGINE THAT MASASHI WILL BE ABLE TO WIN.
Yay.
Soccer team captain, currently in high school, seems kinda incredible
......
But for some reason he was completely confident.
Fairy?
I SEE. OH...
IT'S TRUE THAT THE CAPTAIN IS ONE OF THE FASTER PEOPLE, EVEN ON OUR TEAM.
BUT WHEN YOUR BROTHER WAS RUNNING AROUND LOOKING FOR YOU YESTERDAY, HE WAS REALLY FAST.
I couldn't catch up to him at all.
Suzuki's input is meaningless.
THAT'S JUST BECAUSE YOU'RE SLOW.
!!
AND HEY, LET ME COMPETE, TOO.
EH?
Don't tell me you want to date Miyashita, too?
MIZU-USAWA?!

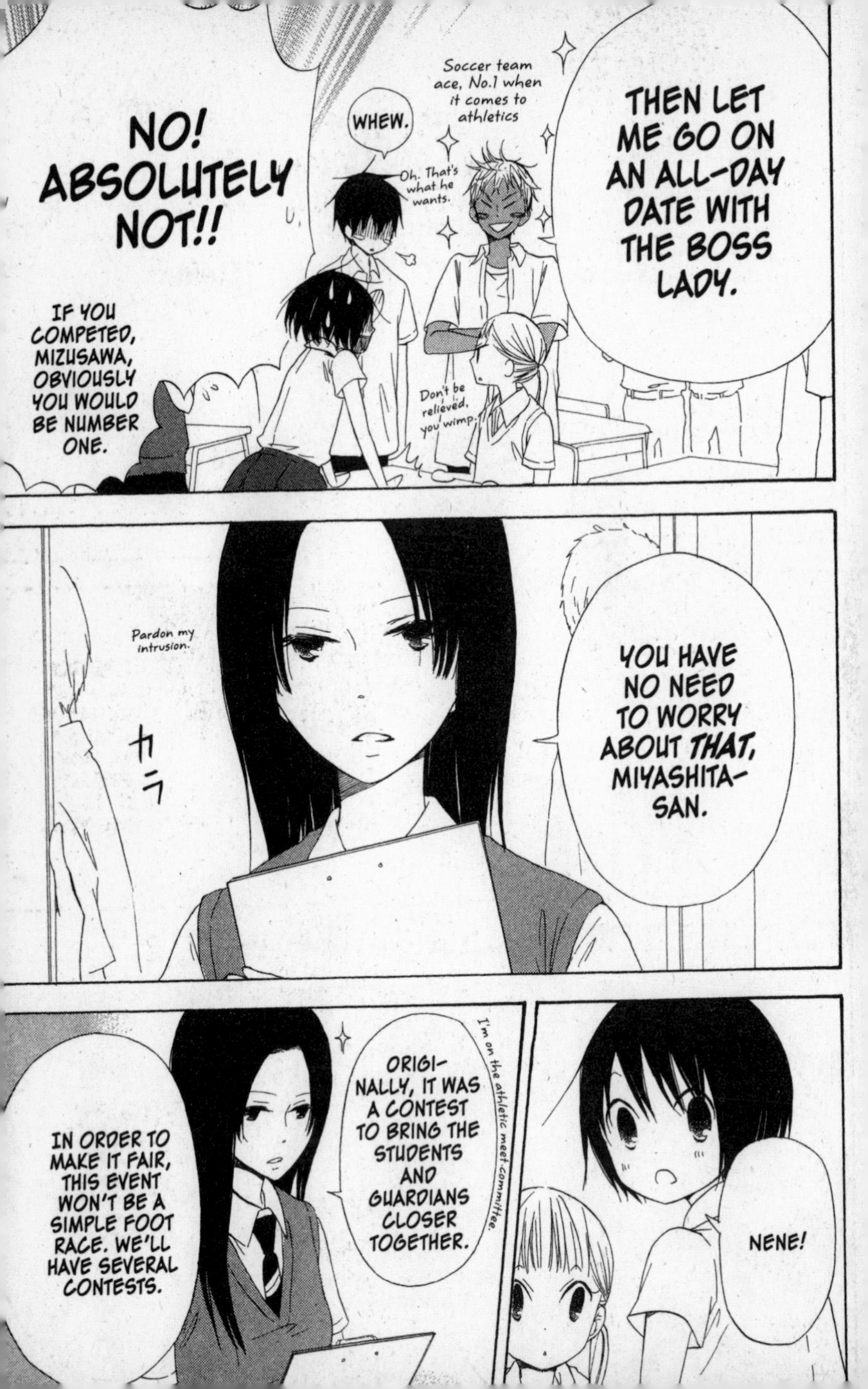
THEN LET ME GO ON AN ALL-DAY DATE WITH THE BOSS LADY.
Soccer team ace, No.1 when it comes to athletics
Oh. That's what he wants.
WHEW.
NO! ABSOLUTELY NOT!!
Don't be relieved, you wimp.
IF YOU COMPETED, MIZUSAWA, OBVIOUSLY YOU WOULD BE NUMBER ONE.
YOU HAVE NO NEED TO WORRY ABOUT *THAT*, MIYASHITA-SAN.
Pardon my intrusion.
カラ
NENE!
I'm on the athletic meet committee.
ORIGI-NALLY, IT WAS A CONTEST TO BRING THE STUDENTS AND GUARDIANS CLOSER TOGETHER.
IN ORDER TO MAKE IT FAIR, THIS EVENT WON'T BE A SIMPLE FOOT RACE. WE'LL HAVE SEVERAL CONTESTS.

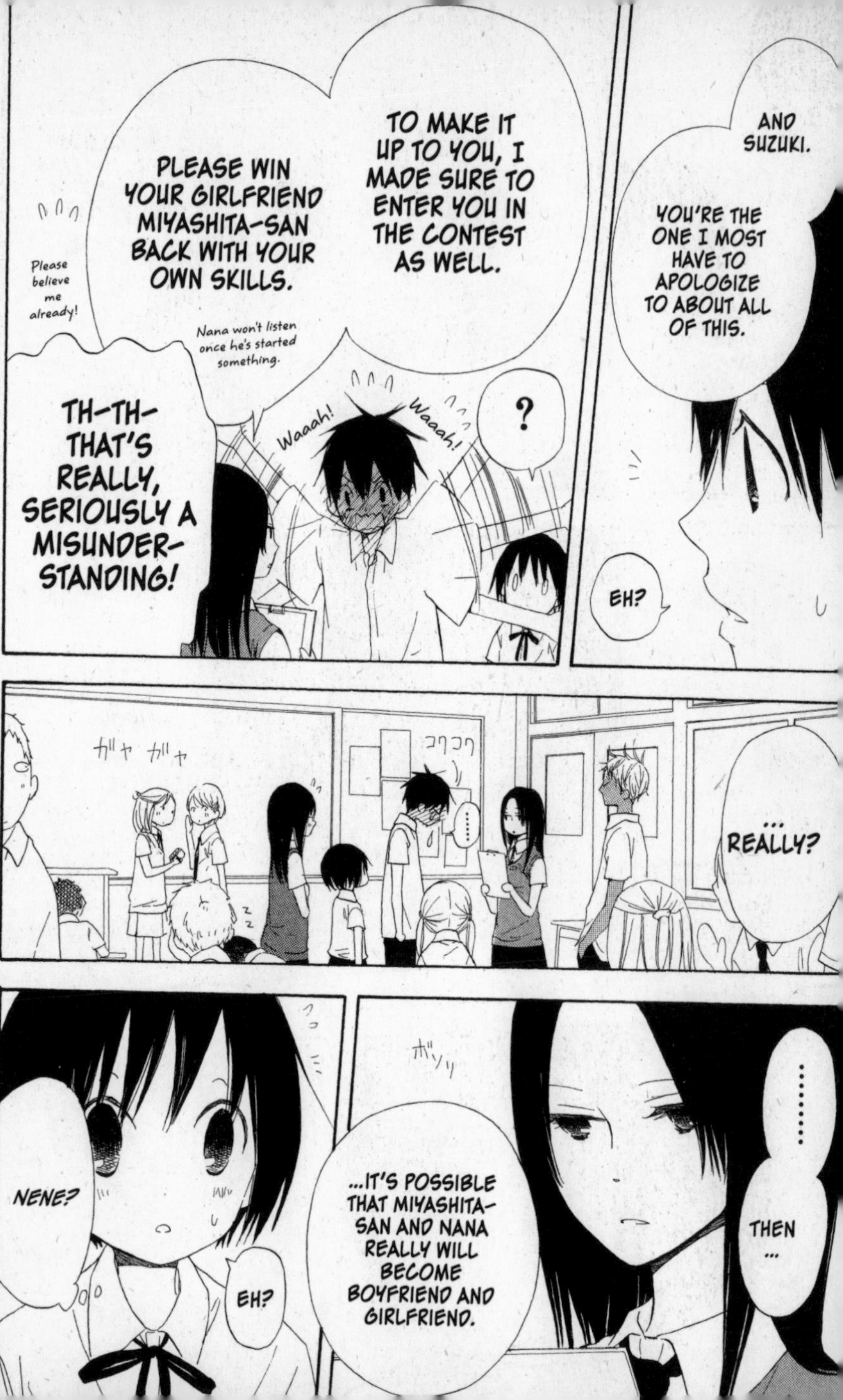
AND SUZUKI.
YOU'RE THE ONE I MOST HAVE TO APOLOGIZE TO ABOUT ALL OF THIS.
EH?
TO MAKE IT UP TO YOU, I MADE SURE TO ENTER YOU IN THE CONTEST AS WELL.
PLEASE WIN YOUR GIRLFRIEND MIYASHITA-SAN BACK WITH YOUR OWN SKILLS.
Please believe me already!
Nana won't listen once he's started something.
?
Waaah!
Waaah!
TH-TH-THAT'S REALLY, SERIOUSLY A MISUNDERSTANDING!
...REALLY?
ガヤ ガヤ
コソコソ
...
......
THEN...
ボソリ
...IT'S POSSIBLE THAT MIYASHITA-SAN AND NANA REALLY WILL BECOME BOYFRIEND AND GIRLFRIEND.
NENE?
EH?

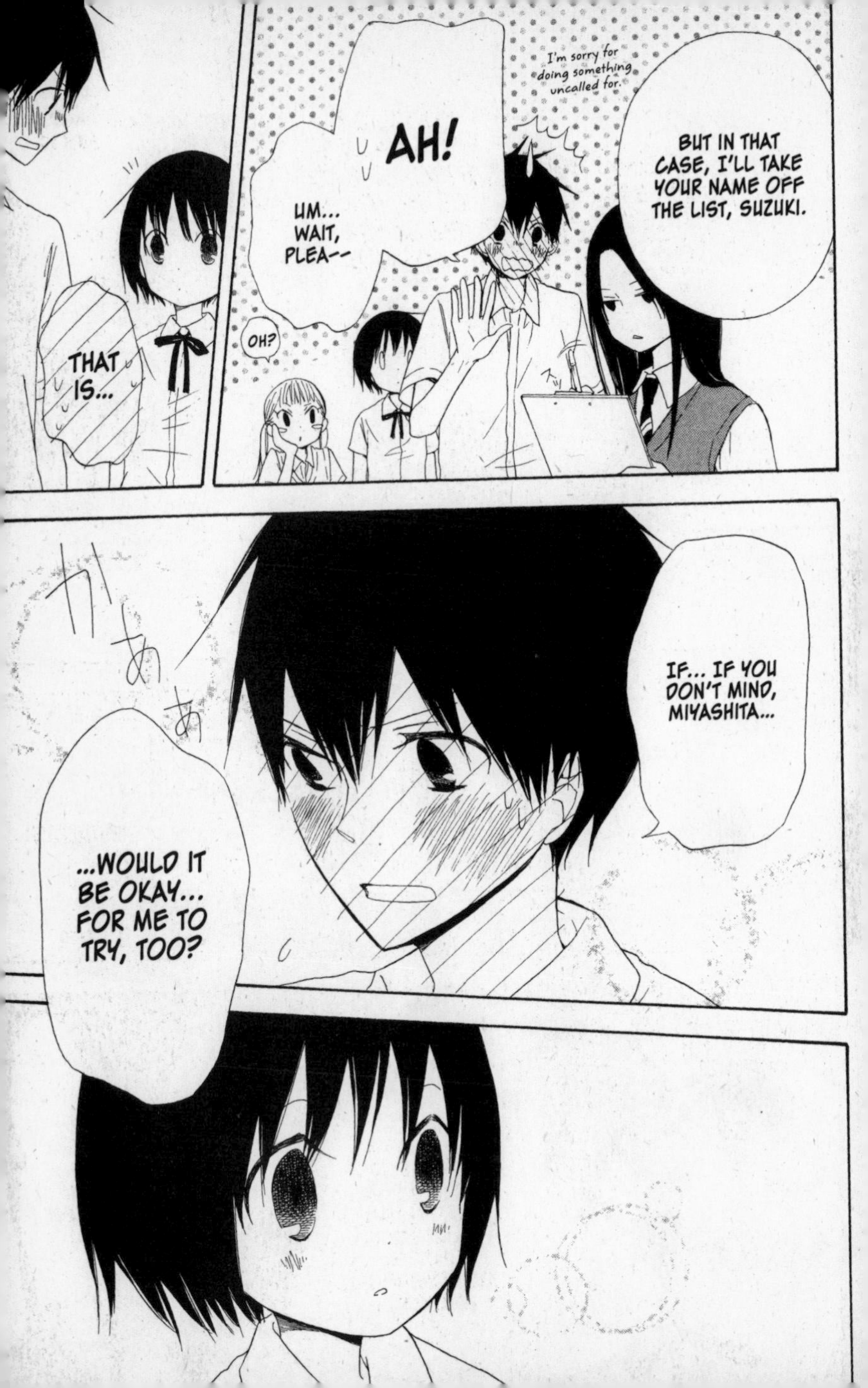
BUT IN THAT CASE, I'LL TAKE YOUR NAME OFF THE LIST, SUZUKI.
I'm sorry for doing something uncalled for.
AH!
UM... WAIT, PLEA--
OH?
THAT IS...
IF... IF YOU DON'T MIND, MIYASHITA...
...WOULD IT BE OKAY... FOR ME TO TRY, TOO?

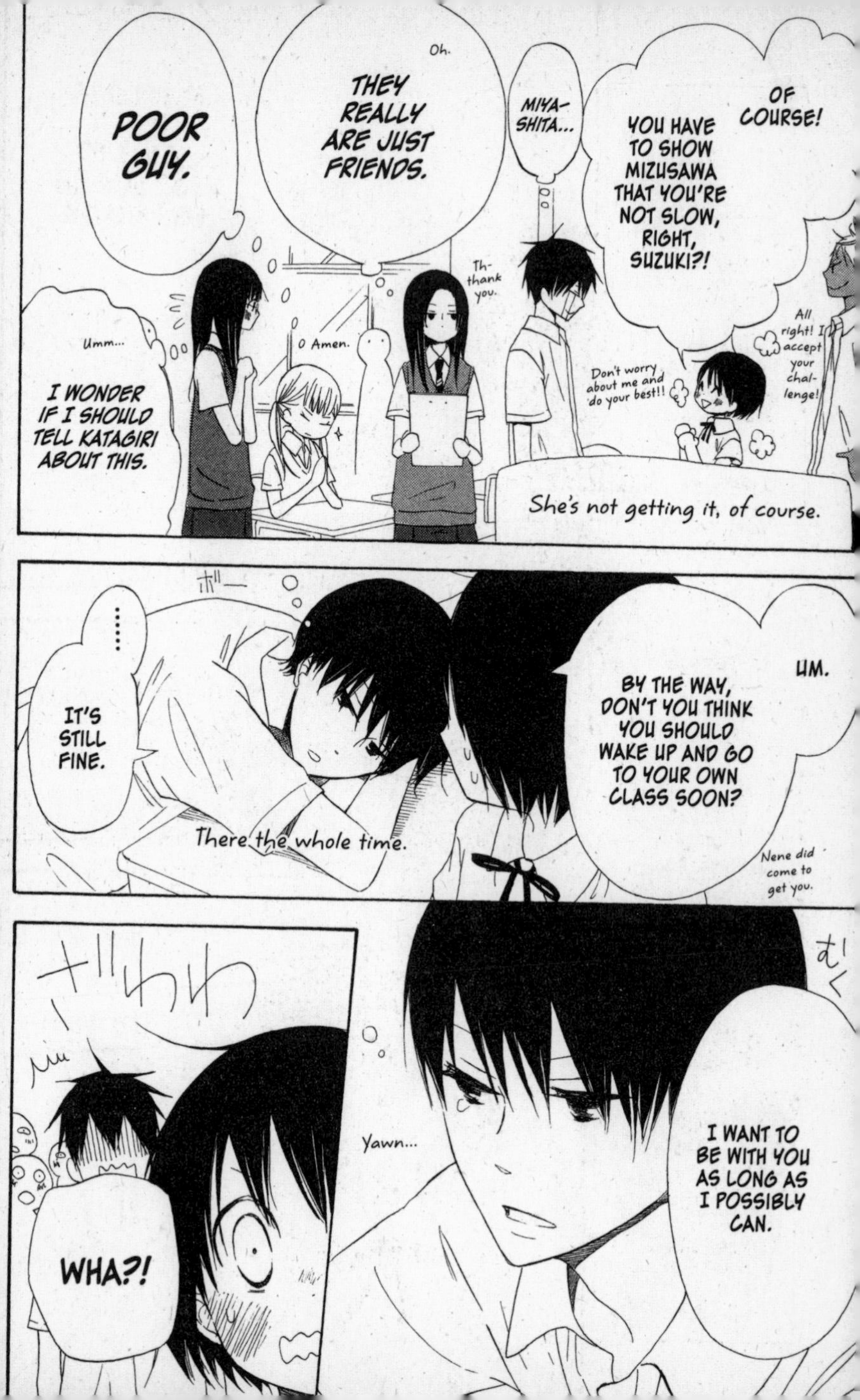
OF COURSE!
YOU HAVE TO SHOW MIZUSAWA THAT YOU'RE NOT SLOW, RIGHT, SUZUKI?!
All right! I accept your challenge!
Don't worry about me and do your best!!
MIYA-SHITA...
Th-thank you.
Oh.
THEY REALLY ARE JUST FRIENDS.
O Amen.
POOR GUY.
Umm...
I WONDER IF I SHOULD TELL KATAGIRI ABOUT THIS.
She's not getting it, of course.
UM.
BY THE WAY, DON'T YOU THINK YOU SHOULD WAKE UP AND GO TO YOUR OWN CLASS SOON?
Nene did come to get you.
ボー
......
IT'S STILL FINE.
There the whole time.
I WANT TO BE WITH YOU AS LONG AS I POSSIBLY CAN.
Yawn...
WHA?!

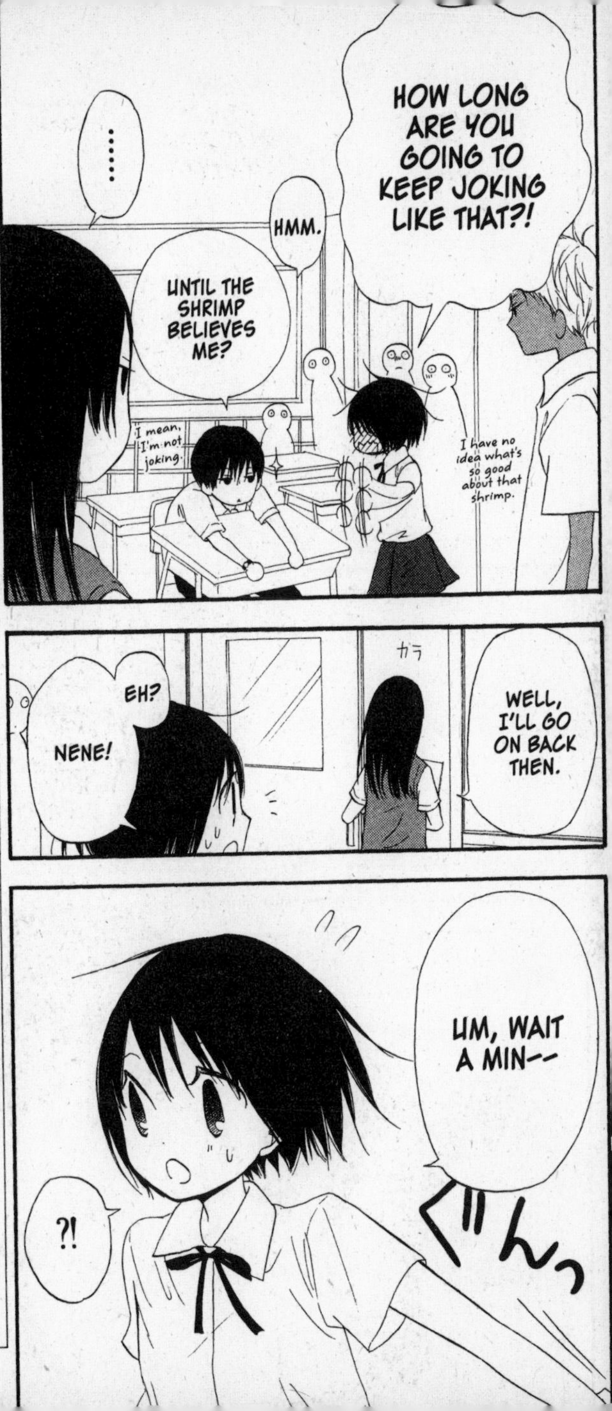
HOW LONG ARE YOU GOING TO KEEP JOKING LIKE THAT?!
I have no idea what's so good about that shrimp.
HMM.
UNTIL THE SHRIMP BELIEVES ME?
......
I mean, I'm not joking.
WELL, I'LL GO ON BACK THEN.
ガラ
EH?
NENE!
UM, WAIT A MIN--
?!

6

Thanks for your hard work! This is the last column!

Thank you very much for sticking with me this long!

I really am happy to reach the commemorative two-digit volume number.

If possible, let's meet again in volume 11.

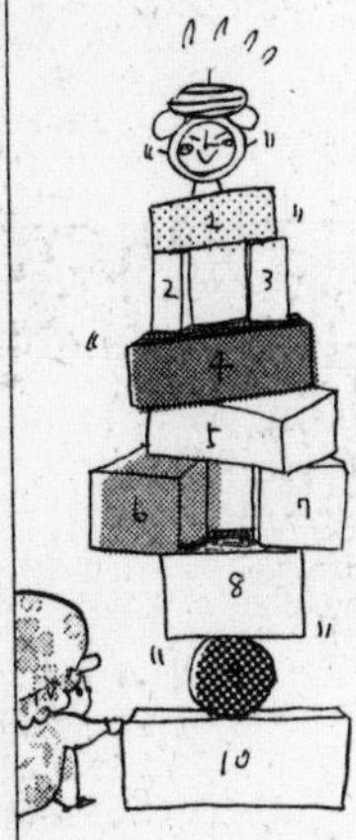

Hari Tokeino

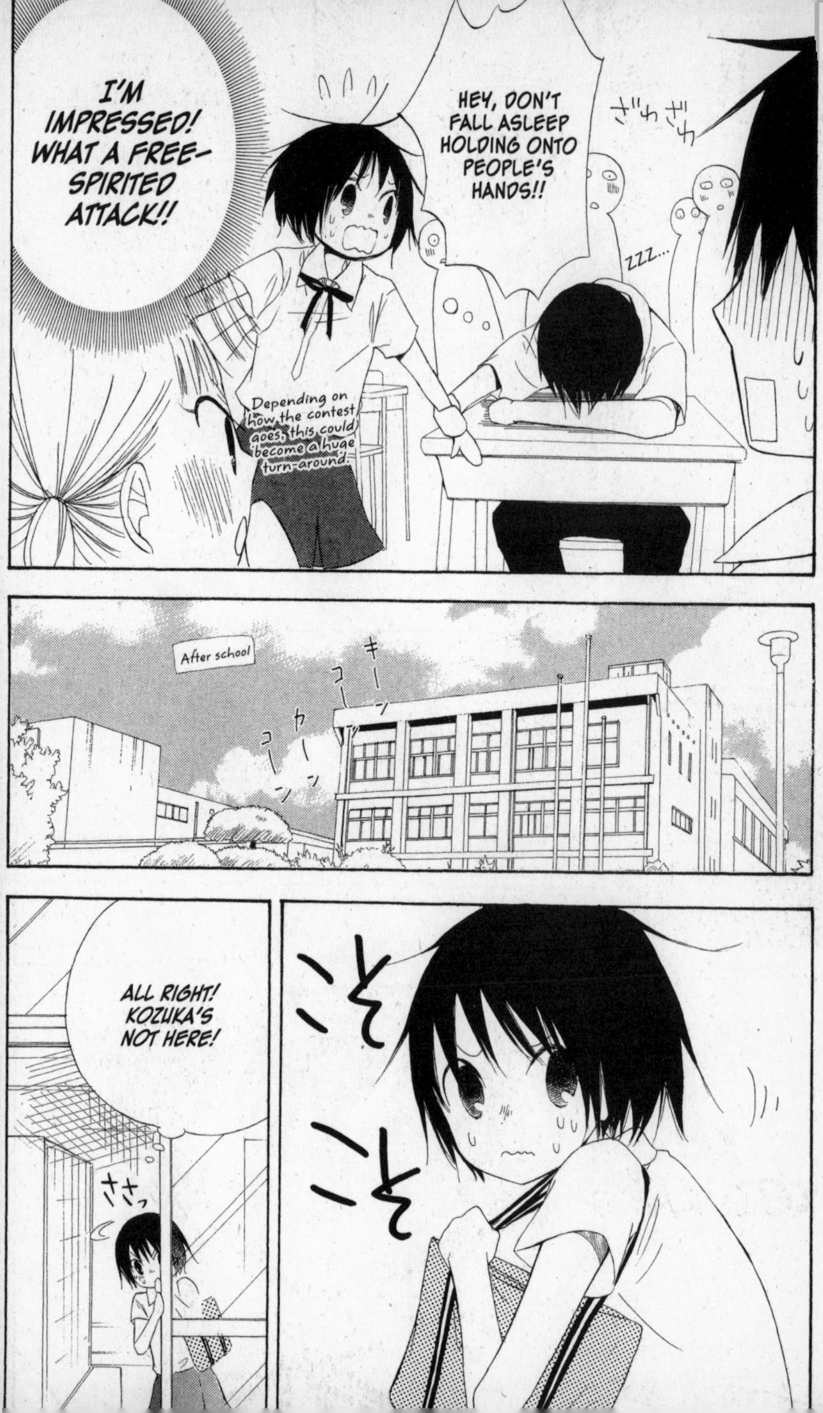
ざわざわ
HEY, DON'T FALL ASLEEP HOLDING ONTO PEOPLE'S HANDS!!
I'M IMPRESSED! WHAT A FREE-SPIRITED ATTACK!!
ZZZ...
Depending on how the contest goes, this could become a huge turn-around.
After school
キーンコーンカーンコーン
こそこそ
ALL RIGHT! KOZUKA'S NOT HERE!
ささっ

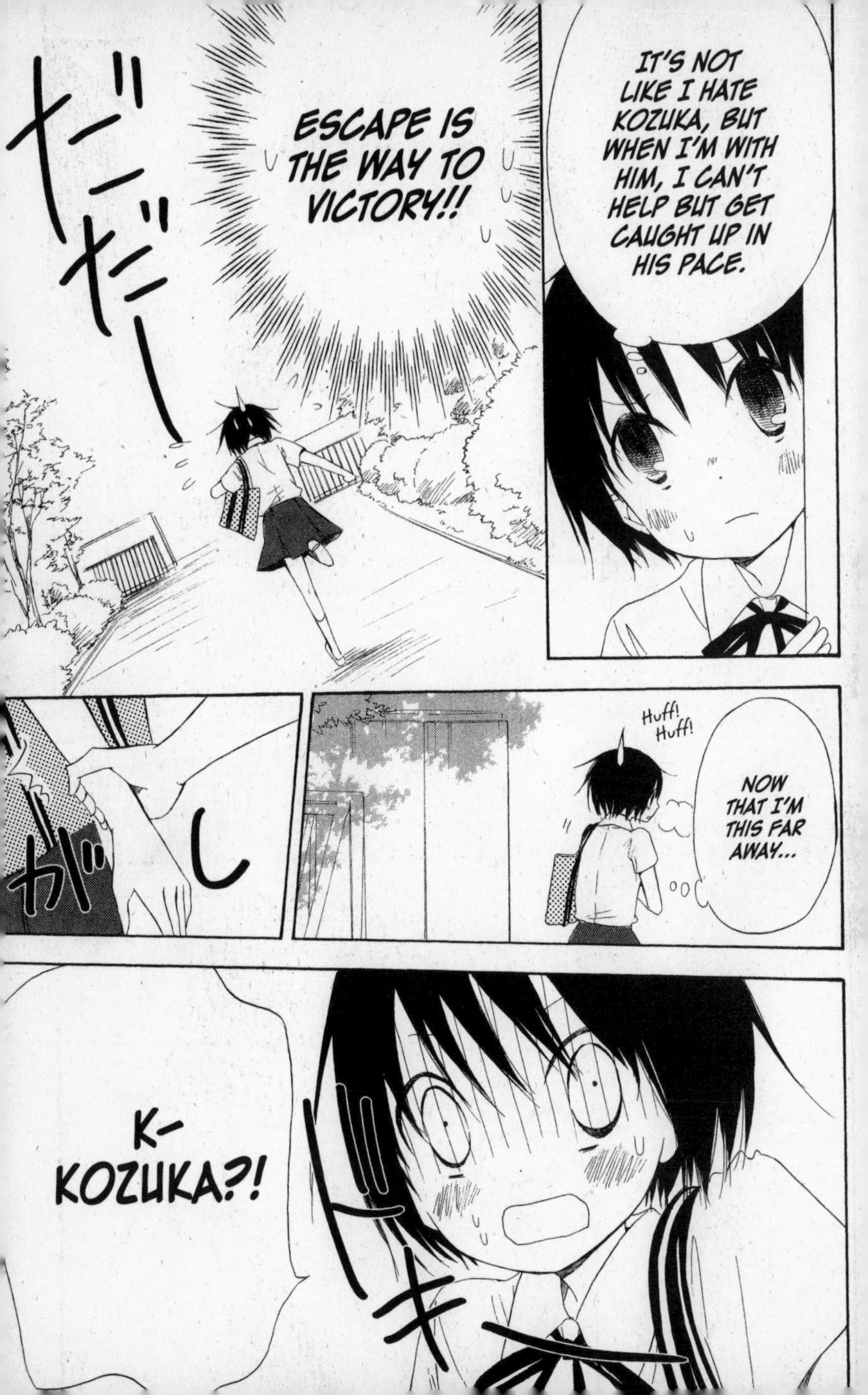
IT'S NOT LIKE I HATE KOZUKA, BUT WHEN I'M WITH HIM, I CAN'T HELP BUT GET CAUGHT UP IN HIS PACE.
ESCAPE IS THE WAY TO VICTORY!!
Huff! Huff!
NOW THAT I'M THIS FAR AWAY...
がし
K-KOZUKA?!
ドキ

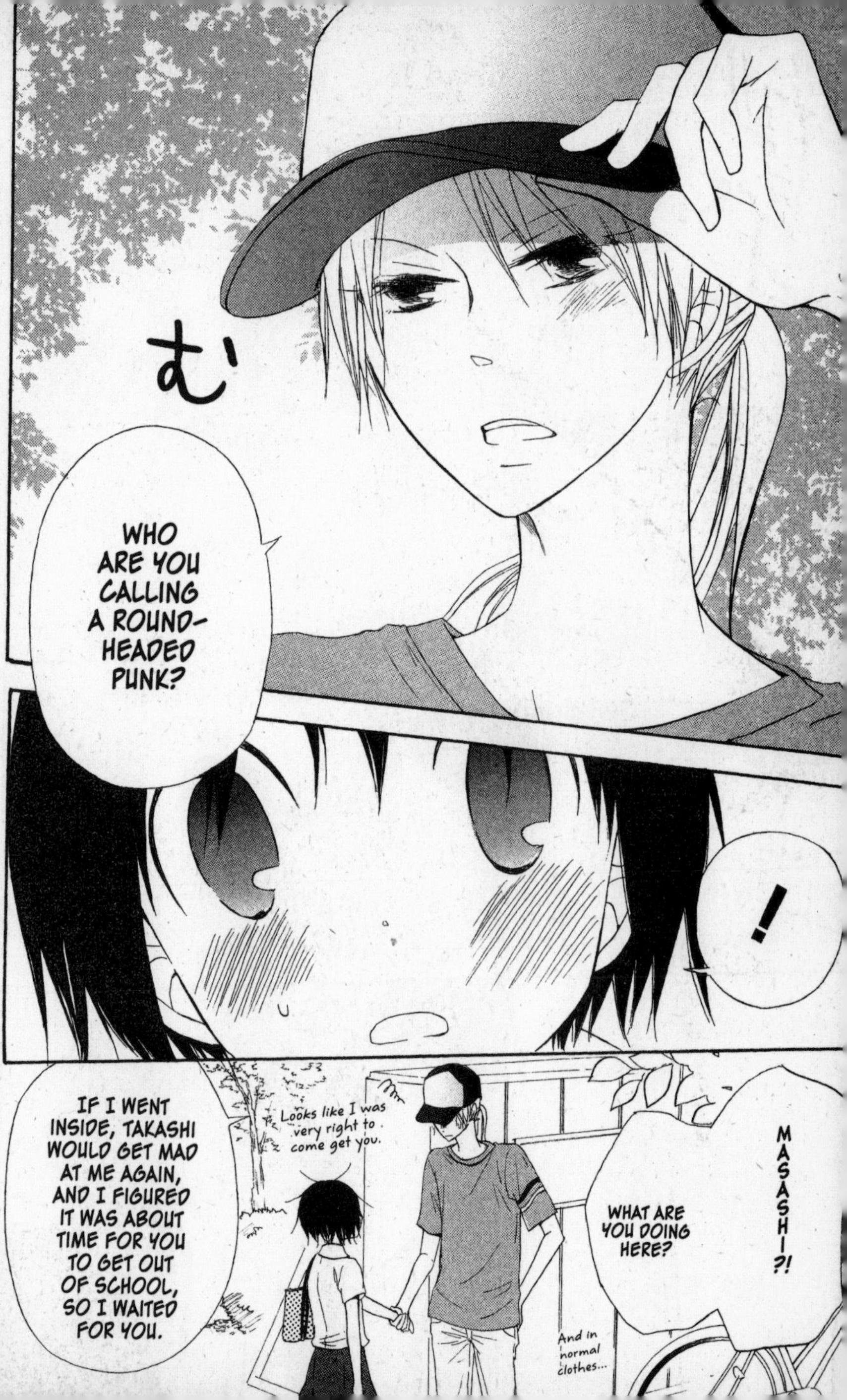
む
WHO ARE YOU CALLING A ROUND-HEADED PUNK?
!
MASASHI?!
WHAT ARE YOU DOING HERE?
And in normal clothes...
Looks like I was very right to come get you.
IF I WENT INSIDE, TAKASHI WOULD GET MAD AT ME AGAIN, AND I FIGURED IT WAS ABOUT TIME FOR YOU TO GET OUT OF SCHOOL, SO I WAITED FOR YOU.

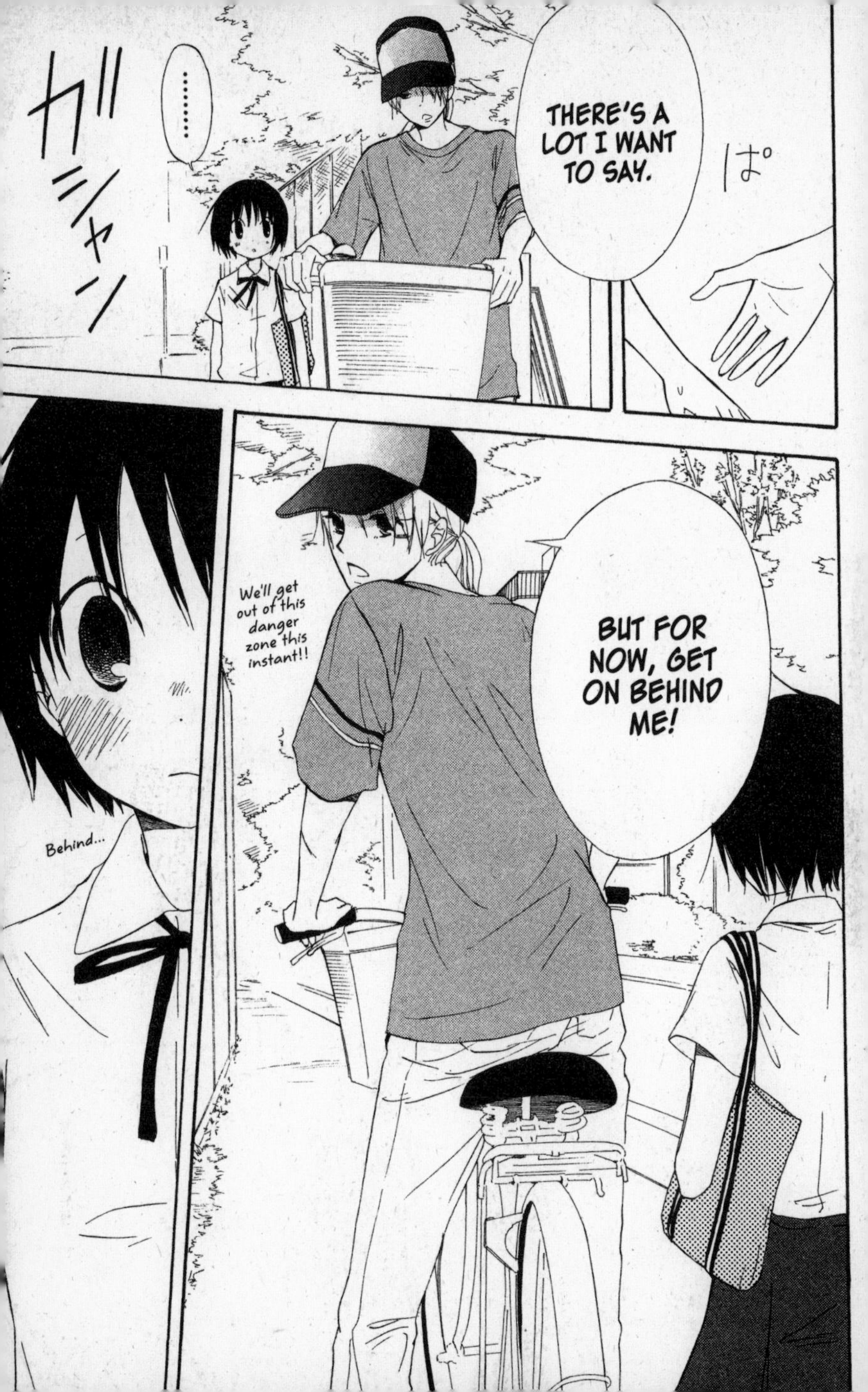
ぱ
THERE'S A LOT I WANT TO SAY.
……
ガシャン
BUT FOR NOW, GET ON BEHIND ME!
We'll get out of this danger zone this instant!!
Behind...

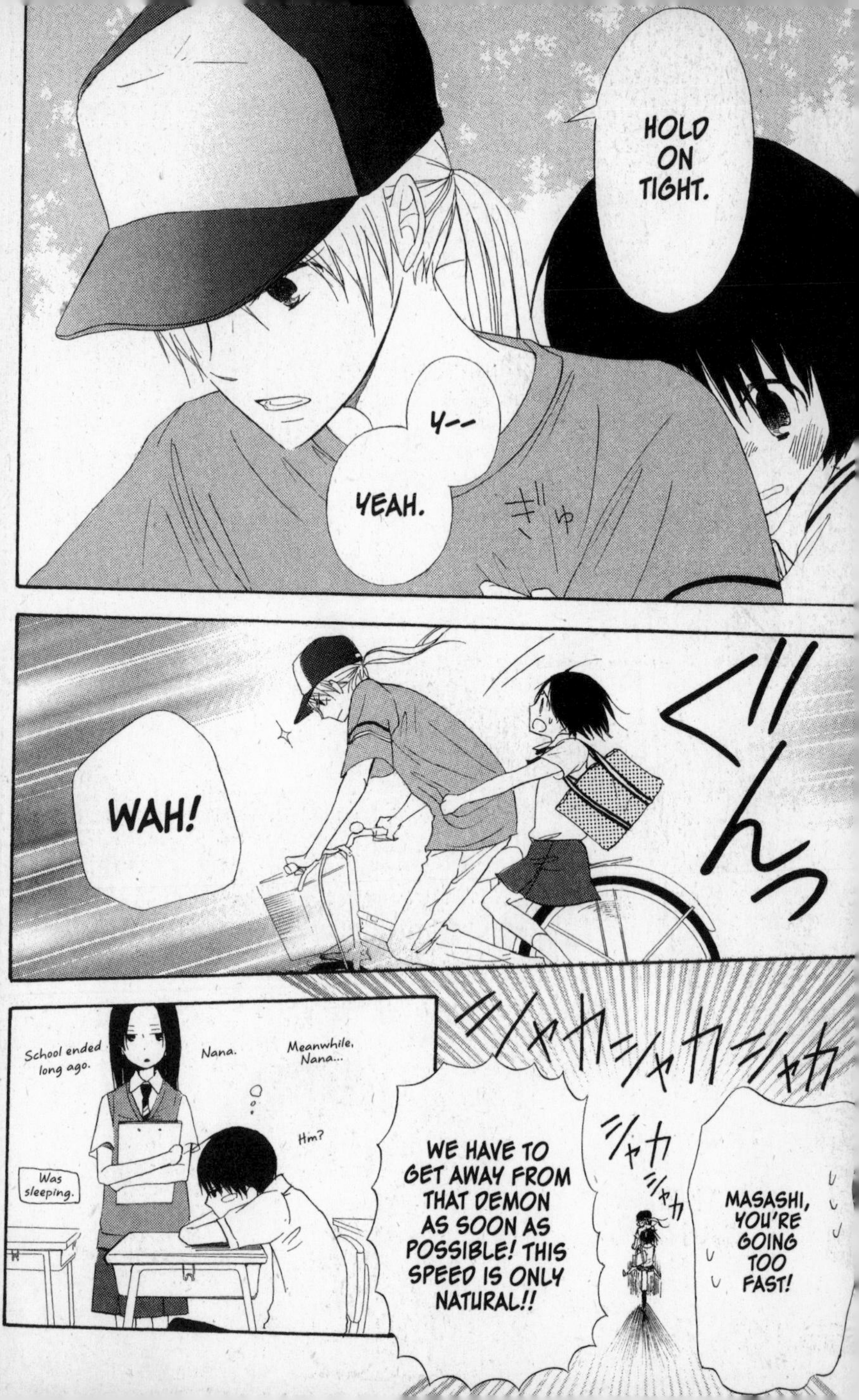
HOLD ON TIGHT.
Y--
YEAH.
ぎゅ
ぐんっ
WAH!
シャカシャカシャカ
MASASHI, YOU'RE GOING TOO FAST!
シャカ
シャカ
WE HAVE TO GET AWAY FROM THAT DEMON AS SOON AS POSSIBLE! THIS SPEED IS ONLY NATURAL!!
Meanwhile, Nana...
Nana.
Hm?
School ended long ago.
Was sleeping.

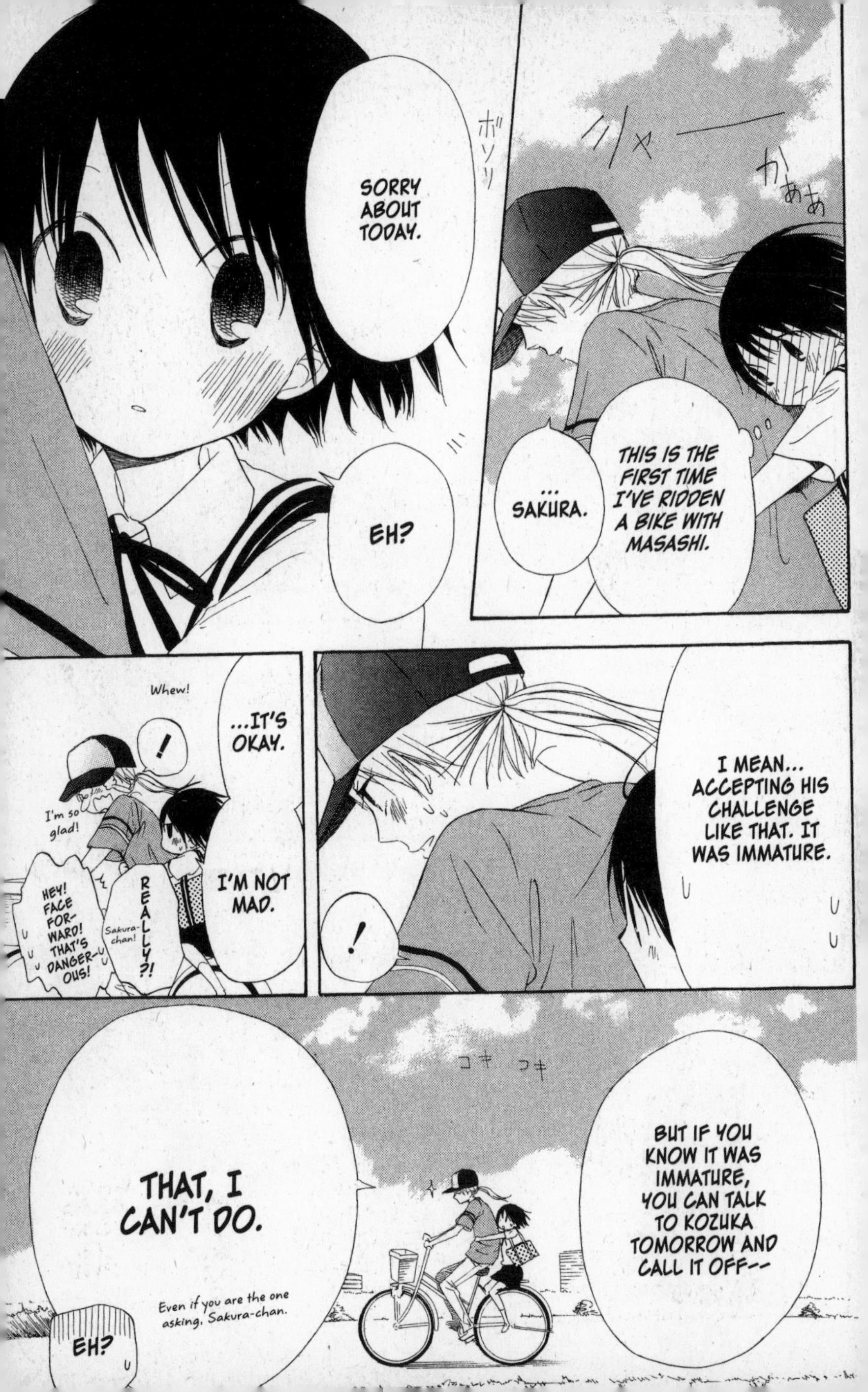
THIS IS THE FIRST TIME I'VE RIDDEN A BIKE WITH MASASHI.
... SAKURA.
ボソッ
SORRY ABOUT TODAY.
EH?
I MEAN... ACCEPTING HIS CHALLENGE LIKE THAT. IT WAS IMMATURE.
!
...IT'S OKAY.
I'M NOT MAD.
!
Whew!
I'm so glad!
REALLY?!
Sakura-chan!
HEY! FACE FORWARD! THAT'S DANGEROUS!
BUT IF YOU KNOW IT WAS IMMATURE, YOU CAN TALK TO KOZUKA TOMORROW AND CALL IT OFF--
コキ コキ
THAT, I CAN'T DO.
Even if you are the one asking, Sakura-chan.
EH?

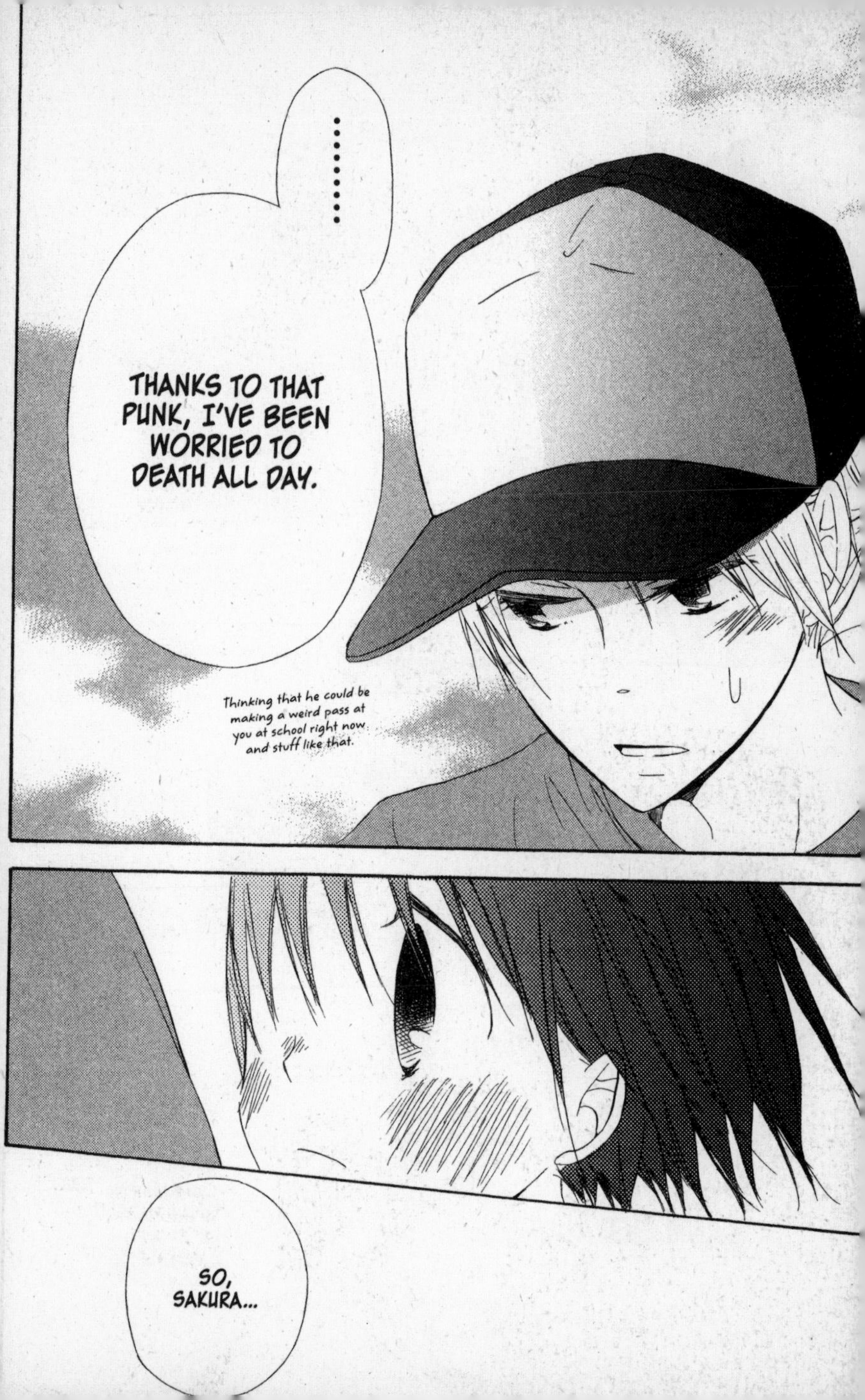
......
THANKS TO THAT PUNK, I'VE BEEN WORRIED TO DEATH ALL DAY.
Thinking that he could be making a weird pass at you at school right now and stuff like that.
SO, SAKURA...

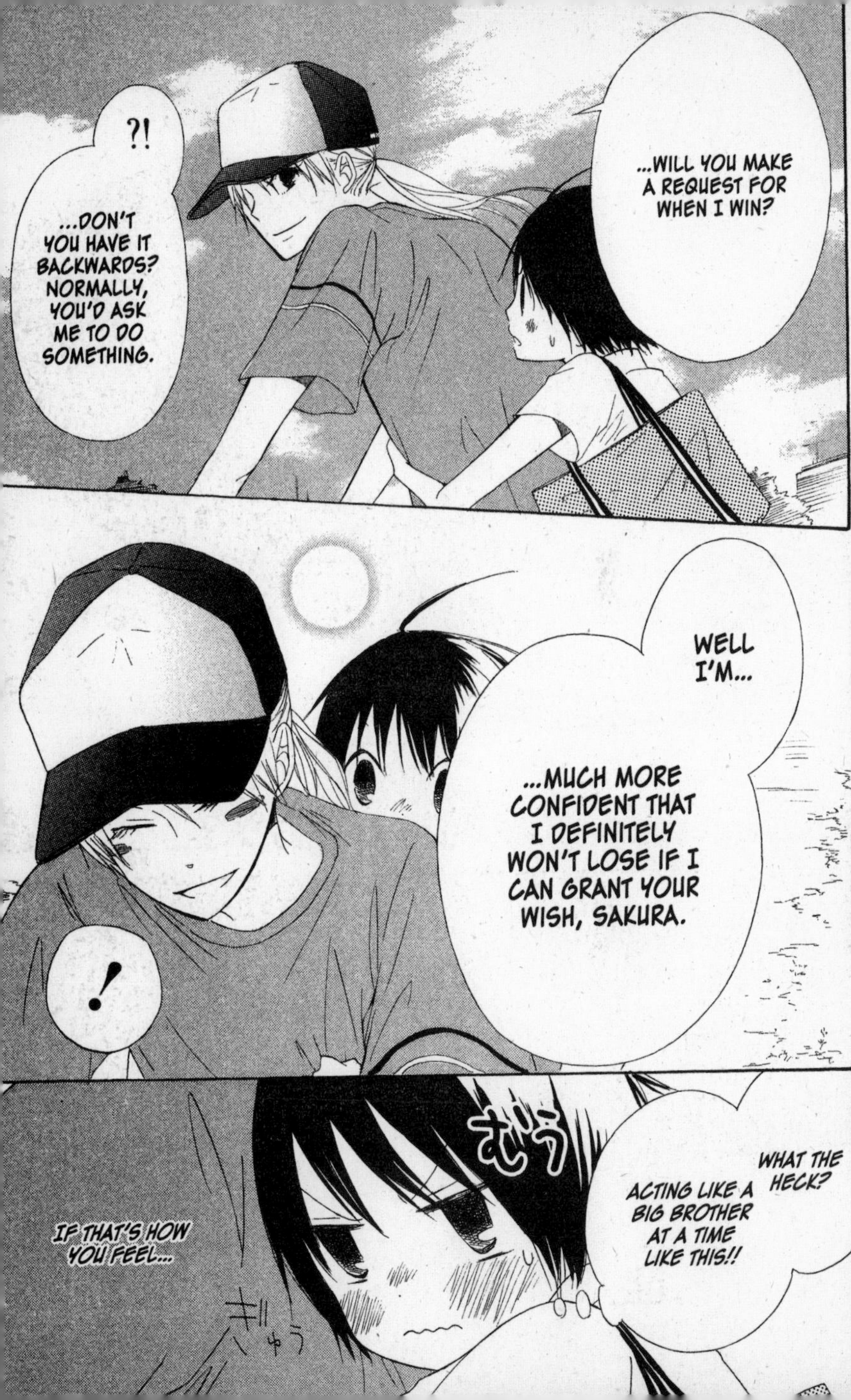
...WILL YOU MAKE A REQUEST FOR WHEN I WIN?
?!
...DON'T YOU HAVE IT BACKWARDS? NORMALLY, YOU'D ASK ME TO DO SOMETHING.
WELL I'M...
...MUCH MORE CONFIDENT THAT I DEFINITELY WON'T LOSE IF I CAN GRANT YOUR WISH, SAKURA.
!
むう
WHAT THE HECK?
ACTING LIKE A BIG BROTHER AT A TIME LIKE THIS!!
IF THAT'S HOW YOU FEEL...
ぎゅう

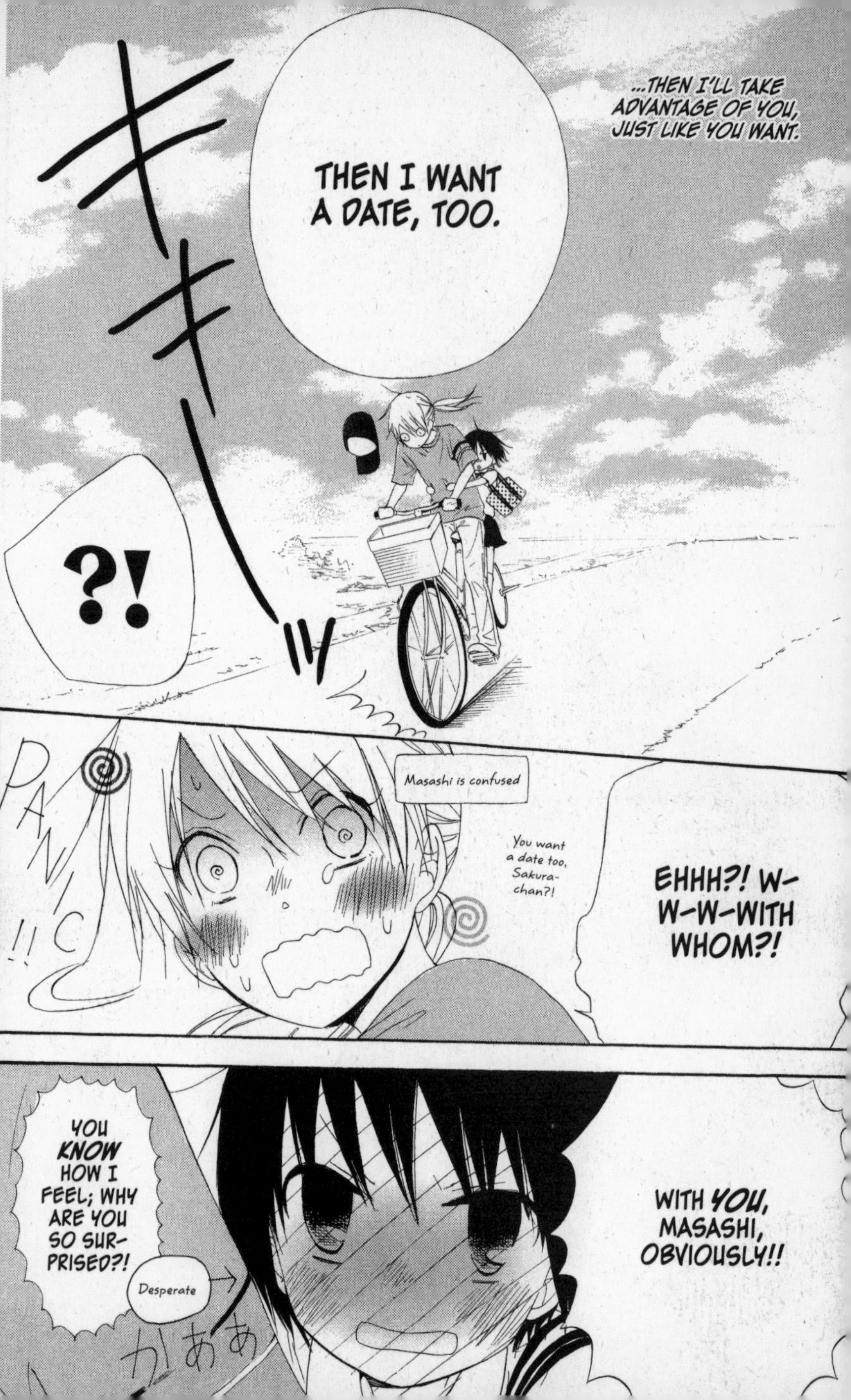
...THEN I'LL TAKE ADVANTAGE OF YOU, JUST LIKE YOU WANT.
THEN I WANT A DATE, TOO.
キキーッ
?!
EHHH?! W-W-W-WITH WHOM?!
You want a date too, Sakura-chan?!
Masashi is confused
PANIC!!
WITH YOU, MASASHI, OBVIOUSLY!!
YOU KNOW HOW I FEEL; WHY ARE YOU SO SURPRISED?!
Desperate
かぁぁ

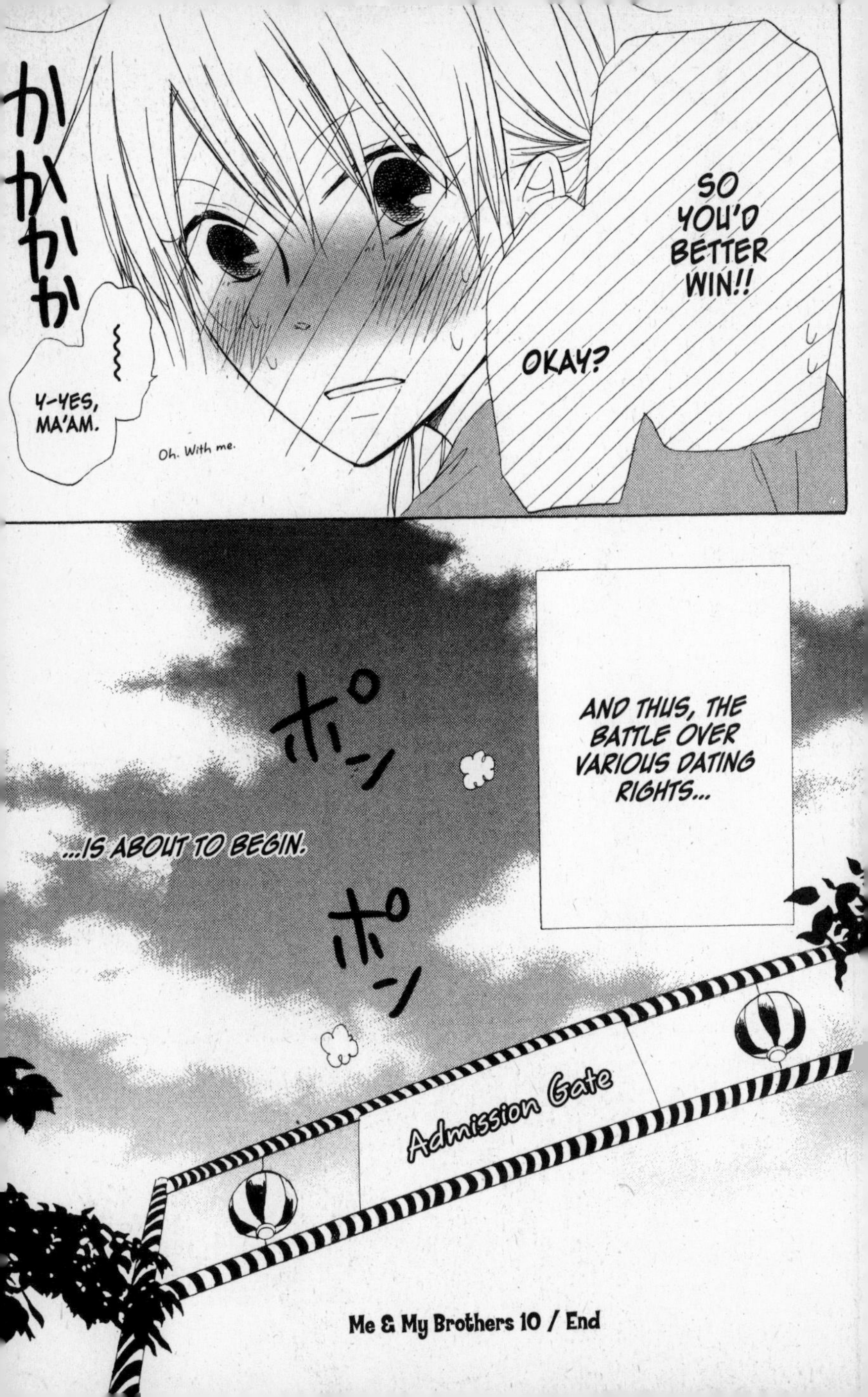
SO YOU'D BETTER WIN!!
OKAY?
かかかか
Y-YES, MA'AM.
Oh. With me.
AND THUS, THE BATTLE OVER VARIOUS DATING RIGHTS...
ポン
ポン
...IS ABOUT TO BEGIN.
Admission Gate

Me & My Brothers 10 / End

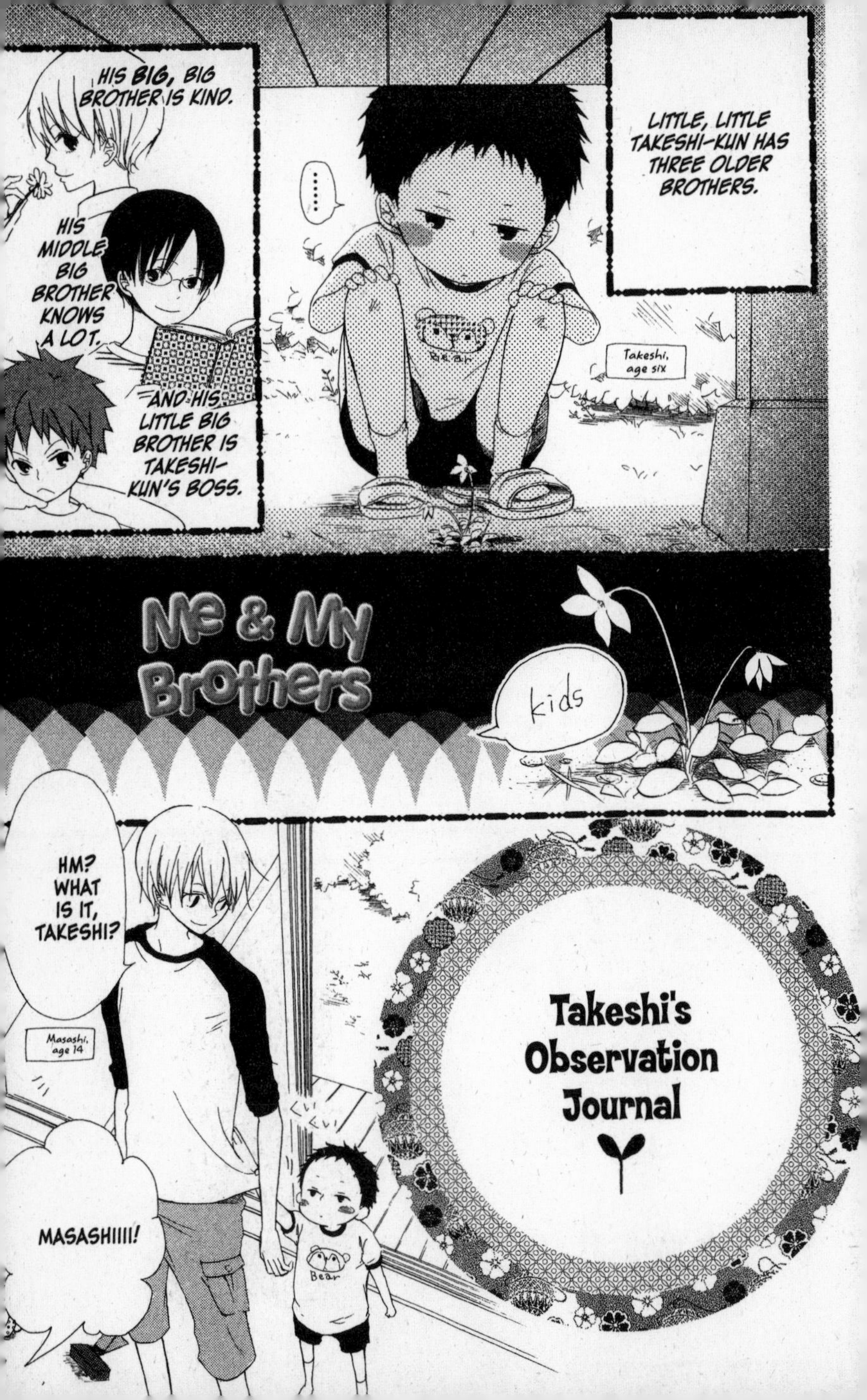
LITTLE, LITTLE TAKESHI-KUN HAS THREE OLDER BROTHERS.
......
Takeshi, age six
HIS BIG, BIG BROTHER IS KIND.
HIS MIDDLE BIG BROTHER KNOWS A LOT.
AND HIS LITTLE BIG BROTHER IS TAKESHI-KUN'S BOSS.
kids
Me & My Brothers
Takeshi's Observation Journal
くい くい
HM? WHAT IS IT, TAKESHI?
Masashi, age 14
MASASHIIIII!

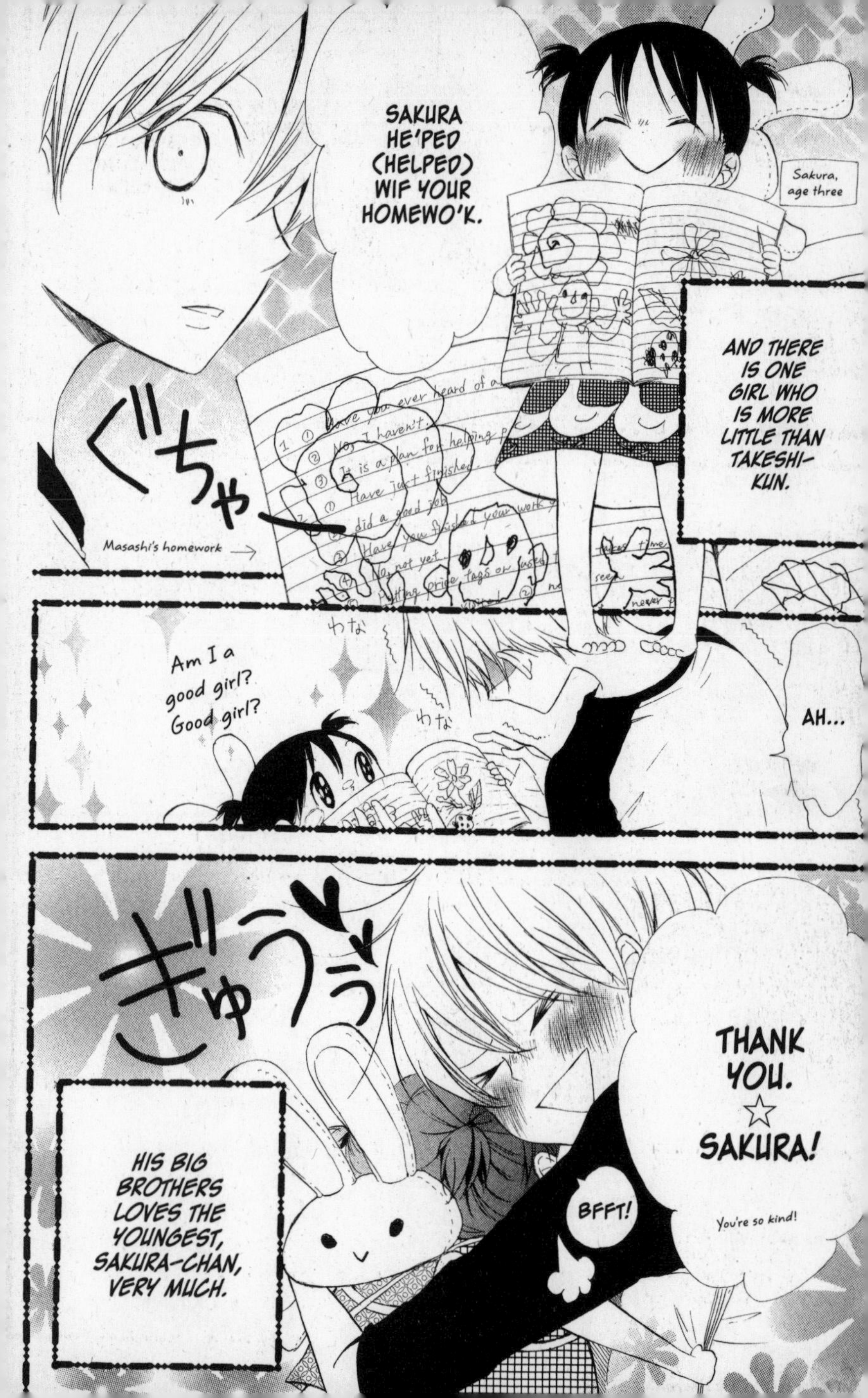

Sakura, age three
AND THERE IS ONE GIRL WHO IS MORE LITTLE THAN TAKESHI-KUN.
SAKURA HE'PED (HELPED) WIF YOUR HOMEWO'K.
ぐちゃー
Masashi's homework →
AH...
わな
わな
Am I a good girl? Good girl?
THANK YOU. ☆ SAKURA!
You're so kind!
ぎゅう
BFFT!
HIS BIG BROTHERS LOVES THE YOUNGEST, SAKURA-CHAN, VERY MUCH.

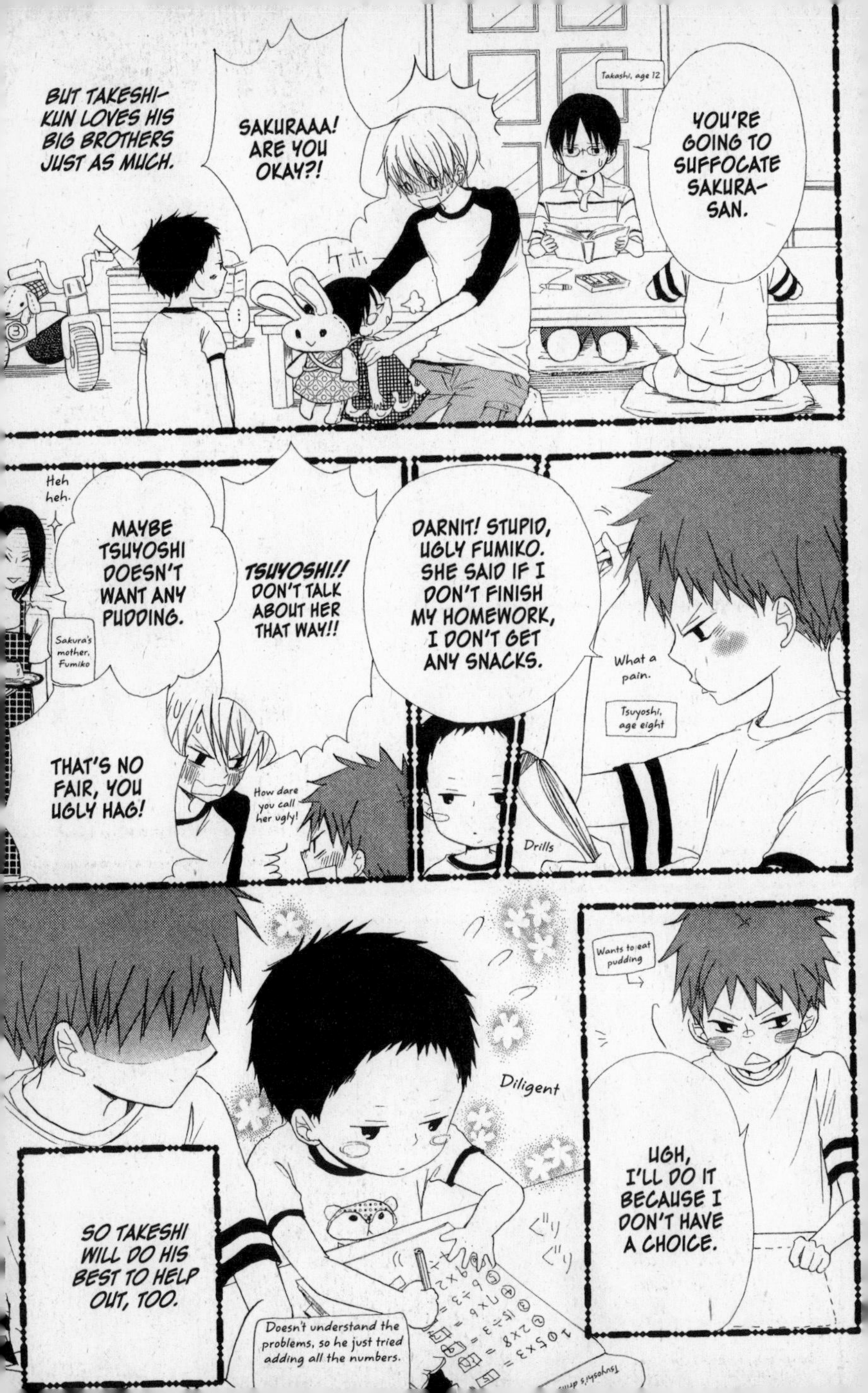
Takashi, age 12
YOU'RE GOING TO SUFFOCATE SAKURA-SAN.
SAKURAAA! ARE YOU OKAY?!
ケホ
...
BUT TAKESHI-KUN LOVES HIS BIG BROTHERS JUST AS MUCH.
What a pain.
Tsuyoshi, age eight
DARNIT! STUPID, UGLY FUMIKO. SHE SAID IF I DON'T FINISH MY HOMEWORK, I DON'T GET ANY SNACKS.
Drills
TSUYOSHI!! DON'T TALK ABOUT HER THAT WAY!!
Heh heh.
MAYBE TSUYOSHI DOESN'T WANT ANY PUDDING.
Sakura's mother, Fumiko
THAT'S NO FAIR, YOU UGLY HAG!
How dare you call her ugly!
Wants to eat pudding
UGH, I'LL DO IT BECAUSE I DON'T HAVE A CHOICE.
Diligent
ぐり ぐり
SO TAKESHI WILL DO HIS BEST TO HELP OUT, TOO.
Doesn't understand the problems, so he just tried adding all the numbers.

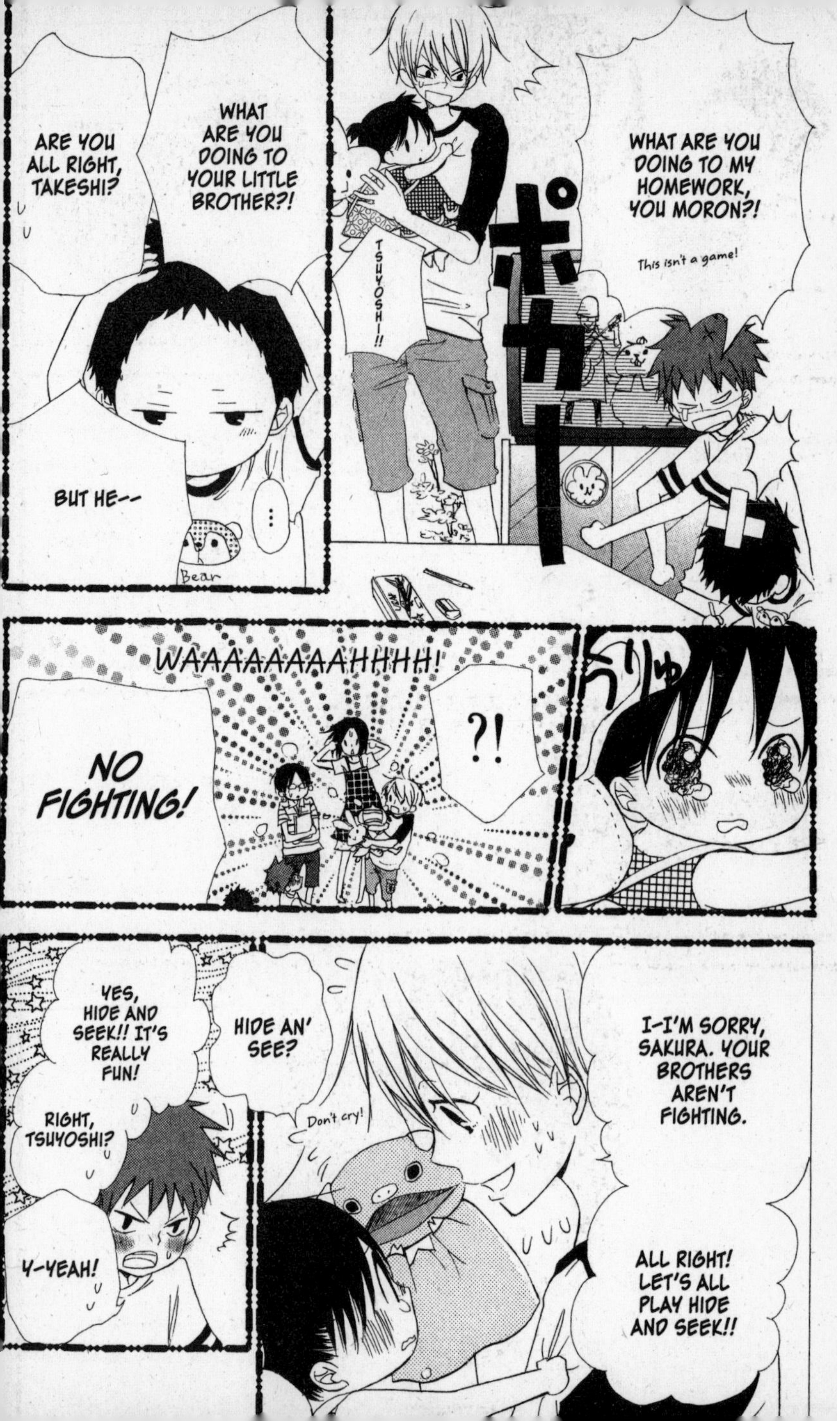
WHAT ARE YOU DOING TO MY HOMEWORK, YOU MORON?!
This isn't a game!
ポカッ
WHAT ARE YOU DOING TO YOUR LITTLE BROTHER?!
TSUYOSHI!!
ARE YOU ALL RIGHT, TAKESHI?
BUT HE--
...
Bear
うりゅ
WAAAAAAAAHHHH!
?!
NO FIGHTING!
I-I'M SORRY, SAKURA. YOUR BROTHERS AREN'T FIGHTING.
Don't cry!
ALL RIGHT! LET'S ALL PLAY HIDE AND SEEK!!
HIDE AN' SEE?
YES, HIDE AND SEEK!! IT'S REALLY FUN!
RIGHT, TSUYOSHI?
Y-YEAH!

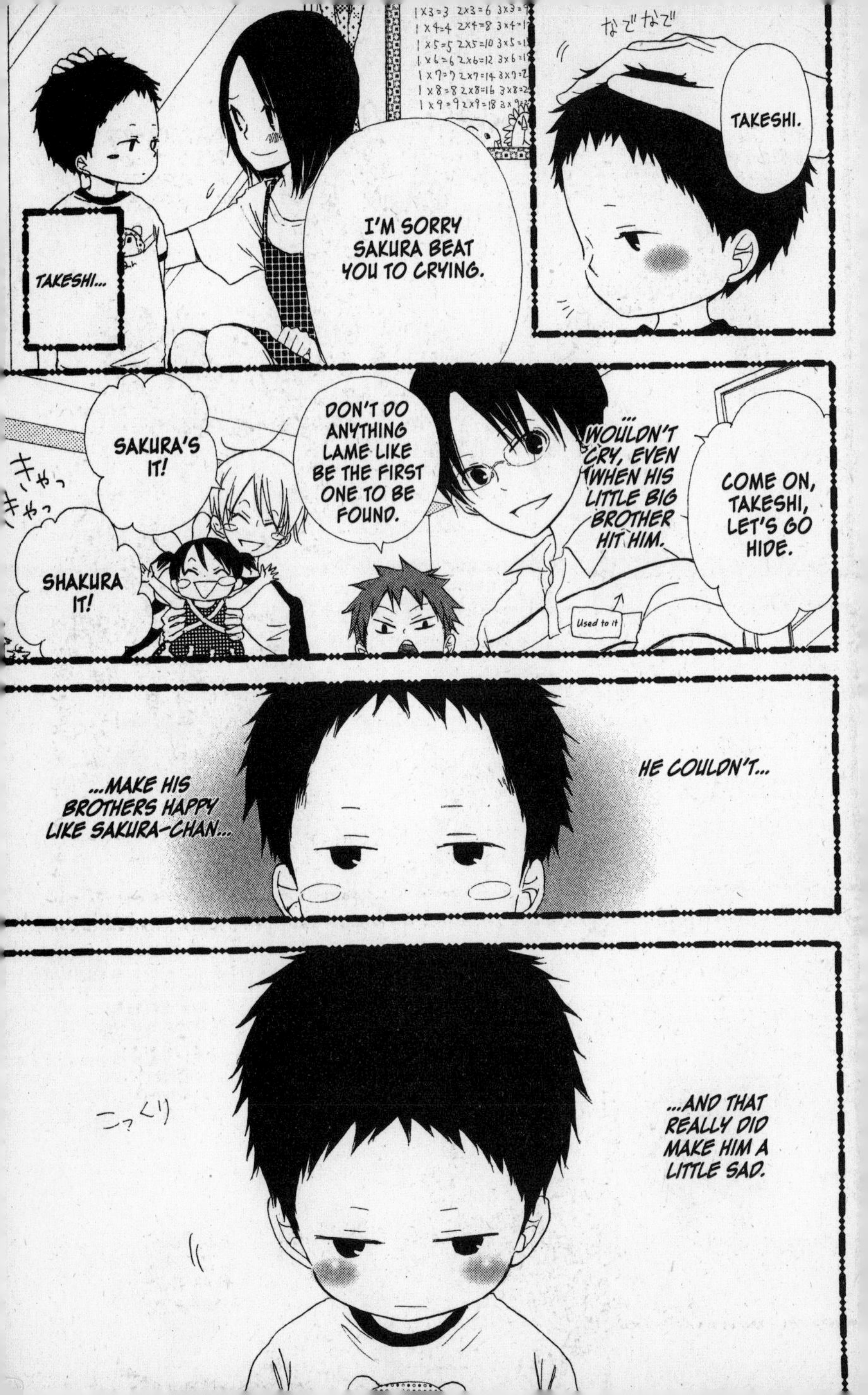
なでなで
TAKESHI.
I'M SORRY SAKURA BEAT YOU TO CRYING.
TAKESHI...
COME ON, TAKESHI, LET'S GO HIDE.
...WOULDN'T CRY, EVEN WHEN HIS LITTLE BIG BROTHER HIT HIM.
Used to it
DON'T DO ANYTHING LAME LIKE BE THE FIRST ONE TO BE FOUND.
SAKURA'S IT!
SHAKURA IT!
きゃっきゃっ
HE COULDN'T...
...MAKE HIS BROTHERS HAPPY LIKE SAKURA-CHAN...
...AND THAT REALLY DID MAKE HIM A LITTLE SAD.
こっくり

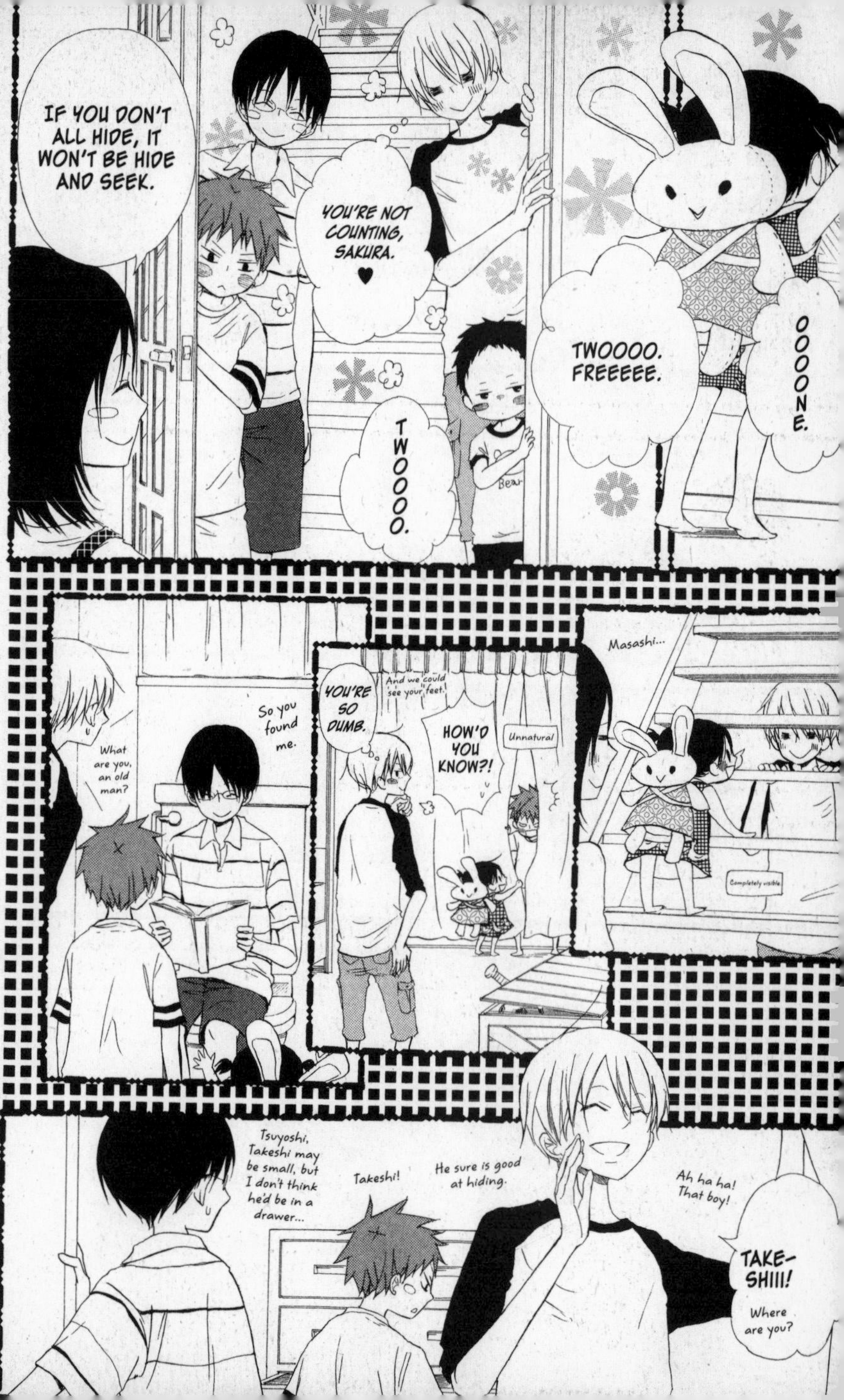
OOOONE.
TWOOOO. FREEEEE.
TWOOOO.
YOU'RE NOT COUNTING, SAKURA. ♥
IF YOU DON'T ALL HIDE, IT WON'T BE HIDE AND SEEK.
Masashi...
Completely visible
HOW'D YOU KNOW?!
Unnatural
YOU'RE SO DUMB.
And we could see your feet.
So you found me.
What are you, an old man?
TAKE-SHIII!
Where are you?
Ah ha ha! That boy!
He sure is good at hiding.
Takeshi!
Tsuyoshi, Takeshi may be small, but I don't think he'd be in a drawer...

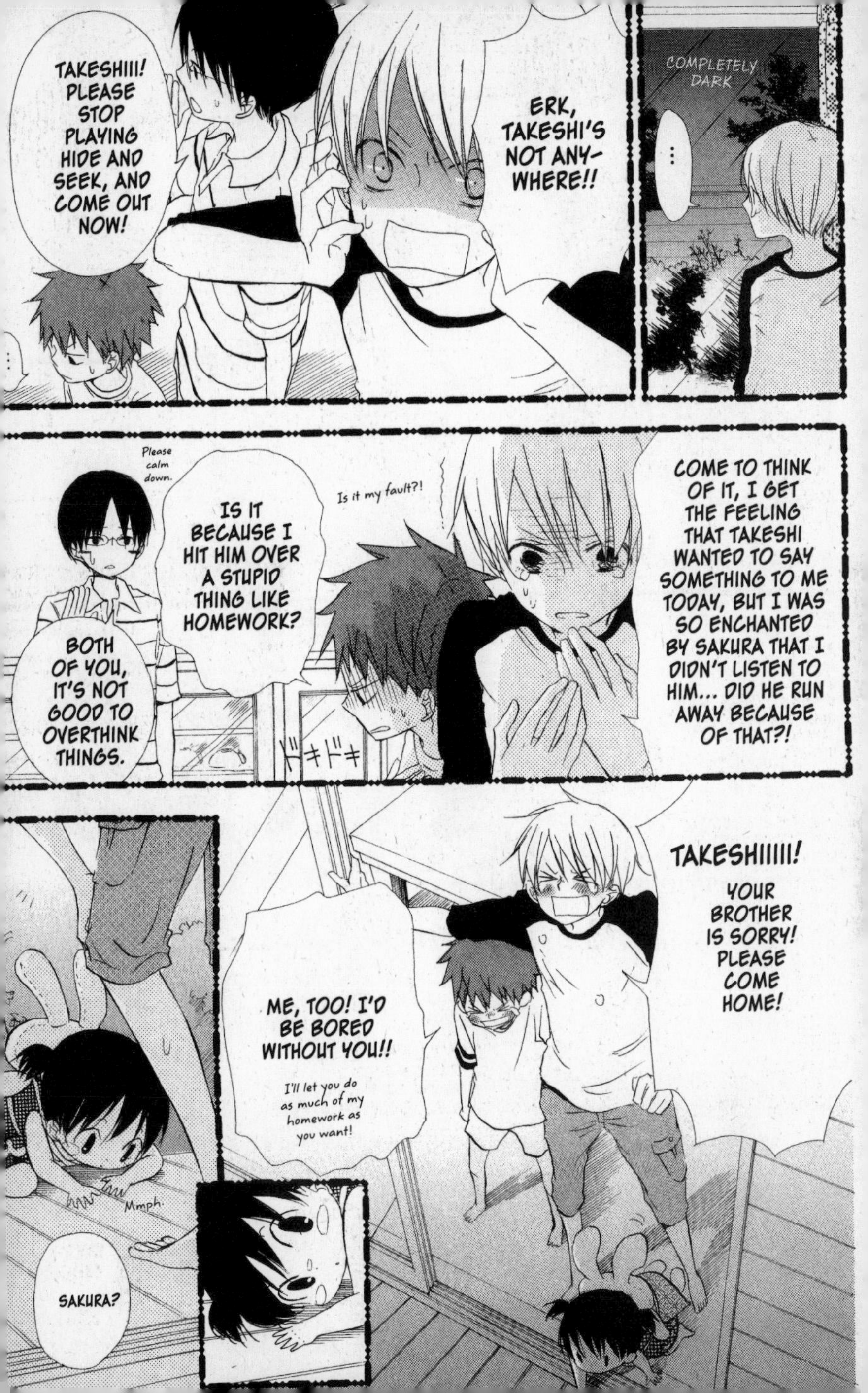
COMPLETELY DARK
...
ERK, TAKESHI'S NOT ANY-WHERE!!
TAKESHIII! PLEASE STOP PLAYING HIDE AND SEEK, AND COME OUT NOW!
...
COME TO THINK OF IT, I GET THE FEELING THAT TAKESHI WANTED TO SAY SOMETHING TO ME TODAY, BUT I WAS SO ENCHANTED BY SAKURA THAT I DIDN'T LISTEN TO HIM... DID HE RUN AWAY BECAUSE OF THAT?!
Is it my fault?!
IS IT BECAUSE I HIT HIM OVER A STUPID THING LIKE HOMEWORK?
Please calm down.
BOTH OF YOU, IT'S NOT GOOD TO OVERTHINK THINGS.
ドキドキ
TAKESHIIIIII!
YOUR BROTHER IS SORRY! PLEASE COME HOME!
ME, TOO! I'D BE BORED WITHOUT YOU!!
I'll let you do as much of my homework as you want!
Mmph.
SAKURA?

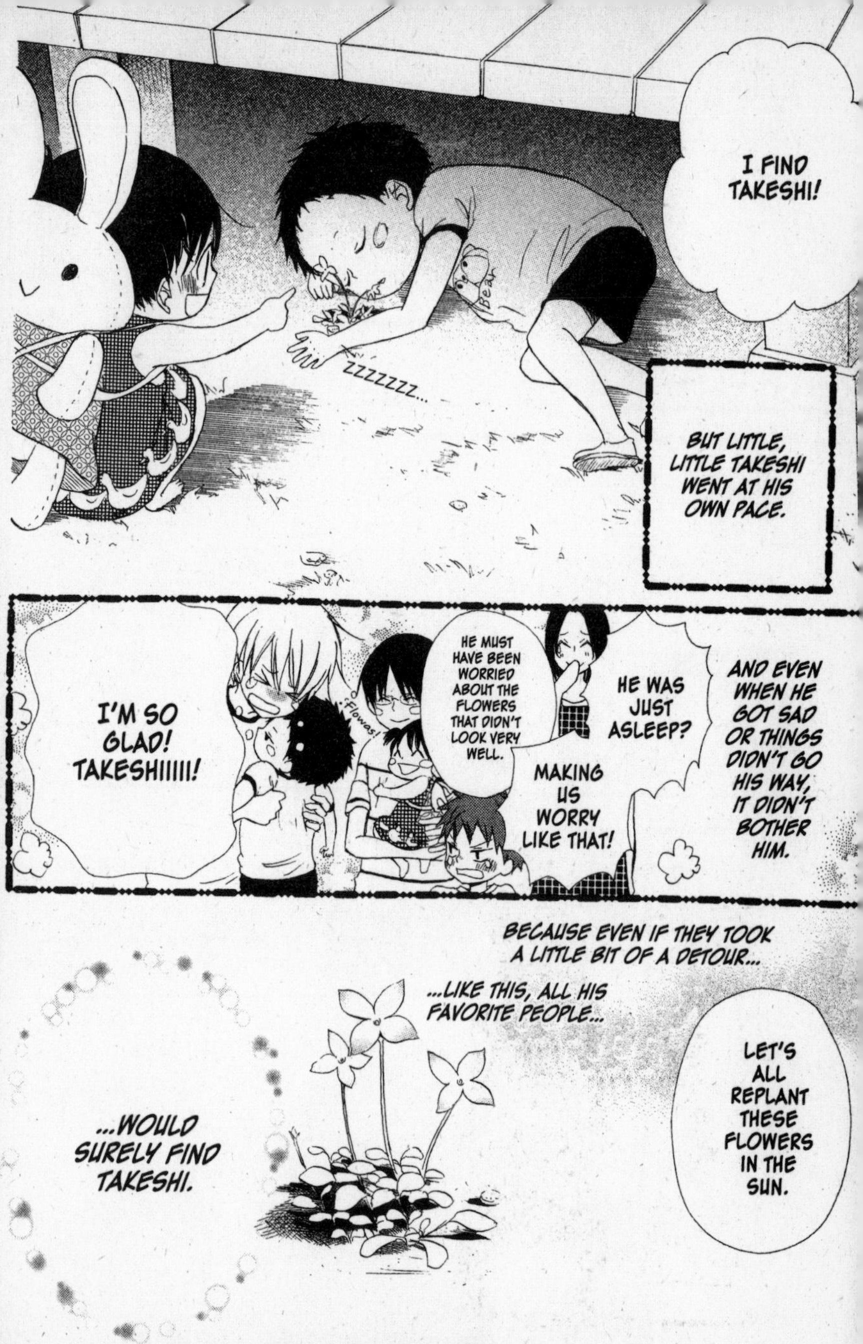
I FIND TAKESHI!
BUT LITTLE, LITTLE TAKESHI WENT AT HIS OWN PACE.
ZZZZZZZ...
Bear
AND EVEN WHEN HE GOT SAD OR THINGS DIDN'T GO HIS WAY, IT DIDN'T BOTHER HIM.
HE WAS JUST ASLEEP?
MAKING US WORRY LIKE THAT!
HE MUST HAVE BEEN WORRIED ABOUT THE FLOWERS THAT DIDN'T LOOK VERY WELL.
Flowas!
I'M SO GLAD! TAKESHIIIIII!
BECAUSE EVEN IF THEY TOOK A LITTLE BIT OF A DETOUR...
LET'S ALL REPLANT THESE FLOWERS IN THE SUN.
...LIKE THIS, ALL HIS FAVORITE PEOPLE...
...WOULD SURELY FIND TAKESHI.

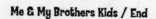

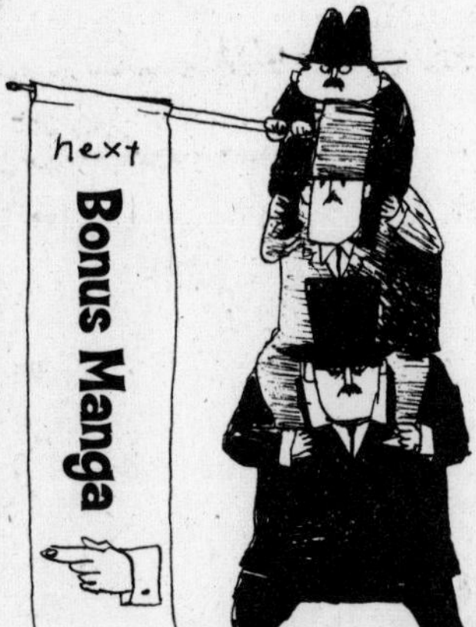
next
Bonus Manga

Bonus Manga

Sonomura and Katagiri

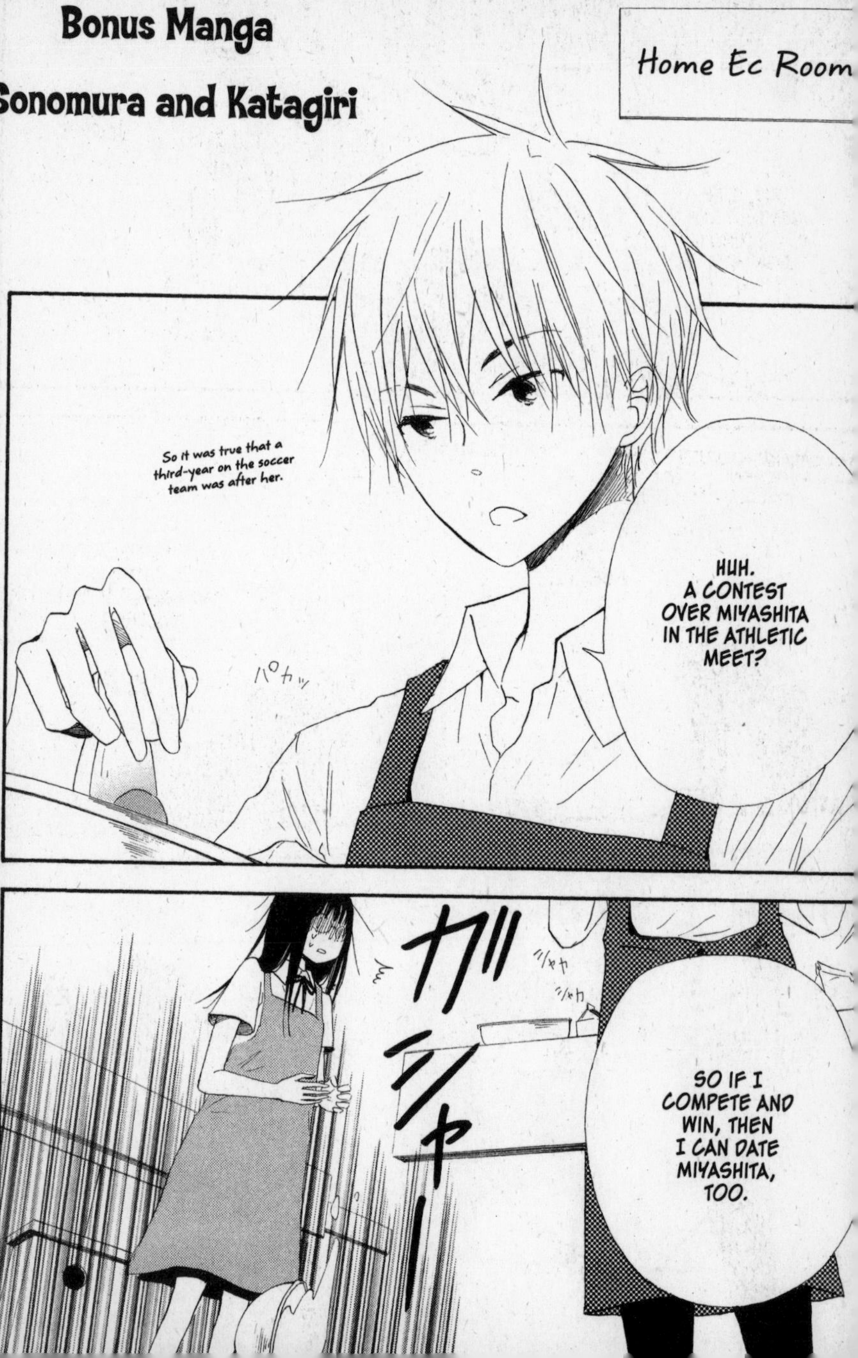
Home Ec Room
HUH. A CONTEST OVER MIYASHITA IN THE ATHLETIC MEET?
So it was true that a third-year on the soccer team was after her.
パカッ
SO IF I COMPETE AND WIN, THEN I CAN DATE MIYASHITA, TOO.
シャカ
シャカ
ガシャー

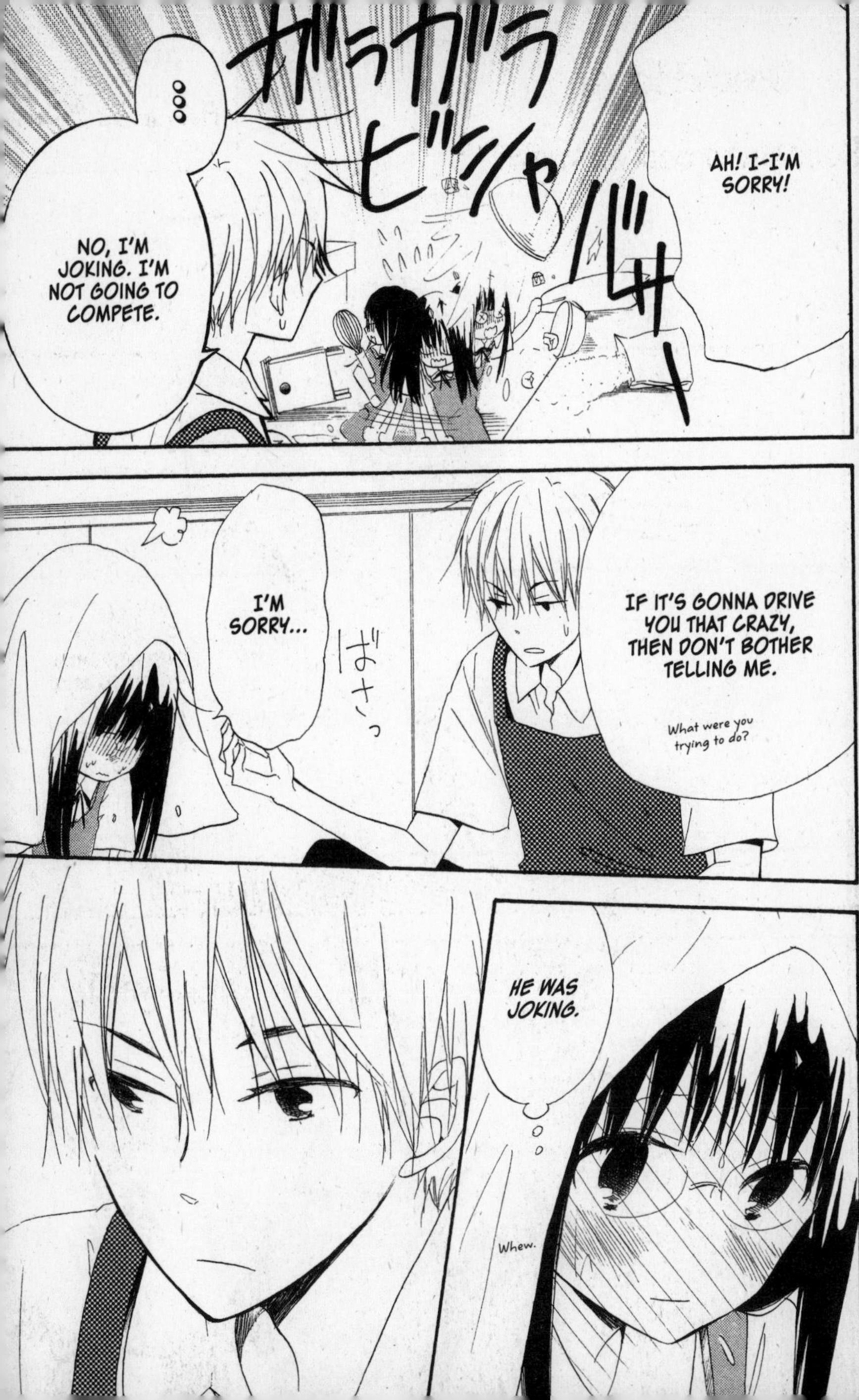
AH! I-I'M SORRY!
ガラガラ
ビシャ
ザー
NO, I'M JOKING. I'M NOT GOING TO COMPETE.
IF IT'S GONNA DRIVE YOU THAT CRAZY, THEN DON'T BOTHER TELLING ME.
What were you trying to do?
ばさっ
I'M SORRY...
HE WAS JOKING.
Whew.

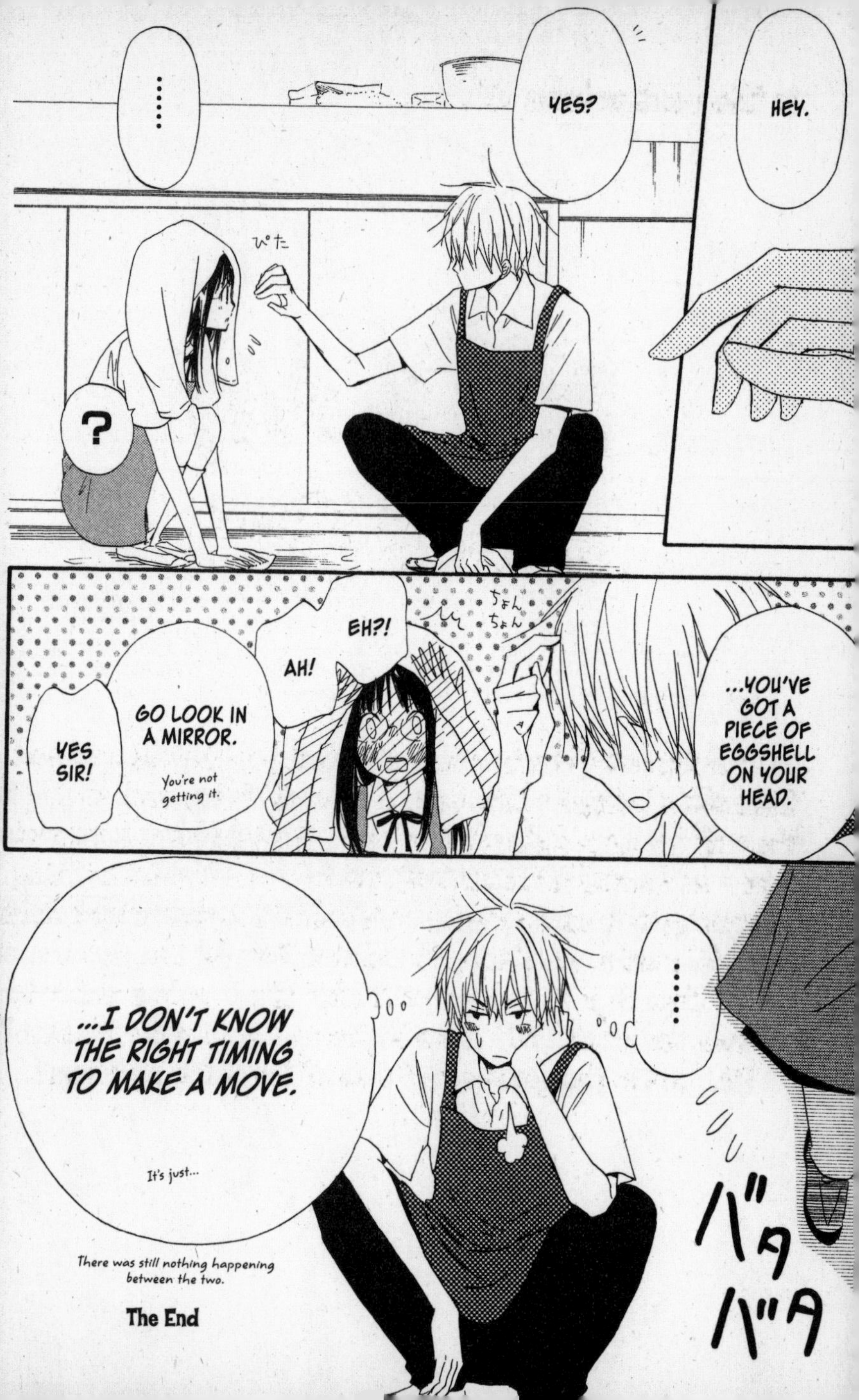
HEY.
YES?
......
ぴた
?
...YOU'VE GOT A PIECE OF EGGSHELL ON YOUR HEAD.
ちょん ちょん
EH?!
AH!
GO LOOK IN A MIRROR.
You're not getting it.
YES SIR!
バタ バタ
......
...I DON'T KNOW THE RIGHT TIMING TO MAKE A MOVE.
It's just...
There was still nothing happening between the two.
The End

In the next volume of...

Me & My Brothers

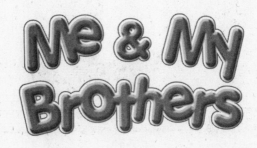

The anticipated high school athletic meet has begun, and the battle between Kozuka and Masashi is on, each giving it their all to win a date with Sakura. Jealous girls, a hilarious race and a sweet moment of victory for... the winner may surprise you! In other events, unexpected occurrences befal Masashi causing confusion to Sakura. Painful feelings are at an all time high as Sakura proclaims she is only a sister to the man she loves. Will Sakura give up her love for Masashi? Find out in the emotional finale of Me & My Brothers!

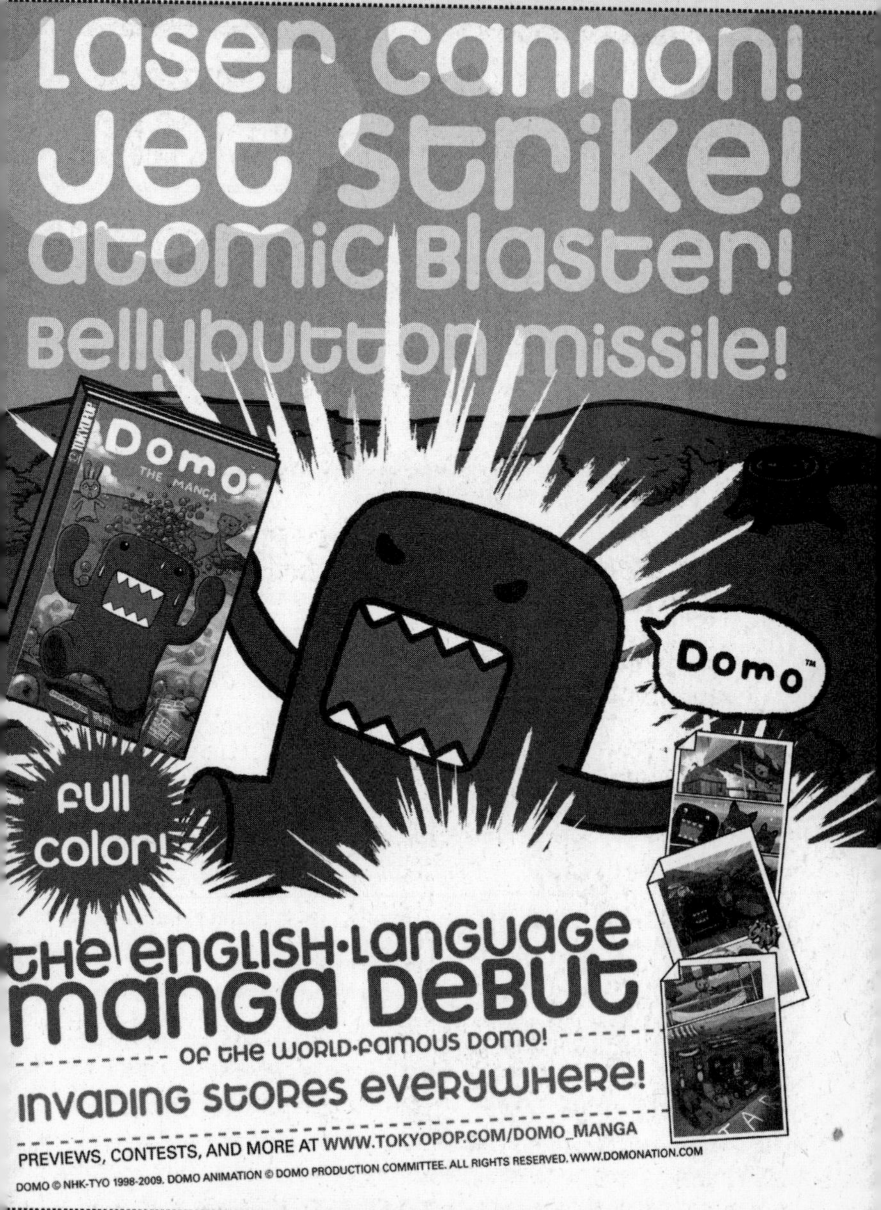
Laser Cannon!
Jet Strike!
Atomic Blaster!
Bellybutton Missile!
TOKYOPOP
Domo THE MANGA
Domo™
Full color!
The English-Language Manga Debut
of the World-Famous Domo!
Invading Stores Everywhere!
PREVIEWS, CONTESTS, AND MORE AT WWW.TOKYOPOP.COM/DOMO_MANGA
DOMO © NHK-TYO 1998-2009. DOMO ANIMATION © DOMO PRODUCTION COMMITTEE. ALL RIGHTS RESERVED. WWW.DOMONATION.COM

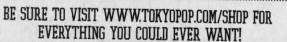

STOP!

This is the back of the book.
You wouldn't want to spoil a great ending!

This book is printed "manga-style," in the authentic Japanese right-to-left format. Since none of the artwork has been flipped or altered, readers get to experience the story just as the creator intended. You've been asking for it, so TOKYOPOP® delivered: authentic, hot-off-the-press, and far more fun!

1
2
3
4
5
6
7
8
9
10

DIRECTIONS

If this is your first time reading manga-style, here's a quick guide to help you understand how it works.

It's easy... just start in the top right panel and follow the numbers. Have fun, and look for more 100% authentic manga from TOKYOPOP®!

THE MANGA REVOLUTION • LEADING

漫画革命